THE
ACCOUNTING
PROFESSIONAL

THE ACCOUNTING PROFESSIONAL

Ethics, Responsibility, and Liability

Floyd W. Windal and Robert N. Corley
University of Georgia

Prentice-Hall, Inc., Englewood Cliffs, New Jersey 07632

Library of Congress Cataloging in Publication Data

Windal, Floyd W.
    The accounting professional.

    Includes bibliographies and index.
    1. Accountant, Professional ethics for.
I. Corley, Robert Neil, joint author. II.
HF5629.W55   170'.9'657   79-9537
ISBN   0-13-003020-1

Editorial/production supervision and
    interior design by Lori E. Wieseneck
Cover design by Edsal Enterprises
Manufacturing buyer: Edmund W. Leone

Printed in the United States of America
10   9   8   7   6   5   4   3   2   1

Prentice-Hall International, Inc., *London*
Prentice-Hall of Australia Pty. Limited, *Sydney*
Prentice-Hall of Canada, Ltd., *Toronto*
Prentice-Hall of India Private Limited, *New Delhi*
Prentice-Hall of Japan, Inc., *Tokyo*
Prentice-Hall of Southeast Asia Pte. Ltd., *Singapore*
Whitehall Books Limited, *Wellington, New Zealand*

Contents

Preface xi

Foreword xiii

PART ONE
PROFESSIONAL ETHICS AND RESPONSIBILITY 1

1

The Accounting Profession 7
Introduction.   The Structure of A Profession.
The Securities and Exchange Commission.   The Congress.
The Commission on Auditors' Responsibilities.   Education Standards.
The Evolution towards Greater Professionalism.   Suggested Additional Readings.

2

Independence, Integrity, and Objectivity   30
Introduction.   The Auditor.
The Management Consultant and The Tax Practitioner.
The Internal Professional.   Commitment to Ethical Conduct.
Perceptions of Independence.
Reporting Lack of Independence: General Standards.
Interpretation of Reporting Standards.   Independence of The Internal Auditor.
Suggested Additional Readings.

3

General and Technical Standards   57
Introduction.   The Auditor.
The Management Consultant and The Tax Practitioner.   The Internal Professional.
The Foundational Concepts.   Detection of Fraud: The Standard.
Illegal Acts By Clients: The Standard.   Letter from Legal Counsel.
The Cost Accounting Standards Board.   Suggested Additional Readings.

4

Responsibilities to Clients, Management, and Owners   92
Introduction.   The Auditor.   The Management Consultant.
The Tax Practitioner.   The Internal Professional.
Internal Control: Responsibilities of The Auditor.
Internal Control and The Financial Executive.
Internal Control and The Computer.   Interim Financial Information.
Unaudited Financial Statements of Public Entities.
Unaudited Financial Statements of Non-Public Entities.
Divisional Reports and The Internal Professional.   Suggested Additional Readings.

5

Responsibility to Colleagues   126
Introduction.   The Auditor.
The Management Consultant and The Tax Practitioner.   The Internal Professional.
Communication between Predecessor and Successor Auditors.
The Discipline of Individuals.   The Discipline of Firms.
The Discipline of A Profession.   Peer Review Programs.
Suggested Additional Readings.

6

Other Responsibilities and Practices 153
Introduction. The Auditor.
The Management Consultant and The Tax Practitioner. The Internal Professional.
Scope of Practice.
Management Advisory Services: Compatibility and Independence.
Dual Practice of Law and Accounting.
The Small Client and Representation Letters. Suggested Additional Readings.

PART TWO
ACCOUNTANTS AND THE LAW 187

7

Accountants and The Law of Contracts 191
Introduction. The Right to Compensation. Agreements Not to Compete.
Exculpatory Clauses, Disclaimers, and Qualifications. Fixing the Price of Services.
Professional License. Suggested Additional Readings.

8

Tort Liability 222
Introduction. Malpractice Theories.
Admissibility of Evidence and Burden of Proof. Expert Testimony. Fraud.
Introduction. Scienter. The Misrepresentations. Justifiable Reliance.
Injury or Damage. Negligence. Examples of Negligence by Accountants.
Contributory Negligence. Liability to Third Parties—The Ultramares Doctrine.
Modifications of The Ultramares Doctrine. Conclusion.
Suggested Additional Readings.

9

Statutory Liability 258
Introduction. The Securities Act of 1933. Coverage.
Liability Under The 1933 Act. Defenses.
The Securities Exchange Act of 1934. Coverage. Liability Under Section 18.
Liability under Section 10b and Rule 10b-5. Material Misrepresentation.
Scienter. Reliance and Due Diligence. Damages. Conclusion.
Suggested Additional Readings.

10

Criminal Liability   287

Introduction.   Securities Act of 1933—Section 24.
Securities Exchange Act of 1934—Section 32(a).   Criminal Intent.
Tax Return Preparation.   Other Criminal Statutes.
Suggested Additional Readings.

11

Privileged and Confidential Communications   311

Introduction.   An Overview of Privileged Communications.
The Attorney-Client Privilege.   The Accountant-Client Privilege.   Introduction.
The Jurisdiction of Federal Courts.   The Law in Federal Question Cases.
The Law in Diversity Cases.   An Overview of State Statutes.
State Statutes—Interpretative Cases.
Private Communications before Administrative Agencies.
Other Privileged Communications and Accountants.   Introduction.
Privileges Based on The Bill of Rights.
The Umbrella of The Attorney-Client Privilege.
The Work-Product Privilege of Attorneys.
The Future of The Accountant-Client Privilege.   Suggested Additional Readings.

12

Unauthorized Practice of Law   335

Introduction.   An Overview of The Practice of Law—State Statutes.
Statutory Exceptions.   Defining The Subject Matter.
Reasons for Prohibiting the Unauthorized Practice of Law.
Theories Used in Deciding Cases.   Introduction.   The Complexity Test.
Additional Approaches to The Tax Problem.   Federal Licensing and State Laws.
Introduction.   Practice before The IRS.   Practice before The Tax Court.
Conclusion.   Suggested Additional Readings.

PART THREE
APPENDIXES   367

1

Rules of Conduct and Interpretations of Rules of Conduct   369

2

Management Advisory Services Practice Standards   396

3

Statements on Responsibilities in Tax Practice   405

4

The Institute of Internal Auditors Code of Ethics   412

5

Statement of Responsibilities of Internal Auditors   415

6

Standards for the Professional Practice of Internal Auditing   418

7

Association of Government Accountants Code of Ethics   421

8

Standards for Audit of Governmental Organizations, Programs, Activities, and Functions   425

9

Statements of Principles With Respect to the Practice of Law Formulated By Representatives of the American Bar Association and the AICPA   432

10

American Bar Association Statement of Policy Regarding Lawyers' Responses to Auditors' Requests for Information   436

Index   445

Preface

"Auditors in the Dock," "The Hill's New Assault on CPAs," "Accounting Firm Settles Fraud Suit for $2.9 Million," "State Jury Awards $30 Million to Firms in (X) Accounting Firm Case," and "Two Auditors Are Convicted of Stock Fraud," are examples of newspaper headlines dealing with contemporary problems facing the accounting profession. Members of Congress, the Securities and Exchange Commission, courts, attorneys, and clients are often critical of the "accounting establishment" and of the quality of service being rendered by many professional accountants. Many members of the profession are also concerned about the ethical standards of the practice of accounting as well as many of the legal aspects such as malpractice. This book has been prepared to assist the student of accounting and the practitioner in developing an understanding of the professional ethics, responsibilities, and liabilities of accountants.

For many years it has been assumed that individuals would somehow just know what was right and what was wrong, that there was no real need for an in-depth study of ethics, responsibility, and the law relating to accountants. As the foregoing headlines attest, that assumption is false. Too often, accountants in industry and public practice are guilty of *not* seeing the obvious wrong, are *not* aware of an accepted standard of practice, and are *not* living up to the moral code expected of professionals. Civil and criminal liability suits, injunctive and enforcement proceedings by the Securities and Exchange Commission, congressional investigations, and possible additional regulation by government are a fact of life for the profession.

We believe that the study of these professional aspects of the practice of accounting is just as essential to the professional education of accountants as similar topics are to the education of doctors and lawyers. The public is demanding more responsibility and higher standards of ethics and competence from all professional persons. Therefore, all who consider themselves to be professional accountants should not only study professional ethics, responsibility, and liability, but should make them a matter of ongoing concern. This work was developed to assist with these studies and reviews.

Some accounting educators across the country have come to the conclusion that a specific college course in Professional Accounting is needed—a course that will address the ethical and legal issues so important to the practice of accounting. It is hoped that this book will provide the basis for such a course. For those already in practice, we believe that the book will provide a ready reference work. It should also prove valuable in the continuing education programs of individual firms and of professional societies. As more and more accountants understand their professional responsibilities and potential liabilities, the need for regulation and the amount of litigation should be significantly decreased.

The authors are very grateful to the University of Georgia for providing released time for Professor Windal to work on the book, and for invaluable secretarial assistance. We are also grateful for the encouragement and support of Dr. Herbert E. Miller, Director of the School of Accounting at the University of Georgia. Thanks also go to our able reviewers, Ray Dockweiler, School of Accountancy, University of Missouri, Columbia, Fred Skousen, Institute of Professional Accountancy, Brigham Young University, and Jeremy Wiesen, Graduate School of Business Administration, New York University. Finally, we are grateful to our wives, Vicky Windal and Elinor Corley, who not only assisted in the typing and proofreading, but also provided moral support well beyond the ordinary.

Floyd W. Windal
Robert N. Corley

Foreword

It is gratifying to participate, even in this small way, in the publication of this text, for I am confident that it will contribute significantly to the literature of accounting and to the academic preparation of students looking forward to careers in the accounting profession. The authors address a broad range of subjects, all closely interrelated and of vital concern to the professional accountant, yet not previously dealt with in such scope and detail within one set of covers.

Essential to preparation for any profession is an awareness of what it means to be a professional, what it demands by way of commitment from the individual. Certainly, this is true of accounting. It is a demanding profession. Accounting and accountability are vital to the functioning of our free enterprise system—and of our democratic society. Thus, the accountant has a key role and it is essential that he or she be keenly aware of its significance, its requirements and responsibilities, and be prepared for and committed to their fulfillment. This contemplates the whole range of duties, responsibilities, and behavioral requirements, the moral and social as well as the legal and pragmatic.

The authors have provided, in this text, the means to meet this need in a comprehensive, yet orderly way. They deal with the subject area as it affects *all* accounting professionals, whether they be management accountants, internal auditors, external auditors, consultants, or tax practitioners. This is as it should be. Each of these functions has significant responsibilities and requirements; some are common to all, while others are specifically identified with a particular function. As one might expect, there tends to be an emphasis on the role of the public accountant, not because it is more important than the others, but rather, because its unique nature inevitably calls for special attention. The role of the public accountant as an independent auditor is indeed unique in its demands for independence and objectivity, the extensive and evergrowing range of standards, rules and regulations to be observed, the breadth of responsibilities and the possible consequences in terms of liability to third parties.

Although the text is directed primarily to the academic preparation of young men and women planning to pursue careers in accounting, it should prove to be a useful refresher and reference work for those already engaged in such careers, both as a reminder of the requirements of their profession and as a compendium of essential information. Certainly, it can contribute significantly to the staff training programs of public accounting firms.

A word of caution is in order. As comprehensive and as current as the text is, the reader must be aware that such matters as professional responsibilities and liabilities, and technical and behavioral standards and rules, are subject to continuing and significant change in the dynamic environment in which we live and practice. Witness in this respect, as but one example, the almost total elimination of restraints on advertising and solicitation by the American Institute of Certified Public Accountants, in response to pressure by governmental agencies and the influence of court decisions.

The reader must be keenly alert to the need to keep current his or her knowledge of this subject area. That, too, is a responsibility of the professional. In this respect, also, the text should prove helpful, for, in addition to providing the basic background needed for such updating, the recommended reading lists suggest publications which can contribute significantly to keeping one's knowledge current. I would suspect and expect that a careful reading of this work will do much to motivate the reader to stay abreast of developments.

Michael N. Chetkovich

THE
ACCOUNTING
PROFESSIONAL

Part One

PROFESSIONAL
ETHICS
AND
RESPONSIBILITY

What is it that impels one person to live by a high moral code and another to disregard such values? Is it true that those engaged in certain human endeavors are, by the very nature of those endeavors, motivated to a higher standard of conduct? It has certainly been true over the centuries that an especially high standard of behavior has been expected of those engaged in one of the learned professions.

How often, however, have those in such positions of trust disappointed us! Time and again, instances of illegal and immoral activity are brought to our attention, leading us to distrust codes of ethics and professional oaths. Is it not true that in the final analysis the man makes the job, rather than the job the man? Only from within can the motivation come to be an honest lawyer, a trustworthy physician, or an independent accountant.

The late Albert J. Harno, for thirty-five years Dean of the College of Law at the University of Illinois, shared his great insight on these issues in a graduation address in 1961. The following excerpts from that address show that it is as valid today as when it was given:

Life for most people is a day-to-day affair; it is "numbered by years, daies and hours." * Men live, seek diversion and comfort, have fleeting glimpses of happiness, are touched by sorrow, and pass from the scene. A few stop to contemplate and to wonder. But now and then there rises from the multitude a prophet, a Plato, an Aristotle, a Jesus of Nazareth, a Beethoven, an Abraham Lincoln, to fashion for us in words, in poetry, in music, and in song, some lasting conception of the eternal verities of life—of the good, the true, and the beautiful—and to formulate for us directives and precepts to guide us on our way.

We live in an age in which materialism and, in many parts of the world, crass materialism prevails. It is a technical age in which men put their faith in mechanized force, in atomic power, missiles, earth satellites, and space ships. We look for guidance and hear only a babel of voices as men give expression to guile, deception, hate, greed, and prejudice. . . .

There is a clash as to the meaning and place of law as a governing force in society. We Americans subscribe, at least outwardly, to the idea and to the ideal that ours is a government of law—that no individuals, no not even our highest governing officials, are above the law. . . .

But law is not the only force that regulates human conduct. I wish to speak about three areas or domains, of human action. I am indebted to an Englishman, Lord Moulton,† for this classification. The development is my own. The *first* is the area of free choice; the *second,* the domain of obedience to the unenforceable; and *third,* the domain of law.

The first, the domain of free choice, is a limited area. I sometimes wonder if we really appreciate how little freedom of choice we have in making decisions; we are constantly under one pressure or another. If we have an evening to ourselves, we may have a choice of reading . . . or of going to a movie. We may be able to choose whether we will or will not take sugar in our coffee. But even that choice may be denied to us by doctor's orders.

The second domain, that of obedience to the unenforceable, is difficult to define. In it there is no law which determines our course of action, and yet we feel that we are not free to choose as we would. It is a very broad area. It covers those actions which we are not compelled to perform but which some inner voice directs us to discharge. It is the realm of kindliness and conscience—the domain of manners, ethics, and morals. It is the realm which recognizes the sway of duty, of fairness, of honest dealings between men, of sympathy, of taste, and of the spirit. It covers all those things that make life beautiful and a good society possible. What other than a call of conscience is it that makes us willing to take part in community enterprises and in matters relating to the public welfare?

It is the realm of courtesy. There is no compelling reason other than the inner voice that prompts us to speak kindly to our fellowmen. It is the domain

* Bartas, Guillaume De Salluste du, *Divine Weekes and Workes,* second week, third day, part two.

† "Law and Manners," *The Atlantic Monthly,* I (July 1924), 134.

of good manners and honest dealings with others. Manners signify good breeding—and more. Manners are the outward expression of an intellectual and moral conviction. Manners are based in that true and deepest self-respect, and they originate in a respect for others. Manners do not make the man, but they reveal the man.

What is it that causes men to maintain self-restraint and consideration for others in the face of danger? Instances come to mind in which many people were faced with impending disaster and death—a shipwreck, fire, or explosion. The way to escape was open to but few. While this has not always been true, often the physically strong have resisted the temptation to fight their way to safety and have permitted the weaker members, the women and children, of the group to escape. Why was this? Law did not require it. Force at that time was not a factor.

It is the realm of tolerance. When men have lost their tolerance for the views and practices of others, they have lost something that is precious to a good society. Tolerance is the premise for some important provisions that have been written into our Constitution—freedom of speech, freedom of worship, freedom of the press.

It is the realm of truth, of ethics, morals, aesthetics, the spiritual, and of those great precepts: Love thy neighbor as thyself; do unto others as you would have them do unto you.

Truly, the full measure of a man can be gauged by the extent to which he gives obedience to these guides to human conduct that are unenforceable. The extent to which its members give credence to these standards is also the measure of the greatness of a people, of the greatness of a nation. It is through obedience of the people to these precepts that a democratic society is made possible. . . .

Observe how closely the last two domains, that of obedience to the unenforceable and that of obedience to law, are interrelated. They intertwine and complement each other. Obedience to law in a free society is of the essence, but law observance would come to naught unless the members of that society were also deeply devoted to the precept of obedience to that which they cannot be forced to obey. . . .

The issue before us is one of values. There are those among us who assert, and with reason, that we have lost our sense of purposeful direction; that we are a drifting people in ideas and ideals; that we are "paralyzed in self-indulgences"; that the impact of technology upon self-government is subjecting "the processes of democracy to a complete change of scale". . . it is imperative that we do not permit ourselves to be deflected from the supreme and enduring values. We must fortify our lives and all of our actions with these values and make them a fighting faith.

We must never waiver in our support of the democratic process, in our adherence to the rule of law, and in our fidelity to the enduring values of life. Thus accoutered, the individual can rise above the confusion of the day. To live by these values marks the supreme measure of a man, of a people, of a nation.

In the chapters that follow, the world of the professional accountant will be explored in great detail. The organization of the profession, its challenges, and its opportunities will be examined in chapter 1. The next five chapters will provide a detailed look at the profession's ethical code and at many of the day-to-day questions which must be answered within its framework. In each chapter, the ethics and responsibility of the auditor, the management consultant, the tax practitioner, and the internal professional will be examined. The chapter headings parallel the subject matter in the American Institute of Certified Public Accountants (AICPA) Code of Ethics. Throughout Part 1 of the book, the discussion is enhanced by excerpts from published articles and by the reproduction of pertinent accounting and auditing standards. Suggested additional readings are provided at the end of each chapter for those who wish to explore the subject further.

Part 2 of the book deals with accountants and the law. The discussion in that section includes the law of contracts; tort liability, fraud and negligence; statutory liability; criminal liability; privileged and confidential communications; and the unauthorized practice of law. In each of the chapters, relevant court cases are briefed and discussed. Because it is essential to a clear understanding of the principles involved, the detailed reasoning of the court is often given. Many of these sometimes long cases involve landmark decisions that are changing the practice of accounting. They provide vivid examples of past mistakes and point the way to future action. A much more complete preview of Part 2 is given in the introduction to that section.

It is the objective of this book to provide the reader with an understanding of professional ethics and responsibility, and of the legal framework within which the professional accountant must operate. The appendices provide ready access to the *AICPA Rules of Conduct* and their interpretations; the *AICPA Management Advisory Services Practice Standards;* the *AICPA Statement on Responsibilities in Tax Practice;* the Institute of Internal Auditors' *Code of Ethics, Statement of Responsibilities, and Standards for the Professional Practice of Internal Auditing; the Code of Ethics of the Association of Government Accountants;* and the comptroller general's *Standards for Audit of Government Organizations, Programs, Activities and Functions.* In addition, the American Bar Association's *Statement of Policy Regarding Lawyer's Response to Auditor's Request for Information,* and the *Statement of Principles With Respect to the Practice of Law* formulated by representatives of the American Bar Association and the AICPA are reproduced.

Chapter 1

The Accounting Profession

INTRODUCTION

Certified public accountants have for many years regarded themselves as professionals, equal in every respect to the more uniformly recognized professions of law, medicine, and theology. In recent years, furthermore, they have come to be regarded by society as deserving of that appellation. As the subject matter with which they are concerned has increased in volume and complexity, in accordance with similar changes in society, their services have become more critical and more in demand. Our industrialized world of today could not get along without this newest member of the learned professions.

Although those in the public practice of accounting are now generally regarded as professionals, it is just becoming recognized that many accountants practicing within an organization are also worthy of that title. Just as many lawyers work for private business and government, so professional accountants can be found in industry, with a governmental agency, or with a not-for-profit organization. Many hold the CPA certificate and are members of the professional associations of those similarly recognized. Others hold the relatively new CMA certificate and refer to themselves as certified management accountants. Still others are certified internal auditors. All of these people, if true to their calling, have the independent outlook and the high standards of performance attributed to professionals.

One outward sign of the increasing stature of accountants is the movement in higher education to establish schools of accounting. These new administrative units have the potential to do for the accounting profession what schools of law have done for the legal profession. Those schools already established and the faculties at universities moving in that direction have already organized a Federation of Schools of Accountancy to further their aims and speed their progress.

THE STRUCTURE OF A PROFESSION

Just what is it that entitles a particular discipline or calling to be referred to as a profession? There are many pretenders to the title, but few are generally so regarded. A profession might be likened to a building, all parts of which are needed in order for it to be complete and ready for occupancy.

The Foundation

Underlying any profession must be a solid foundation consisting of a recognized body of knowledge essential to the well-being of society. Certainly, the subject matter of accounting meets this criterion. The most widely publicized and accepted statement of this foundation of the accounting profession is *Horizons for a Profession,* by Robert H. Roy and James H. MacNeill.[1] A further validation of the existence of a large and at times very technical body of knowledge in accounting can be found in the accounting programs of the many universities offering courses and degrees in accounting.

That this body of knowledge is needed by society can also be easily confirmed. The myriad accounting reports and filings required by the various agencies of municipal, state, and federal governments would be sufficient in themselves to establish society's need for accountants. The requirement by the Securities and Exchange Commission (SEC) that financial reports filed with it be certified by an independent public accountant is also clear evidence. And, of course, the widespread continued demand for college graduates with training in accounting is further proof.

The Framework

The framework erected on a building foundation also has a parallel in the structure of a profession. Three elements comprise this framework: (1) an

[1] Robert H. Roy and James H. MacNeill, *Horizons for a Profession* (New York: American Institute of Certified Public Accountants, 1967).

educational process to acquire and maintain the body of knowledge, (2) an examination and licensing process to test whether individual practitioners have a firm grasp of the subject matter, and (3) a sense of responsibility to society with regard to the use of this knowledge. All three of these elements are essential.

In accounting, the educational process is well established. Schools and programs of accounting are widely available at colleges and universities. In most states, certain minimum formal educational requirements must be satisfied before an individual is allowed to sit for the CPA examination. Those sitting for the CMA examination must hold a baccalaureate degree from an accredited college or university, achieve a satisfactory score on a recognized graduate school admission examination, or already hold a CPA or comparable certificate from a foreign country. Candidates for the CIA examination must hold a baccalaureate or its equivalent from an accredited college-level institution.

Many states now have continuing education requirements for continued practice as a CPA. Furthermore, anyone practicing as a professional accountant with a firm belonging to the Division of CPA Firms of the American Institute of Certified Public Accountants must satisfy a minimum continuing education requirement. Holders of the CMA certificate must also meet a continuing education requirement in order to maintain their certificate, and one of the standards of the Institute of Internal Auditors is that technical competence should be maintained through continuing education.

As pointed out earlier, a very formal examination and licensing process does exist in accounting. Each state has laws for the examination and licensing of CPAs. A uniform national examination is given, with some states adding sections on subject matter of particular interest in their area. Boards of Accountancy in the various states normally are charged with monitoring the practice of accounting. The National Association of State Boards of Accountancy is an association of these boards. Although no licensing is involved, formal examination procedures also exist for awarding the CMA and the CIA certificates.

Finally, the sense of responsibility to society certainly does exist. This is particularly true of the CPA who is practicing as an independent auditor. He is well aware that his opinion on the fairness of financial statements will be relied upon by third parties, and he acts accordingly. The CPA practicing as a management consultant or as a tax practitioner, and the CPA, CMA, or CIA practicing internally are also becoming increasingly aware of their public responsibility. The trial and conviction in recent years of lawyers and accountants working in government and industry, as well as in public practice, have brought these responsibilities to the attention of all.

The Finish

Just as the walls and roof must be attached to the frame to complete a building, so the professional structure needs some additions for its completion. Three elements are needed: (1) professional associations, (2) codes of ethics, and (3) technical standards.

Professional associations abound in the accounting field. The most important of these is probably the American Institute of Certified Public Accountants. Although primarily an organization of individuals, it also has a Division of CPA Firms, with an SEC Practice Section and a Private Companies Practice Section. The CPAs in each of the various states are also organized into state societies, which normally cooperate with the AICPA in the discipline of members, although they are autonomous.

One of the leading associations for management accountants, those internal professionals working primarily in industry and government, is the National Association of Accountants. The Financial Executives Institute is an association of internal professionals who hold senior positions in the accounting and finance area. Other important organizations of practicing professionals are the Institute of Internal Auditors, the Planning Executives Institute, and the Association of Government Accountants. In the academic world, the American Accounting Association is the leading organization.

The American Institute of CPAs has long had a code of professional ethics. It is this code which provides the framework for the discussion of ethics and responsibility in this book. The rules of conduct established under this code and the interpretations of those rules are reproduced in Appendix 1.

The Institute of Internal Auditors has had its own code of ethics and statement of responsibilities for many years. The code is reproduced in Appendix 4 and the statement of responsibilities in Appendix 5.

The technical standards of the profession come from many sources. The primary source for financial accounting standards is the Financial Accounting Standards Board (FASB). This private sector body, which the Financial Accounting Foundation oversees, is assisted by an advisory council. Pronouncements made in prior years by the AICPA Committee on Accounting Research and the Accounting Principles Board are also considered authoritative unless expressly superceded by the FASB. Accounting principles are also promulgated for defense contractors under federal contracts by the Cost Accounting Standards Board, an official governmental body. Finally, the Securities and Exchange Commission, through its rulings and persuasive power, also establishes and influences the establishment of accounting principles.

In the auditing area, accountants must adhere to generally accepted auditing standards which have been approved and adopted by the membership of the AICPA and which are continually interpreted in Statements on Auditing Standards issued by the Auditing Standards Board (formerly this function was performed by the Auditing Standards Executive Committee). The comptroller general of the United States has also issued a set of audit standards to be applied to audits of all governmental organizations, programming activities, and functions. A summary of these standards is reproduced in Appendix 8.

The Institute of Internal Auditors has also approved a set of standards for the professional practice of internal auditing. A summary of these standards is reproduced in Appendix 6.

THE SECURITIES AND EXCHANGE COMMISSION

Of great significance to the professional accountant is the authority and activity of the Securities and Exchange Commission. Established in 1934, this commission has the authority to define the content and form of financial statements and other reports submitted to it, as well as the methods of accounting used in deriving them. It can also require disclosure of all information it considers necessary for investor decisions. Because virtually all large companies must file reports with the SEC, this gives the commission effective control not only over accounting principles, but also over the auditing procedures necessary to insure proper reporting. Certification of financial information by an independent accountant is required by the securities laws.

Fortunately for the accounting profession, the SEC has delegated to the private sector the general responsibility for the establishment of accounting principles. Its Accounting Series Release (ASR) No. 150 reads in part as follows:

. . . Various Acts of Congress administered by the Securities and Exchange Commission clearly state the authority of the Commission to prescribe the methods to be followed in the preparation of accounts and the form and content of financial statements to be filed under the Acts and the responsibility to assure that investors are furnished with information necessary for informed investment decisions. In meeting this statutory responsibility effectively, in recognition of the expertise, energy and resources of the accounting profession, and without abdicating its responsibilities, the Commission has historically looked to the standard-setting bodies designated by the profession to provide leadership in establishing and improving accounting principles. The determinations by these bodies have been regarded by the Commission with minor exceptions, as being responsive to the needs of investors.

The body presently designated by the Council of the American Institute of Certified Public Accountants (AICPA) to establish accounting principles is the Financial Accounting Standards Board (FASB) . . . the Commission intends to continue its policy of looking to the private sector for leadership in establishing and improving accounting principles and standards through the FASB with the expectation that the body's conclusions will promote the interests of investors.

In Accounting Series Release No. 4 (1938) the Commission states its policy that financial statements prepared in accordance with accounting practices for which there was no substantial authoritative support were presumed to be misleading and that footnote or other disclosure would not avoid this presumption. It also stated that, where there was a difference of opinion between the Commission and a registrant as to the proper accounting to be followed in a particular case, disclosure would be accepted in lieu of correction of the financial statements themselves only if substantial authoritative support existed for the accounting practices followed by the registrant and the position of the Commission had not been expressed in rules, regulations or other official releases. For purposes of this policy, principles, standards and practices promulgated by the FASB in its Statements and Interpretations will be considered by the Commission as having substantial authoritative support, and those contrary to such FASB promulgations will be considered to have no such support.

In the exercise of its statutory authority with respect to the form and content of filings under the Acts, the Commission has the responsibility to assure that investors are provided with adequate information. A significant portion of the necessary information is provided by a set of basic financial statements (including the notes thereto) which conform to generally accepted accounting principles. Information in addition to that included in financial statements conforming to generally accepted accounting principles is also necessary. Such additional disclosures are required to be made in various fashions, such as in financial statements and schedules reported on by independent public accountants or as textual statements required by items in the applicable forms and reports filed with the Commission. The Commission will continue to identify areas where investor information needs exist and will determine the appropriate methods of disclosure to meet these needs.

It must be recognized that in its administration of the Federal Securities Acts and in its review of filings under such Acts, the Commission staff will continue as it has in the past to take such action on a day-to-day basis as may be appropriate to resolve specific problems of accounting and reporting under the particular factual circumstances involved in filings and reports of individual registrants. . . .[2]

---

[2] Securities and Exchange Commission, "Statement of Policy on the Establishment and Improvement of Accounting Principles and Standards," *Accounting Series Release No. 150,* December 20, 1973.

As pointed out in the release, the delegation of authority by the SEC is not absolute or complete. The basic rules for the form and content of financial statements filed with the commission are included in its Regulation S-X, and Accounting Series Releases often set forth required accounting and auditing procedures, as well as disclosure requirements. The SEC has fulfilled its promise in ASR 150 to "continue . . . to take such action on a day-to-day basis as may be appropriate to resolve specific problems." As detailed in Accounting Series Release No. 253, for example, the commission overruled a decision of the FASB on the controversial issue of accounting and reporting practices for oil- and gas-producing activities. As a general rule, however, frequent consultation and communication between the SEC and the FASB have avoided such results.

Regulation S-X is also the vehicle for stating the SEC rule on auditor independence. Rule 2-01, dealing with the qualification of accountants practicing before the commission, states in part:

> The Commission will not recognize any certified public accountant or public accountant as independent who is not in fact independent. For example, an accountant will be considered not independent with respect to any person, or any of its parents, its subsidiaries, or other affiliates (1) in which, during the period of his professional engagement to examine the financial statements being reported on or at the date of his report, he or his firm or a member thereof had, or was committed to acquire, any direct financial interest or any material indirect financial interest; or (2) with which during the period of his professional engagement to examine the financial statements being reported on, at the date of his report or during the period covered by the financial statements, he or his firm or a member thereof was connected as a promoter, underwriter, voting trustee, director, officer, or employee, except that a firm will not be deemed not independent in regard to a particular person if a former officer or employee of such person is employed by the firm and such individual has completely disassociated himself from the person and its affiliates and does not participate in auditing financial statements of the person or its affiliates covering any period of his employment by the person. For the purposes of Rule 2-01 the term "member" means all partners in the firm and all professional employees participating in the audit or located in an office of the firm participating in a significant portion of the audit.
>
> In determining whether an accountant may in fact be not independent with respect to a particular person, the Commission will give appropriate consideration to all relevant circumstances, including evidence bearing on all relationships between the accountant and that person or any affiliate thereof, and will not confine itself to the relationships existing in connection with the filing of reports with the Commission.[3]

[3] Securities and Exchange Commission, "Qualifications of Accountants," Regulation S-X, Article 2-01.

Various Accounting Series Releases have provided interpretations and guidelines for the implementation of this rule. In chapter 2, some of these are noted as the issue of independence is explored in great detail.

The SEC has also adopted certain rules of practice applicable to proceedings before the commission, and Rule 2(e) has become the basis for the suspension and disbarment of accountants who fail to meet the commission's standards. That rule reads in part:

> The Commission may deny, temporarily or permanently, the privilege of appearing or practicing before it in any way to any person who is found by the Commission after notice of an opportunity for hearing in the matter (i) not to possess the requisite qualifications to represent others, or (ii) to be lacking in character or integrity or to have engaged in unethical or improper professional conduct, or (iii) to have willfully violated, or willfully aided and abetted the violation of any provision of the federal securities laws . . . , or the rules and regulations thereunder.[4]

THE CONGRESS

On occasion, an accounting issue has become so controversial and its outcome has been of such importance to the affected parties or the economy that Congress has intervened. For example, legislation reinstating an investment credit for federal income tax purposes in the early 1970s included the provision that companies should be free to choose from among alternative methods of accounting, thus precluding the prescription of a particular method by the profession, as had been attempted earlier. More recently, the Congress as a part of Public Law 94-163, *Energy Policy and Conservation Act* (42 U.S. Code, Sec. 6383), empowered the Securities and Exchange Commission either

> to prescribe rules applicable to persons engaged in the production of crude oil or natural gas, or make effective by recognition, or by other appropriate means indicating a determination to rely on accounting practices developed by the Financial Accounting Standards Board, if the Securities and Exchange Commission is assured that such practice will be observed by persons engaged in the production of crude oil or natural gas to the same extent as would result if the Securities and Exchange Commission had prescribed such practices by rule.[5]

[4] Securities and Exchange Commission, *Rules of Practice*, Rule 2(e), par. 201.2.

[5] "Financial Accounting and Reporting by Oil and Gas Companies," *Statement of Financial Accounting Standards No. 19* (Stamford, Conn.: Financial Accounting Standards Board, 1977), par. 75. Copyright © 1977 by Financial Accounting Standards Board, High Ridge Park, Stamford, Connecticut 06905, U.S.A. Reprinted with permission. Copies of the complete document are available from the FASB.

The effect of this provision was to require that an accounting question, over which there was great disagreement, be resolved by a specific date. The Congress was unwilling to allow the private sector to proceed at its own pace with resolving the issue.

Congress has also become directly involved with the accounting profession in recent years as the result of a variety of national concerns. Some of these are detailed in the following introduction to a report of the Subcommittee on Reports, Accounting and Management (Metcalf subcommittee) of the Committee on Governmental Affairs of the United States Senate. The report itself is entitled "Improving the Accountability of Publicly Owned Corporations and their Auditors."

> During the past several years, serious questions have arisen concerning the activities and accountability of publicly owned corporations operating in the United States and throughout the world. These questions have arisen in large part from a series of unexpected failures by major corporations, as well as disclosures of widespread questionable and illegal activities by the managements of many publicly owned corporations. Such problems have contributed to a severe decline of public confidence in the integrity of American business.
>
> Public confidence in the integrity and efficiency of the business community must be restored because such confidence is the key element in making the Nation's economic system function effectively. The Federal Government has certain public policy responsibilities in helping to assure the accountability of publicly owned corporations as set forth in the Securities Act of 1933 and the Securities Exchange Act of 1934. The Federal Government also has an important direct interest in understanding and correcting problems in the business sector. Those problems can lead to substantial Federal assistance programs, as in the cases of Penn Central Corp. and Lockheed Aircraft Corp.
>
> Congress has attempted to meet its responsibilities in this area through various initiatives, both in the enactment of legislation deemed necessary and in the increased oversight activities by appropriate committees.
>
> The Subcommittee on Reports, Accounting and Management is responsible for assuring, among other things, that accounting and financial reporting practices promulgated or approved by the Federal Government are responsive to the needs of the public. Accordingly, this subcommittee has devoted substantial time and effort over the past two years to evaluating the role of such accounting and financial reporting practices as a means of improving the accountability of publicly owned corporations.

The CPA Letter, a semimonthly news report published by the AICPA, summarized the report of this Senate subcommittee as follows:

> Accounting and auditing standards relating to publicly held companies should be set by the accounting profession with close oversight

by the SEC. This is the thrust of the report of the subcommittee on reports, accounting and management of the Senate Committee on Governmental Affairs.

Heading the list of recommendations is the establishment of a self-regulatory organization with disciplinary powers similar to those of the New York Stock Exchange or the National Association of Securities Dealers. All firms that audit publicly held companies would be required to join and meet the organization's performance and behavioral standards. A quality review program would be an essential element. The SEC would have an oversight role to evaluate and determine whether the standards and policies meet established public policies.

The following are among the subcommittee's other recommendations:

> Broaden the basis for representation on standard-setting bodies to include members from small businesses and accounting firms.
>
> Require all firms with publicly held clients to disclose financial data and important operating information.
>
> Require that the profession or the SEC mandate corporate audit committees composed of outside directors.
>
> Limit management advisory services by accounting firms to areas directly related to accounting. The report states that these related activities "are confined to the limited area of providing certain computer and systems analyses that are necessary for improving internal control procedures of corporations."
>
> End artificial professional restrictions against advertising and talking with another firm's clients. Also, employment offers to employees of other firms should be permitted without first consulting with the present employers.
>
> Auditors should be liable to private parties who suffer damages as a result of the auditors' negligence.
>
> Rotate personnel assigned to a specific audit within an accounting firm, pending more study by the profession and the SEC on the desirability of the rotation of firms among publicly held corporations.[6]

In the House of Representatives of the Congress, a similar investigation was undertaken by the Subcommittee on Oversight and Investigations (the Moss subcommittee) of the Committee on Interstate and Foreign Commerce. The outcome of that investigation was the introduction of a bill to further regulate the accounting profession through the establishment of the National Organization of SEC Accountancy (NOSEC). The bill also called for the establishment of an SEC-appointed board which would be authorized to review and investigate auditors registered with NOSEC.

---

[6] "Metcalf Report Calls for Prompt Private Sector Action," *The CPA Letter,* Vol. 57, No. 20, November 28, 1977, p. 1. Copyright © 1977 by the American Institute of Certified Public Accountants, Inc.

Economic sanctions, fines, and other disciplinary actions were provided for in the proposal.

In summary, the accounting profession is under intense congressional scrutiny. Although many of the concerns expressed by the Metcalf and Moss subcommittees have already been addressed, the burden of proof is still on the profession to prove that its own self-regulatory legislation is effective and adequate. Otherwise, new regulatory legislation is likely to be forthcoming.

THE COMMISSION ON AUDITORS' RESPONSIBILITIES

Concurrently with the congressional investigations discussed in the preceding section, a comprehensive study of auditors' responsibilities was conducted under the auspices of the AICPA. An independent commission, chaired by the late Manuel F. Cohen, former chairman of the Securities and Exchange Commission, devoted about three years to the project.

The conclusions and recommendations of the commission, some of which have already been adopted, are complex and do not lend themselves readily to summarization. They deal, however, with the following subjects and are worthy of separate study:

1. The independent auditor's role in society.
2. Forming an opinion on financial presentations.
3. Reporting on significant uncertainties in financial presentations.
4. Clarifying responsibility for the detection of fraud.
5. Corporate accountability and the law.
6. The boundaries of the auditor's role and their extension.
7. The auditor's communication with users.
8. The education, training and development of auditors.
9. Maintaining the independence of auditors.
10. The process of establishing auditing standards.
11. Regulating the profession to maintain the quality of audit practice.[7]

Specific recommendations of the commission will be mentioned throughout the text as various topics are considered.

EDUCATION STANDARDS

In 1969, the AICPA Committee on Education and Experience Requirements for CPAs concluded that at least five years of college study were

[7] *The Commission on Auditor's Responsibilities: Report, Conclusions, and Recommendations* (New York: AICPA, 1978), pp. xvii–xxxiv.

needed to obtain the common body of knowledge for CPAs, set forth in *Horizons for a Profession.*[8] In 1978, the AICPA Task Force on the Report of the Committee on Education and Experience Requirements for CPAs reaffirmed that conclusion, although restating it in terms of 150 semester hours. This task force, in addition to revising the curriculum proposals of the 1969 report, reviewed and reevaluated the recommendations made by that committee. In October 1978, the following ten statements of policy recommended by it were approved by the governing council of the AICPA:

STATEMENTS OF POLICY ON EDUCATION REQUIREMENTS FOR ENTRY INTO THE ACCOUNTING PROFESSION

1. The CPA certificate is evidence of basic competence of professional quality in the discipline of accounting. This basic competence is demonstrated by acquiring the body of knowledge common to the profession and passing the CPA examination.

2. *Horizons for a Profession* is authoritative for the purpose of delineating the common body of knowledge to be possessed by those about to begin their professional careers as CPAs.

3. At least 150 semester hours of college study are needed to obtain the common body of knowledge for CPAs and should be the education requirement. For those who meet this standard, no qualifying experience should be required to sit for the CPA examination.

4. The scope and content of the educational program should approximate what is described in "Academic Preparation for Professional Accounting Careers," and should lead to the awarding of a graduate degree.

5. At the earliest practical date, the states should adopt the 150 semester hour educational requirement. The date by which implementation of this policy may be practical may be dependent upon the following factors: (1) the current education requirement in each jurisdiction; (2) the availability of graduate accounting education in each jurisdiction; and (3) appropriate lead time to permit individuals to meet proposed education requirements.

6. Candidates should be encouraged to take the CPA Examination as soon as they have fulfilled the education requirements, and as close to their college graduation dates as possible. For those graduating in June, this may involve taking the May examination on a provisional basis.

7. Student internships are desirable and are encouraged as part of the educational program.

[8] Report of the Committee on Education and Experience Requirements for CPAs (New York: AICPA, 1969), p. 6; and Robert H. Roy and James H. MacNeill, *Horizons for a Profession* (New York: AICPA, 1967).

8. The AICPA should encourage the development of quality professional programs of accounting (or schools of professional accounting) and participate in their accreditation.

9. Educational programs must be flexible and adaptive, and this is best achieved by entrusting their specific content to the academic community. However, the knowledge to be acquired and abilities to be developed through formal education for professional accounting are proper and continuing concerns of the AICPA.

10. The AICPA should review periodically the standards of admission requirements for CPAs.[9]

"Academic Preparation for Professional Accounting Careers," referred to in statement 4 above, is an Appendix to the report and includes the sample program shown in Table 1.

Another AICPA-appointed group, the Board on Standards for Programs and Schools of Professional Accounting, completed its work in 1977. Its charge was to "identify those standards that, when satisfied by a school, would justify its recognition by the accounting profession." The board acknowledged in its final report that "professional careers in accounting can be pursued in either the private or public sector, that the professional accountant can function as a member of management or as a practicing certified public accountant, that such a person can serve as either an internal or an independent auditor, and that recognition of professional competence and attainment can be achieved by successful performance on an established examination, such as the CPA examination." [10]

The report goes on to identify certain environmental conditions that are essential for a professional program, as well as specific standards dealing with such things as admission and retention of students, curriculum, faculty, financial support, physical plant and equipment, library, computer facilities, and the performance of graduates.

The Committee on Accounting Education of the American Accounting Association also prepared a statement of standards for a professional accounting education. This report is very similar to that of the AICPA and, in fact, borrows freely from it. It goes one step beyond the AICPA report, however, and sets forth standards for a four-year baccalaureate program and for Master of Business Administration programs with an accounting concentration. It points out that while these are not professional programs,

[9] Task Force on the Report of the Committee on Education and Experience Requirements for CPA's, *Education Requirements for Entry Into the Accounting Profession: A Statement of AICPA Policies* (New York: AICPA, 1978). Copyright © 1978 by the American Institute of Certified Public Accountants, Inc.

[10] *Final Report, Board on Standards for Programs and Schools of Professional Accounting* (New York: AICPA, 1977), preface.

TABLE 1

A SAMPLE PROGRAM

	Semester Hours
General Education	
Communication	6–9
Behavioral sciences	6
Economics	6
Elementary accounting	3–6
Introduction to the computer	3
Mathematics and statistics	12
Other general education	24–18
	60
General Business Education	
Economics (theory and the monetary system)	6
The legal and social environment of business	3
Business law	6
Marketing	3
Finance	6
Organization, group, and individual behavior	3–6
Quantitative applications in business	6
Written communication	3
	36–39
Accounting Education *	
Financial accounting theory ⎫	
Applied financial accounting problems ⎬	15
Contemporary financial accounting issues ⎭	
Cost determination and analysis ⎫	
Cost control ⎬	6
Cost-based decision making ⎭	
Tax theory and considerations ⎫	
Tax problems ⎬	6
Audit theory and philosophy ⎫	
Audit problems ⎬	6
Computers and information systems	6
	39 †
Electives	15–12 †
Total semester hours	150

* Includes accounting for both profit-oriented and not-for-profit entities.

† 3 semester hours of the 39 hours of accounting education and 6 hours of the 12–15 hours of electives, or both, might be allotted to an area of specialization.

intent of the rules of conduct. Perhaps this reflected the fact that their practices were still being conducted on a more personal basis and in the form of traditional professional partnerships.

The changes in attitudes that emerged during this era are at the root of the uneasy feeling that the traditional notions about professionalism are in danger of becoming extinct. It had long been accepted that one of the main characteristics of a true profession is a dedication to putting unselfish service to clients and the public ahead of income considerations. The size, structure and operating methods of the largest firms seemed to run counter to this ideal. Partly because of this perception, local firm practitioners have become increasingly critical of the larger firms, whose activities they regard as turning their profession into a commercial business.

The fundamental changes in approach to the practice of public accounting adopted by the larger firms were carried into the 1960s. It was during this decade that the merger movement within the profession began to subside and a period of consolidation took place. At the same time, however, the corporate world was embarking on a spree of mergers and acquisitions, which culminated in the birth of many new large conglomerates.

Some of the people responsible for assembling the conglomerates were a new breed of management who had discovered how to take advantage of alternative accounting principles to reflect earnings on financial statements before such earnings had actually been realized. Others used a similar approach to capitalize on the widespread speculation that was taking place in the securities markets, particularly in such fields as franchising and real estate development.

Because the profession had just come through a period of rapid expansion it was ill-prepared to deal with these new developments. The firms were often inclined to view their responsibilities as running primarily to management, and they generally felt justified in expressing unqualified opinions on financial statements—as long as the statements conformed to one of the alternatives permitted under generally accepted accounting principles. Ultimately, the combination of abuses in the application of accounting principles and the rampant speculation in the securities markets culminated in a series of spectacular business collapses followed by a rash of class action lawsuits against the auditors involved.

Meanwhile, as a result of the collapse of such major corporations as Penn Central, the financial press began to discover that the work of auditors was newsworthy. The importance of accounting principles was quickly identified, and the cry went up that the setting of accounting standards was too important to be left solely to the accounting profession. Members within the profession were also calling for reforms in the standard-setting process, thereby reflecting the differences in views that existed between the national firms. It was in this context that the Study on Establishment of Accounting Principles (the Wheat committee) was set up, which led to the establishment of the present Financial Accounting Foundation and the Financial Accounting Standards Board.

Initially, the profession was slow to realize the full implications of the mounting public concern about accounting principles and the outbreak of lawsuits against auditors. However, as the lawsuits multiplied and the claims for damages assumed monumental proportions, the national firms began to take steps to protect themselves. Extensive training programs were developed, defensive auditing procedures were adopted and intensive systems of quality controls and compliance reviews were installed. The large firms rapidly were becoming acutely conscious of legal liability, and they began building in-house legal departments to cope with the growing volume of litigation.

By the mid-1970s, the pressures of civil liability suits and Securities and Exchange Commission injunctive and enforcement proceedings had brought about significant changes in attitudes within the national CPA firms. Responsibilities to investor and creditor interests came to be more fully recognized, and every precaution was taken to assure that audited financial statements were not based on accounting measurements that reported earnings prematurely. The forces of the marketplace and existing institutions had resulted in correcting the abuses of the 1960s—and they have had a profound and lasting impact on the practice of public accounting as it relates to publicly traded companies.

Not to be overlooked during this period was the combined impact on accounting principles of an aggressive and activist chief accountant of the SEC and the emergence of the FASB. Beginning in 1972, the SEC issued a steady flow of accounting series releases, which greatly increased the amount of disclosures required in financial reporting and which pressed auditors to assume new responsibilities. Reviews of interim financial statements, expressing preferability with respect to alternative accounting principles, disclosures of replacement costs of productive plant and inventories, and reconsideration of the desirability of publishing financial forecasts were among the many issues that were addressed.

Meanwhile, the FASB was shifting into high gear. It issued standards on such long-standing problems as accounting for research and development costs, leases, translation of foreign financial statements and segments of a business. The standing of the FASB's pronouncements was greatly enhanced by the issuance of ASR 150, which acknowledged the SEC's willingness to rely on standards established by the FASB.

In the space of less than five years, these developments caused an enormous growth in both the volume and complexity of financial accounting and reporting standards. This upsurge in activity was a direct result of the demands for better accounting and disclosure that arose from the abuses and business failures of the late 1960s.

Despite the impressive progress achieved in making financial statements more informative and reliable, events occurred that aroused the interest and concerns of congressional committees. Congress discovered that economic data used for establishing national policies was only as reliable as the financial statements on which it was based. This fact became painfully clear when, as a result of the energy crisis, Congress found that financial reports of different oil and gas companies were not comparable because various methods of accounting measurement were used. Congressman John E. Moss (D-Calif.) promptly introduced an amendment to the 1975 energy legislation to mandate the establishment of uniform accounting standards for the petroleum industry. In the process, he raised anew the question of whether accounting standards should be established by a government body instead of relying on the private sector.

Hard on the heels of this development came the disturbing revelations of improper political contributions, illegal bribes and offbook slush funds of hundreds of the nation's largest corporations. The shock waves from disclosures of these practices are still reverberating, and they have raised questions about the performance of independent auditors—questions that have damaged the credibility of the profession.

Out of these and other related events has come the current wave of investigations by various government bodies into the role and performance of our profession. Subcommittees of both houses of Congress, the SEC, the Federal Trade Commission and the Justice Department are all engaged in deliberations about what should be done to make auditors more effective and financial reporting more reliable. Among the concerns being addressed are

1. The establishment of accounting and auditing standards.
2. The independence of auditors.
3. Regulation of independent auditors practicing before the SEC.
4. Anticompetitive practices and concentration within the profession.

Although the profession did not anticipate much of what has happened, it was sufficiently concerned about its growing loss of credibility that an independent commission was appointed in 1974 to study the role and responsibilities of auditors. The final report of this Commission on Auditors' Responsibilities, chaired by the late Manuel Cohen, was issued early this year. It contained over forty recommendations that, if fully implemented, will have a far-reaching effect on how independent auditors discharge their responsibilities.

During the past two years, the profession has thus been confronted with a bewildering and sometimes conflicting array of recommendations for reform emanating from congressional subcommittees, the Cohen commission and CPAs, whose formal statements and testimony have been presented to congressional hearings, the Justice Department and the SEC. Clearly, the profession had to respond to these calls for changes or it ran the real and imminent risk of losing a voice in the shaping of its own destiny. The possibility of federal legislation to impose new layers of regulation on the profession was too serious to be ignored.

Starting in June 1977, the American Institute of CPAs formulated a comprehensive program to respond to criticisms and recommendations that had been made. The key features were

1. Establishment of a division for CPA firms and also to deal with the problems relating to differences in the size of firms and nature of clients served in public practice.

2. Improvement in the effectiveness of the disciplining of individual CPAs.
3. Steps to enhance the independence of auditors.
4. Changes to improve the auditor's report, the setting of auditing standards and corporate accountability through expanding the role of auditors, based largely on recommendations of the Cohen commission.
5. Modifying the profession's rules on advertising, solicitation and other behavioral prohibitions that might be regarded as anticompetitive.
6. Providing for greater public participation in the affairs of the profession by adding public members to the AICPA board of directors and opening meetings of other policy-making bodies to the public.

This extensive overhaul of the profession's structure . . . has not had smooth sailing, . . .

The establishment of a division for CPA firms composed of two sections, one for SEC practice and another for private companies practice, has given formal recognition to the long-standing differences involved in serving clients that are publicly traded and those that are not. Fears have been expressed that institutionalizing these differences will aggravate the competitive problems of the smaller firms and result in a divided profession. A group of 18 practitioners . . . brought a lawsuit against the AICPA . . . to require a referendum of the Institute's membership, presumably with the intention of bringing about changes in the implementation of the division for CPA firms.

The fact is that no amount of pretending that differences in practice do not exist will make them disappear. There is no denying that regulation of firms practicing before the SEC is being demanded, and either the federal government or the profession will establish a mechanism for this purpose. It is clear that the vast volume of complex accounting and auditing standards appropriate for SEC registrants has become excessively burdensome when applied to smaller and privately held companies, and a method of drawing distinctions must be devised. There is little doubt that more competition, not less, is being called for and that artificial devices to protect CPA firms of all sizes from the ravages of competition are not likely to be permitted. Few would deny that there are great pressures to expand the role and responsibilities of auditors as part of a broader demand for greater accountability by publicly traded corporations.

The sooner our profession faces up to these facts of life, the more likely it is that we will avoid becoming obsolete. The social forces that are confronting us are not to be denied, and clinging to the old traditions is not likely to result in maintaining the status quo.

The profession's present program is designed to bring about changes that will deal realistically with the facts which confront us and keep us in harmony with the trends in our society. There is room for debate about specific parts of the program, but those who believe that changes are unnecessary are inviting extensive government intervention.

The SEC is supporting the profession's program, and it is opposing any additional regulatory legislation at this time. However, it is sharply critical of the profession for not going far enough, and it is applying substantial pressure for additional changes.

At the present time, it is difficult to predict with precision the future effects of the developments that have evolved during the past 30 years, and that have converged at a rapidly accelerating pace into the present state of affairs. When viewed in perspective, however, it is possible to conclude that what is happening is the evolution toward greater professionalism, not its death.

In the past, we laid claim to being a profession on the grounds of having all the trappings traditionally identified with those of other professions. However, our preoccupations have been largely with matters within the profession. Our understanding of the true public interest nature of our role has not been as clear as it is now becoming. It has been all too easy to expouse in our literature our dedication to serving the public. Now, however, we are being pressed to make our actions correspond more fully with the ideas that we have articulated in the past.

There are many signs that our professionalism is becoming more substantive. By dropping our bans on advertising and solicitation, we are getting away from the notion that being professional depends in part on such restraints. Instead, we have come to recognize that high levels of skills and expertise are far more important. Greater emphasis is being placed on pre-entry education as well as continuing post-entry education. Independence, quality controls and compliance with standards are being given much greater attention to assure that the highest possible levels of performance are attained.

The impact of liability suits has made it clear that auditors cannot afford to view their role as being primarily responsible to corporate management. The acceptance of a role that is more closely akin to that of a public servant is reflected in the accounting and auditing standards being adopted. Responsibilities to do more than find a way for clients to conform to generally accepted accounting principles are being more widely recognized. The implications of rule 203 of the rules of conduct, which requires the exercise of a judgment about whether financial statements are misleading on an overall basis, are being more fully recognized.

The need for a means to regulate CPA firms in addition to individuals has now gained acceptance and is bringing the profession's disciplinary machinery more squarely in line with the realities of modern practice.

Openly addressing the practical differences in practice between large and small firms and between serving publicly traded companies as compared to small, privately held companies has caused CPAs in public practice to have a growing appreciation of the need for a satisfactory way to deal with these differences. We are trying to do this by working together to establish appropriate practice sections under the umbrella of the AICPA so that we can remain a unified profession on a national basis.

These are all indications that our profession is coming of age. We are tackling the hard problems that have been accumulating since the late 1940s. We are becoming more professional in the sense that we are addressing our public obligations in a more substantive way than ever before. We are developing skills and expertise that far transcend those of earlier times and that give us a more legitimate claim to being professionals.

There is little doubt that much remains to be accomplished and that some of our present initiatives may prove to be wrong in the light of hindsight. But one thing seems certain when viewed in the perspective of events of the past 30 years: our professionalism is far from dead or in danger of becoming extinct. To the contrary, we are moving rapidly in the opposite direction toward making our claim to professional status more soundly based than it has ever been. If we keep this firmly in mind during this difficult period of transition, we will steer a safe course into the future.[12]

>>

1. What are the essential elements of a profession? Discuss each in relation to accounting. Does accounting measure up?

2. Are accountants practicing in industry, government, or with a not-for-profit organization, members of the profession? What is the meaning of CPA, CMA, or CIA after an individual's name?

3. Have any formal codes of professional ethics been adopted within the profession? Who has adopted them? How are technical standards established within the profession?

4. Discuss the role of continuing education in a profession. What requirements are there for continuing education in the accounting profession?

5. Name seven professional associations in the area of accounting. What group of professionals does each serve?

6. What authority does the Securities and Exchange Commission have with regard to accounting principles? How does it exercise it? What other authority does the SEC have over those practicing accounting?

7. Discuss the role which the Congress of the United States has played and is playing in the establishment of accounting principles and auditing standards.

8. What are some of the issues considered by the Commission on Auditors' Responsibilities (Cohen Commission)?

9. What are the ten Statements of Policy on Education Requirements for Entry into the Accounting Profession approved by the governing council of the AICPA? How many semester hours of collegiate education are recommended?

[12] Wallace E. Olson, "Is Professionalism Dead?" *The Journal of Accountancy,* July 1978, pp. 78–82. Copyright © 1978 by the American Institute of Certified Public Accountants, Inc.

10. What types of standards were recommended by the Board on Standards for Programs and Schools of Professional Accounting? Has any other group performed a similar study?

11. What steps have been taken by the AICPA to respond to criticisms and recommendations of the Commission on Auditors' Responsibilities (Cohen Commission), congressional subcommittees, the Justice Department, and the SEC?

SUGGESTED ADDITIONAL READINGS

Committee on Accounting Education, *Standards for Professional Accounting Education.* Sarasota, Florida: American Accounting Association, 1976.

Final Report, Board on Standards for Programs and Schools of Professional Accounting. New York: AICPA, 1977.

SKOUSEN, K. FRED, *An Introduction to the SEC.* Cincinnati, Ohio: Southeastern Publishing Company, 1973.

ROY, ROBERT H., and JAMES H. MACNEILL, *Horizons for a Profession.* New York: AICPA, 1967.

Securities and Exchange Commission, "Adoption of Requirements for Financial Accounting and Reporting Practices for Oil and Gas Producing Activities," *ASR No. 253,* 31 August 1978.

Task Force on the Report of the Committee on Education and Experience Requirements, *Education Requirements for Entry Into Accounting Profession: A Statement of AICPA Policies.* New York: AICPA, 1978.

The Commission on Auditors' Responsibilities: Report, Conclusions, and Recommendations. New York: AICPA, 1978.

Chapter

2

Independence, Integrity, and Objectivity

INTRODUCTION

Independence, in the context of accounting, refers both to the mental attitude of the accountant in approaching a task and to any relationship with the party served which would impair or appear to impair the reliability of the work done. In brief, independence deals with the actual and the perceived ability of the accountant "to act with integrity and objectivity." [1]

The appearance of an independent mental attitude is as important to an auditor as the attitude itself. To the management consultant and the tax practitioner, the mental attitude is primary and appearance secondary. To the internal professional, an independent mental attitude constitutes the whole of independence.

Some of the rules of conduct adopted by the American Institute of Certified Public Accountants and by the various state societies of CPAs in their codes of professional ethics help to insure the presence of independence, integrity, and objectivity, both perceived and actual. These rules, for example, prohibit the expression of an opinion on financial statements when certain financial relationships with clients exist, or when relationships

---

[1] "Concepts of Professional Ethics," AICPA Professional Standards, vol. 2, ET Section 52.02.

exist in which the CPA is virtually a part of management or an employee under management's control. As detailed in Appendix 1, they deal specifically with such issues as directorships, accounting services, family relationships, financial interests, and loans.

Although the CPA is bound to abide by specified rules of conduct, there are also other forces and restraints that cause honest, objective, and independent behavior. The Securities and Exchange Commission, for example, has set forth certain guidelines relating to the independence of accountants who audit and report on financial statements filed with the commission. Violation of these rules can result in loss of the right to practice before the commission. The possibility of legal action is, of course, present if the accountant acts improperly. In addition, improper conduct may cause a loss of the license to practice as a CPA, with the subsequent loss of income and reputation in the community. Perhaps most importantly, the sense of responsibility and pride which goes with being a member of a respected profession acts as an invisible barrier to improper behavior.

Whether or not a particular act or relationship would impair an accountant's independence is often not clear. Interpretations of the rules of conduct are constantly being issued by the AICPA to cover new situations that arise in practice. When in doubt, it is a good rule of thumb for the professional accountant to assume that the proposed relationship or act *would* be in violation of ethical conduct. In this way, any possible embarrassment or censure will be avoided, and there will be no possibility of even the appearance of a lack of independence.

THE AUDITOR

The concept of independence has long been vital to a successful audit practice. When expressing an opinion on the financial statements of a client, the judgment of the certified public accountant must not only be impartial and unbiased, but it must also appear to be so to any outside observer. Great importance is attached to the presence of this state of independence because of the reliance placed upon the work of the auditor by third parties and the general public. Those who rely upon the financial statements of business enterprises as a fair presentation of financial position and of the results of operations must be assured that those statements have been examined and reported upon by someone who is completely objective.

Independence may be impaired because of a financial conflict of interest. For example, assume that as a partner in a large regional public accounting firm, you have been asked by a close friend of yours, who is the chief executive officer of a local bank, whether your firm would be interested in becoming the bank's auditors. Assume that your own home mortgage and that of several of your partners is with this bank, and that the firm has a line of credit with the bank to provide working capital at certain times of the year. Assume also that you have a personal loan from the bank to finance the purchase of some land you are considering developing. Do these facts destroy independence and prevent your accepting the engagement?

Rule of Conduct 101 specifically exempts home mortgages from the general rule that independence will be considered to be impaired if "during the period of his professional engagement, or at the time of expressing his opinion," the member or his firm has "any loan to or from the enterprise" being audited, or from "any officer, director, or principal stockholder thereof." The mortgage must, however, be "made under normal lending procedures, terms, and requirements." A similar exception applies to loans obtained by a member or his firm which are "not material in relation to the net worth" of the borrower, and to "other secured loans, except loans guaranteed by a member's firm which are otherwise unsecured." [2] Thus, independence would probably not be impaired in this case by the line of credit with the bank or by the personal loan.

What if one of the partners had just completed service as executor of an estate that had a direct material financial interest in the bank? The key fact here is that the partner's service as executor has been completed. Independence is not therefore impaired. However, if the service takes place during the period of the engagement or at the time of expressing an opinion, independence would be impaired.[3]

Auditors must also possess the highest integrity. This demand often conflicts with the desire to succeed in one's career. For example, assume that a new senior accountant has been working particularly hard to meet the time budget agreed upon at the start of an audit. It becomes apparent to him that he is not going to make it. While driving home at midnight for the second straight day, it occurs to him that one way of meeting the deadline and still getting the job done would be to work straight through the upcoming long holiday weekend but not record the time on his report.

Would following the contemplated course of action be a violation of the AICPA Code of Professional Ethics? Would it matter if he discussed it with his superior, an audit manager, who tacitly gave his consent? What if he knew that he had not been working at top speed early in the audit and thus had taken longer than normal to complete the earlier phases? Would such action be justified if this were an audit of the United Fund or the Red Cross? While there is no easy answer to this question, the importance of maintaining the very highest standard of integrity leads to the conclusion

---

[2] "Independence," *AICPA Professional Standards*, vol. 2, ET Section 101.01.
[3] Ibid.

that the contemplated action should not be taken under any of the described circumstances.

The receipt of gifts by auditors from clients also raises issues of independence and integrity. Friendships develop in the normal course of events, and social contacts are inevitable. These contacts frequently lead to situations involving ethical problems. For example, assume that an accountant has had a long and friendly relationship with the controller of one of his clients. When the accountant first joined the CPA firm in which he is now a partner, the controller was in a lower level position with his company. The accountant has served over the years as junior, senior, and now partner on the audit of the company. Having moved up together, the two are now good friends. The controller invites the accountant to join him and several other officers of the company on a weekend fishing trip. The accountant offers to pay his share of the expenses, but his friend refuses on the grounds that the company owes it to him for his good service.

Would the accountant be acting in an unethical way if he accepted the offer? If acceptance would not be unethical in this case, what if the offer was for a free trip to Europe? Is the value of the gift significant? Anything "more than a token gift" would at least raise a question as to the appearance of independence, and it might well impair independence itself.[4] The accountant in this case would be wise to insist upon paying his share of the expenses.

Problems such as the foregoing might be avoided or reduced somewhat by rotation of the audit staff on individual engagements. Rotation may not affect the independence of the staff, but it certainly will increase the appearance of independence. The latter is just as important as the former.

Family relationships also create difficult issues for auditors. For example, assume that for many years a partner in a firm has maintained a close relationship with his sister and her husband. The two families have frequently gone on vacations together, and often talked long distance over the phone. The sister is an astute businesswoman and has recently been promoted to an executive position with a client of the firm. Since she is located in a distant city, the partner has nothing to do with the audit. Is the independence of the firm impaired? Is the appearance of independence impaired?

Although independence may not be lacking in this case, the appearance of independence would be. The fact that such a close relative of the auditor has a responsible executive position with the client would impair the appearance of independence, especially in view of the close ties that have been maintained over the years. Had there been both a geographical

---

[4] "Ethics Rulings on Independence, Integrity and Objectivity," *AICPA Professional Standards,* vol. 2, ET Section 191.002.

separation and infrequent contact, the impairment might have been miti-gated.[5]

THE MANAGEMENT CONSULTANT AND THE TAX PRACTITIONER

The management consultant and the tax practitioner should always maintain an independent mental attitude. The accountant's professional judgment should never be subordinated to others even in nonauditing engagements, and all conclusions should be expressed honestly and objectively.

However, when the public accountant is not performing the audit function, the *appearance* of independence need not be maintained. The nonaudit practitioner is, nevertheless, encouraged to avoid the relationships prohibited in the rules of conduct.

Included among the Management Advisory Services Practice Standards is one requiring the practitioner to "act with integrity and objectivity" and to "be independent in mental attitudes." [6] Similarly, some of the statements on responsibilities in tax practice deal with the practitioner's independence, integrity, and objectivity. A tax practitioner's knowledge of an error in return preparation, for example, or of the failure to file a return challenges his independence and integrity. Should he simply keep quiet about the error or is he under an obligation to disclose it? Statement on Responsibilities in Tax Practice No. 6 requires that he advise his client promptly upon learning of the error, but he may not inform the Internal Revenue Service without the client's permission.[7] This issue also relates to the practitioner's responsibility to his client and therefore will be discussed further in chapter 4.

The question is frequently raised as to whether the rendering of management consulting or accounting services to a client would impair independence to the extent that an audit could not be performed for the same client. Assume, for example, that for approximately three years your local CPA firm has been preparing both monthly financial statements and tax returns for a small, but rapidly growing, manufacturing company. One of your staff accountants goes regularly to the client's office and gathers the necessary information maintained there by a part-time bookkeeper. This morning you were asked by the owner of the business to perform a full-fledged audit of the company. You were told by the owner that a

---

[5] "Independence," *AICPA Professional Standards,* vol. 2, ET Section 101.05.

[6] "Management Advisory Services Practice Standards." *AICPA Professional Standards,* vol. 1, MS Section 101.06 (See Appendix 2 for all of the standards).

[7] "Statements on Responsibilities in Tax Practice," *AICPA Professional Standards,* vol. 1, TX Section 161.04 (See Appendix 3 for all of the statements).

local bank has requested the audit, as a precondition to granting an expansion loan.

Is it ethical for you to perform the audit after having been regularly involved in the preparation of the company's financial statements and tax returns? Would it make any difference if you had kept the books and records in your office and done all of the bookkeeping for the company? Generally, the performance of accounting services for an audit client will not impair the auditor's independence. Nevertheless, an accountant "performing accounting services for an audit client must meet the following requirements to retain the appearance that he is not virtually an employee, and therefore lacking in independence in the eyes of a reasonable observer."

1. The CPA must not have any relationship or combination of relationships with the client or any conflict of interest which would impair his integrity and objectivity.

2. The client must accept the responsibility for the financial statements as his own. A small client may not have anyone in his employ to maintain accounting records and may rely on the CPA for this purpose. Nevertheless, the client must be sufficiently knowledgeable of the enterprise's activities and financial condition and the applicable accounting principles so that he can reasonably accept such responsibility, including, specifically, fairness of valuation and presentation and adequacy of disclosure. When necessary, the CPA must discuss accounting matters with the client to be sure that the client has the required degree of understanding.

3. The CPA must not assume the role of employee or of management conducting the operations of an enterprise. For example, the CPA shall not consummate transactions, have custody of assets or exercise authority on behalf of the client. The client must prepare the source documents on all transactions in sufficient detail to identify clearly the nature and amount of such transactions and maintain an accounting control over data processed by the CPA such as control totals and document counts. The CPA should not make changes in such basic data without the concurrence of the client.

4. The CPA, in making an examination of financial statements prepared from books and records which he has maintained completely or in part, must conform to generally accepted auditing standards. The fact that he has processed or maintained certain records does not eliminate the need to make sufficient audit tests.[8]

"When a client's securities become subject to regulation by the Securities and Exchange Commission or some other federal or state regulatory body, responsibility for maintenance of the accounting records, including accounting classification decisions, must be assumed by accounting personnel employed by the client. The assumption of this responsibility must

[8] "Interpretations Under Rule 101—Independence," *AICPA Professional Standards*, vol. 2, ET Section 101.04. Copyright © 1974 by the American Institute of Certified Public Accountants, Inc.

commence with the first fiscal year after which the client's securities qualify for such regulation." [9]

What if it has been the practice of your client to regularly discuss with you the business problems he is facing and to get your advice as to the course of action he should take? What if he usually follows your advice? Again, this type of service normally would not impair independence, whether or not the advice given is followed. Nevertheless, the four requirements stated previously for accounting services would still have to be met.[10]

Another independence question involving a management advisory service engagement arises when the accountant designs an accounting system for a client and then is asked to audit that client. Assume, for example, that you are a partner in the Management Advisory Services Division of a large international CPA firm. You and other members of your firm have just completed an engagement in which you designed a management information system for a medium-sized manufacturing company. As part of this job, you assisted your client in the installation of new data-processing equipment and helped train the client's personnel in its use and in the operation of the new information system. In fact, some of your staff are still at the client's offices until the client's personnel feel competent to operate on their own. The firm also has this company as an audit client. In fact, the systems job arose out of a recommendation from the audit staff.

Was the independence of your firm compromised by the acceptance of this MAS engagement? How can your firm serve as auditor for the system you have designed and installed? What about the presence of your firm's own staff in the client's office? Independence "would not be considered to be impaired under these circumstances provided the client makes all significant management decisions related to the hiring of new personnel and the implementation of the system." The accounting firm must also "take reasonable precautions to restrict its supervisory activities to initial instruction and training of personnel," and it "should avoid direct supervision of the actual operation of the system or any related activities that would constitute undue involvement in or identification with management functions." [11]

The relation of management advisory services to the auditor's independence will be discussed further in chapter 6 in connection with incompatible occupations, and in connection with the management representation letter of a small client.

9 "Interpretations Under Rule 101—Independence," *AICPA Professional Standards*, vol. 2, ET Section 101.04. Copyright © 1974 by the American Institute of Certified Public Accountants, Inc.

10 "Ethics Rulings on Independence, Integrity, and Objectivity," *AICPA Professional Standards*, vol. 2, ET Section 191.015–.016.

11 Ibid, ET Section 191.110.

THE INTERNAL PROFESSIONAL

Internal professional accountants practicing in the private or the public sector must also abide by a high standard of integrity and objectivity. These certified public accountants, certified management accountants, and certified internal auditors cannot, of course, be independent of the company, governmental unit, or association for which they work. They can, however, always perform their duties with honesty and objectivity.

The internal professional who is responsible for the preparation of his company's financial statements would, for example, be obligated to insure that they are not misleading or inaccurate and that no material items are omitted. It should be remembered that external financial statements are representations of the company and not of the auditor who has examined and perhaps approved them. It is extremely important that professional accountants, whether they work as auditors, management consultants, tax practitioners, or internal accountants, be regarded by the public and all those who rely upon their work as persons of integrity and objectivity.

One type of internal professional who is faced with an independence question is the internal auditor. Assume that you are an internal auditor, a member of the Institute of Internal Auditors, and that you subscribe wholeheartedly to the Institute's Code of Ethics, its Statement of Responsibilities of Internal Auditors, and its Standards for the Professional Practice of Internal Auditing.[12] You are considering a job change and are concerned about the organizational arrangement in the company you are thinking of joining. In that company, the internal audit staff reports to the company controller, who in turn reports to the vice president-finance.

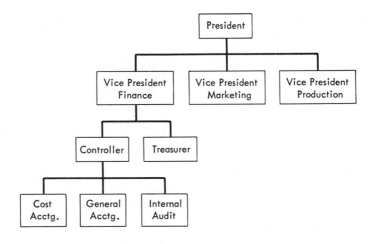

---

[12] See Appendix 4 for the Code of Ethics, Appendix 5 for the Statement of Responsibilities, and Appendix 6 for the Standards.

You find it hard to understand how the internal audit staff can maintain its independence under this arrangement. You are not sure that you will be able to effectively audit the work of the controller if you report directly to him. You are also concerned about your relationship on the organization chart to the treasury operations, which you will also be auditing.

Will the performance of your job under the organizational setup outlined cause you to violate any ethical code? Yes, this arrangement would very likely be in violation of both the Statement of Responsibilities of Internal Auditors and the Standards for the Professional Practice of Internal Auditing. The former states:

> Independence is essential to the effectiveness of internal auditing. This independence is obtained primarily through organizational status and objectivity:
>> The organizational status of the internal auditing function and the support accorded to it by management are major determinants of its range and value. The head of the internal auditing function, therefore, should be responsible to an officer whose authority is sufficient to assure both a broad range of audit coverage and the adequate consideration of and effective action on the audit findings and recommendations.[13]

One of the general standards set forth for the professional practice of internal auditing reinforces the above statement:

> Internal Auditors should be independent of the activities they audit.[14]

One of the specific standards supporting the general standard is:

> The organizational status of the internal auditing department should be sufficient to permit the accomplishment of its audit responsibilities.

Finally, in the detailed discussion of the above specific standard, the point is made that the director of the internal auditing department should have direct communication with the board.[15]

An area in which the internal professional's integrity might be questioned is that relating to the preparation of tax returns. Assume that as the

---

[13] *Statement of Responsibilities of Internal Auditors* (Altamonte Springs, Florida: The Institute of Internal Auditors, Inc.). Copyright by the Institute of Internal Auditors, Inc., 249 Maitland Avenue, Altamonte Springs, Florida 32701 U.S.A. Reprinted with permission.

[14] *Standards for the Professional Practice of Internal Auditing* (Altamonte Springs, Florida: The Institute of Internal Auditors, Inc., 1978). Copyright 1978 by the Institute of Internal Auditors, Inc., 249 Maitland Avenue, Altamonte Springs, Florida 32701 U.S.A. Reprinted with permission.

[15] Ibid.

possessor of a Master's degree in accounting, with specialization in taxes, you have been assigned the primary responsibility for the preparation of your company's federal income tax returns. In your efforts to reduce this year's tax liability to a minimum, you have come upon an item which may or may not be a legitimate deduction. The wording of the tax law is not completely clear, and you are not sure whether or not you should deduct it. You are also concerned about certain items in the return for which you have had to make estimates. They are your best judgment in each case, but you are not particularly confident of their accuracy in a couple of instances.

Are there any ethical considerations in your handling of the doubtful deductions? Can you in good conscience take a deduction that is questionable? Is it acceptable for you to use estimates in your preparation of the return? If so, how accurate do they need to be? Rule of Conduct 102 of the AICPA Code of Ethics, while written to apply to CPAs in tax practice, applies as well to an internal professional preparing a tax return. That rule reads in part as follows:

> "Rule 102-Integrity and objectivity. . . . In tax practice, a member may resolve doubt in favor of his client as long as there is reasonable support for his position." [16]

With regard to the use of estimates, one of the statements on responsibilities in tax practice takes the following position. Again, the statement is written for the CPA in tax practice but applies equally well to the internal professional:

> "A certified public accountant may prepare tax returns involving the use of estimates if said use is generally acceptable or, under the circumstances, it is impractical to obtain exact data. When estimates are used, they should be presented in such a manner as to avoid the implication of greater accuracy than exists. The CPA should be satisfied that estimated amounts are not unreasonable under the circumstances." [17]

COMMITMENT TO ETHICAL CONDUCT

The philosophical foundation upon which the Rules of Conduct of the AICPA are based is expressed in the form of five Ethical Principles. Whereas the Rules of Conduct set forth minimum levels of acceptable conduct and are mandatory and enforceable, the principles suggest behavior which the accountant should strive for. They represent a commitment to

[16] "Integrity and Objectivity," *AICPA Professional Standards*, vol. 2, ET Section 102.

[17] "Statements on Responsibilities in Tax Practice," *AICPA Professional Standards*, vol. 1, TX Section 151.02.

ethical conduct beyond any explicit prohibitions. The following affirmative principle is set forth in the area of independence, integrity, and objectivity.

> "A certified public accountant should maintain his integrity and objectivity, and when engaged in the practice of public accounting, be independent of those he serves." [18]

The nineteen statements which follow are intended by the Institute to provide an elaboration of this principle and rationale for its support.

---

1. The public expects a number of character traits in a certified public accountant but primarily integrity and objectivity and, in the practice of public accounting, independence.

Independence has always been a concept fundamental to the accounting profession, the cornerstone of its philosophical structure. For no matter how competent any CPA may be, his opinion on financial statements will be of little value to those who rely on him—whether they be clients or any of his unseen audience of credit grantors, investors, governmental agencies and the like—unless he maintains his independence.

2. Independence has traditionally been defined by the profession as the ability to act with integrity and objectivity.

3. Integrity is an element of character which is fundamental to reliance on the CPA. This quality may be difficult to judge, however, since a particular fault of omission or commission may be the result either of honest error or a lack of integrity.

4. Objectivity refers to a CPA's ability to maintain an impartial attitude on all matters which come under his review. Since this attitude involves an individual's mental processes, the evaluation of objectivity must be based largely on actions and relationships viewed in the context of ascertainable circumstances.

5. While recognizing that the qualities of integrity and objectivity are not precisely measurable, the profession nevertheless constantly holds them up to members as an imperative. This is done essentially by education and by the Rules of Conduct which the profession adopts and enforces.

6. CPAs cannot practice their calling and participate in the world's affairs without being exposed to situations that involve the possibility of pressures upon their integrity and objectivity. To define and prescribe all such situations would be impracticable. To ignore the problem for that reason, however, and to set no limits at all would be irresponsible.

7. It follows that the concept of independence should not be interpreted so loosely as to permit relationships likely to impair the CPA's integrity or the impartiality of his judgment, nor so strictly as to inhibit the rendering of useful services when the likelihood of such impairment is relatively remote.

---

[18] "Concepts of Professional Ethics," AICPA *Professional Standards*, vol. 2, ET Section 52.
Copyright © 1974 by the American Institute of Certified Public Accountants, Inc.

8. While it may be difficult for a CPA always to appear completely independent, even in normal relationships with clients, pressures upon his integrity or objectivity are offset by powerful countervailing forces and restraints. These include the possibility of legal liability, professional discipline ranging up to revocation of the rights to practice as a CPA, loss of reputation and, by no means least, the inculcated resistance of a disciplined professional to any infringement upon his basic integrity and objectivity. Accordingly, in deciding which types of relationships should be specifically prohibited, both the magnitude of the threat posed by a relationship and the force of countervailing pressures have to be weighed.

9. In establishing rules relating to independence, the profession uses the criterion of whether reasonable men, having knowledge of all the facts and taking into consideration normal strength of character and normal behavior under the circumstances, would conclude that a specified relationship between a CPA and a client poses an unacceptable threat to the CPA's integrity or objectivity.

10. When a CPA expresses an opinion on financial statements, not only the fact but also the appearance of integrity and objectivity is of particular importance. For this reason, the profession has adopted rules to prohibit the expression of such an opinion when relationships exist which might pose such a threat to integrity and objectivity as to exceed the strength of countervailing forces and restraints. These relationships fall into two general categories: (1) certain financial relationships with clients and (2) relationships in which a CPA is virtually part of management or an employee under management's control.

11. Although the appearance of independence is not required in the case of management advisory services and tax practice, a CPA is encouraged to avoid the proscribed relationships with clients regardless of the type of services being rendered. In any event, the CPA, in all types of engagements, should refuse to subordinate his professional judgment to others and should express his conclusions honestly and objectively.

12. The financial relationships proscribed when an opinion is expressed on financial statements make no reference to fees paid to a CPA by a client. Remuneration of providers of services is necessary for the continued provision of those services. Indeed, a principal reason for the development and persistence in the professions of the client-practitioner relationship and of remuneration by fee (as contrasted with an employer-employee relationship and remuneration by salary) is that these arrangements are seen as a safeguard of independence.

13. The above reference to an employer-employee relationship is pertinent to a question sometimes raised as to whether a CPA's objectivity in expressing an opinion on financial statements will be impaired by his being involved with his client in the decision-making process.

14. CPAs continually provide advice to their clients, and they expect that this advice will usually be followed. Decisions based on such advice may have a significant effect on a client's financial condition or operating results. This is the case not only in tax engagements and management advisory services but in the audit function as well.

15. If a CPA disagrees with a client on a significant matter during the course of an audit, the client has three choices—he can modify the financial statements (which is usually the case), he can accept a qualified report or he can discharge the CPA. While the ultimate decision and the resulting financial statements clearly are those of the client, the CPA has obviously been a significant factor in the decision-making process. Indeed, no responsible user of financial statements would want it otherwise.

16. It must be noted that when a CPA expresses an opinion on financial statements, the judgments involved pertain to whether the results of operating decisions of the client are fairly presented in the statements and not on the underlying wisdom of such decisions. It is highly unlikely therefore that being a factor in the client's decision-making process would impair the CPA's objectivity in judging the fairness of presentation.

17. The more important question is whether a CPA would deliberately compromise his integrity by expressing an unqualified opinion on financial statements which were prepared in such a way as to cover up a poor business decision by the client and on which the CPA has rendered advice. The basic character traits of the CPA as well as the risks arising from such a compromise of integrity, including liability to third parties, disciplinary action and loss of right to practice, should preclude such action.

18. Providing advice or recommendations which may or may not involve skills logically related to a client's information and control system, and which may affect the client's decision-making, does not in itself indicate lack of independence. However, the CPA must be alert to the possibility that undue identification with the management of the client or involvement with a client's affairs to such a degree as to place him virtually in the position of being an employee, may impair the appearance of independence.

19. To sum up, CPAs cannot avoid external pressures on their integrity and objectivity in the course of their professional work, but they are expected to resist these pressures. They must, in fact, retain their integrity and objectivity in all phases of their practice and, when expressing opinions on financial statements, avoid involvement in situations that would impair the credibility of their independence in the minds of reasonable men familiar with the facts.[19]

PERCEPTIONS OF INDEPENDENCE

Both the AICPA (see Appendix 1) and the Securities and Exchange Commission have provided illustrations of situations in which the auditor's independence may be questioned.[20] In certain areas, the two appear to disagree. Arguing that both the SEC and the AICPA base their rulings

[19] "Concepts of Professional Ethics," AICPA Professional Standards, vol. 2, ET Section 52.

[20] For example, see Securities and Exchange Commission, "Independence of Accountants," Accounting Series Release 126, July 5, 1972, and Accounting Series Release 234, December 13, 1977.

on perceptions of the opinions of informed third parties, David Lavin of Florida International University conducted an empirical investigation to determine what these opinions really are. In the following excerpts from an article, he describes his research and conclusions.

This paper delves more deeply into the concept of independence by examining particular client-auditor relationships to determine how an informed third party perceives the auditor's independence. . . .

It appears that the present positions of the AICPA and the SEC regarding the concept of independence are not in accord. These two groups disagree in two main areas: electronic data processing and bookkeeping services.

The SEC is of the opinion that an accountant cannot objectively audit books and records which he or she has maintained for a client. Whether these services are accomplished manually or by means of computers and other mechanized instruments, these services ultimately place the accountant in a position of evaluating and attesting to his or her own record keeping. Further, the renting of computer time to a client is a business transaction with a client beyond the customary professional relationship and would, according to the SEC, adversely affect independence. The AICPA is of the opinion that a member can and will objectively audit books and records regardless of the fact that he has maintained them for a client. Members are skilled in applying techniques to audit mechanical accuracy, and the performance of the bookkeeping or data processing function should have no effect on the application of such techniques. Also, according to the AICPA, renting computer time to a client constitutes a business relationship which, in and of itself, will not impair independence.

The AICPA and the SEC supposedly base their rulings on the perceptions of the opinions of informed third parties. Since the concerned groups' positions are not in accord, one of them must have perceived the opinions of third parties incorrectly. If this disagreement between the AICPA and the SEC is not due to misperception of third party opinions, it is likely that the two groups have a different measurement threshold; i.e., one group may be satisfied with a majority of opinion while the other may strive for unanimity. Also, one group may be more aware of the revenue needs of CPAs.

This research provides empirical evidence concerning third parties' opinions on the independence of the auditor. The following questions are studied: (1) Is there a majority of opinion? (2) If there is a majority of opinion, with which authority do the respondent third party groups align themselves? The latter question implies a jurisdictional problem: who will dictate auditing standards, the AICPA or the SEC?

RESEARCH DESIGN

Since both the SEC and the AICPA employ a third party test to determine whether an auditor appears to be independent, the relevant research universe for this study included third parties who utilize audited financial reports in making business decisions. Loan officers of banks and research financial analysts of brokerage houses make use of accounting information in business decision situations . . . Since they occupy strategic decision centers in the financial community, these two sub-groups were chosen as the third-party populations to be studied. Consideration also was given to CPAs who theoretically should be aware of certain standards of independence.

The objective of this study was to arrive at a broad determination of the opinions of third parties and CPAs on the auditor's independence. In order to obtain a wide representation of the opinions of these groups at minimum cost, the medium of a mail survey was chosen. . . .

The subjects were presented with twelve situations, taken from Accounting Series Release No. 126. Each situation involved a different auditor-client relationship, and the subjects were asked to determine whether or not, in their opinion, an accounting firm could be considered independent with respect to a certified audit on the client involved. . . .

The following null hypotheses were tested for each client-auditor situation:

$H_O{}^1$: There is no consensus among AICPA members regarding their perceptions of the concept of independence.

$H_O{}^2$: There is no consensus among bank loan officers regarding their perceptions of the concept of independence.

$H_O{}^3$: There is no consensus among research financial analysts of brokerage houses regarding their perceptions of the concept of independence.

The existence of a consensus is defined operationally as a statistically significant majority of opinion. . . .

In most of the situations, there was some consensus within each experimental group. The hypothesis that there is no consensus among CPA members regarding their perceptions of the concept of independence, $H_O{}^1$, was rejected in every case but one. . . .

$H_O{}^2$, that there is no consensus among loan officers regarding their perceptions of the concept of independence, was rejected in every case except two. . . .

Research financial analysts indicated no consensus for questions one, three and four. . . .

Table 1 summarizes the consensus that occurred within each experimental group in response to each question. These percentages represent an approximate level of agreement within each group. . . .

Table 2 shows the positions taken by the AICPA and the SEC for each question and compares them to the consensus response from Table 1. It appears that the respondents do not concur as a whole with either the AICPA or the SEC; however, they do seem to agree more with the AICPA than with the SEC. . . .

SUMMARY AND CONCLUSIONS

It appears that the consensus of the users and CPAs participating in this study agrees more with the AICPA than with the SEC, and that the authorities, at times, characterize relationships as not independent that the consensus con-

TABLE 1

SUMMARY OF CONSENSUS FOR 12 QUESTIONS

Question	Consensus Response	CPAs %	LO %	RFA %
1	Independent	68	61	60
2	Independent	63	84	88
3*	Not independent	64	—	—
	Independent	—	55	53
4	Independent	59	67	57
5	Not independent	88	58	70
6	Independent	86	70	63
7	Not independent	50	63	75
8	Independent	58	78	69
9	Independent	88	93	96
10	Independent	88	85	87
11	Not independent	75	68	80
12	Not independent	74	73	70

* Only in this question did the CPAs disagree with these financial statement users. CPAs—Not independent; Financial statement users—Independent.

TABLE 2

COMPARISON OF CONSENSUS RESPONSES WITH THE POSITIONS OF THE AICPA AND THE SEC

Question	Consensus Response	AICPA	SEC
1	Independent	Not independent	Not independent
2	Independent	Not independent †	Not independent
3	CPAs—Not independent Users—Independent	Independent	Not independent
4	Independent	Independent	Not independent
5	Not independent	Not independent	Not independent
6	Independent	Independent	Not independent
7	CPAs—No consensus Users—Not independent	Not independent	Not independent
8	Independent	‡	Not independent
9	Independent	Independent	Independent
10	Independent	Independent	Not independent
11	Not independent	Not independent	Not independent
12	Not independent	Not independent	Not independent

† At the time this study was made, the AICPA held that this institution was independent. Recently a new ruling by the Ethics Division has changed this position.

‡ If the auditors are from a different office—Independent. If the auditors are from the same office—Not independent.

siders independent. On the whole, it appears that the SEC's rulings on independence are more conservative than these users feel necessary in these situations. In the twelve situations presented, the SEC deems eleven as non-independent situations, whereas the AICPA characterizes as non-independent a maximum of seven. The respondent users agree more nearly with the AICPA's position. Since the users themselves consider independent seven of the eleven situations that the SEC characterizes as not independent, it appears that the SEC may be overly protective. However, a significant minority indicated standards similar to the SEC.

The SEC supposedly bases its rulings on its perception of the opinions of the financial statement users. This study suggests that in these situations the SEC's perceptions do not agree with the majority of user respondents and, in fact, the AICPA rulings are much closer to the user's opinions. Thus, we have a jurisdictional problem which must be resolved between the concerned groups: who will dictate auditing standards, the AICPA or the SEC?

This problem must be resolved between the concerned groups. Further, there is an ever-increasing abundance of governmental and self-imposed restrictions concerning auditing rules and standards. It is felt that these restrictions need a proper evaluation in terms of their necessity in auditing practice. Further research either to confirm or refute the results of this study is needed in order to resolve this jurisdictional problem. If we fail to respond to the available theory and evidence now, there is little basis for optimism with respect to some of the much more difficult issues that will have to be faced in the future.

Finally, two caveats need to be mentioned. First, the securities acts were designed to make the market operate in line with the perfectly competitive model. Perfect knowledge is an assumption of such a model. Risk-rate-of-return relationships have to be consistent for an efficient allocation of resources. The participants in the market should not have to contend with the risk factor of the auditor's independence. Therefore, the SEC might be correct in its position when it tries to eliminate any type of relationship wherein the auditor's independence might be questioned. Second, the conclusions of this study were based on a statistically significant majority of opinion. Just because the majority disagrees with the SEC does not necessarily invalidate the SEC's position. This survey was conducted among a relatively sophisticated class of statement users whom the SEC may perceive to be able to take care of themselves. If one assumes that a less sophisticated investor might not recognize a non-independent relationship as such, it would appear that the SEC is correct in establishing more conservative standards that would protect the uninformed investor and satisfy the minority of this study which agrees with the SEC position on independence.[21]

Dr. Lavin elsewhere in his article goes into considerable detail as to the limitations of his research. He also presents the exact questions asked and the responses to each by the three groups in his sample.

[21] David Lavin, "Perceptions of the Independence of the Auditor," *The Accounting Review,* January 1976, pp. 41–50.

REPORTING A LACK OF INDEPENDENCE:
GENERAL STANDARDS

In those instances where a certified public accountant is not independent but is still "associated" with the financial statements of a client, he must disclaim an opinion with regard to those statements and state specifically that he is not independent. Association may occur either when the CPA has "consented to the use of his name in a report, document, or written communication containing the statements," or when he has submitted "to his client or others financial statements that he has prepared or assisted in preparing." [22]

Because independence is lacking, *any* procedures performed by the CPA would not be in accordance with generally accepted auditing standards, thus precluding the expression of an opinion. In order to avoid confusing the reader about the importance of the impairment of independence, the reasons for a lack of independence should not be given. The CPA is either independent or he is not. Furthermore, the procedures performed should not be described. Such a description might add unwarranted credibility to the statements. An example of a report setting forth a lack of independence is as follows:

> We are not independent with regard to XYZ Company, and the accompanying balance sheet as of December 31, 19XX, and the related statements of income and retained earnings and changes in financial position for the year then ended, was not audited by us and accordingly we do not express an opinion on them.
>
> (Signature and date) [23]

This report may accompany the financial statements or be placed directly on them. In addition, each page of the statements should be "clearly and conspicuously marked as unaudited." [24]

INTERPRETATION OF REPORTING STANDARDS

Many questions of interpretation have arisen with regard to the disclosure of a lack of independence. D. R. Carmichael of the AICPA staff and J. V. Bencivenga responded to some of them in the following article, which appeared in the *Journal of Accountancy*. Problems associated with the CPA not in public practice were among the several questions discussed.

---

[22] Auditing Standards Board, *Proposed Statement on Auditing Standards: Association with Financial Statements* (New York: American Institute of Certified Public Accountants, 1979), par. 3.

[23] Ibid., par. 9.

[24] Ibid., par. 5.

A greater degree of confidence is given to reports prepared by independent CPAs than to those prepared by CPAs serving as employees of a business concern. Unavoidably, the implication of "audit" attaches itself to CPAs because they are generally known as a profession of auditors. Therefore, an accountant who is serving as an employee rather than an independent contractor, and in so doing is associated with financial statements, must take care not to identify himself in a manner that may lead others to believe he is an independent public accountant. . . .

CPAs NOT IN PUBLIC PRACTICE

Many CPAs are employed by, or otherwise connected with, organizations other than public accounting firms, such as business enterprises and government agencies. When a CPA so engaged allows his name to be associated with financial statements and adds the designation "certified public accountant" or similar title, a reader may erroneously conclude that he is engaged in public practice. Consequently, a CPA not in public practice should avoid that implication by including a narrative which does not resemble the report of an independent CPA. If the CPA is a treasurer, for example, he should preferably sign as "treasurer." As the following inquiry and response illustrate, a simple narrative could be included if a statement of responsibility is desired. This would not be the expression of a professional opinion, but rather a declaration by a member of management since financial statements are the direct responsibility of management. Note that a scope paragraph would not be appropriate. However, a full-time company officer who is incidentally a CPA and is merely listed along with other company officers in a report released to the public would not be deemed to be "associated" with the accompanying financial statements. . . . The following inquiry highlights the problem of CPAs not in public practice.

Inquiry. Recently I assumed the responsibility for the financial audit section of X Company's internal audit division. This section of the audit division has, from time to time, been asked to examine the financial statements and the underlying books and records of small companies related to X Company and to render an opinion as to the fairness of presentation of these statements. These examinations are generally quite thorough and include what would be considered normal auditing procedures. I recognize that an internal auditor, by the very nature of his position, cannot adhere to the generally accepted auditing standards, particularly the second standard on independence, and that phrase would not be included in any scope paragraph. I would like to know, however, if it would be permissible for me (a CPA) to sign an opinion on the financial statements in my capacity as an internal auditor.

Response. . . . if CPAs in public practice are prohibited from adding unwarranted credibility to financial statements when they lack independence, certainly CPAs in private practice should be similarly restricted.

It is not too unusual for a corporate officer to sign a report taking responsibility for financial statements issued by the company, but in doing so he must make clear that he is acting as an officer of the company and not as an independent accountant. Such a statement might read as follows:

Controller's Report

In my opinion, as an officer of the XYZ Company, the accompanying balance sheet and related statements of income and retained earnings present fairly the financial position of the XYZ Company. . . .

By: John Doe, Controller

For a company treasurer, controller or internal auditor, any representations made on behalf of the company should be in the designated capacity of officer or employee.

A CPA cannot serve two masters: he cannot hold himself out to the public in a manner resembling a traditional auditor-client relationship and at the same time serve that client as a controller, treasurer or internal auditor.

RATIONALE AND TERMINOLOGY
OF DISCLAIMER

. . .

Inquiry. We believe that the recommended disclaimer of opinion may raise more questions that it settles. . . . We present the following reasons for our thinking. . . .

If it is thought that the lack of independence must be spelled out, then it would appear to us that the reason for the lack of independence should be set forth. Failure to do so would seem to violate one of our other standards— that of full disclosure. We do not believe that any more credence will be given to the financial statements simply because we explain why we are not indepen- dent, but we think it would help the reader if he were told why we were not independent. We feel quite sure that the vast majority of the readers of financial statements do not understand our Code of Professional Ethics and would only be confused by the statement . . .

We do not believe that the lack of independence is significantly more important than the failure to comply with the other generally accepted auditing standards. It seems to us that if financial statements have not been examined in accordance with generally accepted auditing standards, then they are simply unaudited. We see no particular reason to spell out any one particular item that does not comply with generally accepted auditing standards.

Response. . . . the basic concept of independence is more important than is the reason why independence is lacking. . . . explaining the reason for lack of independence would tend to confuse the reader and cause misleading inferences as to its significance. There are no varying degrees of lack of independence; the auditor is either independent or he is not independent. . . .

You question why the independence standard was deemed to be more important than any of the other standards. . . . the general standards—all three of them—are of such a pervasive nature that when one, or more, of them is not met the remaining seven standards are not really relevant. If inadequately trained people are used in the examination, due professional care is not exercised or independence is lacking, consideration of the field work and reporting stan- dards from a compliance viewpoint has little meaning. To use an incompetent person to evaluate internal control or make decisions requiring professional judgment is not logical. . . . if a CPA lacks independence, there should not be a recitation of procedures performed in order to add credibility to financial statements used by a third party.

PUBLIC UNDERSTANDING OF "INDEPENDENCE"

Several inquiries focused on the public's understanding of independence. The following exchange is representative.

Inquiry. The disclaimer of opinion starts with the phrase, "We are not independent with respect to XYZ Company." I believe the general public is not familiar with the concept of independence which was developed by the profession. Therefore the phrase quoted above would, in my opinion, create confusion or misunderstanding on the part of most of the readers of such a disclaimer. I believe that it would be sufficient if the disclaimer merely stated that the financial statements presented were unaudited and, accordingly, no opinion is expressed on them. I do not feel that a reference to independence is essential and if it is likely not to be understood, it might as well be omitted.

Response. Your premise that the general public is not familiar with the concept of independence is questionable. On the contrary, independence is a rather simple, well-understood concept from the layman's standpoint. An ordinary dictionary definition conveys the meaning quite adequately. On the other hand, specific reasons for lack of independence probably would be difficult for the layman to comprehend and evaluate if he were required to make a judgment as to the importance of a particular reason set forth in a CPA's report.

SERVING AS OFFICER

Several inquiries related to the appropriate wording of a disclaimer when an accountant in public practice serves part-time as an officer of a company as a service to a client. . . .

Inquiry. . . .

Here's an example of a disclaimer released by this office: "The accompanying balance sheet of X Company as of November 30, 1969, and the related statement of income and retained statement of income and retained earnings for the six-month period then ended were prepared by me in the capacity of an officer of the corporation. Accordingly, I cannot express an opinion concerning them in the manner that would be expected had I not served as an officer and had an examination in accordance with generally accepted auditing standards been conducted. (Signed as Treasurer.)" Do you mean to tell me that a disclaimer such as this is more confusing to the stockholders than your recommended disclaimer? . . .

Response. . . . phrases of the sort used in your disclaimer are more confusing because they do not state that an examination was not performed; also the phrase you suggest contains an implication that the only reason for not being able to express an opinion is the fact that as treasurer you are not independent. A reader could infer that you did perform an examination but are barred from stating that you did, or from expressing an opinion, solely because of your "technical" lack of independence. In other words, there is an implication that since you are a member of a CPA firm there is no need for an independent audit because you prepared the statements.

DESCRIPTION OF PROCEDURES

Several inquiries were received concerning the prohibition against describing the procedures the auditor has performed or giving some indication that an examination was performed even though that examination was not in accordance with generally accepted auditing standards because the auditor was not independent.

Inquiry. Why . . . prohibit the CPA from describing the procedures he performed in his report? Why can we not state the facts simply because we are not independent?

Response. The essential reason for requiring the auditor to state in his report that the statements are unaudited, regardless of the extent of procedures performed, was to prevent the association of the CPA's name with financial statements from adding credibility to those statements.

If a client wishes a CPA to perform auditing procedures even though the CPA is not independent, the CPA may furnish this service. In this case, the CPA may function as an internal auditor and provide the client with a service which the client would not otherwise be in a position to obtain. The nature and extent of the procedures may be described in full in an engagement letter. However, the CPA is precluded from including any description of those procedures in his report on the financial statements. If the client's only objective is to have the procedures performed, this objective should be adequately fulfilled by the engagement letter. However, if the client's objective is to add credibility to financial statements for the use of third parties, this is a service which a CPA who is not independent cannot and should not seek to perform. In this case, describing the procedures or otherwise indicating that some type of examination was performed could give a third party reason to believe that the auditor had formed some conclusion on the fair presentation of the statements. The third party would be justified in this belief even though the auditor stated in his report that he was precluded from expressing an opinion because he was not independent. . . .[25]

INDEPENDENCE OF THE INTERNAL AUDITOR

Addressing the problem of stopping illegal acts of businessmen in *The Internal Auditor,* Victor F. DeMarco argues that the independence of the internal auditor is critical and that the director of the Internal Audit Department should report directly to the chairman of the audit committee

[25] D.R. Carmichael and J.B. Bencivenga, "Lack of Independence—Some Reporting Problems," *The Journal of Accountancy,* August 1972, pp. 79–81. Copyright © 1972 by the American Institute of Certified Public Accountants, Inc.

of the board of directors. This committee, in his opinion, should be composed mostly or entirely of outside directors and would provide a vehicle whereby the board of directors could be more than a "rubber stamp" for management's actions. The internal audit staff, under this arrangement, would be independent of management and would be available to perform any special audits or studies desired by the audit committee and to validate the facts of a proposal before it is presented to the entire Board. It would also continue to perform its normal internal audit function.

I believe the emphasis for corporate accountability rests with the Board of Directors. Certified public accountants, the Congress, and the general public must look to the Board for maintenance of integrity. But is the Board capable of assuring corporate integrity?

In an article I wrote for the September/October 1974 edition of *The Internal Auditor,* I said directors are rubber stamps. I specifically described the plight of the outside directors; they are usually appointed by management to meet one day per quarter and are expected to routinely approve all management suggested motions presented to the Board.

Arthur Goldberg, former secretary of labor and former Supreme Court justice, resigned from the Board of Trans World Airlines (T.W.A.) because he felt that without personal staff support it was impossible for the public director, regardless of experience, to perform the functions which, by law and by moral standards, ought to be performed. . . .

Since the public director cannot rely on the public accountant for anything more than an opinion on the fairness of financial statements, the public director receives virtually no input independent of management. Public directors are confronted with complex sets of facts, figures, analyses, and computer printouts provided by management. . . .

So we reach this point: How can the Board of Directors and specifically the outside director act responsibly? . . .

The major innovation needed is to have internal auditors report directly and permanently to the chairman of the Audit Committee, who should be an outside director. The internal auditors' main function would remain the same, and most of their time would continue to be devoted to the review of internal controls. However, they would be available to perform any special audits and studies desired by the chairman of the Audit Committee to validate the facts of a proposal before it is presented to the Board. The auditors would present only facts; they would take no direct part in the decision-making process.

My proposal to have the director of the Internal Audit Department report to the chairman of the Audit Committee is logical. This requires no additional staff; provides the same element of internal control for the chief executive officer who will receive copies of reports; and the service is performed by an element of the company with existing internal working relationships. As an integral part of the company, the Internal Audit Department has day-to-day access to company policies.

Moreover, the internal auditors' task is accepted by the auditees. The auditors have the independence and professionalism to present facts to the Audit Committee chairman; they can provide capability for the outside directors; and they are interested in the welfare of the company because the members of the audit staff are paid employees of the company. Furthermore, internal auditors perform their reviews on a daily basis, not once a year as most outside auditors do. More important, internal auditors are not restricted to purely financial matters which represent the past. They can and do inquire into the past but they review future plans as well.

In an article in the December 1976 issue of *Management Accounting,* "The Internal Auditor and the Annual Audit," the authors recognize the importance of internal auditors and state that reliance can be placed on them. However, the article poses one major question I feel independent auditors must answer. "Is the Internal Audit Department actually independent?"

The authors conclude the internal auditor who is truly independent reports directly to top management—ideally to the Audit Committee of the Board of Directors.

The authors are on the right track, but if they want the CPA to be relieved of the responsibility for illegal acts, they should go one step farther and suggest that the internal auditor report directly to the chairman of the Audit Committee, who should be an outside director who truly represents the stockholders and the public interest. Without this direct line, the internal auditor cannot be considered completely independent and invaluable in assisting public accountants in the detection of illegal acts. I think the rationale is obvious.

Walter E. Hanson, senior partner for Peat, Marwick, Mitchell & Co., in a recent speech entitled "The Changing Role of the Internal Auditor" said, "One of the initial questions we ask when first looking at a new client is, 'to whom does the head of the internal audit section report?' Our rule of thumb is that the higher the reporting relationship goes, the healthier the situation. The best of all possible worlds from our point of view, is when the internal auditors report directly to an Audit Committee composed of independent directors."

If it's so logical, why isn't it done? Because audit committees do not exist in all large companies. Where they do exist, many are dominated by officer/directors. Even when that situation is remedied, the chief executive officers of most large companies view themselves as omnipotent and will not accept a continued examination of their decisions when the results are presented to someone other than themselves. Accordingly, the chief executive will oppose any suggestion he considers an intrusion on his prerogative to manage. He doesn't really want the Board to be too well informed. He wants a "rubber stamp."

But the rubber stamp is cracked. The circumstances causing the most celebrated cases can no longer be ignored or tolerated. The enlightened chief executive officer will move in this direction voluntarily. Unfortunately, others will have to be pressured. That pressure may come from Congress, from outside directors, or from government agencies such as the SEC. But it will come. I hope the public accounting profession will see the wisdom of suggesting that the director of the Internal Audit Department report to the chairman of the Audit Committee, and lead the way. This will materially assist them in arriving at an informed opinion of the business for the public good and may relieve CPAs of their responsibility for illegal acts of their clients.[26]

1. What is the meaning of "independence" in accounting? Is it of significance to the management consultant, the tax practitioner, and the internal professional, as well as to the auditor?

2. What are the various avenues for insuring the presence of independence, integrity, and objectivity?

3. Assume that a particular Savings and Loan Association holds the house mortgage for several members of your firm. Could you ethically serve as its auditor? What is the general rule with regard to loans to or from an enterprise being audited?

4. Will the performance of accounting services for a client impair independence? What are the four requirements that must be met to retain independence and the appearance of independence? Does the Securities and Exchange Commission agree with this position?

5. If you were the management consultant for the design and installation of a company's accounting system, can you ethically serve as that company's auditor? What ground rules must be observed in order to insure independence?

6. What subgroup of internal professional accountants has its own statement of responsibilities and set of standards? What do they have to say about independence?

7. Is it ethical for a tax practitioner to resolve doubts in favor of his client? What if the tax return in question is being prepared by an internal professional rather than a public accountant?

8. What is the distinction between Ethical Principles and Rules of Conduct? What is the Ethical Principle in the area of independence, integrity, and objectivity?

9. Is there any empirical evidence on the perception of independence by third parties? Do third parties agree with the independence rules established by the AICPA and the SEC?

[26] Victor F. DeMarco, "How Internal Auditors Can Help CPAs Stamp Out Illegal Acts," *The Internal Auditor*, February 1978, pp. 60–65. Copyright © 1978 by the Institute of Internal Auditors, Inc., 249 Maitland Avenue, Altamonte Springs, Florida 32701 U.S.A. Reprinted with permission.

10. Assume that you are not independent with respect to a particular client, but have consented to the use of your name in a written communication containing the client's financial statements. What are your reporting requirements? Should you set forth your lack of independence and the reasons for it?

11. If you are working in private industry and your name is associated with your company's financial statements, can you ethically add the designation "certified public accountant" after your name? Would it be appropriate for you to be listed as a CPA in a public report which identifies the officers of the company?

12. If your examination of the financial statements of a particular company was not in accordance with generally accepted auditing standards, can you describe in your report the procedures you did apply? Discuss the reasons for and against such disclosure.

SUGGESTED ADDITIONAL READINGS

American Institute of Certified Public Accountants, "Independence," *AICPA Professional Standards,* vol. 1, AU Section 220 (Statement on Auditing Standards, no. 1).

————, "Personal Characteristics," Statements on Management Advisory Services, *AICPA Professional Standards,* vol. 1, MS Section 110. (See Appendix 2.)

————, "Interpretations of Management Advisory Services Practice Standards: Standard No. 1—Personal Characteristics," *AICPA Professional Standards,* vol. 1, MS Section 110-1.

————, "Consulting Role and Independence," Role in Management Advisory Services, *AICPA Professional Standards,* vol. 1, MS Section 430.26–430.30.

————, "Positions Contrary to Treasury Department or Internal Revenue Service Interpretations of the Code," *AICPA Professional Standards,* vol. 1, TX Section 201.

————, "The Independence of Governmental Auditors and Financial Audits," *The Journal of Accountancy,* May 1978.

KNIGHT, ROGER N., and GREGORY B. TOMLINSON, "The Internal Auditor and the Annual Audit," *Management Accounting,* December 1976.

Securities and Exchange Commission, "Qualifications of Accountants," *Regulation S-X,* Article 2–01.

————, "Independence of Accountants," *Accounting Series Release No. 126,* 5 July 1972.

————, "Notice of Amendments to Require Increased Disclosure of Relationships Between Registrants and their Independent Public Accountants," *Accounting Series Release No. 165,* 20 December 1974. Securities and Exchange Commission, "Independence of Accountants," *Accounting Series Release No. 234,* 13 December 1977.

————, Disclosure of Relationship with Independent Public Accountants," *Accounting Series Release No. 250,* 29 June 1978.

————, "Independence of Accountants, Interpretation and Guidelines Relating to Litigation," *Accounting Series Release No. 251,* 6 July 1978.

Chapter 3

General
and
Technical Standards

INTRODUCTION

All professional accountants, whether they are in the public practice as auditors, management consultants, or tax practitioners or are internal to some organization, must abide by rigorous general standards.[1] First, each professional must undertake only those tasks or engagements which can be completed with *competence*. Second, those tasks which are undertaken must be accomplished with *due professional care*. Third, each engagement or task must have adequate *planning and supervision*. Fourth, *sufficient relevant data* must be obtained to afford a reasonable basis for conclusions or recommendations. And finally, a professional accountant must not permit his name to be used in conjunction with any *forecast* of future transactions in a manner that may lead to the belief that the accountant is vouching for the achievability of the forecast.

In addition to these five general standards, the professional accountant must adhere to certain technical standards. In the area of accounting principles, statements of the Financial Accounting Standards Board are considered authoritative. In addition, any Accounting Research Bulletins

[1] *AICPA Professional Standards*, vol. 2, ET Section 201.

issued by the AICPA Committee on Accounting Research (1939–1959) and any opinions issued by the Accounting Principles Board (1959–1973) should be considered authoritative unless and until they are expressly superceded by the FASB. Also in the area of accounting principles, the standards promulgated by the Cost Accounting Standards Board must be adhered to by defense contractors under federal contracts.

In the area of auditing, the professional accountant must follow generally accepted auditing standards. These standards have been approved and adopted by the membership of the American Institute of Certified Public Accountants and are continually being interpreted by the Auditing Standards Board in their Statements on Auditing Standards. The comptroller general of the United States has also issued a set of audit standards to be applied to audits of all government organizations, programs, activities, and functions. (See Appendix 8) These standards apply to auditors employed by federal, state, and local governments, independent public accountants, and others qualified to perform the work. They are also intended to apply to both internal audits and audits of contractors, grantees, and other external organizations performed by or for a government entity.[2]

THE AUDITOR

The independent external auditor, in addition to adhering to the general standards relating to professional competence, due professional care, planning and supervision, sufficient relevant data, and forecasts, must abide by the technical standards relating to accounting principles and auditing standards. In the area of accounting principles, he may not "express an opinion that financial statements are presented in conformity with generally accepted accounting principles if such statements contain any departure from an accounting principle" promulgated by the FASB which has "a material effect on the statements taken as a whole, unless the member can demonstrate that due to unusual circumstances the financial statements would otherwise have been misleading. In such cases, his report must describe the departure, the approximate effects thereof, if practicable, and the reasons why compliance with the principle would result in a misleading statement." [3]

The following generally accepted auditing standards must be adhered to by the practicing certified public accountant. Although some of them are similar to the general standards outlined earlier, they have special application to the auditor.

---

[2] Comptroller General of the United States, *Standards for Audit of Governmental Organizations, Programs, Activities & Functions* (United States General Accounting Office, 1972), p. 1.

[3] "Accounting Principles," *AICPA Professional Standards*, vol. 2, ET Section 203.

General Standards

1. The examination is to be performed by a person or persons having adequate technical training and proficiency as an auditor.
2. In all matters relating to the assignment, an independence in mental attitude is to be maintained by the auditor or auditors.
3. Due professional care is to be exercised in the performance of the examination and the preparation of the report.

Standards of Field Work

1. The work is to be adequately planned and assistants, if any, are to be properly supervised.
2. There is to be a proper study and evaluation of the existing internal control as a basis for reliance thereon and for the determination of the resultant extent of the tests to which auditing procedures are to be restricted.
3. Sufficient competent evidential matter is to be obtained through inspection, observation, inquiries, and confirmations to afford a reasonable basis for an opinion regarding the financial statements under examination.

Standards of Reporting

1. The report shall state whether the financial statements are presented in accordance with generally accepted accounting principles.
2. The report shall state whether such principles have been consistently observed in the current period in relation to the preceding period.
3. Informative disclosures in the financial statements are to be regarded as reasonably adequate unless otherwise stated in the report.
4. The report shall either contain an expression of opinion regarding the financial statements, taken as a whole, or an assertion to the effect that an opinion cannot be expressed. When an overall opinion cannot be expressed, the reason therefor should be stated. In all cases where an auditor's name is associated with financial statements, the report should contain a clear-cut indication of the character of the auditor's examination if any, and the degree of responsibility he is taking.[4]

To illustrate the application of the general and technical standards, consider the following situations:

(1) Your local CPA firm has been in existence for only three years. After working on the audit staff of a large international firm for six years, you and a former college classmate decided to form a partnership and practice in the small city where you both grew up. You have just finished talking with the city manager of the town, a forward-looking administrator who feels strongly that the city should be audited by an independent CPA.

---

4 "Generally Accepted Auditing Standards," *AICPA Professional Standards,* vol. 1, AU Section 150 (Statement on Auditing Standards No. 1). Copyright © 1977 by the American Institute of Certified Public Accountants, Inc.

You would very much like to have the engagement but have never before been involved with a government audit. Furthermore, because of scheduling problems in school, you were unable to take a governmental accounting course. Are you prohibited from seeking this engagement because of a lack of professional competence? Do the qualifications of your partner or your staff, if any, have any bearing on the question?

The fact that you have never had a governmental accounting course and have never before been involved with a government audit would not necessarily prohibit you or your firm from seeking the engagement. The question to be asked is whether you or your firm "can reasonably expect to complete the engagement with professional competence." [5] If your partner or your staff already have the necessary knowledge and skill, even though you do not, the engagement can be undertaken. Furthermore, you or your staff may be able to acquire the necessary competence through additional research or consultation with others, which would not ordinarily represent a lack of competence. Rather, it would be regarded as "a normal part of the professional conduct of the engagement." [6]

(2) FASB Statement No. 2 (*AICPA Professional Standards*, vol. 3, AC Section 4211) requires that all research and development costs, as defined in the statement, are to be charged as expenses when incurred. Assume that you generally agree with this position but feel strongly that an exception should be made in the case of the enterprise you are now auditing. The research and development costs incurred by this company during the past year are so material in relation to the company's earnings that you feel expensing them would render the financial statements misleading. Can your firm render an opinion that the financial statements of this enterprise are presented in conformity with generally accepted accounting principles if the research and development costs are capitalized rather than expensed? Isn't it permissible to depart from generally accepted accounting principles if following those principles would cause the financial statements to be misleading?

Rule of Conduct 203 does indeed provide that financial statements can contain a departure from an accounting principle promulgated by the FASB if it can be demonstrated that "due to unusual circumstances the statements would otherwise have been misleading." [7] The key question, however, is what constitutes an "unusual" circumstance. The answer is a matter of professional judgment and involves the ability to support the position that adherence to a promulgated principle would be generally regarded by

[5] "General Standards," *AICPA Professional Standards*, vol. 2, ET Section 201.
[6] "Interpretation Under Rule 201—General Standards," *AICPA Professional Standards*, vol. 2, ET Section 201.02.
[7] "Accounting Principles," ET Section 203.

reasonable men as producing a misleading result. An interpretation of Rule of Conduct 203 specifically states, however, that an unusual degree of materiality, as in this case, "would not ordinarily be regarded as unusual." [8] Therefore, you would probably have to qualify your opinion.

(3) Assume that as the partner in charge of the audit of a large department store chain, you are in the process of reviewing the working papers. Included therein is a memo from the senior auditor on the job to the manager entitled "On the Possibility of Fictitious Receivables." In the memo, the senior discusses the reasons for his concern and the logic which led him to conclude that his fears were unjustified. There is a notation by the manager at the bottom of the memo indicating his concurrence with the conclusions of the senior and noting that the amount involved is immaterial. You are inclined to agree with the logic of the senior and the manager but have a nagging doubt that further audit procedures should perhaps be employed to be "absolutely certain" that no fraud exists. After discussing the situation with several of your partners, however, you finally conclude that nothing further needs to be done. Should you raise this issue with the company's management? the Board of Directors? the local sheriff?

If it is concluded in this case that the possible irregularity "could not be so significant as to materially affect the financial statements" under examination, the auditor need not employ any further audit procedures but should refer the matter "to an appropriate level of management that is at least one level above those involved, with the recommendation that the matter be pursued to a conclusion." Also, he should "consider the effect" of the irregularity "as it may relate to other aspects of his examination, such as the role of the personnel involved in the system of internal accounting control." [9] Because of the importance of the subject of errors and irregularities, it will be discussed in greater detail later in this chapter.

THE MANAGEMENT CONSULTANT AND THE TAX PRACTITIONER

All of the general standards requiring professional competence, due professional care, adequate planning and supervision, and sufficient relevant data in connection with engagements apply to the management consultant

---

[8] "Interpretations Under Rule 303—Accounting Principles," *AICPA Professional Standards,* vol. 2, ET Section 203.02.

[9] "The Independent Auditor's Responsibility for the Detection of Errors or Irregularities," *AICPA Professional Standards,* vol. 1, AU Section 327.15 (Statement on Auditing Standards No. 16).

and the tax practitioner, as well as to the auditor. In addition, the management consultant and tax practitioner would be in violation of the AICPA Code of Professional Ethics if they permitted their names to be used in conjunction with any forecast of future transactions in a manner which led to the belief that they vouched for its achievability.

Several of the Statements on Management Advisory Services address the issues raised in the general standards. There are statements dealing with (1) competence, (2) due care, (3) planning, supervision, and control, and (4) sufficient relevant data. (See Appendix 2) Assume that a small manufacturing company has just retained your firm to study the feasibility of purchasing or renting some automated data-processing equipment. Presently, the company relies upon hand-kept records and some bookkeeping machines. In discussing the engagement with the president of the company, you mention that your first step will be to document the details of their operation and of their present system as a prelude to determining the need for a more sophisticated approach. He informs you that another consultant installed the accounting system just a year ago and that all of the information you need is contained in his report. To what extent can you rely upon the information contained in the previous consultant's report? In general, what kind of documentation is needed to support the conclusions and recommendations of a management consulting engagement?

The information contained in the previous consultant's work should not be relied upon without validation. "Before designing a system based on previously assembled facts, the practitioner should assure himself of the adequacy of any underlying systems and the current reliability of the data." [10]

"The amount and formality of documentation needed in a management consulting engagement will vary according to the nature and scope of the engagement. The documentation should demonstrate that due care has been exercised. It should record, as appropriate, (a) the evidential matter obtained and the source, (b) the alternatives considered, and (c) the analytical process leading to specific recommendations." [11]

Several of the Statements on Responsibilities in Tax Practice also have a relationship to the general standards. Assume, for example, that the controller of a company for which your firm is the auditor has asked you to review his federal income tax return. He has completed it himself but would like you to review it before he sends it in. You feel obligated to help him but have several questions about your responsibility. If you

---

[10] "Interpretations of Management Advisory Services Practice Standards: Standard No. 7—Sufficient Relevant Data," AICPA Professional Standards, vol. 1, MS Section 170–1.03.

[11] "Sufficient Relevant Data," AICPA Professional Standards, vol. 1, MS Section 170.02.

complete the review as asked, are you required to sign the return as a preparer? May you sign it? What standards should you adhere to when conducting your review? Will your conduct be affected in any way if, as a result of your review and at your direction, the taxpayer makes substantial changes in the return?

If you are not the preparer of the return, you are not required to sign it. However, you may sign the preparer's declaration on the return if you review the return and, in the course of the review, acquire "knowledge with respect to the return substantially equivalent" to that which you would have acquired had you prepared it. Unless such a review is made, you should not sign it.[12]

If, at your direction, the taxpayer makes "substantial changes" in the return, you are considered to be a "preparer" and should sign the return.[13] Section 1.6065-1(b)(1) of the Income Tax Regulations requires that a preparer sign the declaration "where the return is prepared for a taxpayer for compensation or as an incident to the performance of other services for which compensation is received." Statement on Responsibilities in Tax Practice No. 1 goes even further, however, and states that a preparer should sign the return "whether or not it is prepared for compensation." [14]

THE INTERNAL PROFESSIONAL

As indicated in the introduction to this chapter, every professional accountant, no matter where employed, must abide by rigorous general and technical standards. The internal professional, even if he is not a CPA, must set personal standards that are at least as demanding as those set forth in the AICPA Code of Professional Ethics.

As discussed in chapter 2, one group of internal professionals, members of the Institute of Internal Auditors, has adopted its own code of ethics and its own set of professional standards. (See Appendices 4 and 6) Several of the articles of the code address the general and technical standards discussed earlier.

Article VI. Members, in expressing an opinion, shall use reasonable care to obtain sufficient factual evidence to warrant such expressions. . . .

Article VII. Members shall continually strive for improvement in the proficiency and effectiveness of their service.

12 "Signature of Reviewer: Assumption of Preparer's Responsibility," *AICPA Professional Standards,* vol. 1, TX Section 121.04 (Statement on Responsibilities in Tax Practice No. 2).

13 "Signature of Preparer," *AICPA Professional Standards,* vol. 1, TX Section 111.05 (Statement on Responsibilities in Tax Practice No. 1).

14 Ibid., TX Section 111.03.

Article VIII. Members . . . shall be ever mindful of their obligation
to maintain the high standard of competence, morality, and dignity
which *The Institute of Internal Auditors, Inc.* and its members have
established.

Included among the specific standards for the professional practice of
internal auditing are the following:

* The internal auditing department should provide assurance that the
technical proficiency and educational background of internal auditors are appropriate for the audits to be performed.
* The internal auditing department should possess or should obtain
the knowledge, skills, and disciplines needed to carry out its audit
responsibilities.
* The internal auditing department should provide assurance that
internal audits are properly supervised.
* Internal auditors should possess the knowledge, skills, and disciplines essential to the performance of internal audits.
* Internal auditors should maintain their technical competence through
continuing education.
* Internal auditors should exercise due professioanl care in performing
internal audits.
* Internal auditors should plan each audit.
* The director of internal auditing should establish plans to carry out
the responsibilities of the internal auditing department.
* The director of internal auditing should provide written policies and
procedures to guide the audit staff.[15]

What are some of the issues facing the internal professional in the
area of general and technical standards? Assume that you are the controller for a company that manufactures and markets fruitcakes throughout
the southern part of the country. Having graduated from a prominent
school of accounting in Georgia, you are very conscious of your ethical
responsibility as an accounting professional. One of your responsibilities
as controller is to put together a budget for the next year, as well as a
projection for the ensuing two years. Much of your data is gathered from

[15] *Standards for the Professional Practice of Internal Auditing* (Altamonte Springs, Florida:
The Institute of Internal Auditors, Inc., 1978), pp. 3–4. Copyright © by the Institute of Internal
Auditors, Inc., 249 Maitland Avenue, Altamonte Springs, Florida 32701 U.S.A. Reprinted with
permission.

company personnel in production and sales, but you are the one charged with the final preparation. In fact, your name is the one that will be associated with it, as it is printed and reproduced for all appropriate company personnel. You have some problem with this because you are a CPA, and you vaguely remember something about forecasts in the AICPA Code of Ethics. Does the rule of conduct relating to forecasts apply to you now that you are an internal professional? What if you are a CMA? What if you hold no professional certification? Can your name be associated with the budget?

As pointed out earlier in this chapter, Rule of Conduct 201 of the AICPA Code of Professional Ethics states that a member may not "permit his name to be used in conjunction with any forecasts of future transactions in a manner which may lead to the belief that the member vouches for the achievability of the forecast." [16] Although this rule was formulated for those engaged in the practice of public accounting,[17] the internal professional should still abide by it as a minimum standard of conduct. This is true whether or not you are a CPA, a CMA, or have no certification. The rule, however, would not prevent you, as controller, from having your name associated with the budget. You would, of course, not want to in any way "vouch for the achievability of the forecast." In associating your name with the budget, you should also not leave the impression that you are acting as an independent CPA.

Assume that immediately upon graduating from college you went to work for a local CPA in a medium-sized city near your school. During your four years with the firm, you gained valuable experience and passed the CPA examination. Three years ago, a prominent local business asked you to join them as assistant controller. The financial offer was very attractive and you were promised a promotion to controller as soon as the current controller retired. Just this year you received the promised promotion.

As controller, you now have responsibility for the preparation of the company's financial statements, copies of which are regularly forwarded to the local bank pursuant to a loan agreement. Upon preparing these statements for the first time and after reviewing the statement for the past several months, you note that the earnings picture of the company is rapidly deteriorating. Although you had no trouble putting the statement together, you were surprised to find that the president personally kept the receivables ledger and furnished you with the current balance. When you asked him about it, he pointed out that he handled most of the sales for the company so it was easier for him to maintain it. Are you under any obligation as a

---

16 "General Standards," *AICPA Professional Standards*, vol. 2, ET Section 201.01.

17 "Applicability of Rules," *AICPA Professional Standards*, vol. 2, ET Section 92.04.

professional to verify further the receivables balance and amount of sales before including them on the statement and forwarding the statement to the bank? What obligation do you have as an accounting professional to be alert to the possibility of management misrepresentations or fraud? What action would you take if you strongly suspect that the financial statements are being intentionally distorted?

As an internal professional, you do have an obligation to verify further the figure given to you for inclusion on the statements. The banker receiving them has a right to expect that you exercised due professional care in their preparation. As a professional, you also have an obligation to be alert to the possibility of fraud. Should you strongly suspect that the financial statements are being intentionally distorted, you should discuss the matter with an appropriate level of management, at least one level above those involved. It may even be appropriate to bring the matter to the attention of the Board of Directors or its audit committee. You may even wish to consult legal counsel. Certainly, you should do no less than would be required of an auditor in similar circumstances.[18] The auditor's obligation will be fully discussed later in the chapter.

THE FOUNDATIONAL CONCEPTS

The ethical principle set forth by the American Institute of Certified Public Accountants in the area of general and technical standards is:

> A certified public accountant should observe the profession's general and technical standards and strive continually to improve his competence and the quality of his services.

The following statements elaborate on this principle and provide the rationale for its support.

> 1. Since accounting information is of great importance to all segments of the public, all CPAs whether in public practice, government service, private employment or academic pursuits, should perform their work at a high level of professionalism.
> 2. A CPA should maintain and seek always to improve his competence in all areas of accountancy in which he engages. Satisfaction of the requirements for the CPA certificate is evidence of basic competence at the time the certificate is granted, but it does not justify an assumption that this competence is maintained without continuing effort. Further,

---

[18] "The Independent Auditor's Responsibility for the Detection of Errors or Irregularities," *AICPA Professional Standards*, vol. 1, AU Section 327.14 (Statement on Auditing Standards No. 17).

it does not necessarily justify undertaking complex engagements without additional study and experience.

3. A CPA should not render professional services without being aware of, and complying with, the applicable general or technical standards as interpreted by bodies designated by Council. Moreover, since published general and technical standards can never cover the whole field of accountancy, he must keep broadly informed.

4. Observance of the rule on general and technical standards calls for a determination by a CPA with respect to each engagement undertaken that there is a reasonable expectation it can be completed with the exercise of due professional care, with adequate planning and supervision and with the gathering of sufficient relevant data to afford a reasonable basis for conclusions and recommendations. If a CPA is unable to bring such professional competence to the engagement he should suggest, in fairness to his client and the public, the engagement of someone competent to perform the needed service, either independently or as an associate.

5. The standards referred to in the rules are elaborated and refined to meet changing conditions, and it is each CPA's responsibility to keep himself up to date in this respect.[19]

DETECTION OF FRAUD: THE STANDARD

It is a common misconception that audits are performed primarily for the detection of fraud. This is not the case. The independent auditor's objective in examining financial statements is "to form an opinion on whether the financial statements present fairly financial position, results of operations, and changes in financial position in conformity with generally accepted accounting principles consistently applied."[20] Consequently, the responsibility exists to plan the examination to uncover unintentional mistakes in the statements, as well as intentional distortions. This is not the same, however, as conducting the audit for the purpose of finding such mistakes. Intentional distortions include "deliberate misrepresentations by management, sometimes referred to as management fraud," and "misappropriations of assets, sometimes referred to as defalcations."[21]

In planning and performing this examination, the auditor must have "an attitude of professional skepticism, recognizing that the application of his auditing procedures may produce evidential matter indicating the possibility of errors or irregularities."[22] "An examination made in accordance

---

19 "Concepts of Professional Ethics," *AICPA Professional Standards,* vol. 2, ET Section 53. Copyright © 1978 by the American Institute of Certified Public Accountants, Inc.

20 "The Independent Auditor's Responsibility for the Detection of Errors or Irregularities," *AICPA Professional Standards,* vol. 1, AU Section 327.05 (Statement on Auditing Standards No. 16). Copyright © 1977 by the American Institute of Certified Public Accountants, Inc.

21 Ibid., AU Section 327.03.

22 Ibid., AU Section 327.06.

with generally accepted auditing standards" is, however, "subject to the inherent limitations of the auditing process." Because it is based upon "the concept of selective testing of the data being examined," it is "subject to the inherent risk that material errors or irregularities, if they exist, will not be detected." [23]

"The risk that material errors or irregularities will not be detected is increased by the possibility of management's override of internal controls, collusion, forgery, or unrecorded transactions." Unless his examination reveals "evidential matter to the contrary," however, the auditor's "reliance on the truthfulness of certain representations and on the genuineness of records and documents obtained during the examination" is considered reasonable.[24] The auditor is "not an insuror or a guarantor" against errors and irregularities. If his examination is made "in accordance with generally accepted auditing standards, he has fulfilled his professional responsibility." [25] The viewpoint of the courts on this issue is sometimes different, however, and is fully discussed in chapters 8, 9, and 10. Compliance with generally accepted auditing standards is no guarantee that a judge or jury will hold the auditor guiltless.

Because of the importance of this subject to the professional auditor, the following standard should be studied in its entirety.

---

1. This section provides guidance on the independent auditor's responsibility for detecting errors or irregularities when making an examination of financal statements in accordance with generally accepted auditing standards. It also discusses procedures that the auditor should perform when his examination indicates that material errors or irregularities may exist.

2. The term *errors* refers to unintentional mistakes in financial statements and includes mathematical or clerical mistakes in the underlying records and accounting data from which the financial statements were prepared, mistakes in the application of accounting principles, and oversight or misinterpretation of facts that existed at the time the financial statements were prepared.

3. The term *irregularities* refers to intentional distortions of financial statements, such as deliberate misrepresentations by management, sometimes referred to as management fraud, or misappropriations of assets, sometimes referred to as defalcations.* Irregularities in financial statements may result from the misrepresentation or omission of the effects of events or transactions; manipulation, falsification, or alteration of records or documents; omission of

---

[23] "The Independent Auditor's Responsibility for the Detection of Errors or Irregularities," AICPA *Professional Standards,* vol. 1, AU Section 327.11.

[24] Ibid., AU Section 327.12.

[25] Ibid., AU Section 327.13.

* For guidance on other actions that an independent auditor should consider with respect to the possible illegality of such acts, see section 328, *Illegal Acts by Clients.*

significant information from records or documents; recording of transactions without substance; intentional misapplication of accounting principles or misappropriation of assets for the benefit of management, employees, or third parties. Such acts may be accompanied by the use of false or misleading records or documents and may involve one or more individuals among management, employees, or third parties.

RELATIONSHIP OF INDEPENDENT AUDITS TO OTHER BUSINESS CONTROLS

4. Generally, entities operate with certain controls. Examples of controls for business entities include legal requirements, the monitoring of management activities by boards of directors and their audit committees, the internal audit function, and internal accounting control procedures. Those who rely on financial statements look to entities' controls together with independent audits to provide reasonable assurance that financial statements are not materially misstated as a result of errors or irregularities.

THE AUDITOR'S RESPONSIBILITY

5. The independent auditor's objective in making an examination of financial statements in accordance with generally accepted auditing standards is to form an opinion on whether the financial statements present fairly financial position, results of operations, and changes in financial position in conformity with generally accepted accounting principles consistently applied. Consequently, under generally accepted auditing standards, the independent auditor has the responsibility, within the inherent limitations of the auditing process (see paragraphs 11–13), to plan his examination (see paragraphs 6–10), to search for errors or irregularities that would have a material effect on the financial statements, and to exercise due skill and care in the conduct of that examination. The auditor's search for material errors or irregularities ordinarily is accomplished by the performance of those auditing procedures that in his judgment are appropriate in the circumstances to form an opinion on the financial statements; extended auditing procedures are required if the auditor's examination indicates that material errors or irregularities may exist (see paragraph 14). An independent auditor's standard report implicitly indicates his belief that the financial statements taken as a whole are not materially misstated as a result of errors or irregularities.

THE POSSIBILITY OF ERRORS OR IRREGULARITIES

6. The independent auditor's plan for an examination in accordance with generally accepted auditing standards is influenced by the possibility of material errors or irregularities. The auditor should plan and perform his examination with an attitude of professional skepticism, recognizing that the application of his auditing procedures may produce evidential matter indicating the possibility of errors or irregularities. The scope of the auditor's examination would be affected by his consideration of internal accounting control, by the results of

his substantive tests, and by circumstances that raise questions concerning the integrity of management.

Internal Accounting Control and Substantive Tests

7. Management is responsible for establishing and maintaining internal accounting control procedures including appropriate supervisory review procedures necessary for adherence to adopted policies and prescribed procedures and for identification of errors and irregularities. On the other hand, the auditor evaluates internal accounting control to establish a basis for any reliance thereon in determining the nature, timing, and extent of audit tests to be applied in his examination of the financial statements. Section 320.65–.66 suggests the following approach to the auditor's evaluation of internal accounting control:

A conceptually logical approach to the auditor's evaluation of accounting control, which focuses directly on the purpose of preventing or detecting material errors and irregularities in financial statements, is to apply the following steps in considering each significant class of transactions and related assets involved in the audit:

a. Consider the types of errors and irregularities that could occur.
b. Determine the accounting control procedures that should prevent or detect such errors and irregularities.
c. Determine whether the necessary procedures are prescribed and are being followed satisfactorily.
d. Evaluate any weaknesses—i.e., types of potential errors and irregularities not covered by existing control procedures—to determine their effect on (1) the nature, timing, or extent of auditing procedures to be applied and (2) suggestions to be made to the client.

In the practical application of the foregoing approach, the first two steps are performed primarily through the development of questionnaires, checklists, instructions, or similar generalized material used by the auditor. However, professional judgment is required in interpreting, adapting, or expanding such generalized material as appropriate in particular situations. The third step is accomplished through the review of the system and tests of compliance and the final step through the exercise of professional judgment in evaluating the information obtained in the preceding steps.

In evaluating internal accounting control, the auditor uses accumulated experience and understanding of the points of risk for possible errors and irregularities.

8. Effective internal accounting control reduces the probability that errors or irregularities will occur, but does not eliminate the possibility that they may occur. There are inherent limitations that should be recognized in considering the potential effectiveness of internal accounting control procedures (see section 320.34). Further, whether the objectives of internal accounting control will be achieved depends in substantial part on the competence and integrity of company

personnel (see section 320.35). Consequently, the auditor does not place com-plete reliance on internal accounting control. Section 320.71 states in part:

> The second standard (of field work) does not contemplate that the auditor will place complete reliance on internal control to the exclusion of other auditing procedures with respect to material amounts in the financial statements.

Thus, the auditor's examination includes substantive tests (see section 320.70) that are designed to obtain evidential matter concerning the validity and pro-priety of the accounting treatment of transactions and balances or, conversely, evidential matter indicating the possibility of material errors or irregularities therein even in the absence of material weaknesses * in internal accounting control. Examples of circumstances that may lead the auditor to question whether material errors or possible irregularities exist include the following: (a) discrepancies within the accounting records, such as a difference between a control account and its supporting subsidiary records; (b) differences disclosed by confirmations; (c) significantly fewer responses to confirmation requests than expected; (d) transactions not supported by proper documentation; (e) transactions not recorded in accordance with management's general or specific authorization; and (f) the completion of unusual transactions at or near year end. However, the existence of those circumstances does not necessarily mean that material errors or irregularities do exist.

Integrity of Management

9. The auditor should recognize that management can direct subordinates to record or conceal transactions in a manner that could result in a material mis-statement of the financial statements. Thus, management can perpetrate irregu-larities by other employees. Consequently, the auditor should be aware of the importance of management's integrity to the effective operation of internal accounting control procedures and should consider whether there are circum-stances that might predispose management to misstate financial statements. Such circumstances might include those of a company that is in an industry experiencing a large number of business failures, or that lacks sufficient working capital or credit to continue operations.

10. The auditor should consider the possibility that management may have made material misrepresentations or may have overridden control procedures. The auditor's consideration should include factors such as the nature of the entity being audited, the susceptibility to irregularities of the item or transaction being examined, the degree of authority vested at various management levels, and prior experience with the entity. For example, the following circumstances,

---

* Section 320.68 defines a material weakness as follows: ". . . a condition in which the auditor believes the prescribed procedures or the degree of compliance with them does not provide reasonable assurance that errors or irregularities in amounts that would be material in the financial statements being audited would be prevented or detected within a timely period by employees in the normal course of performing their assigned functions."

although not necessarily indicative of the presence of irregularities, may cause the auditor to be concerned about the possibility that management may have made material misrepresentations or overridden internal control procedures: (a) the company does not correct material weaknesses in internal accounting control that are practicable to correct; (b) key financial positions, such as controller, have a high turnover rate; or (c) the accounting and financial functions appear to be understaffed, resulting in a constant crisis condition and related loss of controls. However, unless the auditor's examination reveals evidential matter to the contrary, it is reasonable for him to assume that management has not made material misrepresentations or has not overridden control procedures.

INHERENT LIMITATIONS OF AN AUDIT

11. An examination made in accordance with generally accepted auditing standards is subject to the inherent limitations of the auditing process. As with certain business controls, the costs of audits should bear a reasonable relationship to the benefits expected to be derived. As a result, the concept of selective testing of the data being examined, which involves judgment both as to the number of transactions to be examined and as to the areas to be tested, has been generally accepted as a valid and sufficient basis for an auditor to express an opinion on financial statements. Thus, the auditor's examination, based on the concept of selective testing of the data being examined, is subject to the inherent risk that material errors or irregularities, if they exist, will not be detected.

12. The risk that material errors or irregularities will not be detected is increased by the possibility of management's override of internal controls, collusion, forgery, or unrecorded transactions. Certain acts, such as collusion between client personnel and third parties or among management or employees of the client, may result in misrepresentations being made to the auditor or in the presentation to the auditor of falsified records or documents that appear truthful and genuine. Unless the auditor's examination reveals evidential matter to the contrary, his reliance on the truthfulness of certain representations and on the genuineness of records and documents obtained during his examination is reasonable. Examples of representations that are normally accepted by the auditor are (a) those of management concerning its intent or knowledge and the completeness of the entity's records and (b) those of third parties, such as confirmations of accounts receivable by debtors and accounts payable by creditors, and confirmations and other documents received from banks or other documents received from banks or other depositaries. Further, the auditor cannot be expected to extend his auditing procedures to seek to detect unrecorded transactions unless evidential matter obtained during his examination indicates that they may exist. For example, an auditor ordinarily would not extend his auditing procedures to seek failures to record the receipt of cash from unexpected sources.

13. In view of those and other limitations on the effectiveness of auditing procedures, the subsequent discovery that errors or irregularities existed during

the period covered by the independent auditor's examination does not, in itself, indicate inadequate performance on his part. The auditor is not an insurer or guarantor; if his examination was made in accordance with generally accepted auditing standards, he has fulfilled his professional responsibility.

PROCEDURES WHEN THE EXAMINATION INDICATES THAT ERRORS OR IRREGULARITIES MAY EXIST

14. If the independent auditor's examination causes him to believe that material errors or irregularities may exist, he should consider their implications and discuss the matter and the extent of any further investigation with an appropriate level of management that is at least one level above those involved. If after such discussions the auditor continues to believe that material errors or irregularities may exist, he should determine that the board of directors or its audit committee is aware of the circumstances. Also, he should attempt to obtain sufficient evidential matter to determine whether in fact material errors or irregularities exist and, if so, their effect. In this regard, the auditor may wish to consult with the client's legal counsel on matters concerning questions of law. If practicable, the auditor should extend his auditing procedures in an effort to obtain such evidential matter. In some circumstances, however, it may be impracticable or impossible to obtain sufficient evidential matter to determine the existence, or related effect, of material errors or possible irregularities, or management may impose a limitation on the scope of the auditor's search for the evidential matter needed to reach a conclusion.* When the auditor's examination indicates the presence of errors or possible irregularities, and the auditor remains uncertain about whether these errors or possible irregularities may materially affect the financial statements, he should qualify his opinion or disclaim an opinion on the financial statements and, depending on the circumstances, consider withdrawing from the engagement, indicating his reasons and findings in writing to the board of directors. In such circumstances, the auditor may wish to consult with his legal counsel.

15. The independent auditor's examination may reveal errors or possible irregularities that he concludes could not be so significant as to materially affect the financial statements he is examining. For example, irregularities involving peculations from a small imprest fund would normally be of little significance because both the manner of operating the fund and its size would tend to establish a limitation on the amount of a loss. The auditor should refer such matters to an appropriate level of management that is at least one level above those involved, with the recommendation that the matter be pursued to a conclusion. Also, the auditor should consider the effect of any immaterial irregu-

---

* For a discussion of the effect of a restriction on the scope of an auditor's examination whether imposed by the client or by circumstances, see section 509.10–13, *Reports on Audited Financial Statements.*

larity as it may relate to other aspects of his examination, such as the role of the personnel involved in the system of internal accounting control.[26]

ILLEGAL ACTS BY CLIENTS: THE STANDARD

Closely related to the auditor's responsibility for the detection of errors or irregularities is his responsibility with regard to client acts that *appear* to be illegal. The determination of whether an act is in fact illegal may, of course, be beyond the auditor's professional competence.

Although "an examination made in accordance with generally accepted auditing standards cannot be expected to provide assurance that illegal acts will be detected," [27] the auditor "should be aware of the possibility that illegal acts may have occurred that may have a material effect on the financial statements. Procedures that are performed primarily for the purpose of expressing an opinion on the financial statements" may "bring possible illegal acts to the auditor's attention." [28]

"If as a result of those procedures, the auditor believes that illegal acts may have occurred, he should enquire of the client's management and consult with the clients' legal counsel or other specialists, as necessary, to obtain an understanding of the nature of the acts and their possible effects on financial statements." [29]

"After it has been determined that an illegal act has occurred, the auditor should report the circumstances to personnel within the client's organization at a high enough level of authority so that appropriate action can be taken by the client." [30] "Deciding whether there is a need to notify parties other than personnel within the client's organization" is the "responsibility of management. Generally, the auditor is under no obligation to notify those parties." [31]

There are a variety of circumstances associated with the discovery of illegal acts on the part of the client when the auditor will need to consider qualifying his opinion, disclaiming an opinion, expressing an adverse opin-

---

[26] American Institute of Certified Public Accountants, "The Independent Auditor's Responsibility for the Detection of Errors and Irregularities," *AICPA Professional Standards*, vol. 1, AU Section 327 (Statement on Auditing Standards No. 17). Copyright © 1977 by the American Institute of Certified Public Accountants, Inc.

[27] "Illegal Acts by Clients," *AICPA Professional Standards*, vol. 1, AU Section 328.03 (Statement on Auditing Standards No. 17). Copyright © 1977 by the American Institute of Certified Public Accountants, Inc.

[28] Ibid., AU Section 328.04.

[29] Ibid.

[30] Ibid., AU Section 328.13.

[31] Ibid., AU Section 328.19.

ion, or withdrawing from the engagement.[32] The following standard discusses the problem of illegal acts and details those situations in which the auditors' report may be affected:

---

1. This section provides guidance for an auditor when client acts that appear to him to be illegal come to his attention during an examination of financial statements in accordance with generally accepted auditing standards. This section also discusses the extent of the attention he should give, when performing such an examination, to the possibility that such acts may have occurred. The types of acts encompassed by this section include illegal political contributions, bribes, and other violations of law and regulations.

2. This section sets forth guidelines for the appropriate conduct of an auditor in fulfilling his obligation to report on financial statements in accordance with professional standards when he becomes aware of an illegal act (paragraphs 4–17). It also offers practical suggestions for an auditor in connection with illegal acts not having a material effect on the financial statements (paragraph 18) and sets forth considerations applicable to notification of other parties of an illegal act (paragraph 19).

3. An examination made in accordance with generally accepted auditing standards cannot be expected to provide assurance that illegal acts will be detected.* In reporting on financial statements, an auditor holds himself out as one who is proficient in accounting and auditing. The determination of whether an act is illegal is usually beyond his professional competence. The auditor's training and experience, however, ordinarily should provide a reasonable basis for an awareness that some client acts coming to an auditor's attention in the performance of his examination might be illegal. Nevertheless, the further removed an illegal act is from the events and transactions specifically reflected in financial statements, the less likely the auditor is to become aware of the act or recognize its possible illegality. For example, violations of the Occupational Safety and Health Act are not ordinarily specifically reflected in financial statements, and the auditor ordinarily does not have a sufficient basis for the awareness needed to recognize the possible illegality of such violations.

PROCEDURES THAT MAY IDENTIFY ILLEGAL ACTS

4. In making an examination in accordance with generally accepted auditing standards, an auditor should be aware of the possibility that illegal acts may have occurred that may have a material effect on the financial statements. Procedures that are performed primarily for the purpose of expressing an opinion on the financial statements that may also bring possible illegal acts to

---

[32] Ibid., AU Section 328.14–328.17.

* See Section 327, *The Independent Auditor's Responsibility for the Detection of Errors or Irregularities,* regarding the limitations of an examination in accordance with generally accepted auditing standards.

the auditor's attention include tests of transactions and balances and the study and evaluation of internal accounting control (paragraphs 5–7), and inquiries of management and others (paragraphs 8 and 9). If as a result of those procedures the auditor believes that illegal acts may have occurred, he should inquire of the client's management and consult with the client's legal counsel or other specialists, as necessary, to obtain an understanding of the nature of the acts and their possible effects on the financial statements. The auditor may also perform additional procedures to investigate such matters.

5. The auditor's tests of transactions and balances, his study and evaluation of internal accounting control, and his tests of compliance if any, with such controls may bring to his attention unauthorized transactions, transactions improperly recorded, or transactions not recorded in a complete or timely manner to maintain accountability for assets. Such transactions may raise questions about the possible existence of an illegal act. The auditor's interest in internal accounting control relates to the authorization, execution, and recording of transactions and accountability for the related assets (see sections 320.27–.40 and 320.43–.48).

6. In conducting his examination, the auditor obtains evidential matter as to the propriety of the accounting treatment of and support for transactions and balances. The procedures performed to obtain such evidential matter include obtaining an understanding of the transactions tested and their business purpose. A transaction that appears to the auditor to have an unusual or questionable purpose may raise questions about the possible existence of an illegal act.

7. As part of his examination, the auditor considers laws and regulations that have a direct effect on the amounts presented in financial statements. For example, tax laws affect accruals and the amount recognized as an expense in the accounting period. Also, applicable laws or regulations may affect the amount of revenue accrued under government contracts.

8. The auditor's examination should include inquiries of the client's management in connection with the accounting for and disclosure of loss contingencies and related communication with the client's legal counsel. The auditor should also inquire about the client's compliance with laws and regulations, the client's policies relevant to the prevention of illegal acts, and internal communications, such as directives issued by the client and periodic representations obtained by the client from management at appropriate levels of authority concerning compliance with laws and regulations. Possible illegal acts may come to the auditor's attention through such inquiries. For example, an auditor may learn of an investigation by a governmental agency or enforcement proceedings concerning violations of laws with respect to occupational safety and health, food and drug administration, truth in lending, environmental protection, price fixing or other anti-trust practices, or violations of laws and regulations of foreign countries.

9. The laws and regulations governing matters such as those indicated in paragraph 8 are highly specialized and complex. Also, they often relate to the operating aspects of an entity rather than its financial or accounting aspects.

Therefore, the auditor's examination cannot reasonably be expected to bring to his attention violations of those types of laws and regulations, unless he becomes aware of external evidence, such as governmental agency investigation or an enforcement proceeding, or obtains information from the client's management or legal counsel drawing his attention to such matters.

EVALUATION OF THE MATERIALITY OF AN ILLEGAL ACT

10. In evaluating the materiality of an illegal act that comes to his attention, the auditor should consider the effects, if any, on the amounts presented in the financial statements, including related contingent monetary effects of the violation. Contingent monetary effects include fines, penalties, and damages. Loss contingencies required to be disclosed should also be considered.

11. Loss contingencies, such as the threat of expropriation of assets, enforced discontinuance of operations in a foreign country, or possible litigation, may arise as a result of an illegal act. The auditor's considerations for evaluating the materiality of those loss contingencies are similar to those applicable to other loss contingencies.*

12. The auditor should also evaluate the adequacy of disclosure in the financial statements of the potential effects of an illegal act on the operations of the entity. If a material amount of revenue or earnings is derived from transactions involving illegal acts, or if illegal acts create significant unusual risks associated with a material amount of revenue or earnings, such as the loss of a significant business relationship, that information ordinarily should be considered for disclosure in the financial statements.

13. After it has been determined that an illegal act has occurred, the auditor should report the circumstances to personnel within the client's organization at a high enough level of authority so that appropriate action can be taken by the client with respect to

    a. consideration of remedial actions;
    b. adjustments or disclosures that may be necessary in the financial statements;
    c. disclosures that may be required in other documents (such as a proxy statement).

In some circumstances, the only persons in the organization of a sufficiently high level of authority to take necessary action may be the audit committee or the board of directors. The auditor should also consider the implications of an illegal act in relation to the intended degree of reliance to be placed on internal accounting control and the representations of management.

---

* Generally accepted accounting principles for the financial accounting for and reporting of loss contingencies are contained in *Statement of Financial Accounting Standards No. 5, Accounting for Contingencies* [AC Section 4311].

EFFECTS ON THE AUDITOR'S REPORT

14. The auditor may not be able to determine the amounts associated with certain events, taken alone or with similar events, of which he becomes aware, or whether an act is, in fact, illegal, because of an inability to obtain sufficient competent evidential matter. For example, the act may have been accomplished by circumventing the internal control system and may not be properly recorded or otherwise adequately documented, or the client's legal counsel may refuse to advise on the illegality of a material act. In those circumstances, the auditor should consider the need to qualify his opinion or disclaim an opinion because of the scope limitation (see section 509.10–.12).

15. If the auditor concludes that the effect of an event, taken alone or with similar events, is material in amount and that the event has not been properly accounted for or disclosed in the financial statements, he should qualify his opinion or express an adverse opinion because of the departure from generally accepted accounting principles (see section 509.15–.17).

16. The auditor may conclude that an illegal act's effects on the financial statements are not susceptible of reasonable estimation. When such an uncertainty exists, the auditor should consider the need to modify his report (see section 509.21–.25).*

17. If the client informs the auditor that it will refuse to accept an auditor's report that has been modified for the reasons cited in paragraphs 14–16, the auditor should withdraw from the current engagement, indicating the reasons for his withdrawal in writing to the board of directors. In such circumstances, the auditor may wish to consult with his legal counsel.

OTHER CONSIDERATIONS REGARDING ILLEGAL ACTS

18. When an illegal act, including one that does not have a material effect on the financial statements, comes to the auditor's attention, he should consider the nature of the act and management's consideration once the matter is brought to their attention. If the client's board of directors, its audit committee, or other appropriate levels within the organization do not give appropriate consideration (see paragraph 13) to the illegal act, the auditor should consider withdrawing from the current engagement or dissociating himself from any future relationship with the client. The auditor's decision as to whether to withdraw or dissociate because of an illegal act, including one not having a material effect on the financial statements, is ordinarily affected by (a) the effects on his ability to rely on management's representations and (b) the possible effects of continuing his association with the client. In reaching a decision on withdrawal or dissociation, the auditor may wish to consult with his legal counsel.

---

* For example, such an uncertainty may exist when it is reasonably possible, or probable, that a loss contingency arising from an illegal act will be resolved by a future event and the amount of the potential loss cannot be estimated. See *Statement of Financial Accounting Standards* No. 5, paragraphs 8–10 [AC Section 4311.08–.10].

19. Deciding whether there is a need to notify parties other than personnel within the client's organization of an illegal act is the responsibility of management. Generally, the auditor is under no obligation to notify those parties. However, if the auditor considers the illegal act to be sufficiently serious to warrant withdrawing from the engagement, he should consult with his legal counsel as to what other action, if any, he should take.[33]

LETTER FROM LEGAL COUNSEL

One particularly difficult standard faced by the auditor concerns loss contingencies. A loss contingency is defined as "an existing condition, situation, or set of circumstances involving uncertainty" as to the possible loss to an enterprise that "will ultimately be resolved when one or more future events occur or fail to occur." [34]

"An estimated loss from a loss contingency" shall be accrued by a charge to income if *both* of the following conditions are met:

a) Information available prior to issuance of the financial statements indicates that it is probable that an asset had been impaired or a liability had been incurred at the date of the financial statements. It is implicit in this condition that it must be probable that one or more future events will occur confirming the fact of the loss.

b) the amount of the loss can be reasonably estimated.[35]

If no accrual is made for a loss contingency because one or both of the above conditions are not met, or if an exposure to loss exists in excess of the amount accrued pursuant to the provisions above, "disclosure of the contingency shall be made when there is at least a reasonable possibility that a loss or an additional loss may have been incurred."[36] Disclosure may also be necessary with regard to losses or loss contingencies coming to the auditor's attention after the date of an enterprise's financial statements, but before those statements are issued.[37]

A major problem arises in connection with pending or threatened litiga-

---

[33] American Institute of Certified Public Accountants, "Illegal Acts by Clients," *AICPA Professional Standards*, vol. 1, AU Section 328 (Statement on Auditing Standards No. 17). Copyright © 1977 by the American Institute of Certified Public Accountants, Inc.

[34] *Statement of Financial Accounting Standards No. 5, Accounting for Contingencies* (Stamford, Conn.: Financial Accounting Standards Board, 1975), par. 1.

[35] Ibid., par. 8.

[36] Ibid., par. 10.

[37] Ibid., par. 11.

tion and actual or possible claims and assessments. How does the auditor assure himself that losses or contingent losses therefrom have been properly accrued or disclosed?

He must look in this regard to management and to the client's lawyer. The following standard discusses this problem.

---

1. This section provides guidance on the procedures an independent auditor should consider for identifying litigation, claims, and assessments and for satisfying himself as to the financial accounting and reporting for such matters when he is performing an examination in accordance with generally accepted auditing standards.

ACCOUNTING CONSIDERATIONS

2. Management is responsible for adopting policies and procedures to identify, evaluate, and account for litigation, claims, and assessments as a basis for the preparation of financial statements in conformity with generally accepted accounting principles.

3. The standards of financial accounting and reporting for loss contingencies, including those arising from litigation, claims, and assessments, are set forth in Statement of Financial Accounting Standards No. 5, "Accounting for Contingencies."

AUDITING CONSIDERATIONS

4. With respect to litigation, claims, and assessments, the independent auditor should obtain evidential matter relevant to the following factors:

   a. The existence of a condition, situation, or set of circumstances indicating an uncertainty as to the possible loss to an entity arising from litigation, claims, and assessments.
   b. The period in which the underlying cause for legal action occurred.
   c. The degree of probability of an unfavorable outcome.
   d. The amount or range of potential loss.

Audit Procedures

5. Since the events or conditions that should be considered in the financial accounting for and reporting of litigation, claims, and assessments are matters within the direct knowledge and, often, control of management of an entity, management is the primary source of information about such matters. Accordingly, the independent auditor's procedures with respect to litigation, claims, and assessments should include the following:

   a. Inquire of and discuss with management the policies and procedures adopted for identifying, evaluating, and accounting for litigation, claims, and assessments.

b. Obtain from management a description and evaluation of litigation, claims, and assessments that existed at the date of the balance sheet being reported on, and during the period from the balance sheet date to the date the information is furnished, including an identification of those matters referred to legal counsel, and obtain assurances from management, ordinarily in writing, that they have disclosed all such matters required to be disclosed by Statement of Financial Accounting Standards No. 5 [AC Section 4311].

c. Examine documents in the client's possession concerning litigation, claims, and assessments, including correspondence and invoices from lawyers.

d. Obtain assurance from management, ordinarily in writing, that it has disclosed all unasserted claims that the lawyer has advised them are probable of assertion and must be disclosed in accordance with Statement of Financial Accounting Standards No. 5 [AC Section 4311]. Also the auditor, with the client's permission, should inform the lawyer that the client has given the auditor this assurance. This client representation may be communicated by the client in the inquiry letter or by the auditor in a separate letter.*

6. An auditor ordinarily does not possess legal skills and, therefore, cannot make legal judgments concerning information coming to his attention. Accordingly, the auditor should request the client's management to send a letter of inquiry to those lawyers with whom management consulted concerning litigation, claims, and assessments.

7. The independent auditor's examination normally includes certain other procedures undertaken for different purposes that might also disclose litigation, claims, and assessments. Example of such procedures are as follows:

a. Reading minutes of meetings of stockholders, directors, and appropriate committees held during and subsequent to the period being examined.

b. Reading contracts, loan agreements, leases, and correspondence from taxing or other governmental agencies, and similar documents.

c. Obtaining information concerning guarantees from bank confirmation forms.

d. Inspecting other documents for possible guarantees by the client.

Inquiry of a Client's Lawyer

8. A letter of audit inquiry to the client's lawyer is the auditor's primary means of obtaining corroboration of the information furnished by management

---

* An example of a separate letter is as follows: We are writing to inform you that (name of company) has represented to us that (except as set forth below and excluding any such matters listed in the letter of audit inquiry) there are no unasserted possible claims that you have advised are probable of assertion and must be disclosed in accordance with *Statement of Financial Accounting Standards* No. 5 [AC Section 4311] in its financial statements at (balance sheet date) and for the (period) then ended. (List unasserted possible claims, if any.) Such a letter should be signed and sent by the auditor.

concerning litigation, claims, and assessments.* Evidential matter obtained from the client's inside general counsel or legal department may provide the auditor with the necessary corroboration. However, evidential matter obtained from inside counsel is not a substitute for information outside counsel refuses to furnish.

9. The matters that should be covered in a letter of audit inquiry include, but are not limited to, the following:

a. Identification of the company, including subsidiaries, and the date of the examination.

b. A list prepared by management (or a request by management that the lawyer prepare a list) that describes and evaluates pending or threatened litigation, claims, and assessments with respect to which the lawyer has been engaged and to which he has devoted substantive attention on behalf of the company in the form of legal consultation or representation.

c. A list prepared by management that describes and evaluates unasserted claims and assessments that management considers to be probable of assertion, and that, if asserted, would have at least a reasonable possibility of an unfavorable outcome, with respect to which the lawyer has been engaged and to which he has devoted substantive attention on behalf of the company in the form of legal consultation or representation.

d. As to each matter listed in item b, a request that the lawyer either furnish the following information or comment on these matters as to which his views may differ from those stated by management, as appropriate:

(1) A description of the nature of the matter, the progress of the case to date, and the action of the company intends to take (for example, to contest the matter vigorously or to seek an out-of-court settlement).

(2) An evaluation of the likelihood of an unfavorable outcome and an estimate, if one can be made, of the amount or range of potential loss.

(3) With respect to a list prepared by management, an identification of the omission of any pending or threatened litigation, claims, and assessments or a statement that the list of such matters is complete.

e. As to each matter listed in item c, a request that the lawyer comment on those matters as to which his views concerning the description or evaluation of the matter may differ from those stated by management.

f. A statement by the client that the client understands that whenever, in the course of performing legal services for the client with respect to a matter recognized to involve an unasserted possible claim or assessment that may call for financial statement disclosure, the lawyer has formed

---

* It is not intended that the lawyer be requested to undertake a reconsideration of all matters upon which he was consulted during the period under examination for the purpose of determining whether he can form a conclusion regarding the probability of assertion of any possible claim inherent in any of the matters so considered.

a professional conclusion that the client should disclose or consider disclosure concerning such possible claim or assessment, the lawyer, as a matter of professional responsibility to the client, will so advise the client and will consult with the client concerning the questions of such disclosure and the applicable requirements of Statement of Financial Accounting Standards No. 5 [AC Section 4311].

g. A request that the lawyer confirm whether the understanding described in item f is correct.

h. A request that the lawyer specifically identify the nature of and reasons for any limitation on his response.

Inquiry need not be made concerning matters that are not considered material, provided the client and the auditor have reached an understanding on the limits of materiality for this purpose.

10. In special circumstances, the auditor may obtain a response concerning matters covered by the audit inquiry letter in a conference, which offers an opportunity for a more detailed discussion and explanation than a written reply. A conference may be appropriate when the evaluation of the need for accounting for or disclosure of litigation, claims, and assessments involves such matters as the evaluation of the effect of legal advice concerning unsettled points of law, the effect of uncorroborated information, or other complex judgments. The auditor should appropriately document conclusions reached concerning the need for accounting for or disclosure of litigation, claims, and assessments.

11. In some circumstances, a lawyer may be required by his Code of Professional Responsibility to resign his engagement if his advice concerning financial accounting and reporting for litigation, claims, and assessments is disregarded by the client. When the auditor is aware that a client has changed lawyers or that a lawyer engaged by the client has resigned, the auditor should consider the need for inquiries concerning the reasons the lawyer is no longer associated with the client.

Limitations on the Scope of a Lawyer's Response *

12. A lawyer may appropriately limit his response to matters to which he has given substantive attention in the form of legal consultation or representation. Also, a lawyer's response may be limited to matters that are considered individually or collectively material to the financial statements, provided the lawyer and auditor have reached an understanding on the limits of materiality for this purpose. Such limitations are not limitations on the scope of the auditor's examination.

13. A lawyer's refusal to furnish the information requested in an inquiry letter either in writing or orally (see paragraphs 9 and 10) would be a limitation on the scope of the auditor's examination sufficient to preclude an unqualified

---

* The American Bar Association has approved a "Statement of Policy Regarding Lawyer's Response to Auditors' Requests for Information," which explains the concerns of lawyers and the nature of the limitations an auditor is likely to encounter. (See Appendix 10.)

opinion (see section 509.10–.11).* A lawyer's response to such an inquiry and the procedures set forth in paragraph 5 provide the auditor with sufficient evidential matter to satisfy himself concerning the accounting for and reporting of pending and threatened litigation, claims and assessments. The auditor obtains sufficient evidential matter to satisfy himself concerning reporting for those unasserted claims and assessments required to be disclosed in financial statements from the foregoing procedures and the lawyer's specific acknowledgement of his responsibility to his client in respect of disclosure obligations (see paragraph 9g). This approach with respect to unasserted claims and assessments is necessitated by the public interest in protecting the confidentiality of lawyer-client communications.

Other Limitations on a Lawyer's Response

14. A lawyer may be unable to respond concerning the likelihood of an unfavorable outcome of litigation, claims, and assessment or the amount or range of potential loss, because of inherent uncertainties. Factors influencing the likelihood of an unfavorable outcome may sometimes not be within a lawyer's competence to judge; historical experience of the entity in similar litigation or the experience of other entities may not be relevant or available; and the amount of the possible loss frequently may vary widely at different stages of litigation. Consequently, a lawyer may not be able to form a conclusion with respect to such matters. In such circumstances, the auditor ordinarily will conclude that the financial statements are affected by an uncertainty concerning the outcome of a future event which is not susceptible of reasonable estimation. If the effect of the matter on the financial statements could be material, the auditor ordinarily will conclude that he is unable to express an unqualified opinion (see section 509.21–.26).[38]

THE COST ACCOUNTING STANDARDS BOARD

The Cost Accounting Standards Board is a relatively new presence in the standard-setting process. Its origin, its accomplishments, and its relation to the other standard-setting bodies are discussed in the following excerpts

---

* A refusal to respond should be distinguished from an inability to form a conclusion with respect to certain matters of judgment (see paragraph 14). Also, lawyers outside the United States sometimes follow practices at variance with those contemplated by this section to the extent that different procedures from those outlined herein may be necessary. In such circumstances, the auditor should exercise judgment in determining whether alternative procedures are adequate to comply with the requirement of this section.

[38] "Inquiry of a Client's Lawyer Concerning Litigation, Claims, and Assessments," AICPA *Professional Standards*, vol. 1, AU Section 337 (Statement on Auditing Standards No. 12). Copyright © 1976 by the American Institute of Certified Public Accountants, Inc.

from an article by C. Howell of the Martin Marietta Aerospace Corporation.

Government contract cost accounting regulations started at least as far back as 1934 when the Vinson-Trammel Act was passed limiting the profits on aircraft and naval vessel contracts.* The next activity took place after World War II when Treasury Decision 5000 applying to subsidized ships was issued. These were replaced in 1949 when the Armed Services Procurement Regulation (ASPR) was issued. Although ASPR has been revised once and amended and supplemented many times it is still in effect today.

In the late Sixties, the Vietnam war was escalating and so was the defense budget. Large cost overruns were common. Conflicting opinions accompanied by strong feeling centered around the war, the draft, the defense budget and the changing life styles of the times created considerable unrest. It was in this setting in 1968 that Vice Admiral Rickover appeared before the House Banking and Currency Committee. He testified strongly and colorfully that it was impossible to determine the profit being made on defense contracts because of lack of control and inconsistencies in treatment of contract costs.

As a result of Rickover's urgings for Congress to provide accounting standards, Congress passed P.L. 90-370 setting up a General Accounting Office study to see if such standards were feasible.† In 1970 the GAO reported back that it was feasible and recommended that such standards apply to all government contracts, not just defense contracts.

CONGRESS CREATES THE CASB

Acting on the results of the feasibility study, Congress in 1970 passed P.O. 91-379 amending the Defense Procurement Act of 1950 to provide for the establishment of a Cost Accounting Standards Board (CASB).‡ The Board was to report and act as an agent of Congress. The law further provided that the Board would promulgate cost accounting standards to achieve uniformity and consistency in the cost accounting principles followed by defense contractors under Federal contracts.

The law specified that the Comptroller General would be the chairman and that he should appoint four members; one from industry, one from a Federal agency and two from the accounting profession. . . . The Board has a professional staff . . . of CPAs, attorneys, former professors, controllers and government auditors. //

The CASB has specified that all contractors receiving defense contract or

---

* *Cost Accounting Standards for Defense Contracts,* Arthur Anderson & Co., 1972, p. 4.

† *Cost Accounting Standards Guide,* Commerce Clearing House, Inc., Chicago, Ill., 1975, p. 2023.

‡ *CAS for Defense Contracts,* p. 83.

// *CAS Guide,* p. 2102.

subcontract awards exceeding $10 million within a fiscal year must submit a disclosure statement, and has prescribed a formalized procedure for doing this.* However, this should not be construed as the limits of the CASB's jurisdiction. The actual limit is the first contract exceeding $500,000 in a fiscal year and all subsequent contracts greater than $100,000. . . .

ASSESSMENT OF THE PROMULGATION PROCESS

There are varied opinions about the procedures followed by the CASB in promulgating standards and the results obtained. As might be expected the opinions of the Board and its staff are not precisely shared by the contractors, the industry and various associated interests. Then there is a somewhat middle ground stand taken by those who are not associated with either the government or the defense industry.

From the Board Point of View

Board member Robert Mautz has been one of the more prolific expounders of the Board's promulgation procedure. In a speech before the Cost Accounting Symposium, Mr. Mautz, presumably speaking in his capacity as a member of the CASB, discussed the Board's function.† He stated that the Board's first concern is to do the job prescribed by Congress, the promulgating of standards to achieve uniformity and consistency. The Board's performance has apparently satisfied Congress, since no standard has been struck down by that body as provided for in the law. Mr. Mautz summed up the Board's method of determining when adequate research had been performed as ". . . when the Board is convinced that the stated solution to a given issue is the best that can be devised." ‡ On the CASB's relationship with other authoritative bodies such as the FASB, the SEC, etc., Mr. Mautz stated that close liaisons were maintained and certainly no conflict is desired. He made it clear, however, that possible conflict with another authority would not deter the Board from its mandate to promulgate standards. Mr. Mautz gave little hope that the Board would soon promulgate a standard dealing with concepts and closed his remarks by soliciting advice and cooperation from all concerned.

In a later speech to an AICPA meeting Mr. Mautz let his hair down a little. // After reviewing the various development stages a standard goes through from problem identification to final acceptance, Mr. Mautz proceeded to provide some insight into his personal and somewhat pragmatic philosophy of setting standards. He pointed out that truth is, in his opinion, not the only consideration in developing a standard. He stated that ". . . an accounting standard is a social agreement that must be acceptable to the majority to be

---

* CAS for Defense Contracts, p. 83.

† Ibid., p. 8350. Mr. Mautz has since left the board.

‡ Ibid., p. 8352.

// Robert K. Mautz, "Other Accounting Standards Board," *Journal of Accountancy*, February 1974.

effective . . ." and as a result ". . . may be nothing more than the best compromise that can be reached . . ." The practical answer, he feels, lies somewhere between an ". . . ideal solution that is unacceptable to the majority" and an innocuous solution ". . . that offends no one." *

Mr. Arthur Schoenhaut, Executive Secretary of the CASB, says that much interaction has taken place between the Board and outsiders concerned with cost accounting standards.† He feels that comments have received and will continue to receive careful consideration by the Board and staff in developing standards. In an evaluation of the cooperation received, Mr. Schoenhaut said that the individual contractors have been most helpful and constructive while the industry associations have generally provided the most "negative attitude possible." He pointed out, however, that such a negative attitude is helpful because it requires good research work and sound evidence gathering to combat it. As a by-product he feels better standards no doubt result.

One of the most concise explanations of the standards development procedure was presented by CASB staff member Paul McClenon in the *Journal of Accountancy*.‡ Basically the procedure consists of six steps which are:

1. Identification of a problem area.
2. Extensive research to determine the severity.
3. Development of the most promising solution.
4. Test the solutions in practical situations at contractor locations.
5. Develop the exposure draft and publish in Federal Register.
6. Review comments, revise regulation as needed, republish revised draft if necessary or publish in final form in the Federal Register. . . .

As Seen from Outside the CASB

How do those interested in the standards, but not associated with the Board, view the promulgation procedures? . . . Professor Howard Wright pointed out some general imperfections in the CASB promulgation procedures in a speech at the Financial Executives Institute Conference. // He felt that some standards had been determined by popular votes cast by government agencies rather than on merit. Professor Wright saw no evidence of the Board's inclination to act on its pledge to modify or correct any standard that needs it. Like many others, Mr. Wright believed the Board should publish a total conceptual framework which all could use as a guide. He further complained that the Board prescribes methods rather than standards and ignores ". . . the fact that indirect cost allocations are but approximations at best." #

* Robert K. Mautz, "Other Accounting Standards Board," *Journal of Accountancy*, February 1974.

† Arthur Schoenhaut, "CASB—Past, Present and Future," *Financial Executive*, September 1973.

‡ Paul R. McClenon, "Operations of the Cost Accounting Standards Board," *Selected Studies In Modern Accounting*, AICPA, 1973, pp. 62–66.

// Howard W. Wright, "FASB—CASB—Similarities and Differences," *Financial Executive*, September 1973.

Ibid.

In a communication to the Board, the Aerospace Industries Association (AIA) expressed several items of criticism.* The AIA requested that the Board publish the criteria it uses to determine the need for standards. They also requested that research methods and results be published for evaluation. The AIA in complaining of the rigidity of standards said, "there were more procedures than standards." It also believed that they cost too much to administer. . . .

The most favorable comment from outside the CASB has been to compliment the Board's solicitation of active participation and ideas from all sources. Many also feel the Board and staff are sincerely attempting to do a good job.†

Other groups that have evidenced constructive attitudes toward the CASB are: American Institute of Certified Public Accountants, National Association of Accountants, American Accounting Association, Federal Government Accountants Association and Financial Executives Institute.

GAUGING THE IMPACT OF THE CASB

The CASB has made its presence felt. Hundreds of thousands of man-hours and millions of dollars have been expended by the CASB and the defense industry on the development, promulgation and implementation of cost accounting standards since 1970. Most contractors have set up staffs to review CASB communications, submit comments and to analyze disclosure statements looking for possible standard violations. Accounting systems have had to be revised in some cases to fit the new standards. Whenever this requires computer programming and system changes, considerable expense results. A particularly time-consuming task occurs when it is necessary or desirable to make a change that affects the disclosure statement or when it is determined that there has been an inadvertent noncompliance with the disclosure statement. Any resulting cost impact must be determined by contract and must be reported to the cognizant contract officer.‡

The CASB seems to be moving with each new standard further into the depths and details of accounting. It also is concerning itself with broader areas of accounting. The CASB has also indicated a desire to extend its coverage to include government contracts beyond the defense category. With Congressional approval the CASB may widen its area of authority and influence until it meets strong resistance from other authoritative groups. The force of law is more influential in a business situation than are principles promulgated by a professional group. It follows then that in a clash between the CASB and the FASB, the CASB will no doubt prevail. However, should the conflict be between the CASB and the SEC, the CASB would probably come out second-best. Under favorable conditions then it is conceivable that the CASB may expand to the point where it will be contained by the boundaries of authority of other regulatory bodies, primarily of legal origin.

---

* CAS Guide, p. 8557.

† Louis Bisgay, "MAP and CASB," Management Accounting, August 1973.

‡ Fred R. Lang, "Cost Accounting Standards and Financial Auditing," Management Accounting, April 1975.

CONCLUSION

The CASB has vigorously followed its mandate to promulgate standards. It has sincerely solicited comments and participation from all concerned. But some believe that built-in biases have surfaced during their now-public deliberations and are evidenced in standards promulgated thus far. Industry representatives feel that CASB promulgations have been too theoretical and impractical. The results, they say, have been increased cost to the government, reduced incentive and curtailed innovation in the industry and the forcing of some contractors out of the defense business. Such objections have had little apparent restraining effect on the CASB. Instead, there are indications that the CASB will move to expand its authority and influence. In the present political climate any such move will most likely receive Congressional blessing.[39]

1. What are the five general standards which all professional accountants must follow?

2. What should be your authority in the area of accounting principles? Your own good judgment? Are opinions issued by the Accounting Principles Board still valid? What about the Cost Accounting Standards Board?

3. As an auditor expressing an opinion on the financial statements of a client, is it ever ethical for you to sanction a departure from "generally accepted accounting principles?" What reporting responsibilities do you have if such a departure takes place?

4. What are the seven generally accepted auditing standards? Where did these standards originate and who interprets them?

5. Are any general or technical standards addressed in the Statements on Management Advisory Services? the Statements on Responsibilities in Tax Practice? What are they?

6. Under what circumstances should you, as a tax practitioner, sign the return of a client? What is the authority for your answer?

7. What general and technical standards are addressed in the Code of Ethics of the Institute of Internal Auditors? In the Standards for the Professional Practice of Internal Auditing?

8. Assume that you are both a certified management accountant and the controller of a large manufacturing company. What ethical standards, if any, should you abide by with regard to forecasts of future transactions?

[39] Cloyd Howell, "CASB: An Assessment," *Management Accounting*, April 1977, pp. 23–26.

9. As an audit partner with a large CPA firm, you have assumed a major role in practice development. In a discussion with the Audit Committee of a prospective client, it becomes apparent to you that the committee regards the detection of fraud as one of an auditor's main responsibilities. How would you respond to them? What are the auditor's responsibilities in this area according to the written standards of the profession?

10. To what extent can an auditor rely upon the representations of management? Is it reasonable for him to assume that no material misrepresentations have been made and that control procedures have not been overridden?

11. What is the auditor's obligation when his examination causes him to believe that material errors or irregularities may exist? With whom should he discuss the matter? Should he extend his audit procedures? Under what circumstances should he consider withdrawing from the engagement?

12. How does an auditor assure himself that losses or contingent losses from pending or threatened litigation have been properly accrued or disclosed? What audit procedures are needed? What is the role of a letter of inquiry to the client's lawyer? Are there any limitations on the scope of a lawyer's response?

SUGGESTED ADDITIONAL READINGS

ALLEN, BRANDT, "The Biggest Computer Frauds: Lessons for CPAs," *The Journal of Accountancy,* May 1977.

American Institute of Certified Public Accountants, "The Auditors' Study and Evaluation of Internal Control," *AICPA Professional Standards,* vol. 1, AU Section 320 (Statement on Auditing Standards No. 1).

————, "Adequacy of Planning and the Timing of Field Work," *AICPA Professional Standards,* vol. 1, AU Section 310 (Statement on Auditing Standards No. 1).

————, "Planning and Supervision," *AICPA Professional Standards,* vol. 1, AU Section 311 (Statement on Auditing Standards No. 22).

————, "Training and Proficiency of the Independent Auditor," *AICPA Professional Standards,* vol. 1, AU Section 210 (Statement on Auditing Standards No. 1).

————, "Exhibit II—American Bar Association Statement of Policy Regarding Lawyer's Responses to Auditors' Requests for Information," *AICPA Professional Standards,* vol. 1, AU Section 337C. (See Appendix 10.)

American Institute of Certified Public Accountants, "Inquiry of a Client's Lawyer Concerning Litigation, Claims and Assessments: Auditing Interpretations of AU Section 337," *AICPA Professional Standards,* vol. 1, AU Section 9337.

ANDREWS, WESLEY T., "Obtaining the Representations of Legal Counsel," *The CPA Journal,* August 1977.

Responsibilities to Clients, Management, and Owners

INTRODUCTION

Every professional accountant has certain responsibilities to the party or parties he serves. If in public accounting, that party is a client. If practicing internally, it may be top management, a board of directors, and owners. One of the ethical principles adopted by the AICPA, although written in the context of responsibilities to clients, serves well to describe the obligation of all professionals to those they serve.

> "A certified public accountant should be fair and candid with his clients and serve them to the best of his ability, with professional concern for their best interests, consistent with his responsibilities to the public." [1]

Five statements elaborating this principle have been adopted by the AICPA. Although some of them relate primarily to those in public practice, they are significant for all accountants.

[1] "Concepts of Professional Ethics," *AICPA Professional Standards,* vol. 2, ET Section 54.

1. As a professional person, the CPA should serve his clients with competence and with professional concern for their best interests. He must not permit his regard for a client's interest, however, to override his obligation to the public to maintain his independence, integrity and objectivity. The discharge of this dual responsibility to both clients and the public requires a high degree of ethical perception and conduct.

2. It is fundamental that the CPA hold in strict confidence all information concerning a client's affairs which he acquires in the course of his engagement. This does not mean, however, that he should acquiesce in a client's unwillingness to make disclosures in financial reports which are necessary to fair presentation.

3. Exploitation of relations with a client for personal advantage is improper. For example, acceptance of a commission from any vendor for recommending his product or service to a client is prohibited.

4. A CPA should be frank and straightforward with clients. While tact and diplomacy are desirable, a client should never be left in doubt about the CPA's position on any issue of significance. No truly professional man will subordinate his own judgment or conceal or modify his honest opinion merely to please. This admonition applies to all services including those related to management and tax problems.

5. When accepting an engagement, a CPA should bear in mind that he may find it necessary to resign if conflict arises on an important question of principle. In cases of irreconcilable difference, he will have to judge whether the importance of the matter requires such an action. In weighing this question, he can feel assured that the practitioner who is independent, fair and candid is the better respected for these qualities and will not lack opportunities for constructive service.[2]

THE AUDITOR

While an auditor generally cannot disclose confidential information obtained in the course of a professional engagement without the consent of the client, the rule has several exceptions. For example, the auditor is required to comply with generally accepted auditing standards and to describe departures from these standards. He is also required to describe departures from generally accepted accounting principles.

It would not be a violation of responsibility to a client, for example, if an auditor qualified his opinion and disclosed the fact that a client had dividend arrearages or liens on some of his assets.[3] It would also not be a violation of the auditor's responsibility to a client if it were disclosed that a client capitalized research and development costs, for example, rather

[2] "Concepts of Professional Ethics," *AICPA Professional Standards,* vol. 2, ET Section 54. Copyright © 1978 by the American Institute of Certified Public Accountants, Inc.

[3] "Adequacy of Informative Disclosure," *AICPA Professional Standards,* vol. 1, AU Section 430.01–.02 (Statement on Auditing Standards No. 1).

than expensing them as required by generally accepted accounting principles.[4]

The rule requiring auditors not to disclose confidential information is not used (a) "to affect in any way his compliance with a validly issued subpoena or summons enforceable by order of a court," (b) "to prohibit review of a member's professional practices as part of voluntary quality review under Institute authorization" or (c) "to preclude a member from responding to any inquiry made by the ethics division or Trial Board of the Institute, by a duly constituted investigative or disciplinary body of a state CPA society, or under state statutes."[5] Chapter 11 contains a complete discussion of the law regarding privileged and confidential communications.

The auditor also has definite responsibilities to the client arising out of the study and evaluation of internal control made in connection with an audit. First, such a study is required under generally accepted auditing standards.[6] Second, any material weaknesses in internal accounting control discovered as a part of the study and evaluation must be communicated to "senior management and to the board of directors or its audit committee."[7] The question of internal control and the auditor's duties will be more thoroughly discussed in a later section of this chapter.

THE MANAGEMENT CONSULTANT

Statements on Management Advisory Services 4, 5, and 8 have a direct relation to the accountant's responsibility to the client. (See Appendix 2.) "Before accepting an engagement," a practitioner should "notify the client of any reservations he has regarding" its "anticipated benefits." Furthermore, if during the course of the engagement, "the relationship between anticipated benefits and costs changes significantly, the client should be informed."[8] Assume, for example, that you have been asked by a small manufacturing company in your area to conduct a detailed study and evaluation of their cost accounting system. Having just completed an

---

[4] *Statement of Financial Accounting Standards No. 2, Accounting for Research and Development Costs* (Stamford, Conn.: Financial Accounting Standards Board, 1974) par. 12, and "Adherence to Generally Accepted Accounting Principles," *AICPA Professional Standards,* vol. 1, AU Section 410 (Statement on Auditing Standards No. 1).

[5] "Confidential Client Information," *AICPA Professional Standards,* vol. 2, ET Section 301.

[6] "Generally Accepted Auditing Standards," *AICPA Professional Standards,* vol. 1, AU Section 150 (Statement on Auditing Standards No. 1).

[7] "Required Communication of Material Weaknesses in Internal Accounting Control," *AICPA Professional Standards,* vol. 1, AU Section 323 (Statement on Auditing Standards No. 20).

[8] "Client Benefit," *AICPA Professional Standards,* vol. 1, MS Section 140 (Statement No. 4).

audit of the company less than six months ago, you are very familiar with the system and are convinced that it is a sound one. Should you accept the engagement?

Clearly, you would have an obligation in this case to communicate your reservations about the need for a review to the client. If the client still wants you to conduct the study, you may do so. Even though no direct financial benefit may come from the study, it may reassure the client that his system is a good one, and only he can decide whether that kind of benefit is worthwhile.[9]

"Before undertaking an engagement," a practitioner should "inform the client of all significant matters related to the engagement." This would include "(a) the engagement's objectives, (b) its scope, (c) the approach, (d) the role of all personnel, (e) the manner in which results are to be communicated, (f) the timetable, and (g) the fee. These matters should be recorded in writing, particularly for engagements of significant duration or complexity. This can be done in a formal contract, in a letter of understanding, or in a file memorandum summarizing the terms of an oral agreement with the client." [10] When an engagement is completed, "all significant matters" relating to its results should be communicated to the client. This communication may be written or oral, but when a written report is not issued the practitioner should "prepare a file memorandum documenting the significant recommendations and other pertinent information discussed with the client." [11]

What about a situation in which a management consultant attains expertise as a result of work for one client and is then engaged by another client with a similar problem? Assume, for example, that you have just completed an evaluation of the feasibility of purchasing a particular computer system. This study, which led you to a negative conclusion as regards Client A, also suggests a negative conclusion with regard to Client B. Can you disclose to Client B the information and conclusions you reached with regard to Client A? Should you disclose the facts of your prior study without the conclusions?

Rule of Conduct No. 301 provides that "a member shall not disclose any confidential information obtained in the course of a professional engagement except with the consent of the client." [12] "Knowledge and

9 "Interpretations of Management Advisory Services Practice Standards: Standard No. 4—Client Benefit," *AICPA Professional Standards,* vol. 1, MS Section 140-1.02.

10 "Understanding with Client," *AICPA Professional Standards,* vol. 1, MS Section 150 (Statement No. 5).

11 "Communication of Results," *AICPA Professional Standards,* vol. 1, MS Section 180 (Statement No. 8).

12 "Confidential Client Information," *AICPA Professional Standards,* vol. 2, ET Section 301.

expertise which result in a special competence in a particular field" can be provided to a client, however, without violating the confidence of another client. The reservations you have concerning the purchase of the computer system should be communicated to Client B, but the details of the other engagement should not be disclosed. If the circumstances are such that Client B would "clearly know the origin of the information" on which the advice is based and "such information is sensitive," the engagement should not be accepted without clearance from Client A.[13]

THE TAX PRACTITIONER

A tax practitioner, upon learning of an error in a client's previously filed tax return, or of the failure of a client to file a required return, is faced both with a problem of maintaining his independence and integrity and with fulfilling his responsibility to the client. The basic position taken in one of the Statements on Responsibilities in Tax Practice is that the client should be promptly advised of the error. "The CPA is neither obligated to inform the Internal Revenue Service nor may he do so without his client's permission." [14]

Another area of concern to the tax practitioner deals with the setting of his fees. Would it be ethical for example to tie the amount of the fee to the amount of taxes saved? Clearly, this would not be proper. Rule of Conduct 302 states that "professional services shall not be offered or rendered under an arrangement whereby no fee will be charged unless a specified finding or result is attained, or where the fee is otherwise contingent upon the findings and results of such services." [15] Furthermore, "a properly prepared tax return results in a proper tax liability, and there is no basis for computing a savings. To make a fee contingent upon the amount of taxes saved presumes a tax liability has been established which an accountant is attempting to reduce, whereas all persons concerned with the preparation of a tax return should attempt to determine only the correct tax liability." [16] The rule prohibiting contingent fees does not, of course, prevent a member from varying his fee according to "the complexity of the service rendered." [17]

---

[13] "Ethics Rulings on Responsibilities to Client," *AICPA Professional Standards*, vol. 2, ET Section 391.029.

[14] "Knowledge of Error: Return Preparation," *AICPA Professional Standards*, vol. 1, TX Section 161 (Statement No. 6).

[15] "Contingent Fees," *AICPA Professional Standards*, vol. 2, ET Section 302.

[16] "Ethics Rulings on Responsibilities to Clients," *AICPA Professional Standards*, vol. 2, ET Section 391.023.

[17] "Contingent Fees," ET Section 302.

THE INTERNAL PROFESSIONAL

The internal professional has a responsibility to be fair and candid with management, directors, and owners, and to serve them to the best of his ability, with professional concern for their best interests, consistent with his responsibilities to the public. It is important to note that an internal professional, even though not in the public practice, still has a responsibility to the public. Just as a lawyer working for a corporation or the government still has an ethical and moral responsibility to the public and to the courts, so does the accountant. External parties should be able to rely upon financial statements prepared internally because they were prepared by accounting professionals and, therefore, were prepared correctly and honestly.

One area where management and directors must place great reliance upon their internal professional accountants is in the establishment of an accounting system and a system of internal control. The Foreign Corrupt Practices Act of 1977 amended the Securities Exchange Act of 1934 to require that:

> Every issuer which has a class of securities registered pursuant to section 12 of this title and every issuer which is required to file reports pursuant to section 15(d) of this title shall—
> (A) make and keep books, records, and accounts, which, in reasonable detail, accurately and fairly reflect the transactions and dispositions of the assets of the issuer; and
> (B) devise and maintain a system of internal accounting controls sufficient to provide reasonable assurances that—
> (i) transactions are executed in accordance with management's general or specific authorization;
> (ii) transactions are recorded as necessary (I) to permit preparation of financial statements in conformity with generally accepted accounting principles or any other criteria applicable to such statements, and (II) to maintain accountability for assets;
> (iii) access to assets is permitted only in accordance with management's general or specific authorization; and
> (iv) the recorded accountability for assets is compared with the existing assets at reasonable intervals and appropriate action is taken with respect to any differences.

Failure to comply with these provisions subject management and others to possible fines and imprisonment. It is very important, therefore, for the internal professional to fulfill his responsibility in this area.

What responsibility does the internal professional have with regard to internal reports? Assume, for example, that you are the accountant putting together the budget for your division. You become aware that some of the cost estimates submitted by department heads in the division are deliberately overstated. Should you simply include the figures without question and forward the budget to corporation headquarters? Clearly, to do so would be a violation of professional ethics. The internal professional must always act with integrity, and he would have a responsibility in this case to question the department heads and determine the correct figures to use.

INTERNAL CONTROL:
RESPONSIBILITIES OF THE AUDITOR

As indicated earlier, the external auditor has definite responsibilities to his client with regard to internal control. The second auditing standard of field work is as follows:

> There is to be a proper study and evaluation of the existing internal control as a basis for reliance thereon and for the determination of the resultant extent of the tests to which auditing procedures are to be restricted.[18]

Internal control includes controls which may be characterized as either accounting or administrative, as follows:

> *Administrative control* includes, but is not limited to, the plan of organization and the procedures and records that are concerned with the decision processes leading to management's authorization of transactions.* Such authorization is a management function directly associated with the responsibility for achieving the objectives of the organization and is the starting point for establishing accounting control of transactions.
>
> *Accounting control* comprises the plan of organization and the procedures and records that are concerned with the safeguarding of assets and the reliability of financial records and consequently are designed to provide reasonable assurance that:
> a. Transactions are executed in accordance with management's general or specific authorization.
> b. Transactions are recorded as necesssary (1) to permit preparation of financial statements in conformity with generally accepted accounting principles or any other criteria applicable to such statements and (2) to maintain accountability for assets.

---

[18] "The Auditor's Study & Evaluation of Internal Control," *AICPA Professional Standards,* vol. 1, AU Section 320.01 (Statement on Auditing Standards No. 1). Copyright © 1974 by the American Institute of Certified Public Accountants, Inc.

* This definition is intended only to provide a point of departure for distinguishing accounting control and, consequently, is not necessarily definitive for other purposes.

c. Access to assets is permitted only in accordance with management's authorization.

d. The recorded accountability for assets is compared with the existing assets at reasonable intervals and appropriate action is taken with respect to any differences.

The foregoing definitions are not necessarily mutually exclusive because some of the procedures and records comprehended in accounting control may also be involved in administrative control. For example, sales and cost records classified by products may be used for accounting control purposes and also in making management decisions concerning unit prices or other aspects of operations. Such multiple uses of procedures or records, however, are not critical for the purposes of this section because it is concerned primarily with clarifying the outer boundary of accounting control. Examples of records used solely for administrative control are those pertaining to customers contacted by salesmen and to defective work by production employees maintained only for evaluating personnel performance.[19]

Accounting control, as defined above, is "within the scope of the study and evaluation of internal control contemplated by generally accepted auditing standards, while administrative control is not."[20] It should be remembered, however, that the overriding criterion is "the bearing which particular controls have on the reliability of financial statements, regardless of their classification as accounting or administrative controls. For practical purposes, this is tantamount to including within the definition of accounting controls any administrative controls that have an important bearing on the reliability of the financial statements."[21]

The study and evaluation of internal control includes two phases: (1) "knowledge and understanding of the procedures and methods prescribed" and (2) "a reasonable degree of assurance that they are in use and are operating as planned." Although these phases are separated, "they are closely related in that some portions of each may be performed concurrently and may contribute to the auditor's evaluation of the prescribed procedures and of the compliance with them."[22]

In fulfilling the second phase of a study and evaluation of internal control, the auditor conducts certain *tests of compliance*. These tests are concerned primarily with the questions: "Were the necessary procedures performed, how were they performed, and by whom were they performed."[23]

The tests of compliance are closely interrelated with what are called *substantive tests*. In fact, as pointed out earlier, the reason for a review of

19 "The Auditor's Study & Evaluation of Internal Control," *AICPA Professional Standards*, vol. 1, AU Section 320.27–.29 (Statement on Auditing Standards No. 1).

20 Ibid., AU Section 320.49.

21 Ibid., AU Section 320.12.

22 Ibid., AU Section 320.50.

23 Ibid., AU Section 320.57.

internal control is to obtain a "basis for reliance thereon and for the determination of the *resultant extent of the tests to which auditing procedures are to be restricted* (emphasis added)." These substantive tests involve two general classes of auditing procedures: (1) "tests of details of transactions and balances," and (2) "analytical review of significant ratios and trends and resulting investigation of unusual fluctuations and questionable items." [24] These substantive tests are closely linked to the tests of compliance in that they often "concurrently provide evidence of compliance with accounting control procedures as well as evidence required for substantive purposes." [25]

Generally accepted auditing standards require that the auditor "communicate to senior management and the board of directors or its audit committee material weaknesses in internal accounting control that come to his attention during an examination of financial statements." [26] However, it should be noted that the auditor does not conduct a comprehensive review of the entire system of internal accounting controls. Therefore, he is not in a position to make a judgment as to whether the internal accounting controls are in compliance with requirements of the Foreign Corrupt Practices Act of 1977.

A "material weakness" is defined in Statement on Auditing Standards No. 1 as:

> . . . a condition in which the auditor believes the prescribed procedures or the degree of compliance with them does not provide reasonable assurance that errors or irregularities in amounts that would be material in the financial statements being audited would be prevented or detected within a timely period by employees in the normal course of performing their assigned functions.[27]

One clear example of a material weakness would be where cash is received, recorded, and deposited by the same person. Assuming that cash receipts are material in amount, the prescribed procedure does not provide reasonable assurance that a theft of cash would be prevented or detected within a timely period by employees in the normal course of performing their assigned functions.

SEC Requirement

Auditors will very probably be further involved with the internal control systems of their SEC clients in fiscal years ending after December 31, 1980.

---

[24] "The Auditor's Study & Evaluation of Internal Control," AICPA *Professional Standards,* vol. 1, AU Section 320.70.

[25] Ibid., AU Section 320.56.

[26] "Required Communication of Material Weaknesses in Internal Accounting Control," AICPA *Professional Standards,* vol. 1, AU Section 323.01.

[27] "The Auditors' Study & Evaluation of Internal Control," AU Section 320.68.

The Securities and Exchange Commission has proposed that management, in connection with its responsibilities under the Foreign Corrupt Practices Act of 1977, be required to state in their annual shareholders report and Form 10-K their opinion as to whether their internal accounting control system provided reasonable assurance for the fiscal year that the accounting control objectives of the Act were achieved. It has also proposed that a report from the independent accountant be required which expresses an opinion as to (1) whether the representations of management are consistent with the results of management's evaluation and (2) whether such representations are reasonable with respect to transactions and assets in amounts which would be material when measured in relation to the registrant's financial statements.

INTERNAL CONTROL AND
THE FINANCIAL EXECUTIVE

The role of the internal accounting professional as it relates to internal control is discussed in the following excerpts from an article by Harvey V. Guttry, Jr. and Jesse R. Foster of the Times Mirror Company. The authors also outline the approach being taken in their company to ensure compliance with the Foreign Corrupt Practices Act of 1977.

Recent developments have necessitated a reexamination of the role of internal controls in the efficient and orderly conduct of today's corporations. This reexamination must be based on an understanding that internal control is the composite of a company's arrangements to attain its objectives including maximizing the return on owners' investment; protecting the company's assets; providing a safe and fulfilling work environment for its employees; reporting properly and adequately to owners, regulators, and taxing authorities; and acting as a good citizen.

The internal control arrangements adopted by a company will vary according to its own complex mix of objectives as well as the nature and size of its business. While there is a tendency, particularly among the independent auditors, to stress procedures, internal control effectiveness is primarily dependent on the people involved. No matter how extensive a company's framework of policies and procedures are, that framework can only be effective to the extent that there are competent people exercising good judgment in the implementation of policies and procedures.

RECENT LEGISLATION

Internal control has taken on a new dimension with the signing of the "Foreign Corrupt Practices Act of 1977" by President Carter. This new statute is a lasting outgrowth of the questionable payments campaign of the Securities and

Exchange Commission.* As the name of the Act implies, it prohibits the bribing of foreign officials and establishes severe penalties for offending corporations and corporate personnel. Of potentially greater concern to corporations and their auditors are the additional provisions pertaining to internal accounting controls.

The internal control provisions of the new law seem innocuous enough. The provisions include four required objectives of internal accounting control that are borrowed from the AICPA's definition as expressed in the Institute's Statement on Auditing Standards No. 1.

When the internal control provisions were proposed, the AICPA and FEI took the positive approach of supporting the proposals provided certain refinements in the language were made. The Congress was generally amenable to these suggestions. Further, as recommended by the AICPA and FEI, related provisions pertaining to deceiving the auditors were dropped completely as being inappropriate.[28]

The SEC staff is disappointed that the new law does not include specific language requiring internal controls to prevent bribery. However, such emphasis on corporate rules and procedures is misplaced. Not only does internal control, per se, have limitations as a means to assuring reliable financial statements and safeguarding assets, but there are serious defects in depending on internal control as the means of preventing questionable payments and questionable acts. There has been no evidence presented that the companies who reported questionable acts did not have satisfactory internal accounting controls in the view of their independent auditors. In fact, the evidence indicates that a large percentage of the questionable payments and acts were accomplished by simple override of the controls through executive authority.

While there are some serious definitional and implementational problems posed in the internal control provisions of the statute, the overall thrust of these provisions does not unduly infringe upon individual and institutional freedoms. Rather, the requirements, when supported by additional guidance generated in the private sector, should be effective in emphasizing management's responsibility for internal control. The legislation goes beyond the concept of appropriate internal accounting controls in the context of the auditor's work and places a definite, explicit duty on the publicly held corporation.

Contrary to the expectations of some users of audited financial statements, independent auditors normally limit their review of internal controls to determining how much reliance can be placed on such controls in conducting their audit. As required by auditing standards, management and directors are alerted

---

* At the end of the major phase of its questionable payments campaign, the SEC summarized its conclusions and recommendations in a report entitled "Report on Questionable and Illegal Corporate Payments and Practices." Since the report was prepared for Senator Proxmire's committee, it has become known as the "Proxmire Report." This report recommended anti-bribery legislation containing internal control requirements as well as penalties for deceiving the independent auditors.

[28] Subsequent to the passing of the Act, the SEC issued regulations making it illegal for an officer or director to make false or incomplete statements to an auditor.

when flagrant deficiencies in internal control are detected. However, additional scrutiny by management is required. To achieve adequate surveillance of controls at a reasonable cost, large enterprises should utilize internal specialists in internal control just as internal expertise is already employed in the areas of taxation, financial reporting, and management services.

THE MOSS SUBCOMMITTEE REPORT

In addition to serving as the genesis for the foreign corrupt practices legislation, the SEC's conclusions and recommendations in the Proxmire Report were ironically used in an attack on the SEC itself.

A much publicized report prepared under the direction of Congressman Moss relies heavily on the Proxmire Report for evidence that internal controls have been inadequate and ineffective, and that corporate accountability to shareholders and to the public has broken down in too many instances. Among a multitude of other recommendations, the subcommittee's report recommends that the SEC require uniformity of financial controls.

The Moss Subcommittee Report also recommended a SEC requirement that independent auditors publicly report on the quality of internal controls and their enforcement. . . .

THE COHEN COMMISSION'S CONCLUSIONS

Public reporting on internal controls is also being advocated by some financial analysts. In a recent survey, a group of financial analysts indicated that they were not interested in a simple statement on the adequacy of internal control as is already being provided by a few major corporations in their annual reports. Rather, they would prefer a detailed report describing all material weaknesses in internal control.

The analysts believe that comprehensive information on internal controls can be significant to the investment decision-making process. Such information, it is felt, could give some indication of the reliability of information used for internal decision-making and of the reliability of interim and other unaudited information.

Furthermore, the Commission on Auditor's Responsibilities (the Cohen Commission), after studying the needs and expectations of those who rely on the auditor's work, is recommending voluntary public disclosures relative to internal controls. The Cohen Commission envisions management placing a "Report by Management" in the annual report to acknowledge management's responsibility for the financial statements and to describe the status of internal controls.

The Cohen Commission is also recommending an expanded auditor's report that will focus on the company's representations contained in the report by management. The Commission recognizes that before issuing this expanded auditor's report, the auditors would have to expand their study and evaluation of internal control. Also to meet the expectations of users, the auditors would be expected to actively search for fraud, rather than simply being alert for it. . . .

MANAGEMENT'S RESPONSIBILITY

Regardless of where the definitional boundaries of internal accounting controls are placed, it must be emphasized that so-called administrative controls have the most bearing on the success of a business. Management has to avoid the pitfall of overstressing accounting controls at the expense of the administrative or operational controls. The importance of proper attention to both administrative and accounting controls should be conveyed in the criteria for internal control from management's perspective.

Management's concept of internal control should begin with explicit acknowledgement of its overall responsibilities. For example, in its "report by management" representation, management could summarize its objectives and corporate policies and other controls designed to achieve those objectives. Then management can speak to the adequacy of the company's internal accounting controls.

Management's definition of internal accounting control has to go beyond the boundaries established for the auditor's benefit in Statement on Auditing Standards No. 1. From the point of view of the managements of large corporations, the definition of internal accounting control should be broad enough to include all external corporate reporting including business statistics such as volume data presented to the public. While management can take the broadest view in making its representation, the auditors can limit their opinion to the adequacy of the internal accounting controls tested in conjunction with their audit of the financial statements.

It must be recognized that the largest determinant of the effectiveness of any system of internal control is the people who are responsible for the functioning of the controls. Therefore, in evaluating internal control, management must keep uppermost the competence of personnel. Evaluating personnel performance is, of course, difficult because of subjective aspects and the potential for rapid and significant change in human performance. Good management practices, however, have always included adequate attention to employee evaluation and any review of the adequacy of a system of controls to detect and prevent errors must include sufficient consideration of how personnel performance affects the performance of the system.

The importance of the human element is such that management cannot afford to leave its control and ethical objectives to undirected perceptions and interpretations throughout the company. To effectively accomplish its objectives, top management must continuously communicate its philosophy as explicitly and as often as is reasonable.

While society should be reasonably tolerant of occasional internal control malfunctioning, management should assure itself that it is doing enough within the perspective of cost versus benefit. The effort for internal control excellence can be most effective if senior management is fully committed to the goal, and if key operating officers are actively supporting the chief financial and accounting officers by conveying a high degree of concern for the quality of internal controls. Management's philosophy on internal controls and corporate ethics, as perceived throughout the corporation, sets the tempo for internal control performance on every level.

As a key part of this communication, but certainly not a substitute for periodic discussions, board of directors and senior management should adopt a policy statement on internal controls. This statement should be disseminated throughout the company. It should convey to employees that just as they are expected to follow certain standards of accountability to higher management, the directors and senior management are committed to a standard of accountability to the shareholders and to the public.

ONE COMPANY'S APPROACH

At Times Mirror, while planning our approach and generally striving to increase the effectiveness of our system of internal controls, we seek to follow the basic philosophy of our senior management toward the subsidiaries—i.e., the best performance is obtained when operating management is free to make its own business decisions. Also, there is a commitment to the concept of decentralized accounting records and accounting controls that fit the unique aspects of the individual operating units. Of course, the operating units must conform their practices to corporate policies and to sound accounting and reporting requirements as set forth by the company's chief accounting officer.

The company's accounting management continuously considers the adequacy of controls. In addition to the normal controls at the operating levels, significant controls include the following:

* Organizational structure and reporting lines designed to preclude any single member of management from overriding the system of internal controls.
* A qualified and informed audit committee of the board of directors.
* A clear and concise corporate policy manual.
* Annual planning and budgeting at all operating units with subsequent monitoring of actual performance against budget plans on a period-by-period basis. (This program also provides for capital expenditure control.)
* An accounting policy manual which describes significant accounting policies to be followed throughout the company.
* Segregation of functions within the controller's organization, which includes a "policy and control" function and the company's primary internal audit function.
* Quarterly letters of representation from chief operating and accounting officers of divisions and subsidiaries encompassing, in addition to comprehensive representations as to the financial statements, statements of compliance with company policy, and representations covering compliance with public law.
* Mandatory rotation of audit personnel in accordance with audit committee policy.
* Pre-audit/post-audit conferences attended by representatives of the corporate accounting staff, independent auditors, and the management of the operating units.

* A post-audit closing conference of the company's senior management and the independent auditors as well as a meeting of the auditors with the audit committee.
* A corporate audit staff which historically has reviewed internal accounting controls and compliance with company policy and performs annual EDP audits and reviews of EDP systems during their development.

Additional controls being considered are:

* Even greater coordination of internal and independent audit resources to maximize audit effectiveness.
* A log of all accounting practice changes to formally document acknowledgement by the company's management of all accounting changes.

Experimenting with Monitoring and Evaluation Techniques

Beyond these contemplated refinements, the most revolutionary innovation being considered is a process of monitoring internal controls that provides for the measurement of risk. It is still undecided as to how formal and detailed a monitoring mechanism needs to be. However, in any company, the importance of internal controls needs to be stressed to operating management beyond the emphasis that comes through from the audit process. Most probably, the discipline of a monitoring process can help corporate and subsidiary management assign and maintain the proper priorities in addressing internal control deficiencies.

The guidelines for this monitoring program were adapted from Statement on Auditing Standards No. 1 and the audit manuals of several CPA firms. This approach calls for identifying all significant types of transactions and considering the types of errors that could occur with each. Using detailed systems descriptions, all of the pertinent controls will be matched with the error types and weaknesses will then be identified. Compensating controls will be considered before a bona fide deficiency in controls will be considered to exist. Once a control deficiency is identified, the risk of not eliminating the deficiency or weakness will be quantified. Then the cost of the additional controls needed to eliminate the weakness will be estimated. Finally, management will consider the risk and cost relationship and make a decision on whether the additional controls should be implemented.

CONCLUSION

The purpose of Times Mirror's experiment is to search for a means for operating management to make a comprehensive assessment of internal controls. Since the effectiveness of controls, administrative and accounting, is management's responsibility, management should make the primary representation concerning the adequacy of the controls. The auditor's role should be limited to reviewing and testing those controls which are pertinent to their examination of the financial statements and using the results of such audit work as a basis for commenting on management's representation. Just as the auditors should not be expected to verify certain subjective financial disclosures, they should not be expected to report on the controls that have no significant bearing on their examination of the financial statements.

Operating management should be able to benefit from a requirement to monitor controls if a method that does not create an undue burden can be devised. Operating management and senior management should have reasonable assurance that controls designed to achieve the company's objectives are in place and working. Shareholders and other external users of the company's information are entitled to know that adequate attention is being given to internal controls.[29]

INTERNAL CONTROL AND THE COMPUTER

The advent of electronic data-processing systems has complicated the internal control problems of business, and made theft easier and more difficult to detect. It has also made more difficult the job of conducting an audit. The following excerpts from an article by Elise G. Jancura and Fred L. Lilly discuss the evaluation of internal control when an electronic data-processing system is in use, and the generally accepted auditing standard related to it.[30]

Computers and their related support equipment have not in any significant way altered established accounting theory as it relates to the kind of data to be collected or the manner in which such data should be organized for reporting purposes. But the computer has substantially altered the methods by which that theory is put into practice. As the collection and subsequent uses of data are changed from manual procedures performed by individuals familiar with both the data and the accounting process to high volume, automated techniques performed by individuals unfamiliar with both the data and accounting practices, the opportunities for personal review and clerical checking have declined.

Statement on Auditing Standards No. 3 describes "the effects of the use of EDP on the various characteristics of accounting control and on an auditor's study and evaluation thereof." * It does this by defining EDP accounting controls and the auditor's responsibility for reviewing those controls. SAS No. 3

---

[29] Harvey V. Guttry, Jr. and Jesse R. Foster, "Internal Controls and the Financial Executive," *Financial Executive*, April 1978, pp. 42–48.

[30] "The Effects of EDP on the Auditor's Study and Evaluation of Internal Control," *AICPA Professional Standards*, vol. 1, AU Section 321 (Statement on Auditing Standards No. 3).

* Statement on Auditing Standards No. 3, "The Effects of EDP on the Auditor's Study and Evaluation of Internal Control" (New York: AICPA, 1974), par. 5.

also provides "a framework for the development of further guidance concerning auditing procedures in examining financial statements of entities that use EDP in accounting applications.*

The introduction of data-processing equipment requires that the recording and processing functions be concentrated in departments that are separate from the origin of the data; it may also eliminate the separation of responsibilities that previously characterized the record keeping function. A trend toward the integration of operating and financial data into corporate information systems or data bases also eliminates independent records that might previously have provided a source of comparative data. At the same time, such integrated information systems can become the basis for more vital and timely management decisions.

Computerization has reduced substantially the time available for the review of transactions before their entry into the accounting records. As a result, in poorly controlled systems the opportunity for discovering errors before they have an impact on operations has been reduced or even eliminated, especially in the case of real time systems. This has increased the importance of internal control procedures.

Many records are no longer stored in hard copy that is intelligible to human beings. Data is often stored instead in a machine-readable format, and intermediate results may not be printed. Changes in the recording media and the elimination of many clerical procedures have combined to eliminate many of the traditional audit trails by which individual records can be traced to final reports or to the original transaction. There is also an educational lag that makes it difficult for persons without training and experience in data processing to understand the system and evaluate its performance.

Computer-based accounting systems add special emphasis to three basic auditing standards from Statement on Auditing Standards No. 1. These are the first general standard, which is concerned with adequate technical training and proficiency; the second field standard, which covers the study and evaluation of internal control; and the third field standard on collection of competent evidential matter.

THE AUDITOR'S TECHNICAL PROFICIENCY

The first general standard states that "the examination is to be performed by a person or persons having adequate technical training and proficiency as an auditor." † While this standard has been in effect for a long time, its scope has broadened recently because of the development of EDP auditing. The Institute has not made a formal pronouncement of the knowledge required for auditing computer records, but two articles about this subject have appeared in the *Journal of Accountancy* and are the most authoritative standards available. These articles both suggested three levels of EDP technical proficiency: the

---

* Statement on Auditing Standards No. 3, "The Effects of EDP on the Auditor's Study and Evaluation of Internal Control" (New York: AICPA, 1974), Footnote 4.

† Statement on Auditing Standards No. 1, "Codification of Auditing Standards and Procedures" (New York: AICPA, 1973), par. 150.02.

general audit staff member, the computer audit specialist, and the data-processing specialist.*

The general staff auditor has the basic audit responsibility for the examination of the financial statements of clients, including full responsibility for the review and evaluation of internal control and the development and execution of the audit plan. In order to perform properly the required tasks of reviewing and evaluating internal control and performing subsequent substantive tests of the financial data, the minimum EDP knowledge requirements of the general staff auditor should include

1. A basic understanding of computer systems, including equipment components and their general capabilities.
2. A basic understanding of widely installed computer operating systems and software.
3. A general familiarity with file processing techniques and data structures.
4. Sufficient working knowledge of computer audit software to use existing standardized audit packages.
5. The ability to review and interpret systems documentation including flowcharts and record definitions.
6. Sufficient working knowledge of basic EDP controls to
   a. Identify and evaluate the controls in effect in the client's installation.
   b. Determine the extent to which such controls should be tested and to evaluate the results of such tests (although not necessarily to execute such tests).
7. Sufficient knowledge of EDP systems to develop the audit plan and supervise its execution.
8. A general familiarity with the dynamics involved in developing and modifying programs and processing systems.

Many audit situations will call for a level of EDP knowledge above that of the general audit staff member; for these situations an auditor at the level of a computer audit specialist will be required. The computer audit specialist is an auditor specially trained in data processing who may serve as the accountant in charge of the engagement or as a specialist who supplements the skills and abilities of that person. In either case, use of an auditor with special training in data processing may be appropriate in meeting the first general auditing standard.

The computer audit specialist can provide assistance in the use of computers to perform the compliance and substantive tests in technically sophisti-

---

* See Richard M. Cutting and others, "Technical Proficiency for Auditing Computer Processed Accounting Records," *Journal of Accountancy*, Oct. 1971, pp. 76–78. This article was prepared by a task force of the AICPA computer auditing subcommittee and published with the committee's permission, although it was never designated as an official committee position paper. See also Elise G. Jancura, "Technical Proficiency for Auditing Computer Processed Accounting Records" (an update), *Journal of Accountancy*, Oct. 1975, pp. 46–59. This article was prepared at the request of the AICPA computer education subcommittee.

cated systems. The primary distinction between the staff auditor and computer audit specialist should be in the depth—not the breadth—of their EDP knowledge and proficiency in the use of the computer.

Although the level of ability of the computer audit specialist would normally meet the requirements of the first general standard, there may be audit situations that require the abilities of the data processing specialist. Although this specialist is not an auditor, he or she can provide the same type of extremely specialized technical services to the auditor as the appraiser or actuary.

In building on this requirement, SAS No. 3 states that some situations "will require that the auditor apply specialized expertise in EDP in the performance of the necessary audit procedure." * This wording is designed to follow SAS No. 1 and at the same time permit the auditor to make use of specialists in performing his work.

INTERNAL CONTROL IN
AN EDP ENVIRONMENT

The second standard of field work states that "there is to be a proper study and evaluation of the existing internal control as a basis for reliance thereon and for the determination of the resultant extent of the tests to which auditing procedures are to be restricted." †

This standard requires a review of internal control without distinguishing between manual and computer systems. Further, reference to SAS No. 1 indicates that the basic concepts of accounting control are expressed in terms of objectives and are independent of whether the records are maintained manually or electronically.‡ The auditor is therefore required to review internal control in an EDP system.

The purpose of this review is to permit the auditor to determine the extent to which internal controls can be relied on. Presumably, the auditor could choose to perform a 100 percent examination of all transactions and thus not rely on internal controls. The second standard of field work does not mention this possibility and, therefore, provides no exemption from the requirement to review the controls in an EDP system. However, the possibility of not relying on internal controls is mentioned in SAS No. 3; the Statement also requires a preliminary review of the EDP system even if the auditor is not going to rely on internal controls.

Accounting controls are distinguished from administrative controls in SAS No. 1; the auditor is put on notice that although the review of internal control is normally concerned only with accounting controls, there may be cases when some of the controls frequently thought of as administrative controls fall within the definition of accounting controls. //

In practice, the distinction between accounting controls and administrative controls is often minor, for the procedures adopted and the controls employed

---

* Statement on Auditing Standards No. 3, par. 4.

† Statement on Auditing Standards No. 1, par. 150.02.

‡ Ibid., par. 320.33.

// Ibid., par. 320.12.

can serve both purposes. Often administrative controls have a substantial impact on the reliability of the financial records. SAS No. 1 defines administrative controls as the plan of organization and the procedures that are concerned with operational efficiencies and adherence to management policies, and accounting controls as the plan of organization and the procedures that are concerned with the safeguarding of assets and the reliability of financial records.* Frequently, both types of controls are implemented by the same procedures.

The introduction of SAS No. 3 states that evaluation of administrative controls is not contemplated by generally accepted auditing standards. This would appear to relieve the auditor of the responsibility of reviewing many of the controls maintained over computer systems, but in fact it does not. The auditor's responsibilities have been defined to include most of the typical EDP controls; paragraphs 6 through 9 indicate that when a computer is being used, many of the controls normally associated with computer center operations are actually EDP accounting rather than administrative controls. This is true regardless of whether these procedures are performed in the EDP department or in a user department.

A computer-based accounting system may make use of both manual and electronic activities in maintaining accounting records. Paragraph 3 of SAS No. 3 states that control procedures may be manual or may be performed by the EDP process itself. The auditor may thus be called on to recognize a control procedure actually taking place within the computer. This may be true whether the use of EDP in the system is limited or extensive and whether the processing is done on the company's premises or at a service bureau.

Controls for which the auditor is responsible are described in paragraphs 7 and 8 of SAS No. 3 as being divided between general controls and application controls. General controls are defined as procedures that relate to all EDP activities and application controls as procedures that relate only to specific accounting tasks. The significance of this division to the auditor is that application controls are effective in only those programs or applications (e.g., inventory, accounts receivable or payrolls) where they have been implemented. For this reason, review and compliance testing of application controls must be done separately for each application involved.

In the review of controls, SAS No. 3 alerts the auditor to the problem of incompatible functions. Computerized techniques frequently bring about centralization and a greater integration of processing steps into fewer departments. This eliminates some of the safeguards previously associated with the segregation of functions performed by employees at different points in the organizational structure. Because of the concentration of accounting procedures within the computer, computer programs may perform duties which, if performed by one person, would result in that person's performing incompatible functions. Any person who has the ability to modify such a program without supervision or review is himself performing incompatible functions. This may also be true of a programer who maintains the computer supervisory programs and whose work is not subject to review.

* Statement on Auditing Standards No. 1, par. 320.10.

The concept of compensating controls is introduced in paragraph 15 of SAS No. 3, the first official recognition in the professional literature of this concept. In a computer-based accounting system, the possibilities for accounting control are so great that it is possible to maintain one or more controls that will effectively compensate for the lack of an otherwise important control. SAS No. 3 does not give specific examples of compensating controls but suggests that user departments may be able to maintain controls that can compensate for missing or ineffective controls within data processing. For example, if the payroll department maintains batch controls over hours worked for the pay period and control totals for the payroll master file, including number of active employees and hash totals of pay rates, this may compensate for a lack of control over access to data files in the data center.

In describing the recording of transactions, SAS No. 3 states that errors may be introduced into the accounting system as part of the initial recording process. For this reason, the auditor should consider the need for control over entry of data into the system. Paragraph 18 tells the auditor that a computer program may be used not only to record but also to initiate transactions. Using the computer to initiate transactions should be done only in accordance with management's authorization; the auditor should know the points, if any, in the client's system at which the computer is authorized to initiate transactions and the controls maintained over this process.

REVIEWING, EVALUATING AND TESTING THE SYSTEM OF INTERNAL CONTROL

The preliminary phase of the auditor's review of internal control is described in paragraph 25; the auditor is told that review "should be designed to provide an understanding of the flow of transactions through the accounting system. . . ." *

In addition to this level of understanding, the auditor is expected to determine the extent to which EDP is used in each significant accounting application and the basic structure of accounting control. This preliminary review is important to the auditor as a requirement that is effective regardless of whether or not internal controls are to be relied on in establishing the scope of examination. Paragraph 26 spells out the options open to the auditor after completion of the preliminary review.

After the preliminary review, the auditor may decide to (1) complete the review of controls and, if warranted, place reliance on the system of controls or (2) perform the audit without completing the review of controls and without placing reliance on the controls. The auditor would choose the second course of action if he or she concludes that the system of controls is so ineffective that such reliance would be impossible. SAS No. 3 also says that the auditor may choose not to complete the review of controls and thus not rely on internal

---

* Statement on Auditing Standards No. 1, pars. 320.19–320.25, describes the flow of transactions.

controls even though they appear to be adequate. Without limiting the possible reasons for this action, the Statement cites two examples of cases where the auditor concludes that (1) it would be more costly to review and test controls than to forgo reliance on controls and that (2) EDP controls would duplicate manual controls maintained by users. Although both of these situations would be unusual for an accounting system large enough to require a sophisticated computer system for processing records, no mention is made in SAS No. 3 of the extent of substantive testing when no reliance is placed on internal control.

The Statement does not mention the action to be taken by an auditor who, after completing the preliminary review, finds that the controls appear adequate but decides not to complete his review and rely on controls because his own level of technical proficiency is not adequate to complete the review and perform appropriate compliance tests. In such a situation, if the auditor is able to perform substantive testing to the extent that reliance on controls is not necessary, some auditors may feel that it is possible to avoid conflict with the first general standard by not performing the remaining part of the review. In such a case, the auditor would, however, have to be careful not to be in conflict with the second standard of field work.

If the auditor decides to rely on the system of internal control, sufficient tests of compliance must be performed to establish a reasonable degree of assurance that the system of internal control is in use and operating as planned. Tests of compliance may be applied on a subjective or a statistical basis. The extent of testing done and the level of assurance deemed acceptable or reasonable are matters of auditing judgment. The degree of assurance achieved is a function of the results of the tests. It is the auditor's responsibility to judge what control procedures are appropriate to the client's system, to test whether they operate as intended and to assess any weaknesses resulting from the absence of a needed control procedure or the failure of prescribed procedures to function as intended.

Frequently, tests of compliance are closely interrelated with substantive tests. Specific auditing procedures may concurrently provide evidence of compliance with accounting control procedures as well as substantive evidence of accurate records. In some cases, actual data may be used as the auditor samples the results of processing for the existence of conditions that should have been detected by program controls. While some of the compliance testing procedures may use actual data, others may introduce simulated (test) data for purposes of tracing the way in which the system handles the simulated data. Whatever procedures are used, the primary purpose of compliance testing is to test the system, not the data. In addition, direct observation of the installation operations and installation records can also function as a test of the installation's internal controls.

COMPETENT EVIDENTIAL MATTER

The third statement of field work requires that "sufficient competent evidential matter is to be obtained through inspection, observation, inquiries and confirmations to afford a reasonable basis for an opinion regarding the financial statements under examination." *

Evidential matter is defined as that including the books of original entry, the general ledger and subsidiary ledgers.† In a computer-based accounting system, these records can be machine-readable media such as magnetic tapes and discs. This fact is recognized in SAS No. 3, paragraph 13, and may require the auditor to make use of computer programs to read the basic data files. (As recognized in SAS No. 3, this concept is mentioned in connection with changing the data records rather than examining basic accounting records although the same principle is involved.)

Evidential matter in a system that is dependent on computerized controls and processing procedures draws heavily on the documentation of the system's processing procedures and programs. This documentation frequently consists of record layouts, program listings, flowcharts, decision tables and run manuals. The documents represent the client's formal description of his system, and an understanding of these materials can help the auditor to design the test program. Also important are the listings and calculations assembled by the auditor as he examines and evaluates the client's system and data. Since much client data is in machine-readable form, the auditor may be required to use computer-assisted audit techniques to test those machine records in order to verify their accuracy as a part of the compliance test of internal controls or the substantive test of the accounting records.

CONCLUSION

SAS No. 3 is a bold first step in defining auditing standards for EDP systems. It not only prescribes a required level of EDP internal control review and understanding of the system but it also alerts the auditor to numerous potential control problems in EDP systems and identifies situations where it may be appropriate, or even necessary, for the auditor to make use of the computer in performing tests.[31]

INTERIM FINANCIAL INFORMATION

In addition to examining annual financial statements in accordance with generally accepted auditing standards, accountants are frequently called upon to review interim financial statements or information. The objective of such reviews is to provide the accountant with "a basis for reporting whether material modifications should be made for such information to

---

* Statement on Auditing Standards No. 1, par. 150.02.

† Ibid., par. 330.04.

[31] Elise G. Jancura and Fred Lilly, "SAS No. 3 and the Evaluation of Internal Control," *The Journal of Accountancy*, March 1977, pp. 69–74. Copyright © 1977 by the American Institute of Certified Public Accountants, Inc.

conform with generally accepted accounting principles." [32] They do not provide the basis for an expression of opinion on the financial statements taken as a whole, but consist primarily of inquiries and analytical review procedures concerning significant accounting matters. The procedures ordinarily applied are:

a. Inquiry concerning (1) the accounting system, to obtain an understanding of the manner in which transactions are recorded, classified, and summarized in the preparation of interim financial information and (2) any significant changes in the system of internal accounting control, to ascertain their potential effect on the preparation of interim financial information.

b. Application of analytical review procedures to interim financial information to identify and provide a basis for inquiry about relationships and individual items that appear to be unusual. Analytical review procedures, for purposes of this section, consist of (1) comparison of the financial information with comparable information for the immediately preceding interim period and for corresponding previous period(s), (2) comparison of the financial information with anticipated results, and (3) study of the relationships of elements of financial information that would be expected to conform to a predictable pattern based on the entity's experience. In applying these procedures, the accountant should consider the types of matters that in the preceding year or quarters have required accounting adjustments.

c. Reading the minutes of meetings of stockholders, board of directors, and committees of the board of directors to identify actions that may affect the interim financial information.

d. Reading the interim financial information to consider, on the basis of information coming to the accountant's attention, whether the information to be reported conforms with generally accepted accounting principles.

e. Obtaining reports from other accountants, if any, who have been engaged to make a review of the interim financial information of significant components of the reporting entity, its subsidiaries, or other investees.

f. Inquiry of officers and other executives having responsibility for financial and accounting matters concerning (1) whether the interim financial information has been prepared in conformity with generally accepted accounting principles consistently applied,

---

[32] "Review of Interim Financial Information," *AICPA Professional Standards*, vol. 1, AU Section 721.03 (Statement on Auditing Standards No. 24).

(2) changes in the entity's business activities or accounting practices, (3) matters as to which questions have arisen in the course of applying the foregoing procedures, and (4) events subsequent to the date of the interim financial information that would have a material effect on the presentation of such information.

g. Obtaining written representations from management concerning its responsibility for the financial information, completeness of minutes, subsequent events, and other matters for which the accountant believes written representations are appropriate in the circumstances.[33]

These procedures apply to "reviews of interim financial information presented alone, including interim financial statements and summarized financial data," and to "reviews of interim financial information included in a note to audited financial statements of a public or non-public entity." They do not apply to "an accountant's involvement with interim financial information included in documents filed with the Securities and Exchange Commission pursuant to the Securities Act of 1938, unless the accountant has examined and reported on financial statements which include the interim financial information in a note." [34]

The accountant's report accompanying interim financial information that he has reviewed, which is presented other than in a note to audited financial statements, should consist of the following:

1. a statement that the review of interim financial information was made in accordance with the standards for such reviews,
2. an identification of the interim financial information reviewed,
3. a description of the procedures for a review of interim financial information,
4. a statement that a review of interim financial information is substantially less in scope than an examination in accordance with generally accepted auditing standards, the objective of which is an expression of opinion regarding the financial statements taken as a whole, and accordingly, no such opinion is expressed, and
5. a statement about whether the accountant is aware of any material modifications that should be made to the accompanying financial information so that it conforms with generally accepted accounting principles.[35]

[33] "Review of Interim Financial Information," *AICPA Professional Standards,* vol. 1, AU Section 721.06.

[34] Ibid., AU Section 721.02. The accountant's procedures concerning such interim financial information for periods subsequent to the periods reported on are discussed in AU Section 630, "Letters for Underwriters," and AU Section 710, "Filings Under Federal Securities Statutes."

[35] Ibid., AU Section 721.17.

As indicated above, this kind of report gives limited assurance regarding the interim information, but disclaims an expression of opinion. The interim information is unaudited and each page should be so marked.

"When interim financial information designated as unaudited is presented in a note to audited financial statements, the auditor need not modify his report on the audited financial statements to make reference to his review or to the selected interim information." [36] However, if the scope of his review of the interim financial information was restricted or if the information does not appear to be presented in conformity with generally accepted accounting principles, the report should be expanded as appropriate.[37]

UNAUDITED FINANCIAL STATEMENTS OF PUBLIC ENTITIES

A public accountant sometimes has a responsibility to assist a public entity [38] with the preparation of unaudited financial statements or perhaps to prepare them entirely. In fulfilling this responsibility he may become *associated* with the statements. As indicated in Chapter 2, this *association* occurs when "he has consented to the use of his name in a report, document, or written communication containing the statements" or has submitted "to his client or others financial statements that he prepared or assisted in preparing." [39]

The danger with association lies in the possible misinterpretation by third parties that the financial statements have been audited, and that the accountant is in some way vouching for their accuracy and correctness. Generally accepted auditing standards require that a disclaimer of opinion accompany unaudited financial statements with which the CPA is associated. As pointed out in the preceding section, this includes interim statements which have been "reviewed" in accordance with Statement on Auditing Standards No. 24 (AU Section 721).

The form of report to be issued when an accountant is associated with

---

[36] "Review of Interim Financial Information," *AICPA Professional Standards*, vol. 1, AU Section 721.26.

[37] Ibid., AU Section 721.27.

[38] A public entity is defined as any entity (a) whose securities trade in a public market either on a stock exchange (domestic or foreign), or in the over-the-counter market, including securities quoted only locally or regionally or (b) that makes a filing with a regulatory agency in preparation for the sale of any class of its securities in a public market. See "Review of Interim Financial Information," *AICPA Professional Standards*, vol. 1, AU Section 721.02 (Statement on Auditing Standards No. 24).

[39] Auditing Standards Board, *Proposed Statement on Auditing Standards: Association With Financial Statements* (New York: American Institute of Certified Public Accountants, 1979), par. 3.

the annual financial statements of a public entity, but has not audited or reviewed [40] them, is as follows:

> The accompanying balance sheet of X Company as of December 31, 19X1, and the related statements of income and retained earnings and changes in financial position for the year then ended were not audited by us and accordingly we do not express an opinion on them.
>
> (Signature and date) [41]

This report "may accompany the unaudited financial statements or it may be placed directly on them. In addition, each page of the financial statements should be clearly and conspicuously marked as unaudited." [42] When issuing this type of opinion, the accountant has no obligation to apply any procedures, nor should he describe any procedures that have been applied. Such a description might cause the reader to believe the statements have been audited or reviewed.

"If the accountant is aware that his name is to be included in a client-prepared written communication of a public entity containing financial statements that have not been audited or reviewed, he should request (a) that his name not be included in the communication or (b) that the financial statements be marked as unaudited and that there be a notation that he does not express an opinion on them. If the client does not comply, the accountant should advise the client that he has not consented to the use of his name and should consider what other actions might be appropriate." [43]

"If the accountant concludes on the basis of facts known to him that the unaudited financial statements on which he is disclaiming an opinion are not in conformity with generally accepted accounting principles, which include adequate disclosure, he should suggest appropriate revision; failing that, he should describe the departure in his disclaimer of opinion. This description should refer specifically to the nature of the departure and, if practicable, state the effects on the financial statements or include the necessary information for adequate disclosure." [44]

---

[40] If an accountant is requested to "review" the interim or annual statements of a public entity that does not have its annual financial statements audited, he should look to Statements on Standards for Accounting and Review Services for the standards and procedures and form of report applicable to such an engagement. See "Compilation and Review of Financial Statements," AICPA Professional Standards, vol. 1, AR Section 100.

[41] Auditing Standards Board, Proposed Statement on Auditing Standards: Association with Financial Statements, par. 5.

[42] Ibid.

[43] Ibid., par. 6.

[44] Ibid., par. 10.

"When a departure from generally accepted accounting principles involves inadequate disclosure, it may not be practicable for the accountant to include the omitted disclosures in his report. For example, when management has elected to omit substantially all of the disclosures, the accountant should clearly indicate that in his report, but the accountant would not be expected to include such disclosures in his report." [45]

"If the client will not agree to revision of the financial statements or will not accept the accountant's disclaimer of opinion with the description of the departure from generally accepted accounting principles, the accountant should refuse to be associated with the statements and, if necessary, withdraw from the engagement." [46]

UNAUDITED FINANCIAL STATEMENTS
OF NON-PUBLIC ENTITIES

The Accounting and Review Services Committee is the senior technical committee of the American Institute of Certified Public Accountants designated to issue pronouncements in connection with unaudited financial statements or other unaudited financial information of a non-public entity. Statements on Auditing Standards still provide guidance to the accountant who performs services in connection with the unaudited statements of a public entity.

In its first official statement on Standards for Accounting and Review Services, the committee defined two types of engagements leading to reports: (1) compilation of financial statements, and (2) review of financial statements.[47] Specific standards were established for each type of engagement.

Compilation of financial statements is defined by the committee as "presenting in the form of financial statements information that is the representation of management (owners) without undertaking to express any assurance on the statements." *Review* of financial statements is defined as "performing inquiry and analytical procedures that provide the accountant with a reasonable basis for expressing limited assurance that there are no material modifications that should be made to the statements

---

[45] Auditing Standards Board, *Proposed Statement on Auditing Standards: Association with Financial Statements, par. 11.*

[46] Ibid., par. 12.

[47] "Compilation and Review of Financial Statements," *AICPA Professional Standards,* vol. 1, AR Section 100.

in order for them to be in conformity with generally accepted accounting principles or, if applicable, with another comprehensive basis of accounting." [48]

As indicated previously, the statement sets forth standards for the guidance of accountants in both compilation and review engagements. It requires the issuance of a report, including an appropriate disclaimer of opinion, whenever a compilation or review is completed in compliance with these standards, and prohibits a report when they are not followed. The accountant, furthermore, is not allowed to submit unaudited statements to clients or to others unless the standards have been met. Merely typing or reproducing financial statements as a service to a non-public client is prohibited. Should the accountant "consent to the use of his name in a document or written communication containing unaudited financial statements of a non-public entity" for which he has issued no report, the financial statements must be "accompanied by an indication that the accountant has not compiled or reviewed the financial statements and that he assumes no responsibility for them.[49]

Following the standards and procedures set forth for compilations and reviews will enable the accountant to comply with the general standards of the profession set forth in AICPA Rule of Conduct No. 201. The only one of the general standards not covered by the statement is that dealing with forecasts, which is not applicable to these types of engagements.

The inquiry and analytical procedures set forth for a "review of financial statements" are similar to the "review" requirements found in Statement on Auditing Standards No. 24, Review of Interim Financial Information (AU Section 721). They are:

a. Inquiries concerning the entity's accounting principles and practices and the methods followed in applying them.
b. Inquiries concerning the entity's procedures for recording, classifying, and summarizing transactions, and accumulating information for disclosure in the financial statements.
c. Analytical procedures designed to identify relationships and individual items that appear to be unusual. For the purposes of this statement, analytical procedures consist of (1) comparison of the financial statements with statements for comparable prior period(s), (2) comparison of the financial statements with anticipated results, if available (for example, budgets and forecasts), and (3) study of the relationships of the elements of the financial statements that

---

[48] Ibid., AR Section 100.04. See Statement on Auditing Standards No. 14, AU Section 621.04, for the definition of "another comprehensive basis of accounting." One example is "a basis that the reporting entity uses or expects to use to file its income tax return for the period covered by the financial statements."

[49] Ibid., AR Section 100.06.

would be expected to conform to a predictable pattern based on the entity's experience. In applying these procedures, the accountant should consider the types of matters that required accounting adjustments in preceding periods. Examples of relationships of elements in financial statements that would be expected to conform to a predictable pattern may be the relationships between changes in sales and changes in accounts receivable and expense accounts that ordinarily fluctuate with sales, and between changes in property, plant, and equipment and changes in depreciation expense and other accounts that may be affected, such as maintenance and repairs.

d. Inquiries concerning actions taken at meetings of stockholders, board of directors, committees of the board of directors, or comparable meetings that may affect the financial statements.

e. Reading the financial statements to consider, on the basis of information coming to the accountant's attention, whether the financial statements appear to conform with generally accepted accounting principles.

f. Obtaining reports from other accountants, if any, who have been engaged to audit or review the financial statements of significant components of the reporting entity, its subsidiaries, and other investees.

g. Inquiries of persons having responsibility for financial and accounting matters concerning (1) whether the financial statements have been prepared in conformity with generally accepted accounting principles consistently applied, (2) changes in the entity's business activities or accounting principles and practices, (3) matters as to which questions have arisen in the course of applying the foregoing procedures, and (4) events subsequent to the date of the financial statements that would have a material effect on the financial statements.[50]

The objective of these and other procedures is to provide the accountant with "a reasonable basis for expressing limited assurance that there are no material modifications that should be made to the financial statements." [51] This is quite different from the objective of a compilation, in which no expression of assurance is contemplated.

For a compilation, the accountant is not required to "make inquiries or perform other procedures to verify, corroborate or review information supplied by the entity." [52] However, he must possess or acquire a "level of knowledge of the accounting principles and practices of the industry in which the entity operates that will enable him to compile financial statements that are appropriate in form for an entity operating in that industry.[53]

[50] Ibid., AR Section 100.27.
[51] Ibid., AR Section 100.04.
[52] Ibid., AR Section 100.12.
[53] Ibid., AR Section 100.10.

In addition, the accountant must possess or acquire "a general understanding of the nature of the entity's business transactions, the form of its accounting records, the stated qualifications of its accounting personnel, the accounting basis on which the financial statements are to be presented, and the form and content of the financial statements.[54] Before issuing his report, the accountant should read the compiled financial statements and consider whether they appear to be "appropriate in form and free from obvious material errors." [55]

DIVISIONAL REPORTS AND
THE INTERNAL PROFESSIONAL

The following article sets forth a problem which may be encountered by the internal professional. When preparing internal reports, what responsibility does the accountant have to his immediate supervisor, to the central office, to top management, to the owners, to himself?

A MORAL DILEMMA

A young accountant was recently told by his superior that he would have to drop his moralistic notions about accounting reports if he hoped to be a success with the company. He was informed that it was normal practice to have some hidden bookkeeping dollars to adjust the reported figures for his division, and thus present it in a more favorable light to the central office. This was not wrong, he was told, because the dollars used were not fictitious, but only handled in a way that was timely and advantageous to the division.

This young man was unable to live with this kind of arrangement, and subsequently left the company. Who was right, he or his superior?

WHAT IS THE ACCOUNTANT'S ROLE?

At issue here are the basic objectives and purposes of accounting. Is the accountant primarily a manipulator of figures, an advocate of his particular division or segment of the company? Or is he a professional expert, interpreting the activities of the division in an unbiased manner to all concerned? Should he be an unwilling middle man, caught between his inherent desire to present the facts as clearly as he can perceive them, and the will of his immediate superior to present the division in a favorable, though perhaps inaccurate, light?

It is submitted here that the accountant should be regarded as a professional expert, and allowed to present the facts in as accurate and honest a manner as he is able.

---

[54] Ibid., AR Section 100.11.
[55] Ibid., AR Section 100.13.

THE SANCTION OF GENERAL ACCEPTANCE

There are, of course, a number of gray areas associated with the problem. It is well known that many different practices and procedures fall under the umbrella of "generally accepted accounting principles." Should the accountant be chastised for not using that generally accepted practice which presents his division most favorably? Maybe so. Perhaps the fact that the practice giving the more favorable result is generally accepted is sufficient grounds to insist on its use by the division accountant, even though he personally feels that an alternate practice presents the facts more accurately. Perhaps the general acceptability of the more favorable practice is prima facie evidence that the accountant's preference is merely a personal judgment and not binding.

It does appear clear, however, that figure juggling outside of the umbrella of generally accepted accounting principles should be loudly denounced by all accountants.

WHO IS TO BLAME?

At whose doorstep can this problem be laid? Is it the fault of the division superior who insists that his accountant comprise conscience for the good of the division? Is it the accountant himself for submitting to this pressure? Is it an excessive emphasis placed on divisional cost or profit reports by central office executives? Many of the control advantages claimed for these reports may be strictly paper advantages if figure manipulation is practiced. Surely, if the reports generated by the system are inaccurate, much of the control is fictitious. It is submitted that central office executives, division managers, and division accountants are all partly to blame.

A SUGGESTION FOR IMPROVEMENT

What can be done to improve the situation? Basic to the problem is the necessity for a change of attitude on the part of all concerned. First, and perhaps most important, must come a change of approach by top-level management. These people set the tone for the entire business organization. If they are inflexible about budget and profit deviations, never giving any credence to the circumstances surrounding a particular period's report, their subordinates will adapt their reporting procedures to fit this attitude. If explainable deviations are met with the same critical attitudes that would face unjustified deviations, every effort will be made to conceal deviations, whatever their nature.

An attitude of cooperation and professionalism needs to be engendered throughout the organization. Divisions should not be made to feel they are separate from the parent organization, but rather that they are an integral part of the whole. Although it is frequently useful to compute profit by division, this end figure should not be the sole criterion of success for a division. Nor should it become the single basis of reward to a division manager. Such a policy is short-sighted and can create unhealthy attitudes throughout the company.

Let's hire back the young man with the high standards and let the kind of thinking he embodies permeate the entire company.[56]

[56] Floyd W. Windal, "A Problem of Integrity," *Managerial Planning*, May/June 1969, pp. 26–27.

1. Are there any limits to an auditor's obligation not to disclose confidential information obtained in the course of a professional engagement? If so, what are they? Give specific examples of situations where the obligation does not apply.

2. Management Advisory Services Practice Standard No. 5 states that before undertaking an engagement, a practitioner should inform the client of all significant matters related to the engagement. What are some examples of these "significant matters?"

3. What is the ethical responsibility of a tax practitioner upon learning of an error in a client's previously filed tax return or of the failure of a client to file a required return?

4. Is it proper for a tax practitioner to accept an engagement under an arrangement whereby his fee will be related to the amount of tax he saves the client? Explain the rationale underlying your answer.

5. Does the Foreign Corrupt Practices Act of 1977 have any relevance to the internal accounting professional? If so, what provisions are pertinent and why?

6. Explain the difference between administrative control and accounting control.

7. What are the responsibilities of the external auditor with regard to the internal control system of a client? Does his examination determine its adequacy? What reporting obligations does he have?

8. What are the recommendations of the Commission on Auditor's Responsibilities (the Cohen Commission) with regard to disclosure of internal control adequacy?

9. What are the three suggested levels of EDP technical proficiency which have been discussed in the professional literature? What are the minimum EDP knowledge requirements of the general staff auditor? Is any higher level of knowledge necessary in order for a firm to meet the first general auditing standard?

10. Is an auditor required to study and evaluate the existing internal control of a client when the client has a "computer" rather than a "manual" system? What if the auditor is not going to rely upon the internal controls in performing the audit but is going to satisfy himself by other means?

11. What is the purpose of the "disclaimer of opinion" which must accompany unaudited financial statements? What if the accountant has come to the conclusion as a result of his work that the statements are not in conformity with generally accepted accounting principles?

12. What is meant by a "review" of interim financial information? What is its purpose? What should be included in the auditor's report following such an examination?

13. What is meant by the "compilation of financial statements?"

14. Who is responsible for the issuance of pronouncements in connection with unaudited financial statements of a non-public entity? What is meant by a "review" of such statements? What standards have been established for a review?

15. Does the internal professional have any ethical responsibility for the correctness of the financial information he provides for management's use?

SUGGESTED ADDITIONAL READINGS

American Institute of Certified Public Accountants, "Review of Interim Financial Information," *AICPA Professional Standards,* vol. 1, AU Section 721 (Statement on Auditing Standards No. 24).

————, "Letters for Underwriters," *AICPA Professional Standards,* vol. 1, AU Section 630 (Statement on Auditing Standards No. 1).

————, "Filings under Federal Securities Statutes," *AICPA Professional Standards,* vol. 1, AU Section 710 (Statement on Auditing Standards No. 13).

————, "Client Benefit," *AICPA Professional Standards,* vol. 1, MS Section 140. (See Appendix 2.)

————, "Understanding with Client," *AICPA Professional Standards,* vol. 1, MS Section 150. (See Appendix 2.)

————, "Communication of Results," *AICPA Professional Standards,* vol. 1, MS Section 180. (See Appendix 2.)

————, "Knowledge of Error: Return Preparation," *AICPA Professional Standards,* vol. 1, TX Section 161. (See Appendix 3.)

————, "Knowledge of Error: Administrative Proceedings," *AICPA Professional Standards,* vol. 1, TX Section 171. (See Appendix 3.)

————, "Advice to Clients," *AICPA Professional Standards,* vol. 1, TX Section 181. (See Appendix 3.)

BERESFORD, DENNIS R., and JAMES D. BOND, "The Foreign Corrupt Practices Act—Its Implication to Financial Management," *Financial Executive,* August 1978.

CUTTING, RICHARD W., RICHARD J. GUILTINAN, FRED L. LILLY, JR., and JOHN F. MULLARKEY, "Technical Proficiency for Auditing Computer Processed Accounting Records," *Journal of Accountancy,* October 1971.

JANCURA, ELISE G., "Technical Proficiency for Auditing Computer Processed Accounting Records," *Journal of Accountancy,* October 1975.

Chapter

5

Responsibility to Colleagues

INTRODUCTION

The Biblical admonition "As ye would that men should do to you, do ye also to them likewise" [1] is an appropriate standard for relationships among accounting professionals. These relationships encompass a broad range of activities and include the relationship between the auditor and the internal professional whose financial statements he is examining, between the management consultant designing an accounting system and the controller of the concerned company, and between a division accountant and his superior at corporate headquarters. All such relationships must be carried out in an atmosphere of mutual respect and honesty.

The ethical principle set forth by the American Institute of Certified Public Accountants in this area of responsibility to colleagues is as follows:

> "A certified public accountant should conduct himself in a manner which will promote cooperation and good relations among members of the profession." [2]

---

[1] Luke 6:31.

[2] "Responsibilities to Colleagues," AICPA Professional Standards, vol. 2, ET Section 55.

The following seven statements provide an elaboration on this principle, and even though written with the CPA in mind, are appropriate for the consideration of all accounting professionals.

---

1. The support of a profession by its members and their cooperation with one another are essential elements of professional character. The public confidence and respect which a CPA enjoys is largely the result of the cumulative accomplishments of all CPAs, past and present. It is, therefore, in the CPA's own interest, as well as that of the general public, to support the collective efforts of colleagues through professional societies and organizations and to deal with fellow practitioners in a manner which will not detract from their reputation and well-being.

2. Although the reluctance of a professional to give testimony that may be damaging to a colleague is understandable, the obligation of professional courtesy and fraternal consideration can never excuse lack of complete candor if the CPA is testifying as an expert witness in a judicial proceeding or properly constituted inquiry.

3. A CPA has the obligation to assist his fellows in complying with the Code of Professional Ethics and should also assist appropriate disciplinary authorities in enforcing the Code. To condone serious fault can be as bad as to commit it. It may be even worse, in fact, since some errors may result from ignorance rather than intent and, if let pass without action, will probably be repeated. In situations of this kind, the welfare of the public should be the guide to a member's action.

4. While the Code proscribes certain specific actions in the area of relationships with colleagues, it should be understood that these proscriptions do not define the limits of desirable intraprofessional conduct. Rather, such conduct encompasses the professional consideration and courtesies which each CPA would like to have fellow practitioners extend to him.

5. It is natural that a CPA will seek to develop his practice. However, in doing so he should not seek to displace another accountant in a client relationship by any means which will lessen the effectiveness of his technical performance or lessen his concern for the rights of third parties to reliable information. Further, he should not act in any way that reflects negatively on fellow practitioners.

6. A CPA may provide service to those who request it, even though they may be served by another practitioner in another area of service, or he may succeed another practitioner at a client's request. In such circumstances it is always desirable and required in some situations before accepting an engagement that the CPA who has been approached should advise the accountant already serving the client. Such action is indicated not only by considerations of professional courtesy but by good business judgment.

7. A client may sometimes request services requiring highly specialized knowledge. If the CPA lacks the expertise necessary to render such services, he should call upon a fellow practitioner for assistance or refer the entire engagement to another. Such assistance or referral brings to bear on the client's needs both the referring practitioner's knowledge of the client's affairs and the technical expertise of the specialist brought into the engagement. If both serve the client best in their own area of ability, all parties are well served as is the public.[3]

The relevance of these general guidelines to the day-to-day practice of accounting is shown in the following sections.

THE AUDITOR

There are many occasions in which an auditor has formal or informal contact with his fellow professionals. He, of course, will associate with them in the various professional societies in which they are active. As clients previously audited by another are acquired, or as present clients move on to another, the successor and predecessor auditors will need to communicate and to rely upon one another. In the area of practice development which results in the acquisition of new clients, the auditor must be extremely careful not to violate the ethical code governing such activity.

Assume, for example, that you are a partner in a medium-sized regional firm. You belong to a fashionable country club and regularly play golf with the president of a corporation which has its home office in your city. After a particularly stimulating round of golf one Saturday afternoon in which you lost by one stroke to your friend, he asks if you would be willing to give him some advice on how to handle an especially difficult accounting matter. Although his company is being audited by another accounting firm, he would like your advice. Is it ethical to give it?

You would be able to accept the engagement, but would be well advised to first consult with the other accountant to ascertain that you are aware of all the available relevant facts. If your friend is merely "shopping for an accounting principle," you would not want to be a party to it.

Sometimes an auditor is required to express an opinion on combined or consolidated financial statements which include a subsidiary, branch, or other component, audited by another public accountant. Should his insistence upon auditing any such component in order to express an overall opinion be interpreted as an unethical encroachment upon the practice of a colleague?

---

[3] "Responsibilities to Colleagues," *AICPA Professional Standards,* vol. 2, ET Section 55. Copyright © 1975 by the American Institute of Certified Public Accountants, Inc.

No, an auditor should insist upon auditing such a component when, in his judgment, it is necessary to warrant the expression of an opinion. Generally accepted auditing standards must always be complied with. Insistence upon auditing an unreasonably large portion of the financial statements might, however, lead to an assertion that the auditor's judgment is part of a plan or design to deceptively solicit a client. Rule of Conduct 502 specifically prohibits any solicitation that is false, misleading, or deceptive.[4]

What are the guidelines for reporting on financial statements when the independent auditor utilizes the work and reports of another independent auditor who has examined the financial statements of a component, such as a subsidiary? Should he make reference to the other auditor in his report? How does he satisfy himself that the work of the other auditor is reliable?

"If the principal auditor decides to assume responsibility for the work of another auditor insofar as that work relates to the principal auditor's expression of an opinion on the financial statements taken as a whole, no reference should be made to the other auditor's examination. On the other hand, if the principal auditor decides not to assume that responsibility, his report should make reference to the examination of the other auditor and should indicate clearly the division of responsibility between himself and the other auditor in expressing his opinion on the financial statements. Regardless of the principal auditor's decision, the other auditor remains responsible for the performance of his own work and for his own report." [5]

In satisfying himself that the other auditor's work can be relied upon, the principal auditor "should make inquiries" as to his "professional reputation and independence," and "should adopt appropriate measures to assure the coordination of his activities with those of the other auditor in order to achieve a proper review of matters affecting the consolidating or combining of accounts in the financial statements." [6]

THE MANAGEMENT CONSULTANT AND
THE TAX PRACTITIONER

One area presenting ethical questions to the management consultant and the tax practitioner is that of referrals. Assume, for example, that you are a sole practitioner with an audit, tax, and management consulting practice.

---

4 "Advertising and Other Forms of Solicitation," *AICPA Professional Standards*, vol. 2, ET Section 502.01.

5 "Part of Examinations Made by Other Independent Auditors." *AICPA Professional Standards*, vol. 1, AU Section 543.03 (Statement on Auditing Standards No. 1). Copyright © 1974 by the American Institute of Certified Public Accountants, Inc.

6 Ibid., AU Section 543.10.

You have been serving a particular business since its inception, preparing the necessary tax returns and acting as a management consultant. The business has now grown to such an extent that a public issuance of stock is to be made, entailing involvement with a variety of government regulations and reports. You have no desire to review that area in depth, although you would still like to continue your service as general management consultant to the business. Should you prepare the needed reports as best you can in order not to lose your consulting job with the client?

Clearly, you have a responsibility to see that your client gets competent assistance in this case. As pointed out in one of the Statements on Management Advisory Services, "referral of management advisory services work to other independent accounting firms is an alternative course of action to that of developing individual or firm capability. . . . The referral arrangement may provide for a joint effort or provide for the services to be performed solely by the referee brought in for that purpose. . . . to the extent that the independent accounting firm finds an effective way to co-operate with others, it may thereby expand its own knowledge and extend its own scope of service toward providing the full range of management advisory services." [7]

What if you were the accountant called in to assist in this case, and after completing your assignment, the client asked if you would be willing to advise him on another aspect of the business? Can you accept such an engagement? Would it be ethical for you to make an inquiry of the client about engaging you to assist with another problem you uncovered as a part of your work on the referred job?

It would be ethical for you to extend your service beyond the specific engagement, and to make an inquiry regarding an additional job. Professional courtesy, however, would dictate that you notify the referring accountant of your intentions. This is one of the instances where the practitioner must look to his own sense of fairness for an answer, rather than to a specific Rule of Conduct.

The management consultant and the tax practitioner often interface with their colleagues on the audit staff. They also may interface with the audit staff of another firm of independent certified public accountants. It goes without saying that such contacts should be carried out in an atmosphere of cordiality, with full cognizance that the work being done will be relied upon by another.

What if you, as management consultant for a particular nonaudit client, become aware that the financial statements of that client, audited by another independent CPA, deviate substantially from accepted professional

---

[7] "Tentative Description of the Nature of Management Advisory Services by Independent Accounting Firms," *AICPA Professional Standards*, vol. 1, MS Section 410.12.

standards? Do you have any ethical obligation to bring this to the attention of anyone?

A professional accountant does have an obligation to assist his colleagues "in complying with the Code of Professional Ethics." [8] Probably the first step in this case would be to determine whether the client is aware of the violation of accepted standards. Perhaps such an inquiry will correct the situation. If it reveals, however, that the deviation is being done willfully, some action may be called for. One possibility would be to refer the financial statements to the Practice Review Committee of the AICPA. The charge of this committee is "to review specific reports and related financial statements that appear to deviate from accepted standards, and to communicate to the reporting accountant or accounting firm the committee's comments or questions about the report or related financial statements." [9]

The committee does not refer cases to the Professional Ethics Division except that "it may refer a case under either of the following circumstances:

(a) A member, after reasonable notice, fails or refuses to make a substantive response to a letter or inquiry from the committee.
(b) A member, without reasonable grounds, fails to comply subsequently with technical standards with respect to a specific client where major deficiencies in such technical standards have previously been called to his or her attention by the committee." [10]

The committee will not disclose the source of a report submitted to it and will deal with each report on a confidential basis.[11]

THE INTERNAL PROFESSIONAL

A major area of contact between the internal professional and other professionals is provided by the external audit. The work of the controller and his staff comes under intensive scrutiny by the independent certified public accountant, and it is very important that each party respect the professionalism of the other. And, of course, each party must perform his work in a manner that will justify such respect.

The possible reliance of the external auditor upon the work of the internal auditor is one instance of direct contact. The external auditor "should acquire an understanding of the internal audit function as it relates to his study and evaluation of internal accounting control. The

[8] "Responsibilities to Colleagues," *AICPA Professional Standards*, vol. 2, ET Section 55.03.

[9] "Implementing Resolutions Under Section 3.6 'Committees,'" *AICPA Professional Standards*, vol. 2, BL Section 360R.03.

[10] Ibid.

[11] Ibid.

work performed by internal auditors may be a factor in determining the nature, timing, and extent" of the external auditor's procedures. If the external auditor "decides that the work performed by internal auditors may have a bearing on his own procedures, he should consider the competence and objectivity of internal auditors and evaluate their work." [12]

"When the work of the internal auditors is expected to be significant to the independent auditor's study and evaluation of internal accounting control, the external auditor should, at the outset of the engagement, inform internal auditors of the reports and working papers he will need. He should also consult with internal auditors concerning work they are performing, since work not yet completed may also have a bearing on his examination. Also, work done by internal auditors will frequently be more useful to the external auditor if plans for the work are discussed in advance." [13]

The external auditor may also use the internal auditor to provide direct assistance, such as in performing substantive tests or tests of compliance. When the external auditor employs internal auditors in this way, he "should consider their competence and objectivity and supervise and test their work to the extent appropriate in the circumstances." [14]

Assume that you are the controller of a small manufacturing company and that the company's federal income tax return is being examined by the Internal Revenue Service. What should your behavior be toward the internal professional working for the IRS? What is your obligation with regard to questions raised by the agent?

Clearly, you should behave with the same integrity and objectivity that you would in interacting with any other professional. This is not to imply that you should not work for the best interests of the company, but only that you should be honest in your answers and should not deliberately mislead or misinform. You should also not allow an untruth or misinterpretation to remain uncorrected, even though you are not directly responsible for it.

COMMUNICATION BETWEEN PREDECESSOR AND SUCCESSOR AUDITORS

In order to provide guidance on communications between predecessor and successor auditors when a change has taken place or is in process,

---

[12] "The Effect of an Internal Audit Function on the Scope of the Independent Auditor's Examination," AICPA Professional Standards, vol. 1, AU Section 322.04 (Statement on Auditing Standards No. 9). Copyright © 1977 by the American Institute of Certified Public Accountants, Inc.

[13] Ibid., AU Section 322.09.

[14] Ibid., AU Section 322.10.

Statement on Auditing Standards No. 7 was issued. A portion of this important statement follows:

---

1. The purpose of this section is to provide guidance on communications between predecessor and successor auditors when a change of auditors has taken place or is in process. The term "predecessor auditor" refers to an auditor who has resigned or who has been notified that his services have been terminated. The term "successor auditor" refers to an auditor who has accepted an engagement or an auditor who has been invited to make a proposal for an engagement. This section applies whenever an independent auditor has been retained, or is to be retained, to make an examination of financial statements in accordance with generally accepted auditing standards.

2. The initiative in communicating rests with the successor auditor. The communication may be either in writing or oral. Both the predecessor and successor auditors should hold in confidence information obtained from each other. This obligation applies whether or not the successor accepts the engagement.

3. Prior to acceptance of the engagement, the successor auditor should attempt certain communications that are described in paragraphs 4 through 7. Other communications between the successor and the predecessor, described in paragraphs 8 and 9 are advisable. However, their timing is more flexible. The successor may attempt these other communications either prior to acceptance of the engagement or subsequent thereto.

COMMUNICATIONS BEFORE SUCCESSOR ACCEPTS ENGAGEMENT

4. Inquiry of the predecessor auditor is a necessary procedure because the predecessor may be able to provide the successor with information that will assist him in determining whether to accept the engagement. The successor should bear in mind that, among other things, the predecessor and the client may have disagreed about accounting principles, auditing procedures, or similarly significant matters.

5. The successor auditor should explain to his prospective client the need to make an inquiry of the predecessor and should request permission to do so. Except as permitted by the Rules of Conduct, an auditor is precluded from disclosing confidential information obtained in the course of an audit engagement unless the client consents. Thus, the successor auditor should ask the prospective client to authorize the predecessor to respond fully to the successor's inquiries. If a prospective client refuses to permit the predecessor to respond or limits the response, the successor auditor should inquire as to the reasons and consider the implications of that refusal in deciding whether to accept the engagement.

6. The successor auditor should make specific and reasonable inquiries of the

predecessor regarding matters that the successor believes will assist him in determining whether to accept the engagement. His inquiries should include specific questions regarding, among other things, facts that might bear on the integrity of management; on disagreements with management as to accounting principles, auditing procedures, or other similarly significant matters; and on the predecessor's understanding as to the reasons for the change of auditors.

7. The predecessor auditor should respond promptly and fully, on the basis of facts known to him, to the successor's reasonable inquiries. However, should he decide, due to unusual circumstances such as impending litigation, not to respond fully to the inquiries, he should indicate that his response is limited. If the successor auditor receives a limited response, he should consider its implications in deciding whether to accept the engagement.

OTHER COMMUNICATIONS

8. When one auditor succeeds another, the successor auditor must obtain sufficient competent evidential matter to afford a reasonable basis for expressing his opinion on the financial statements he has been engaged to examine as well as on consistency of the application of accounting principles in that year as compared with the preceding year. This may be done by applying appropriate auditing procedures to the account balances at the beginning of the period under examination and in some cases to transactions in prior periods. The successor auditor's examination may be facilitated by (a) making specific inquiries of the predecessor regarding matters that the successor believes may affect the conduct of his examination, such as audit areas that have required an inordinate amount of time or audit problems that arose from the condition of the accounting system and records and (b) reviewing the predecessor auditor's working papers. In reporting on his examination, however, the successor auditor should not make reference to the report or work of the predecessor auditor as the basis, in part, for his own opinion.

9. The successor auditor should request the client to authorize the predecessor to allow a review of the predecessor's working papers. It is customary in such circumstances for the predecessor auditor to make himself available to the successor auditor for consultation and to make available for review certain of his working papers. The predecessor and successor auditors should agree on those working papers that are to be made available for review and those that may be copied. Ordinarily, the predecessor should permit the successor to review working papers relating to matters of continuing accounting significance, both current and noncurrent, and those relating to contingencies. Valid business reasons, however, may lead the predecessor auditor to decide not to allow a review of his working papers. Further, when more than one successor auditor is considering acceptance of an engagement, the predecessor auditor should not be expected to make himself or his working papers available until the successor has accepted the engagement.

FINANCIAL STATEMENTS REPORTED ON
BY PREDECESSOR

10. If during his examination the successor auditor becomes aware of information that leads him to believe that financial statements reported on by the predecessor auditor may require revision, he should request his client to arrange a meeting among the three parties to discuss this information and attempt to resolve the matter. If the client refuses or if the successor is not satisfied with the result, the successor auditor may be well advised to consult with his attorney in determining an appropriate course of further action.[15]

THE DISCIPLINE OF INDIVIDUALS

The American Institute of CPAs has established specific procedures for the discipline of its members. This discipline ranges from an administrative reprimand to expulsion. Action taken by the AICPA may in turn lead to action by a state board of accountancy or other governmental authority to suspend or revoke the member's CPA certificate or license to practice. In other cases, action by the governmental authority may precede action by the institute.

Membership in the institute is suspended without a hearing if a judgment of conviction for any of the following is filed with the secretary of the institute. Membership is terminated upon the similar filing of a final judgment of conviction.

1. A crime defined as a felony under the law of the convicting jurisdiction.
2. The willful failure to file any income tax return which he, as an individual taxpayer, is required by law to file.
3. The filing of a false or fraudulent income tax return on his or a client's behalf.
4. The willful aiding in the preparation and presentation of a false and fraudulent income tax return of a client.[16]

Membership in the institute may also be suspended or terminated without a   hearing "should a member's certificate as a certified public

[15] "Communications Between Predecessor and Successor Auditor," AICPA *Professional Standards*, vol. 1, AU Section 315 (Statement on Auditing Standards No. 7). Copyright © 1973 by the American Institute of Certified Public Accountants, Inc.

[16] "Disciplinary Suspension and Termination of Membership Without Hearing," AICPA *Professional Standards*, vol. 2, BL Section 730.01.

accountant, or license or permit to practice as such or to practice public accounting" be suspended or revoked "as a disciplinary measure by any governmental authority." In such cases, however, the member has the right to petition that this provision not be applied.[17] Only "expectional or unusual circumstances" which would make automatic suspension or termination inequitable would result in the approval of such an appeal.[18] In such a case, the matter would be transmitted to the Professional Ethics Division of the AICPA to take whatever action it deemed appropriate in the circumstances.[19]

About 80 percent of the state societies and other eligible jurisdictions have entered into an agreement with the AICPA for the joint handling of disciplinary matters. A complaint regarding professional ethics might thus be submitted to the Professional Ethics Division of the institute or to an ethics committee (or its equivalent) of a state society of certified public accountants. In some cases, the Professional Ethics Division will refer complaints to the appropriate state society committee for investigation and recommendation.

If either the Professional Ethics Division or a state society ethics committee concludes that there is a prima facie case showing a violation of any applicable bylaws of the institute or any provision of the Code of Professional Ethics of the Institute or of the involved state society, or showing any conduct discreditable to a certified public accountant, they will report the matter to what is called the Joint Trial Board Division.[20] This division consists of a system of regional trial boards and a National Review Board.[21] The various regional trial boards are "created for each appropriate geographical region as agreements are entered into between the Institute and the various state societies." [22]

Normally, cases are referred to the appropriate regional trial board, which may "admonish, suspend for a period of not more than two years, or expel the member against whom the complaint is made." In any case in which the board finds that "a member has departed from the profession's ethical standards, it may also direct the member concerned to complete specified professional development courses and to report to the Professional

[17] Ibid.

[18] "Implementing Resolution Under Section 7.3 Disciplinary Suspension and Termination of Membership Without Hearing," AICPA Professional Standards, vol. 2, BL Section 730R.09.

[19] Ibid., BL Section 730R.08.

[20] "Implementing Resolution Under Section 7.4 Disciplining of Member by Trial Board," AICPA Professional Standards, vol. 2, BL Section 740R.01.

[21] "Implementing Resolutions Under Section 3.6 Committees," AICPA Professional Standards, vol. 2, BL Section 360R.05.

[22] Ibid., BL Section 360R.06.

Ethics Division upon such completion." [23] In a case decided by a regional trial board, the member concerned may request a review by a panel of the National Review Board. Such a review is not a matter of right, however, and an ad hoc committee appointed by the chairman of the National Review Board will decide whether or not to grant it.

A member also has the right to request that his case be heard by a panel of the National Review Board, rather than by a regional trial board. Again, such requests are not granted as a matter or right but must be considered by an ad hoc committee of the National Review Board.[24]

In those cases when the Professional Ethics Division concludes that "a prima facie violation of the Code of Professional Ethics or bylaw is not of sufficient gravity to warrant further formal action, it may issue an administrative reprimand." In such cases, there will be no publication of the reprimand and the member concerned must be "notified of his right to a hearing on the issues before the appropriate trial panel." [25] In cases involving departures from any section of the Code of Professional Ethics, the division may also "direct the member or members concerned to complete specified professional development courses." [26]

THE DISCIPLINE OF FIRMS

The primary vehicle within the profession for the discipline of firms, as distinguished from individual members, is the AICPA Division for CPA Firms. Within this division of the AICPA, there are two sections: the SEC Practice Section and the Private Companies Practice Section. Although membership in the division is voluntary, it is expected that most firms will belong to one or both of its sections. Both sections require their members to (1) "adhere to quality control standards established by the AICPA Quality Control Standards Committee," (2) submit to peer reviews of their "accounting and audit practice every three years or at such additional times as designated" by their executive committees, (3) ensure that all of their professionals participate in continuing professional education, and (4) maintain "minimum amounts and types of liability insurance."

The SEC Practice Section requires, in addition, that its members (1) rotate audit partners on SEC engagements, (2) "ensure that a concurring review of the audit report by a partner other than the audit partner in charge of an SEC engagement is required before issuance" of the report,

[23] "Implementing Resolutions Under Section 7.4 Disciplining of Members by Trial Board," *AICPA Professional Standards,* vol. 2, BL Section 740R.03.

[24] Ibid.

[25] Ibid., BL Section 740R.04.

[26] Ibid., BL Section 740R.05.

(3) file with the section annually specified information about the firm to be available for public inspection, (4) "report annually to the audit committee or board of directors (or its equivalent in a partnership) of each SEC audit client on the total fees received from the client for management advisory services during the year under audit and a description of the types of such services rendered," (5) "report to the audit committee or board of directors (or its equivalent in a partnership) of each SEC audit client on the nature of disagreements with the management of the client on financial accounting and reporting matters and auditing procedures which, if not satisfactorily resolved, would have caused the issuance of a qualified opinion on the client's financial statements," and (6) "adhere to the portions of the Code of Professional Ethics and Management Advisory Services Practice Standards dealing with independence in performing management advisory services for audit clients whose securities are registered with the SEC." They must also "refrain from performing for such clients services that are inconsistent with the firm's responsibilities to the public." [27]

The executive committee of each section has the authority to impose sanctions on member firms either on its own initiative or on the basis of recommendations from its peer review committee. The following types of sanctions may be imposed for failure to maintain compliance with the membership requirements.

(a) Require corrective measures by the firm including consideration by the firm of appropriate actions with respect to individual firm personnel.
(b) Additional requirements for continuing professional education.
(c) Accelerated or special peer reviews.
(d) Admonishments, censures, or reprimands.
(e) Monetary fines.
(f) Suspension from membership.
(g) Expulsion from membership.[28]

The SEC Practice Section has a Public Oversight Board, composed of prominent individuals of high integrity and reputation, with the following responsibilities and functions:

(a) Monitor and evaluate the regulatory and sanction activities of the peer review and executive committees to assure their effectiveness.
(b) Determine that the peer review committee is ascertaining that firms are taking appropriate action as a result of peer reviews.

[27] AICPA Division for CPA Firms SEC Practice Section Peer Review Manual (New York: American Institute of Certified Public Accountants, 1978), pp. 1–5 to 1–8. Copyright © 1978 by the American Institute of Certified Public Accountants, Inc. Item No. 6 is a revision of the rule contained in the original published document.

[28] Ibid., p. 1–12.

(c) Conduct continuing oversight of all other activities of the section.

(d) Make recommendations to the executive committee for improvements in the operations of the section.

(e) Publish an annual report and such other reports as may be deemed necessary with respect to its activities.

(f) Engage staff to assist in carrying out its functions.

(g) Have the right for any or all of its members to attend any meetings of the executive committee.[29]

The Executive Committee of the Private Companies Practice Section, should it so choose, has the authority to establish a Public Oversight Board for that section.

THE DISCIPLINE OF A PROFESSION

In the following article, Wallace E. Olson, president of the American Institute of Certified Public Accountants, addresses the many problems associated with disciplining the members and firms comprising the public accounting segment of the profession.

One of the hallmarks of a profession is an accreditation or licensing process before an applicant is permitted to practice or hold himself out as a member of the group. In general, either the state or the federal government establishes right-to-practice requirements to assure consumers that licensees have met minimum standards.

The notion that there should be an effective system for the ongoing regulation and disciplining of a profession is a natural effect of the monopoly that is granted to a qualified group under the law. It is rooted in the belief that initial qualification requirements, standing alone, are not sufficient to protect the consuming public from malpractice. The threat of punishment of licensees for wrongdoing is an essential part of the total scheme for public protection.

The sanctions provided under the licensing laws are normally restricted to suspensions or revocations of rights to practice. Redress for civil damages or punishment for criminal acts relating to malpractice must be sought under the civil liability and criminal laws, which are designed for application to a much wider range of activities than that of professionals.

Given this combination of regulation by threats of revocation of rights to practice, civil damages and criminal penalties, one might wonder why an organized profession either desires or is expected to impose on itself additional forms of discipline or sanctions. One answer might be that professions have membership organizations in the private sector designed to enhance both the quality of practice of its members and the stature of the profession in the eyes of the public. A code of ethics is an important means of achieving these

[29] *AICPA Division For CPA Firms SEC Practice Section Peer Review Manual* (New York: American Institute of Certified Public Accountants, 1978), pp. 1–11.

objectives, and some form of disciplinary mechanism is necessary to put teeth in the code.

Another answer might be that a profession usually prefers to keep governmental intervention in its affairs at a minimum. An effective system of self-regulation is believed to be the best way to achieve this objective, although it is by no means a guarantee that a profession will be left alone to handle its affairs.

Professionals voluntarily assume the threat of disciplinary sanction by the organized group because they believe the alternative—greater governmental involvement—would be more onerous. If one accepts this premise, it follows that, to be effective, a system of self-regulation must be accompanied by a serious and continuing threat of additional forms of outside regulation.

In general, a disciplinary system is necessary to assure that practitioners adhere to the high ideals of a professional. However, if a profession is composed of professionals capable of individual self-restraint, why is a disciplinary system necessary?

Perhaps the answer is that the behavior of professionals is not much different from that of everyone else. An essential ingredient in improving the behavior of professionals, like that of all human behavior, is the threat of punishment for wrongdoing.

Even the threat of punishment has been of questionable effectiveness in curbing the misdeeds of individuals who lack respect for authority and the law. Nevertheless, most people are likely to behave better as a result of the threat of punishment for wrongdoing. Thus, "How should a profession be disciplined?" is really a question of what kinds of punishment and how great a threat of punishment of professionals is necessary to assure expected levels of performance.

This is a complex matter because it involves an evaluation of the strength of pressure that might cause a breakdown in performance and the identification of the performance that can reasonably be expected of the average practitioner. These involve subjective judgments, which make decisions about individual cases or the effectiveness of a disciplinary system difficult at best.

THE PUBLIC ACCOUNTING PROFESSION

It would be interesting to know what would happen if the public accounting profession abandoned all efforts to discipline itself. Would the quality of performance decline substantially? Would the number of alleged audit failures increase? Would the states or the federal government rush in with legislation to establish an additional disciplinary system that would provide for sanctions, such as monetary fines, which would go beyond the present suspensions or revocations of rights to practice?

The answers to these questions are not clear, but it is safe to assume that the elimination of all self-disciplinary efforts would be unacceptable to the profession and the public alike, even though such efforts may not be wholly successful. Accordingly, assuming that a system of self-discipline is necessary, and that the combined internal and external disciplinary systems ought to be as effective as possible in protecting the public from malpractice, it is appropriate to address these questions:

1. Who should be disciplined?
2. What types of misconduct should give rise to discipline?
3. What types of sanctions should be imposed?
4. Which institutions should impose discipline and how much?

The balance of this article discusses these questions.

WHO SHOULD BE DISCIPLINED?

Because state accountancy statutes are all designed to regulate the accreditation and practice of CPAs as individuals, the provisions for suspension or revocation of a CPA certificate apply only to individuals. In some states CPA firms must also register to practice. For all practical purposes, however, the disciplinary machinery of state boards of accountancy is directed at individuals.

Most practice is carried on today in the names of firms, not in the names of individual practitioners. CPAs have surrendered their individual identities to the firm entities that sign auditors' reports, set policies and carry on multilocation practices as partnerships or professional corporations. If a substandard performance occurs, it raises questions about who was at fault. Was it a defect in the firm's policies? If not, did an individual in the firm fail to adhere to its policies? If the firm's policies were deficient, should top management be disciplined as the responsible individuals or should a sanction be imposed on the entire firm, or both?

Lately it has been recognized that the way the practice of accounting is conducted calls for a means of disciplining firms as well as individuals. Until now the only attempts of regulators to deal with firms were those of the Securities and Exchange Commission under rule 2(e) proceedings and injunctive actions. When a very large CPA firm was involved, the SEC found it impractical to suspend it from practice before the commission because of the harm such action would impose on the firm's innocent SEC clients. Therefore, alternative sanctions were developed such as suspensions of single offices of firms, mandated peer reviews and agreements not to add new SEC clients for specified periods. Of course, SEC injunctive actions against firms also spawned civil liability suits, which are a severe and effective form of discipline of firms.

Until recently, the disciplinary machinery of the American Institute of CPAs and the state CPA societies confined itself to bringing actions against individuals only; there was no basis on which firms could be disciplined as entities.

The AICPA has now established a division for firms with two sections, one for SEC practice and another for private companies practice. Each section can impose sanctions on its particular firms for not meeting the requirements for participation. This is a significant step because it brings firms within a self-disciplinary scheme for the first time. It represents a voluntary surrender of a considerable degree of autonomy on the part of the participating firms.

This development recognizes that an effective system of discipline for the public accounting profession must deal with both individual CPAs and CPA firms as separate entities, depending on the cause of the substandard performance giving rise to the need for disciplinary action. Thus, the answer to the question "Who should be disciplined?" seems to be individuals, firms or both.

WHAT TYPES OF MISCONDUCT SHOULD GIVE RISE TO DISCIPLINE?

At first blush it might appear to be a simple matter to determine what types of misconduct should give rise to discipline. Most people believe that they know misconduct when they see it. But when it comes to evaluating the performance of practicing CPAs, there are many degrees of misconduct that make disciplinary decisions difficult. Indeed, in deciding on the circumstances for which auditors should be held liable, even the courts have had difficulty in defining where the dividing lines should be.

Most people would agree that a conscious violation of the profession's technical standards or a knowing participation in the issuance of misleading audited financial statements calls for disciplinary action. Less clear is whether an honest oversight or mistake by an auditor should result in a sanction. Even if it should not, is there a point where the negligence is so gross or the act so reckless that a sanction should be imposed? Where should the line be drawn? Also, to what extent should it be required that harm resulted before the disciplinary process comes into play?

In most cases involving questionable technical performance, there is a further complication—the difficulty in determining the technical standard to which the practitioner should be held. For example, when a management fraud has not been detected by an auditor, it is seldom clear whether a normally prudent auditor exercising due care would have uncovered the fraud.

Often, the technical standards are not sufficiently defined to be able to measure performance. . . . The *Continental Vending* case (*U.S.* v. *Simon*) is an example of a case where a main issue was whether there was an appropriate standard that should have been applied in an audit.

A tribunal faced with making a decision about the adequacy of technical performance, whether it be a court, the SEC, a state board of accountancy, or one of the profession's regional trial boards, often finds itself making subjective judgments about what the defendant auditor should have done under the circumstances. Such judgments are always made after it is known that a mistake was made and what caused it. It would take a body of saints to prevent such knowledge from causing a bias in the judgment about what the auditor should have done at a time when the present information was unknown.

Under these circumstances, it seems clear that the standards for determining misconduct are, to a large extent, established ad hoc by subjective judgments made with the benefit of hindsight. Broad concepts such as negligence, recklessness and scienter may be followed, but applying them to a specific set of facts is largely a subjective process. Thus, the accounting profession is in a position of having to accept, as a risk of doing business, the fact that it will be held responsible for meeting a shifting set of standards subjectively determined by hindsight, and usually by an uninformed laity, if litigation is involved. This is not to say that the standards of the profession are useless or ignored for disciplinary purposes. But compliance with them is no guarantee that under particular circumstances an auditor will be held blameless. There is simply no substitute for vigilance and good judgment when it comes to avoiding blame.

In addition to requiring adherence to technical standards, the state boards of accountancy and the profession's state and national organizations have included a series of rules on general behavior in their codes of conduct. These rules have as their principal objective fostering harmony and courtesy within the profession, ostensibly to assure that the public is well served.

Because many of the rules place a degree of restraint on unfettered competition, it has been charged in recent times that they may be in violation of the antitrust laws. Rules restricting advertising and solictiation are now seen to be improper restraints on competition unless they involve false claims or deception. Other rules . . . are likely to be subject to the same kind of attack.

Perhaps the only behavioral rules likely to survive the test of current perceptions about what serves the public interest are those that deal with potential conflicts of interest or rights of privacy. These include the rules on independence, receipt or payment of commissions, and confidentiality of client information.

The foregoing observations lead to the conclusion that the professional organizations and the state boards of accountancy are likely to be restricted to imposing discipline for the following types of offenses:

1. Performing services without competence or due care or failing to adhere to technical standards.
2. Knowingly engaging in deceptive practices or misrepresenting facts in the practice of public accounting.
3. Failing to adhere to rules on independence and commissions when reporting on audits of financial statements as an independent auditor.
4. Being found guilty of a felony for acts whether or not related to the practice of public accounting.
5. Violating the confidences of clients except as technical standards, the law, peer reviews or disciplinary proceedings require such disclosure.
6. Any unspecified acts, whether or not related to the practice of public accounting, that bring discredit on the entire profession.

Only the first three of these offenses are the bases for disciplinary sanctions by the SEC, although presumably an auditor might be found to be unfit and suspended from practice under the fourth or sixth categories. The first three offenses are also recognized by the courts as providing bases for either civil liability or criminal penalties, depending on a showing of willfulness or deliberate intent to engage in a fraud or conduct so reckless as to be its equivalent.

As previously noted, it is one thing to describe in a general way what types of misconduct should give rise to discipline but it is quite another to make judgments about whether in a specific case misconduct that should result in discipline has occurred. Nevertheless, the profession, the courts and governmental regulatory bodies must do their best to impose punishment fairly for offenses under these broad categories, however imprecise they may be.

WHAT TYPES OF SANCTIONS
SHOULD BE IMPOSED?

The range of sanctions that have been imposed against members or firms of the profession include

1. Private or public censure by the profession's organizations.
2. Remedial actions including peer reviews and attendance at specified educational courses.
3. Suspension or expulsion from membership in the profession's organizations.
4. Injunctions against continuing violations of the federal securities laws.
5. Suspension or revocation of a CPA's certificate and right to practice.
6. Money damages in civil liability suits.
7. Fines and/or imprisonment for criminal acts.

Until recently, when the AIPCA's division for firms was established, the sanctions that could be imposed by the profession's disciplinary actions were the least effective of those of the various disciplinary bodies. Members who are expelled from the profession's organizations may still practice if their licenses are not revoked. This is not to say that the profession's sanctions have been wholly ineffective. Practitioners have consistently taken the profession's disciplinary actions against them very seriously because of the damage such actions can do to their reputations and their abilities to recruit and hold a qualified staff. Also, the profession's sanctions are brought to the attention of state boards of accountancy, and the result can be suspension or revocation of the license to practice.

The AICPA's new division for firms has adopted a range of sanctions that includes the possible imposition of fines for failure to maintain appropriate quality controls. This goes beyond the traditional types of punishment that the profession has imposed in the past. Even the SEC and the state boards of accountancy do not have the authority to impose fines on CPAs or CPA firms.

The most severe penalties are those that can be imposed by the licensing bodies and the courts. Revocation of rights to practice and fines or imprisonment are the most extreme measures that can be taken. Only slightly less severe are the money damages resulting from civil liability suits. Even though there are widely varying judgments about when and to whom auditors should be held liable for money damages, this form of sanction has had a significant effect on improving the profession's performance. The threat of unlimited liability has caused most practitioners to take the quality of their work very seriously.

Based on experience to date, it is clear that each of the seven types of sanctions listed above is necessary to provide gradations of penalties to fit the differing degrees of professional misconduct that may be encountered in practice. The principal problem is not identifying the types of sanctions to impose. The greatest difficulty is determining how to apply, on a consistent basis, the range of sanctions to the varying degrees of misconduct.

WHICH INSTITUTIONS SHOULD IMPOSE
DISCIPLINE AND HOW MUCH?

A major question to be resolved is whether the present forms of discipline are sufficient to assure the levels of performance that can reasonably be expected, given the nature of the functions involved. The Commission on Auditors' Responsibilities addressed this question and concluded: ". . . the total system as it now exists, including litigation and actions by regulatory bodies, provides a reasonable level of protection to the public. Nevertheless, improvements in the system are warranted and should be implemented."

At the hearings of the House Commerce Committee's Subcommittee on Oversight and Investigations chaired by Congressman John E. Moss (D-Calif.) on January 31 through February 2, 1978, contrary views were expressed. Clearly, the SEC and members of Congress believe that a more stringent system of regulation of CPA firms practicing before the SEC is necessary, either within the AICPA or by a quasi-governmental body under the oversight of the SEC.

It can be argued that the threat of unlimited legal liability is sufficient to assure that the profession will take all reasonable steps to avoid audit failures. A number of practitioners have questioned whether it makes sense for the profession to add its own layer of discipline on top of legal liability, SEC sanctions and suspension or revocation of the CPA certificate by state boards of accountancy. Although this addition may not be necessary from the standpoint of needed restraining pressures, it is likely, as previously noted, that neither the profession nor the public is prepared to accept a complete abdication of disciplinary responsibility by the profession. To the contrary, there are strong pressures to increase the amount of self-regulation and make it more effective. Presumably, this is based on the view that the profession has an obligation to protect the public through preventive measures, thereby minimizing the need for resorting to the courts for redress.

Some have said that the amount of auditors' legal liability should be limited because the threat of unlimited liability causes the profession to be excessively defensive and to shun new responsibilities out of fear of increased exposure to lawsuits.

It seems unlikely that any relief will be granted by a Congress that is demanding greater regulation of the profession. Even if a limitation of liability was granted, it would almost certainly be accompanied by a quid pro quo of some new form of federal regulation. The profession would be unlikely to find such a trade-off acceptable.

It seems certain that all the present institutions involved in disciplining the profession will continue to function for the foreseeable future. The question is not whether any will be eliminated but, rather, how they will be made more effective and what additional forms and layers of discipline will be added. If the AICPA-sponsored division for CPA firms is successful in its efforts to regulate and impose sanctions on firms, perhaps the SEC and Congress will be persuaded that additional federal regulation is unnecessary. If not, creation of a National Association of Securities Dealers type of regulatory body under the direct oversight of the SEC becomes a likely possibility.

A key problem to be resolved if more governmental regulation is to be avoided is finding a way to take disciplinary action immediately even though litigation is involved in an alleged case of substandard audit performance. Because the AICPA does not have subpoena powers, it has found litigation to be an insurmountable barrier to prompt action. It cannot compel production of witnesses or evidence, and its files are open to discovery by adverse parties in litigation.

Most CPA firms take the position that the profession should not attempt to preempt the judicial system and thereby jeopardize the due process rights of the individuals involved. On the other hand, the SEC, members of Congress and other critics of the profession's disciplinary efforts find unacceptable the profession's policy of deferring action pending a determination through litigation.

Where litigation is involved, it might be expected that the threat of substantial money damages would force CPA firms to exercise reasonable precautions against malpractice. Immediate additional discipline should not be necessary. Unfortunately, much of today's criticism is based on appearances, and the critics are not always persuaded by the substance.

To solve the litigation problem and avoid a new federal regulatory body, somebody will have to give ground. Either the SEC and members of Congress will have to be persuaded by the merits of the profession's position or the CPA firms will have to accept immediate disciplinary proceedings under whatever protection can be secured to prevent unfair influence on pending litigation.

This issue may have to be addressed and resolved at an early stage by the public oversight board of the SEC practice section of the new division for firms. Thus, within the next few months the die is likely to be cast that will determine whether the SEC will continue to support the profession's new self-regulatory system for firms in lieu of new regulatory legislation.

The institution that has received the least attention is the state board of accountancy. Historically, the state boards, with few exceptions, have been ineffective in meeting their disciplinary responsibilities. This stems in part from a lack of funds and investigative staff.

Because the boards can suspend or revoke the right to practice, they offer a fertile possibility for increasing the disciplinary pressures on the profession. Perhaps the profession should turn its attention to improving the capabilities of the boards as a means of satisfying the critics. It is questionable, however, whether this would satisfy members of Congress who have a natural inclination to solve the perceived problems at the federal level through its creation, the SEC. In any event, the firms might find effective and immediate state regulation to be almost as distasteful as federal regulation and would, no doubt, opt for self-regulation. Otherwise, there would be the likely result of incurring additional sanctions at both levels of government.

To sum up, the outlook is for more disciplinary machinery, not less. The question of whether a new federal regulatory scheme will be established through legislation hangs in the balance, pending an appraisal of the effectiveness of the AICPA division for firms.

Whether the many layers of disciplinary pressures are all necessary is open to question, but in the present environment any argument for reduction is likely to fall on deaf ears. Suggestions for relief from unlimited legal liability are likely to be similarly received.

Under these circumstances, practitioners and firms are well advised to maintain the highest possible quality controls. If they wish to avoid sanctions that can flow from as many as five different sources for the same offense, they will take increasingly defensive positions in resolving problems with their clients.

SUMMARY AND CONCLUSIONS

The present system for disciplining the public accounting profession is scattered among a number of institutions—the government, the private sector and, perhaps most important, the courts. While there are some limited inter-relationships among these institutions, significant portions of the overall disciplinary scheme function wholly independently of the others. As a result, there are multiple layers of punishment for the same offense, and the severity of the sanctions imposed can vary widely, depending on the disciplinary body.

Because in recent years the profession's performance has been judged by its critics to be unsatisfactory, there have been demands for additional and more effective discipline. The assumption is made that more aggressive punishment will bring about a significant improvement in the effectiveness of audits.

No doubt there were instances of audit failures in the late 1960s and early 1970s, but not all of the business failures during this period were attributable to poor auditing performance by the profession. Some were the result of well-executed management fraud, and others occurred simply because bad management decisions led to bankruptcy. Others occurred because the profession was too inclined to permit accounting treatments that conformed to generally accepted accounting principles even though the circumstances called for different treatments to make financial statements not misleading.

A rapid increase in the number of lawsuits against accounting firms occurred during this period. The firms may have been slow to recognize the significance of this development in the early stages, but there is little doubt that today they are expending great effort toward preventive measures. Also, the firms have become far less prone to bend to management pressures, and the emergence of stronger client audit committees has significantly strengthened the independent position of auditors.

To the extent that such preventive measures have already been taken because of the pressures under the existing system of discipline, it is at least debatable whether additional layers of discipline will yield any significant degree of improvement in performance. The penalties for malpractice are already so severe that few firms are likely to be careless about the quality of their work.

Nevertheless, there is generally a considerable lag in time between the occurrence of poor performance by a profession and the point at which public concern becomes sufficiently aroused to take corrective action. Seldom is the barn door locked before the horse is stolen. When action is taken, however, it tends to go further than necessary and sometimes ignores the fact that in the interim the identified problem has already been resolved by the actions of existing institutions.

There is little reason to believe that the public accounting profession's experience will vary from this pattern. Indeed, it is already virtually a certainty that a new layer of discipline will be imposed either through the AICPA-sponsored division for CPA firms, the SEC or a newly legislated regulatory body. It is also possible that some combination of these alternatives will evolve.

The eventual outcome depends to a substantial degree on how far the profession elects to go in imposing on itself or its clients a number of cures for past failures in corporate accountability. Principal among these are

1. Required independent audit committees for audit clients.
2. Reports to the public on deficiencies in the systems of internal control of audit clients.
3. Restrictions on the scope of consulting services provided to audit clients.

The SEC is aggressively pressing the profession to act on each of these matters. If the profession falls short of expectations in its response, there is the clear implication that the SEC will take action on its own through rule making or by seeking legislation if additional authority is required.

In addition to these immediate challenges, the profession continues to be faced with the crucial problem of what to do with respect to disciplinary proceedings when litigation is involved.

The proposed actions on all these matters are the subject of controversy within the profession, and it remains to be seen how far the profession will go toward accommodating its critics in Congress and the wishes of the SEC. Whatever happens, the tide of sentiment for reforms in corporate accountability and in the effectiveness of auditors is running so strong that additional governmental regulation of the profession will be difficult to avoid.

In the end, it may make little difference whether existing forms of discipline are adequate to provide as much public protection from malpractice as is reasonably attainable. When extensive wrongdoing occurs in the business community—such as the recent revelations about illegal political contributions, bribes and off-book slush funds—new forms of regulation are devised and superimposed on existing systems of discipline. When unheralded dramatic business failures occur in the future, additional steps are likely to be taken to place even further corrective pressure on the auditing profession. This search for total assurance against error is likely to continue even though the goal is clearly unattainable.

In the past, the belief that governmental intervention would solve most of our country's problems led to a huge bureaucracy that touches nearly every facet of our lives. Lately, however, there is a growing recognition that this belief is not entirely warranted by our experience with big government. Even so, it will be a major achievement if the profession's actions toward self-regulation prove to be successful in convincing its critics that additional governmental regulation is unnecessary.

Self-regulation is a worthy objective, but it requires being able to transcend the norms of human behavior as well as having the will to take timely action to satisfy the aroused concerns of legislators. It is to be fervently hoped that the public accounting profession will successfully meet the test and strike a small blow for preserving free enterprise in our society.[30]

PEER REVIEW PROGRAMS

As indicated in the discussion of the discipline of firms, one responsibility those practicing public accounting have to their colleagues is to assist in one of the various peer review programs. In addition to the mandatory peer review required of those firms in the AICPA Division for CPA firms, the institute has a Voluntary Quality Control Review Program.[31] In this program, firms may choose to submit to a review by their peers, the satisfactory conclusion of which will indicate their compliance with the quality control standards of the profession.

The AICPA Quality Control Standards Committee is the senior technical committee of the Institute designated to issue pronouncements on quality control standards. The following nine elements of quality control are enumerated in a statement proposed for issuance.

1. *Independence.* Policies and procedures should be established to provide the firm with reasonable assurance that persons at all organizational levels maintain independence to the extent required by the rules of conduct of the AICPA. Rule 101 of the rules of conduct contains examples of instances wherein a firm's independence will be considered to be impaired.

2. *Assigning Personnel to Engagements.* Policies and procedures for assigning personnel to engagements should be established to provide the firm with reasonable assurance that work will be performed by persons having the degree of technical training and proficiency required in the circumstances. In making assignments, the nature and extent of supervision to be provided should be taken into account. Generally, the more able and experienced the personnel assigned to a particular engagement, the less is the need for direct supervision.

3. *Consultation.* Policies and procedures for consultation should be established to provide the firm with reasonable assurance that personnel will seek assistance, to the extent required, from persons having appropriate levels of knowledge, competence, judgment, and authority. The nature of the arrangements for consultation will depend on a number of factors,

---

[30] Wallace E. Olson, "How Should a Profession Be Disciplined?" *Journal of Accountancy,* May 1978, pp. 59–66. Copyright © 1978 by the American Institute of Certified Public Accountants, Inc.

[31] "Voluntary Quality Control Review Program for CPA Firms," *AICPA Professional Standards,* vol. 2, QC Section 100.

including the size of the firm and the levels of knowledge, competence, and judgment possessed by the persons performing the work.

4. *Supervision.* Policies and procedures for the conduct and supervision of work at all organizational levels should be established to provide the firm with reasonable assurance that the work performed meets the firm's standards of quality. The extent of supervision and review appropriate in a given instance depends on many factors, including the complexity of the subject matter, the qualifications of the persons performing the work, and the extent of consultation available and used. The responsibility of a firm for establishing procedures for supervision is distinct from the responsibility of a person to adequately plan and supervise the work on a particular engagement.

5. *Hiring.* Policies and procedures for hiring should be established to provide the firm with reasonable assurance that those employed possess the appropriate characteristics to enable them to perform competently. The quality of a firm's work ultimately depends on the integrity, competence, and motivation of personnel who perform and supervise the work. Thus, a firm's recruiting programs are factors in maintaining such quality.

6. *Professional Development.* Policies and procedures for professional development should be established to provide the firm with reasonable assurance that personnel will have the knowledge required to enable them to fulfill responsibilities assigned. Continuing professional education and training activities enable a firm to provide personnel with the knowledge required to fulfill responsibilities assigned to them and to progress within the firm.

7. *Advancement.* Policies and procedures for advancing personnel should be established to provide the firm with reasonable assurance that those selected for advancement will have the qualifications necessary for fulfillment of the responsibilities they will be called on to assume. Practices in advancing personnel have important implications for the quality of a firm's work. Qualifications that personnel selected for advancement should possess include, but are not limited to, character, intelligence, judgment, and motivation.

8. *Acceptance and Continuance of Clients.* Policies and procedures should be established for deciding whether to accept or continue a client in order to minimize the likelihood of association with a client whose management lacks integrity. Suggesting that there should be procedures for this purpose does not imply that a firm vouches for the integrity or reliability of a client, nor does it imply that a firm has a duty to anyone but itself with respect to the acceptance, rejection, or retention of clients. However, prudence suggests that a firm be selective in determining its professional relationships.

9. *Inspection.* Policies and procedures for inspection should be established to provide the firm with reasonable assurance that the procedures relating to the other elements of quality control are being effectively applied. Procedures for inspection may be developed and performed by individuals acting on behalf of the firm's management. The type of inspection

procedures used will depend on the controls established by the firm and the assignment of responsibilities within the firm to implement its quality control policies and procedures.[32]

In order to provide guidance in the establishment of quality control procedures to those firms intending to participate in the Voluntary Quality Control Review Program of the AICPA, some quality control policies and procedures were developed.[33] These guidelines are not intended as interpretations or modifications of statements of the AICPA Quality Control Standards Committee but merely as assistance in following them. Although they were developed for the Voluntary Quality Control Review Program, the guidelines are also being used as the requirements to be met in connection with reviews conducted under the authority of the Peer Review Committees of the AICPA Division of CPA firms.[34] The seven elements of quality control enumerated above are the basis for the discussion of guidelines.

1. As a practicing CPA, is it ethical for you to offer your audit services to a company already being audited by another firm? What if that company approaches you about the services?

2. As auditor for a large conglomerate, can you ethically insist upon auditing a subsidiary already audited by another firm? What are the guidelines for reporting if you decided to rely upon the work of another auditor? How do you satisfy yourself that the work of the other auditor can be relied upon?

3. Is it ethical for one practitioner to refer work to another? What if a referral is made and the client then requests an extension of the service beyond the specific engagement? Should the practitioner receiving the referral seek additional engagements from the client?

4. What is the function of the Practice Review Committee of the AICPA? Under what circumstances may it refer a matter to the Professional Ethics Division of the Institute?

---

[32] AICPA Quality Control Standards Committee, *Proposed Statement on Quality Control Standards: System of Quality Control for a CPA Firm* (New York: American Institute of Certified Public Accountants, 1979), pp. 5–6.

[33] "Quality Control Policies and Procedures for Participating CPA Firms," *AICPA Professional Standards*, vol. 2, QC Section 200.

[34] AICPA, *Division for CPA Firms SEC Practice Section Peer Review Manual* (New York: American Institute of Certified Public Accountants, 1978), p. A–14.

5. Under what circumstances is it permissible for an external auditor to utilize work done by an internal auditor? Is it necessary to audit the internal auditor before relying upon his work?

6. What communications is a successor auditor required to attempt under generally accepted auditing standards prior to accepting an engagement? What additional communications are advisable?

7. Membership in the AICPA may be terminated without a hearing upon the filing of a final judgment of conviction for any of four actions. What are they? What other occurrence may result in a member's suspension without a hearing?

8. What is the function of the Joint Trial Board Division of the AICPA? What roles are played by the Professional Ethics Division of the Institute, the state societies, the Regional Trial Boards and the National Review Board?

9. What four membership requirements are common to both the SEC Practice Section and the Private Companies Practice Section of the AICPA Division for CPA Firms?

10. What are the responsibilities and functions of the Public Oversight Board of the SEC Practice Section?

11. What three separate peer review programs are operated under the auspices of the AICPA? What are the nine elements of quality control applicable to all firms?

SUGGESTED ADDITIONAL READINGS

American Institute of Certified Public Accountants, "The Effect of an Internal Audit Function on the Scope of the Independent Auditor's Examination," *AICPA Professional Standards,* vol. 1, AU Section 322 (Statement on Auditing Standards No. 9).

———, "Part of Examination Made by Other Independent Auditors," *AICPA Professional Standards,* vol. 1, AU Section 543 (Statement on Auditing Standards No. 1).

———, *Division for CPA Firms SEC Practice Section Peer Review Manual* (New York: AICPA, 1978).

———, "Voluntary Quality Control Review Program for CPA Firms": *AICPA Professional Standards,* vol. 2, QC Section 100.

———, "Quality Control Considerations for a Firm of Independent Auditors," *AICPA Professional Standards,* vol. 1, AU Section 160.

———, "Quality Control Policies and Procedures for Participating CPA Firms," *AICPA Professional Standards,* vol. 2, QC Section 200.

COOPERS & LYBRAND, "Good Audit Committee and Internal Audit Communications are Essential," *Journal of Accountancy,* April 1978.

Chapter 6

Other Responsibilities and Practices

INTRODUCTION

It is impossible to list every possible circumstance in which the professional accountant may face an ethical question. His responsibilities and practice are so varied that he must be alert at all times to see that his motives and behavior are on the highest possible level.

The last ethical principle set forth by the AICPA in its Code of Professional Ethics encompasses all the responsibilities and practices not previously addressed:

> "A certified public accountant should conduct himself in a manner which will enhance the stature of the profession and its ability to serve the public." [1]

The following eleven statements elaborate on this principle:

---

1. In light of the importance of their function, CPAs and their firms should have a keen consciousness of the public interest and the needs

[1] "Other Responsibilities and Practices." *AICPA Professional Standards*, vol. 2, ET Section 56.

of society. Thus, they should support efforts to achieve equality of opportunity for all, regardless of race, religious background or sex, and should contribute to this goal by their own service relationships and employment practices.

2. The CPA is beneficiary of the organization and character of his profession. Since he is seen as a representative of the profession by those who come in contact with him, he should behave honorably both in his personal and professional life and avoid any conduct that might erode public respect and confidence.

3. Solicitation to obtain clients through false, misleading and deceptive statements or acts is prohibited under the Rules of Conduct because it will lessen the professional effectiveness and the independence toward clients which is essential to the best interests of the public.

4. Advertising, which is false, misleading and deceptive, is also prohibited because such representations will mislead some of the public and thereby reduce or destroy the profession's usefulness to society. A CPA should seek to establish a reputation for competence and character, through actions rather than words. There are many ways this can be done such as by making himself known through public service, by civic and political activities, and by joining associations and clubs. It is desirable for him to share his knowledge with interested groups by accepting requests to make speeches and write articles. Whatever publicity occurs as a natural by-product of such activities is entirely proper.

5. In his work, the CPA should be motivated more by desire for excellence in performance than for material reward. This does not mean that he need be indifferent about compensation. Indeed, a professional man who cannot maintain a respectable standard of living is unlikely to inspire confidence or to enjoy sufficient peace of mind to do his best work.

6. In determining fees, a CPA may assess the degree of responsibility assumed by undertaking an engagement as well as the time, manpower and skills required to perform the service in conformity with the standards of the profession. He may also take into account the value of the service to the client, the customary charges of professional colleagues and other considerations. No single factor is necessarily controlling.

7. Clients have a right to know in advance what rates will be charged and approximately how much an engagement will cost. However, when professional judgments are involved, it is usually not possible to set a fair charge until an engagement has been completed. For this reason CPAs should state their fees for proposed engagements in the form of estimates which may be subject to change as the work progresses.

8. Other practices prohibited by the Rules of Conduct include using any firm designation or description which might be misleading, or practicing as a professional corporation or association which fails to comply with provisions established by Council to protect the public interest.

9. A member, while practicing public accunting, may not engage in a business or occupation which is incompatible therewith. While certain occupations are clearly incompatible with the practice of public accounting, the profession has never attempted to list them, for in most cases the individual circumstances indicate whether there is a problem. For example, there would be a problem of conflict of interest if a practicing CPA were to serve on a tax assessment board since he would be open to accusations of favoring his clients whether this was done or not. Moreover, they might, under some circumstances, create a conflict of interest in the CPA's independent relationship with his clients.

10. Paying a commission to outsiders is prohibited in order to eliminate the temptation to compensate anyone for referring a client. Receipt of a commission is proscribed since practitioners should look to the client, and not to others, for compensation for services rendered. The practice of paying a fee to a referring CPA irrespective of any service performed or responsibility assumed by him is proscribed because there is no justification for a CPA to share in a fee for accounting services where his sole contribution was to make a referral.

11. Over the years the vast majority of CPAs have endeavored to earn and maintain a reputation for competence, integrity and objectivity. The success of these efforts has been largely responsible for the wide public acceptance of accounting as an honorable profession. This acceptance is a valuable asset which should never be taken for granted. Every CPA should constantly strive to see that it continues to be deserved.[2]

THE AUDITOR

For over half a century prior to March 31, 1978, members of the organized public accounting profession in the United States were prohibited by their Code of Professional Ethics from advertising. From March 31, 1978, until March 31, 1979, the prohibition extended only to advertising or other forms of solicitation that were "false, misleading, or deceptive," and to "'a direct uninvited solicitation of a specific potential client." Effective March 31, 1979, the latter prohibition was removed.[3]

Assume that your firm is relatively small but over the years has developed great expertise in working with small to medium-sized retail businesses. You not only audit these companies, but prepare their tax returns and serve as their management consultant. Would it be proper for you to advertise your special competence in this area?

---

2 "Other Responsibilities and Practices," *AICPA Professional Standards,* vol. 2, ET Section 56. Copyright © 1978 by the American Institute of Certified Public Accountants, Inc.

3 "Advertising and Other Forms of Solicitation," *AICPA Professional Standards,* vol. 2, ET Section 502.01.

No, you may not claim to be "an expert or specialist" in a particular area. Because "no AICPA program with methods for recognizing competence in specialized fields" has been developed, "self-designations would be likely to cause misunderstanding or deception." [4]

What if your firm is asked by a local chapter of the National Association of Accountants to place an ad in their monthly newsletter as a means of financing that publication? Could you do so? Would there be any restriction on the size of your ad, its style, or placement?

Yes, you could place the ad, as long as it is informative, objective, in good taste, and professionally dignified. There are no restrictions as to the frequency of placement, size, artwork, or type style.[5] Some examples of informative and objective content are:

1. Information about the member and the member's firm, such as—
   a. Names, addresses, telephone numbers, number of partners, shareholders or employees, office hours, foreign language competence, and date the firm was established.
   b. Services offered and fees for such services, including date and place of certifications, schools attended, dates of graduation, degrees received, and memberships in professional associations.
2. Statements of policy or position made by a member or a member's firm related to the practice of public accounting or addressed to a subject of public interest.[6]

Paying a commission "to obtain a client" or accepting a commission "for a referral to a client of products or services of others" are practices specifically prohibited by the Rules of Conduct.[7] Suppose, for example, that you have a small audit and tax practice, while your wife practices law. From time to time, in the course of your audits, you come upon matters which require a client to seek legal advice. Would it be ethical for you to refer these matters to your wife?

No, Rule of Conduct 503 would prohibit such a referral, since you would be receiving the economic benefit from any fees paid to your wife and would therefore be receiving compensation from a third party.[8] This

---

[4] "Interpretations under Rule 502—Advertising and Other Forms of Solicitation," AICPA *Professional Standards,* vol. 2, ET Section 502.05. Copyright © 1978 by the American Institute of Certified Public Accountants, Inc.

[5] Ibid., ET Section 502.02.

[6] Ibid.

[7] "Commission," AICPA *Professional Standards,* vol. 2, ET Section 503.

[8] "Ethics Rulings on Other Responsibilities and Practices," AICPA *Professional Standards,* vol. 2, ET Section 591.255 —.266

would be a violation of the profession's position that practitioners should look to their clients for compensation for services rendered.[9]

THE MANAGEMENT CONSULTANT AND THE TAX PRACTITIONER

The advertising question is of significance to the management consultant and the tax practitioner, as well as to the auditor. Suppose, for example, that your firm wished to sponsor a radio program on taxation issues during tax season. Listeners could call in with questions, and you would present a tax tip of interest to small businessmen in the area. Or what if your management consulting group wanted to sponsor a seminar on cash flow analysis to show businessmen how to better budget and control their cash flows. Are either of these activities acceptable?

"CPAs may engage in a variety of activities to enhance their reputations and professional stature with the objective of expanding their clientele. Such indirect forms of solicitation, which include giving speeches, conducting seminars, distributing professional literature, and writing articles and books, are considered to be in the public interest and are permitted." [10] Sponsoring a radio program would probably also fall in this category.

Are there any ground rules for determining if a particular piece of advertising is "false, misleading, or deceptive?" Is it permissible, for example, for you as a successful management consultant to quote your satisfied clients? Can you compare the quality of your services in a particular area with those of your competitors? You might point out, for example, that 90 percent of your tax staff served previously with the Internal Revenue Service, as compared with a 25 percent rate for other firms.

One of the official interpretations of Rule of Conduct 502 offers some guidance on these questions. Example of activities that would be prohibited are those that:

1. Create false or unjustified expectations of favorable results.
2. Imply the ability to influence any court, tribunal, regulatory agency, or similar body or official.
3. Consist of self-laudatory statements that are not based on verifiable facts.
4. Make comparisons with other CPAs.
5. Contain testimonials or endorsements.

9 "Other Responsibilities and Practices," *AICPA Professional Standards*, vol. 2, ET Section 56.10.
10 "Interpretations Under Rule 502—Advertising and Other Forms of Solicitation," *AICPA Professional Standards*, vol. 2, ET Section 502.04. Copyright © 1978 by the American Institute of Certified Public Accountants, Inc.

6. Contain any other representations that would be likely to cause a reasonable person to misunderstand or be deceived.[11]

You could not, therefore, quote your satisfied clients, nor could you compare your staff with that of your competitors.

The form of your practice is also governed by the Rules of Conduct. Suppose, for example, that your firm engages in a great deal of write-up work and provides accounting services to many clients. You have the opportunity to acquire a 75 percent interest in a corporation which offers data-processing services to the public. You would be able to better serve your own clients if you had control of this data-processing installation. Would such a step be a violation of the Code of Ethics?

Rule of Conduct 505 states that "a member may practice public accounting whether as an owner or employee, only in the form of a proprietorship, a partnership, or a professional corporation whose characteristics conform to resolutions of Council." [12]

These characteristics are:

1. **Name.** The name under which the professional corporation or association renders professional services shall contain only the names of one or more of the present or former shareholders or of partners who were associated with a predecessor accounting firm. Impersonal or fictitious names, as well as names which indicate a specialty, are prohibited.
2. **Purpose.** The professional corporation or association shall not provide services that are incompatible with the practice of public accounting.
3. **Ownership.** All shareholders of the corporation or association shall be persons engaged in the practice of public accounting as defined by the Code of Professional Ethics. Shareholders shall at all times own their shares in their own right, and shall be the beneficial owners of the equity capital ascribed to them.
4. **Transfer of Shares.** Provisions shall be made requiring any shareholder who ceases to be eligible to be a shareholder to dispose of all of his shares within a reasonable period to a person qualified to be a shareholder or to the corporation or association.
5. **Directors and Officers.** The principal executive officer shall be a shareholder and a director, and to the extent possible, all other directors and officers shall be certified public accountants. Lay directors and officers shall not exercise any authority whatsoever over professional matters.
6. **Conduct.** The right to practice as a corporation or association shall not change the obligation of its shareholders, directors, officers and other employees to comply with the standards of professional con-

---

[11] Ibid., ET Section 502.03.
[12] "Form of Practice and Name," *AICPA Professional Standards*, vol. 2, ET Section 505.01.

duct established by the American Institute of Certified Public Accountants.

7. Liability. The stockholders of professional corporations or associations shall be jointly and severally liable for the acts of a corporation or association, or its employees—except where professional liability insurance is carried, or capitalization is maintained, in amounts deemed sufficient to offer adequate protection in the public. Liability shall not be limited by the formation of subsidiary or affiliated corporations or associations each with its own limited and unrelated liability.[13]

"A member may have a financial interest in a commercial corporation which performs for the public services of a type performed by public accountants and whose characteristics do not conform to resolutions of Council, provided such interest is not material to the corporation's net worth, and the member's interest in and relation to the corporation is solely that of an investor." [14] The proposed 75 percent material interest in the data-processing corporation would, therefore, probably be a violation of the code. Your interest would certainly be material to the corporation's net worth, and your relation to the corporation would not be solely that of an investor. Furthermore, the corporation does not appear to have the requisite characteristics of a professional corporation.

THE INTERNAL PROFESSIONAL

One responsibility of the internal professional which places his integrity and reputation squarely on the line is his signature on management representation letters. The chief financial officer of a corporation, as well as its chief executive officer, are normally asked to sign these letters on behalf of management.

One type of management representation letter is required by the independent auditor as part of his examination. These representations, involving some matters which are the direct responsibility of the internal professional accountant, comprise part of the evidential matter the auditor obtains. They "ordinarily confirm oral representations given to the auditor, indicate and document the continuing appropriateness of such representations, and reduce the possibility of misunderstanding concerning matters that are the subject of the representations." [15] The casual signing of such

13 "Council Resolution Permitting Professional Corporations or Associations," AICPA *Professional Standards*, vol. 2, ET Appendix C.

14 "Interpretation Under Rule 505—Form of Practice and Name," AICPA *Professional Standards*, vol. 2, ET Section 505.02.

15 "Client Representations," AICPA *Professional Standards*, vol. 1, AU Section 333.02 (Statement on Auditing Standards No. 19).

a letter by an internal professional, without substantive knowledge that all of the statements in it are correct, would certainly be an act discreditable to the profession. A CPA acting in such a fashion would be in violation of Rule of Conduct 501,[16] and a CMA would certainly be in violation of the high standard of his calling.

Another management representation letter which the internal professional is likely to have to sign and vouch for is one advocated by the Financial Executives Institute. Its committee on corporate reporting has endorsed a recommendation made by the Commission on Auditors' Responsibilities (Cohen Commission) that financial statements should be accompanied by a management report. The committee stated that "we believe that such reports will further public understanding of the respective roles of management and the outside auditor, and that the 'report' should emphasize that the primary responsibility for financial statements and representations related thereto rests with management, and not with the Certified Public Accountant, whose role is one of independent verification." Included in such a report would be comments on the system of internal accounting controls, the preparation and presentation of the financial statements in conformity with generally accepted accounting principles appropriate in the circumstances, and the quality of the data in the statements, all of which fall within the purview of the internal professional.[17]

Can an internal professional concurrently engage in another occupation? For example, would it be ethical for the assistant controller of a manufacturing company to accept engagements as a systems consultant for other companies? Could an internal professional working for the Internal Revenue Service moonlight as a tax consultant?

Perhaps the guiding standard in arriving at an answer to these questions can be borrowed from Rule of Conduct 504, which governs CPAs in public practice:

"A member who is engaged in the practice of public accounting shall not concurrently engage in any business or occupation which would create a conflict of interest in rendering professional services." [18]

The decision would be clear-cut in the case of the Internal Revenue Service employee. Certainly, moonlighting as a tax consultant would create a conflict of interest with his primary job. As one working for the tax collection agency, he could not at the same time counsel the one being

16 "Acts Discreditable," AICPA Professional Standards, vol. 3, ET Section 501.

17 "FEI Calls for 'Management Reports' in Annual Reports," Journal of Accountancy, August 1978, pp. 14, 20.

18 "Incompatible Occupations," AICPA Professional Standards, vol. 2, ET Section 504.

taxed. The case of the assistant controller is not quite so easy. So long as the companies with which he consults are not in competition with his own company, and his employer does not object, there would appear to be no reason why he could not engage in such activity. If he is a CPA, he would, of course, need to abide by all of the other Rules of Conduct in connection with his consulting practice.

SCOPE OF PRACTICE

Rule of Conduct 504, cited in the previous section, is one of the guidelines to be followed in determining the proper scope of practice and the acceptability of a particular concurrent occupation. For an independent auditor, another major guideline is the one discussed in Chapter 2, the avoidance of any loss of independence or any loss of the appearance of independence.

Concern is often centered on firms with both an audit practice and a management advisory services practice. Some have argued strongly that some of these services are not really the practice of public accounting, that some of them impair auditor independence and are in essence incompatible occupations.

The Public Oversight Board of the SEC Practice Section has taken the position that "mandatory limitations on the scope of services should be predicated only on the determination that certain services, or the role of the firm performing certain services, will impair the member's independence in rendering an opinion on the fairness of a client's financial statements or present a strong likelihood of doing so." [19] The Board further states that the profession "should be careful not to impose unnecessarily prophylactic rules with regard to MAS and independence" because of the "many potential benefits to be realized by permitting auditors to perform MAS for audit clients." [20]

Many avenues are available to insure the independence of auditors performing management advisory services. Various sections of the AICPA Code of Professional Ethics and of the Statements on Management Advisory Services address the independence issue. In addition, disclosure of the extent and nature of management advisory services carried out by an individual firm is now required. The Securities and Exchange Commission requires companies to disclose in proxy materials all nonaudit engagements and the fees therefrom as a percentage of the audit fee. It further

[19] Public Oversight Board, *Scope of Services by CPA Firms* (New York: American Institute of Certified Public Accountants, 1979), p. 4.
[20] Ibid.

requires disclosure of whether the company's audit committee or board of directors approved such engagements and whether the approval was granted before or after commencement of the agreement.[21]

Members of the SEC Practice Section, as a requirement of membership, must disclose their gross fees for accounting and auditing, tax, and MAS expressed as a percentage of total gross fees. In addition, they must disclose the gross fees for both MAS and tax services performed for SEC audit clients expressed as a percentage of total fees charged to all SEC audit clients.[22]

Peer review is of course required for all members of the AICPA Division for CPA firms, thus providing an avenue for determining adherence to the prescribed principle of independence.

The Executive Committee of the SEC Practice Section, with the support of the Public Oversight Board, has prohibited certain types of executive recruiting services. These types of services are perceived by some as having a strong likelihood of impairing independence. In addition, certain limitations have been set forth relative to the rendering of actuarially oriented advisory services to audit clients. These positions are set forth in Appendix A of the SEC Practice Section Organizational Document.[23]

EXECUTIVE RECRUITING SERVICES

The hiring of persons for managerial, executive, or director positions is a function which is properly the client's responsibility. Accordingly, the role of a member firm in this function should be limited. In serving an audit client whose securities are registered with the SEC, a member firm should not:

1. Accept an engagement to search for, or seek out, prospective candidates for managerial, executive, or director positions with its audit clients. This would not preclude giving the name of a prospective candidate previously known to someone in the member firm.
2. Engage in psychological testing, other formal testing or evaluation programs, or undertake reference checks of prospective candidates for an executive or director position.
3. Act as a negotiator on the client's behalf, for example, in determining position status or title, compensation, fringe benefits, or other conditions of employment.

---

[21] Ibid., p. 42. See also Securities and Exchange Commission, "Disclosure of Relationship with Independent Public Accountants," Accounting Series Release No. 250, June 29, 1978.

[22] This latter provision was added to the original membership requirements by action of the Executive Committee of the Section in March, 1979.

[23] This Appendix was added to the Organizational Document by the Executive Committee in March, 1979, at which time original Appendices A and B were deleted.

4. Recommend, or advise the client to hire, a specific candidate for a specific job. However, a member firm may, upon request by the client, interview candidates and advise the client on the candidate's competence for financial, accounting, administrative, or control positions.

When a client seeks to fill a position within its organization which is related to its system of accounting, financial, or administrative controls, the client will frequently approach employees of the member firm directly as candidates or seek referral of the member firm's employees who may be considering employment outside of the profession. Such employment from time to time is an inevitable consequence of the training and experience which the public accounting profession provides to its staff, is beneficial to all concerned, including society in general, and therefore is not proscribed.

INSURANCE ACTUARIAL SERVICES

Actuarial skills are both accounting and auditing related. The bodies of knowledge supporting the actuarial and accounting professions have a substantial degree of overlap. Both professions involve the analysis of various factors of time, probability and economics, and the quantification of such analysis in financial terms. The results of their work are significantly inter-related. Their professions are logical extensions of each other; indeed, they have practiced jointly for many years and even shared the same professional society in Scotland prior to their becoming established in the United States.

The work of actuarial specialists generally is necessary to obtain audit satisfaction in support of insurance policy and loss reserves. To assist them in meeting their audit responsibilities, a number of CPA firms have hired qualified actuaries of their own.

The actuarial function is basic to the operation and management of an insurance company. Management's responsibility for this function cannot be assumed by the CPA firm without jeopardizing its independence. Because of the special significance of a CPA firm's appearance of independence when auditing publicly held insurance companies:

1. The CPA firm should not render actuarially oriented advisory services involving the determination of policy reserves and related accounts to its audit clients unless such clients utilize their own actuaries or third party actuaries to provide management with the primary actuarial capabilities. This does not preclude the use of the CPA firm's actuarial staff in connection with the auditing of such reserves.

2. Whenever the CPA firm renders actuarially oriented advisory services, it must satisfy itself that it is acting in an advisory capacity and that the responsibility for any significant actuarial methods and assumptions is accepted by the client.

3. The CPA firm should not render actuarially oriented advisory services when the CPA firm's involvement is continuous since such a relationship

might be perceived as an engagement to perform a management function.

Subject to the above limitations it is appropriate for the CPA firm to render certain actuarially oriented advisory services to its audit clients. Such services include:

1. Assisting management to develop appropriate methods, assumptions, and amounts for policy and loss reserves and other actuarial items presented in financial reports based on the company's historical experience, current practices and future plans.
2. Assisting management in the conversion of financial statements from a statutory basis to one conforming with generally accepted accounting principles.
3. Analyzing actuarial considerations and alternatives in federal income tax planning.
4. Assisting management in the financial analyses of various matters such as proposed new policies, new markets, business acquisitions and reinsurance needs.[24]

MANAGEMENT ADVISORY SERVICES: COMPATIBILITY AND INDEPENDENCE

Stanley R. Klion, an experienced management consultant with Peat, Marwick, Mitchell & Co., discusses in the following article the relationship of management advisory services to the audit practice of a CPA firm, as well as the value of such services to clients, shareholders, and society at large.

It is likely that few other professions in modern times have been exposed to public scrutiny to the degree that the accounting profession is at present. Indeed, it seems fair to suggest that the profession is at the most critical stage in its history. Every aspect of it is under review—from its professional organizational structure to its independence and ethics to the basic principles by which it performs its various functions.

And if the accounting profession in its entirety is under attack, certainly management advisory services have not escaped notice. MAS practitioners find themselves defending the scope of their practice, the impact of their activities on audit independence, indeed their very reason for being. I cannot speak for

---

[24] *"Appendix A," Organizational Structure and Functions of the SEC Practice Section of the AICPA Division for CPA Firms* (New York: American Institute of Certified Public Accountants, 1979).

all of the 7,000 to 8,000 full-time MAS practitioners who work in a CPA environment; . . . But I have been actively involved in MAS for more than twenty years with a large international CPA firm, and I have served three terms on the AICPA MAS executive committee, . . . Accordingly, I believe I can speak from personal experience and knowledge of the realities of MAS practice. In my view, it is important that the position set forth in this article be presented because the bulk of the public pronouncements, articles, research reports and the like, has presented what I believe to be a distorted and erroneous appraisal of MAS activities.

Let's start with my conclusions:

1. *MAS practice is an integral part of the public accounting profession* and has been since it was organized more than eighty years ago. Today, there is hardly a practice unit, from the national firms to the sole practitioner, that does not provide business counsel to its clients. Businessmen look to their CPAs for business insight and advice because the CPA has demonstrated his competence in this field for many years.

2. *The critical relationship between the CPA as an MAS practitioner and his client relates to his role as an advisor* rather than to the subject matter or technical component of any particular engagement.

3. *MAS capabilities are increasingly important in enhancing the quality of audits,* and the absence or proscription of such skills in a CPA environment will adversely affect audit performance.

4. *There are demonstrable advantages to clients in obtaining MAS from their CPAs.*

5. *Examination of the impact of MAS activities on auditors' independence has yet to produce the first hard instance of compromise,* although this question has been one of the most thoroughly researched subjects in the profession. The most recent example of such research can be found in the report of the Commission on Auditors' Responsibilities (the Cohen commission), which states: "If the empirical evidence were the only consideration, the Commission's conclusion would be clear: *The evidence does not support the theory.* No prohibition of management services is warranted." (Emphasis added.) *

Let's look at each of these matters in turn.

MAS PART OF THE PUBLIC
ACCOUNTING PROFESSION

From the beginning of the accounting profession, the businessman has looked to his CPA to provide business advice and insight in a number of areas. Obviously, the CPA renders bookkeeping and accounting advice, but he is also the source of counsel on a great many business management matters, including

---

* *Commission on Auditor's Responsibilities, Report, Conclusions, and Recommendations* (New York: AICPA, 1978), p. 102.

organization, costing, inventory control, data processing, internal control, administrative procedures and other business functions. In many cases, the businessman also looks to the accountant to assist him in locating accounting and administrative personnel. These services were, and continue to be, sought because the CPA is in the unique position of serving many business enterprises, and his clients wish to avail themselves of the knowledge and experience that the CPA obtains through his exposure to business needs and concerns. To this day, this generalized description of services rendered by a CPA to his clients probably refers to the bulk of the accounting profession in public practice.

There is nothing sinister or devious in a businessman's seeking such counsel from his CPA; indeed, as the businessman profits from this advice, stockholders and society should be the better for it. In turn, the CPA carefully guards the integrity and independence of this relationship. His reputation and livelihood depend on his ability to advise clients in confidence and with competence. One result of this "advice-giving" has been the expansion of the number of individuals or groups of MAS practitioners to be found in CPA practice units of all sizes.

In our economic system, such growth can take place only if the services rendered serve a specific need and are of a quality to demand their expansion. To suggest, as did one witness before the late Senator Lee Metcalf's Subcommittee on Reports, Accounting and Management of the Senate Committee on Governmental Affairs, that the CPA takes unfair advantage of his overall client relationship to render such services is to deny the logic that the client makes the final judgment on obtaining counsel from among all the sources available; the MAS practitioner does not provide it as a right. Were the CPA not considered a prime source of MAS, clearly these services would not have grown as they have. If the business community may look only to certain persons for its business counseling and not to others, irrespective of competence, competition is not fostered; it is restricted. And one need only attend any bidders' conference of a public or private sector request for proposal to dismiss the erroneous allegation that real competition does not exist within the profession and between CPA firms and other providers of MAS.

Current professional literature recognizes the wide variety of services rendered by CPAs to their clients. Structured services are described fully. The AICPA also speaks of informal advice as a major service that most businessmen seek from their CPA's, in both large and small firms.* The need for such services, both informal and structured, is best tested in the marketplace. When the services cease to be of value, the businessman will cease to obtain them from his CPA.

THE ROLE OF THE MAS PRACTITIONER

The role of the CPA in providing advisory services is the most efficient criterion for identifying the types of MAS that are appropriate for CPAs to render to both audit and nonaudit clients. Basically, this role is to provide

---

* Committee on Management Services, "Statement on Management Advisory Services No. 3, Role in Management Advisory Services," (New York: AICPA, 1969), par. 24.

advice and technical assistance but to avoid assuming the responsibilities of client management to make decisions. The concept of his role is considered in depth in the AICPA Statements of Management Advisory Services Nos. 1 and 3.* Stated briefly: "The role of an independent accounting firm in performing management advisory services is to provide advice and technical assistance, and should provide for client participation in the analytical approach and process. Specifying this as the proper role recognizes both the appropriate place of management advisory services and the realities of practice. This is the only basis on which the work should be done and it is the only basis on which responsible management should permit it to be done." †

This description of the MAS role is simply an articulation of a concept which was included in the literature on MAS long before these statements were issued and which continues to permeate professional literature.‡ The concept has traditionally been respected by practitioners and is in one way or another clearly mandated in the written operating procedures of all major accounting firms. Moreover, it is not unique to CPAs; similar policies are in effect in most of the major management consulting firms. Finally, this concept has been officially recognized by the Securities and Exchange commission. //

Attempts to establish relatively objective criteria based on factors other than role have been fruitless. Typically, these other factors have involved either the functional or the technical aspects of the services provided. The functional aspects relate to the client's operational functions, e.g., finance, manufacturing, engineering, marketing, industrial relations, etc. Technical aspects are concerned with the particular academic discipline or skill on which the service is based, e.g., systems analysis, data processing, management sciences, etc. Because most MAS engagements involve many different operational functions and a variety of technical disciplines, useful advisory services might cease if they were to be curtailed in these terms. Even such traditional and relatively uncontroversial services as the design of a management information or inventory control system might not be performed properly if the CPA's fact-finding and recommendations for procedural improvements were confined to the client's accounting or finance department and could not extend to the marketing, distribution, engineering and manufacturing functions. Similarly, the CPA's services would probably

---

* Committee on Management Services, Statement on Management Advisory Services No. 1, *Tentative Description of the Nature of Management Advisory Services by Independent Accounting Firms* (New York: AICPA, 1969), and MAS Statement No. 3.

† MAS Statement No. 1, par. 1.

‡ See, for example, *Statements on Management Advisory Services* (New York: AICPA, 1974), p. 4, par. 4, and p. 21 ff.

// "Independence of Accountants," Accounting Series Release 126 (Washington, D.C.: Securities and Exchange Commission, 1972): "A part of the rationale which underlies any rule on independence is that managerial and decision-making functions are the responsibility of the client and not of the independent accountant. . . . However, it is the role of the accountant to advise management and to offer professional advice on their problems. Therefore, the problem posed by this dilemma is to ascertain the point where advice ends and managerial responsibility begins."

be of limited value if he restricted the skills he applies to those traditionally associated with a narrow definition of accounting, ignoring the benefits his client might often realize from the use of, for example, sophisticated mathematical techniques.

It is important to recognize that the role of MAS practitioners is to counsel and to make recommendations to their clients. It is not to participate in management decision-making. A proper understanding of this relationship should lay to rest the concern of some that MAS somehow compromises the independence of the auditor.

ENHANCING THE QUALITY OF AUDITS

The performance of MAS enhances the quality of audits. In most CPA firms, audits of clients and sophisticated information systems depend significantly on the technical skills of the personnel employed and trained primarily for MAS work. MAS assistance in designing or improving clients' control systems results in more reliable financial information. It is not uncommon for work performed as part of an MAS engagement to lead directly to improvements in financial statements or in the auditing procedures applied to them.

When an auditor (or auditing firm) provides MAS to a client, the reliability of the client's financial statements and the quality and effectiveness of the audit are directly enhanced in five ways:

1. *Controls incorporated in the design of a financial information system.* Because of the CPA's "control consciousness," financial information systems designed and installed by CPAs can be expected to have better controls and greater auditability than systems designed by others. This is equally true for information systems that are oriented primarily toward operations but that produce accounting by-products, such as inventory management or production planning and scheduling systems.

   A reasonable extension of this concept strongly indicates that other advisory services, when performed by auditors, can effectively enhance the client's financial controls. For example, the auditor's assistance can be particularly valuable in evaluating the technical qualifications of senior accounting personnel because of the CPA's own technical competence and his strong motivation to have highly qualified personnel prepare the financial statements on which he will express an opinion.

2. *Correction of control deficiencies.* A key audit procedure is the study and evaluation of internal control. It would be counterproductive to prohibit the auditor from communicating to the client any weaknesses or defects he observes. It would be just as unsound to prohibit the auditor from making specific recommendations for improvement, because no one is better qualified to do so. Any restrictions on the auditor's assistance in implementing the improvements would also be illogical. The auditor's affirmative participation in such circumstances results in improved controls on financial information and, consequently, in improved reliability of financial statements.

3. *Effective conduct of the audit.* MAS work enables the auditor to understand better his client and the client's operations and information systems. This increased familiarity results in more effective audit procedures, more perceptive analytical reviews and greater sensitivity to problem areas that deserve intensive scrutiny.

4. *Utilization of MAS technical skills.* The auditor's need to rely on specialized competencies not normally included in a narrow definition of accountancy has increased greatly in recent years, and this growth can be expected to continue. It might be argued that the auditor is responsible for providing those skills, either from within his organization or from outside experts, regardless of inconvenience. Auditors normally do just that. However, their ability or inclination to do so could be seriously diminished if they are unable to maintain the needed skills within their own organizations while, at the same time, they are held professionally responsible for the results.

Computer auditing provides the most obvious example. Some CPA firms customarily call on their MAS personnel to provide the needed technical skills. Others have computer audit specialists, but even these firms often involve their MAS personnel in particularly difficult or sensitive investigations because of the MAS staff's broader technical knowledge and experience. Moreover, computer audit software, typically employed in audits of even modest sophistication, is the direct result of MAS competence resident in the various firms that develop or use this important audit tool.

Accounting firms would find it uneconomical, and even impossible, to maintain sufficient expertise within their organizations if such personnel could not be used on, and stimulated by, consulting assignments. And securing appropriate assistance from an outside expert is often an unsatisfactory last resort because of cost, decentralized responsibility, lack of direct control over the outside expert's activities and uncertainty about his full understanding of the audit function. Indeed, it is ironic that, at the very time when the SEC is seeking to have auditors report publicly on their clients' systems of internal control and become involved in forecasting, there is a movement afoot to cut back or proscribe the specific talents that auditors require to perform these activities.

5. *Enhancement of the auditor's image.* If the profession would limit its professional services to only those that constitute an essential part of audits, it would become much narrower and more highly specialized than it is today. The resultant deterioration of the image of the CPA profession would diminish its auditing effectiveness in two distinct ways.

The first would be to discourage the entry of many highly qualified graduates into auditing firms. Graese stated it well in 1967, and I believe it is not less true today: "To anyone who has engaged in college recruiting, particularly at the graduate level, it goes without saying that the embracing of management [advisory] services by the CPA firms has been a major factor in enhancing the general status of the CPA profession. Any profession, in order to survive, needs to attract promising young men to its ranks." *

The second detrimental effect of the CPA's diminished image concerns financial statement users' perceptions of the auditor's overall competence. It could be difficult for auditors to maintain a useful level of credibility if the public viewed their function as simply limited to vouching and confirming transaction samples, checking the logic and arithmetic of transaction compilations and evaluating the application of generally accepted accounting principles. Such auditors might appear to be operating in an artificial environment, insulated from the real world of business. Their credibility in attesting to the overall fairness of presentation, and in relating their conclusions to the broad economic and operating factors affecting their clients' financial health, could be sharply diminished.

In contrast, the knowledge that businesses frequently turn to their auditors for advice and assistance in translating information about economic events into usable management information reinforces the image of auditors as competent, knowledgeable and constructive professionals.

ADVANTAGES TO CLIENTS

When a client requires MAS, he can turn to his auditor, to another consulting organization or do without the services. Here are five benefits that, in most cases, the auditor can best provide:

1. *Familiarity with client.* The accounting firm is already familiar with the client and his objectives, operations, finances, organization and personnel. MAS personnel have ready access to additional details, either by referring to workpapers or by direct contact with audit personnel. At the very least, this enables the consulting project to get under way more quickly and more efficiently. In many circumstances, it will result in a more responsible and effective end product.

2. *Confidence of client.* The final objective of most consulting engagements is some sort of action. If such action does not occur, the engagement is of questionable value. Accordingly, the consultant who is most effective at stimulating appropriate action is the one who usually produces the greatest client benefit.

   A consultant's effectiveness at stimulating action is directly related to the client's confidence in him. All things being equal, the client's confidence in his accounting firm, usually built up, maintained and reinforced over years of professional association, will usually exceed his confidence in a firm that lacks this continuing relationship.

---

* C. E. Graese, "Management Services and the Independence Issue," *New York Certified Public Accountant,* June 1967, p. 436. This article reprinted with permission from *The CPA Journal,* published by the New York State Society of Certified Public Accountants.

3. *Follow-through.* Since the accounting firm continues in close contact with the client after completion of the consulting engagement, it will have greater opportunity to monitor and appraise the implementation of the recommended course of action. This follow-through is critical to successful results.

4. *Incentive for quality.* In most instances a recurring annual audit fee is of much greater commercial value to the accounting firm than the fee for a consulting engagement. Therefore, good business practice compels the accountant to avoid overselling his services or undertaking a job for which he lacks competence. And he has a powerful incentive to produce work of the highest quality, regardless of whether the cost of the engagement exceeds his original expectations.

5. *Audits of efficiency, economy and program results.* Although the majority of CPA firms are not at present involved in government auditing for efficiency and effectiveness, those firms that do participate extensively, and those that expect to in the future, must have the necessary skills. These are spelled out in the U.S. General Accounting Office's definition of the first general standard for governmental auditing:

> "The full scope of an audit of a governmental program, function, activity, or organization should encompass:
>
> **1.** An examination of financial transactions, accounts, and reports, including an evaluation of compliance with applicable laws and regulations.
> **2.** A review of efficiency and economy in the use of resources.
> **3.** A review to determine whether desired results are effectively achieved.
>
> ". . . those responsible for authorizing governmental audits are charged with the knowledge that, for most governmental programs, their full responsibility for obtaining audit work is not discharged unless the full scope of audit work set forth in the standard is performed." *

CPAs traditionally have recognized that they often supplement the GAO's audit staff in conducting government audits, especially of state and local entities and programs and of grant recipients. It is doubtful that CPA firms could maintain the necessary technical competencies if it were not for the requirements of their MAS practice.

An illustration of the diversity of skills demanded by the generally broader scope audits usually performed by the GAO can be found in the

---

* *Standards for Audit of Governmental Organizations, Programs, Activities & Functions* (Washington, D.C.: U.S. General Accounting Office, 1972), p. 10.

facts that the GAO's professional staff is comprised of about 60 percent accountants and 40 percent nonaccountants and that their audit hours are distributed as follows:

Financial and compliance	20%
Economy and efficiency	50
Program results or effectiveness	30
	100% *

MAS ACTIVITIES AND
AUDITORS' INDEPENDENCE

The fundamental issue encountered in evaluating the relationship of MAS to the audit function is the possibility that, by providing MAS to an audit client, a CPA might somehow jeopardize either the substance or the appearance of his independence as auditor.

Independence traditionally has been defined by the CPA profession as the ability to act with integrity and objectivity. In this sense, integrity is equivalent to honesty or to trustworthiness and incorruptibility even in the face of strong pressures. Objectivity is lack of bias and resistance of any conscious or subconscious influences toward action, inaction, conclusions or statements that are based on anything other than an impartial evaluation of the best available evidence.

Few aspects of the practice of accountancy have been questioned more frequently or scrutinized more closely than the potential effects of MAS on audit independence. Criticisms of MAS, based on a perceived detriment to audit independence primarily among academicians, reached a high point in the late 1960s. It appeared to subside shortly after the publication in 1969 of the final report of the AICPA ad hoc committee on independence, which was charged to search for information about audit failures resulting from the performance of MAS.† The committee found no such evidence. As a result, also in 1969, the AICPA published statements on Management Advisory Services nos. 1, 2 and 3, which described the nature of MAS, the requirement for competence and the role of the CPA in providing MAS. These publications appeared to have reassured most critics until recently, with the advent of such bodies as the Metcalf subcommittee, the Cohen commission and the House Commerce Committee's Subcommittee on Oversight and Investigations (the Moss subcommittee). Quite clearly, the matter is again under intensive review.

Many of the researchers who questioned the independence of an auditor who performs MAS seem to have started with the hypothesis that auditing and

---

* Stephen C. Dilley, "Expanded Scope Audits—Untapped Opportunities?" *CPA Journal,* Dec. 1975, p. 31.

† "Final Report of Ad Hoc Committee on Independence," *Journal of Accountancy,* Dec., 1969, p. 51.

MAS are somehow incompatible. Using questionnaires, information was com-piled on the attitudes of informed users of financial statements toward this hypothesis. Little attention appears to have been paid to whether MAS did in fact jeopardize audit independence, and "the concern of users decreases as their familiarity with the nature of the services offered by public accounting firms increases. . . .* Even so, none of these studies developed research findings, rationale or any specific instance which would justify curtailment of MAS as currently performed by auditing firms. And most significantly, the Cohen commission has once again confirmed the absence of such empirical evidence.

Despite more than fifteen years of research—much of which conducted by persons, however sincere their motives, with an apparent preconception about the impropriety of MAS—the record of MAS practice as it relates to audit independence is unblemished: *Not a single compromising instance has been presented.* Both equity and reason would seem to suggest that the question has been answered adequately.

As to the argument that MAS created the appearance of lack of indepen-dence of the auditor, no relationship between the offeror and the user of professional services can be totally immune from such perceptions. Payment of fees, personal friendship, joint service in community activities—these and many other factors might conceivably affect the auditor's independence, however slightly. But given the ethical and professional constraints placed on practition-ers by the AICPA, the state CPA societies and the state boards of accountancy, the internal control procedures of auditing firms regarding MAS activities and the integrity and objectivity that are the cornerstones of every professional's reputation and career, one must ask, What more is necessary? At what point may the profession provide services requested by and beneficial to its clientele? The continuing unsubstantiated suggestion that there is something vaguely wrong with MAS activities must adversely affect the MAS practitioner. Ultimately, these allegations, although unproved, will produce a result that scholarly research has failed to justify: the diminution of MAS skills in auditing firms to the detriment of all who are involved—the professional, his client, shareholders and society at large.

Academicians, congressional committees, AICPA commissions—all have set out to examine the problem. None had found a substantiation of the allegation that MAS activities impair independence. The profession should be permitted to practice its skills in a free marketplace, subject to current regula-tions, ethical codes and practice standards—unless hard evidence is produced that our independence has actually been impaired. So far, no such evidence has been produced. From the intensity of recent scrutiny, I suspect that none will be. Therefore, it is time for the profession to move ahead with MAS—not retreat.[25]

---

* *Report, Conclusions, and Recommendations*, p. 96.

[25] Stanley R. Klion, "MAS Practice: Are the Critics Justified?" *Journal of Accountancy*, June 1978, pp. 72–78. Copyright © 1978 by the American Institute of Certified Public Accountants, Inc.

DUAL PRACTICE OF LAW AND ACCOUNTING

Another question arising in connection with incompatible occupations is whether or not it is ethical to practice law and accounting concurrently. The only possible basis under the AICPA Code of Professional Ethics for charging that the practice of law is incompatible with the practice of accounting is that it creates a "conflict of interest" [26] or that it "impairs the member's objectivity." [27] It might also be asserted that it impairs the auditor's independence and thus is a violation of another section of the code (Rule of Conduct 101).

The assertion that the dual practice of law and accounting, in and of itself, creates a conflict of interest, impairs a member's objectivity, or impairs his independence is probably not supportable. While it is easy to imagine particular circumstances that would cause a conflict or impairment. it is equally easy to imagine other circumstances with no such effect.

A management consulting engagement for an accounting client might, for example, be conducted concurrently with the preparation of legal documents for another client, with no code violation. Similarly, an accounting tax practitioner might at the same time practice law in the area of trusts and estates. On the other hand, a conflict of interest and an impairment of objectivity and independence would clearly result if a lawyer/accountant served as legal counsel for a company bringing action against his audit client. There would also be a serious question as to whether an auditor's independence could be maintained if he served as legal counsel for his client. Thus, while the AICPA Code of Ethics does not prohibit the dual practice of law and accounting, it does raise some serious questions about the nature of that practice.

The American Bar Association, likewise, does not prohibit dual practice. Certain restrictions are imposed, however. DR 2-102(E) of its Code of Professional Responsibility reads:

> A lawyer who is engaged in the practice of law and another profession or business shall not so indicate on his letterhead, office sign, or professional card, nor shall he identify himself as a lawyer in any publication in connection with his other profession or business.

Further explaining the ABA position on joint practice, the ABA Ethics Committee stated in its Opinion 328:

> . . . he may practice from the same office as a lawyer and as . . . an accountant . . . if he complies not merely with DR 2-102(E) but

[26] "Incompatible Occupations," *AICPA Professional Standards,* vol. 2, ET Section 504.01.

[27] "Interpretations Under Rule 504—Incompatible Occupations," *AICPA Professional Standards,* vol. 2, ET Section 504.02.

with all provisions of the Code of Professional Responsibility while conducting his second, law-related occupation.

In view of the recent trend in the law relative to advertising by accountants and lawyers, it is possible that the ABA restriction regarding letterheads, office signs, and professional cards will soon be removed. It is clear, however, that from the viewpoint of both the legal and accounting professions, dual practices should be approached very cautiously and with careful attention to the ethical codes of both professions.

THE SMALL CLIENT AND REPRESENTATION LETTERS

The representation letter required by auditors from their clients, which was discussed earlier in the chapter in the context of the responsibility of the internal professional, is of particular concern to the small practitioner and his client. In the following article, the author discusses the usefulness of such a letter in establishing the client's responsibility for his own financial statements, as well as in establishing the auditor's independence. The desirability of an engagement letter is also discussed.

Your field work is completed; you have just finished reviewing the pencil copy of the annual financial statements with your client. Before you leave his office, you give him the client representation letter for his signature. You put on your hat and coat and stand, briefcase resting on the edge of the desk, waiting for the final document which will allow you to complete the audit and have the report typed for distribution to banks and other credit grantors.

"Wait a minute," says the client. "I am not 'responsible for the fair presentation in the . . . financial statements of financial position, results of operations and changes in financial position in conformity with generally accepted accounting principles.' * You are. You prepare my unaudited quarterly financial statements, and you prepare my audited annual financial statements. You decide what accounting principles to use—I don't. I don't know what generally accepted accounting principles are, let alone whether my statements are prepared in conformity with them. I won't sign the letter unless you eliminate this section."

You close your briefcase, remove your hat and coat and sit down. Patiently you say, "Although I have prepared the financial statements, they are yours. They are your representations prepared from your books and records which summarize transactions you initiated or participated in. I must have your

* Statement on Auditing Standards No. 19, *Client Representations* (New York: AICPA, 1977), p. 8.

signature on this letter or I cannot issue a clean opinion on your financial statements."

Your client thinks for a moment and responds, "I run a $5 million a year manufacturing company; I purchase, I sell and I supervise production. I have a head bookkeeper and four clerks who keep my books and records. I depend on you to review their work, correct their errors and tell them how to record unusual transactions. I rely on you for financial and tax advice. If you want me to sign that letter, you'll have to give me a better explanation of why I must sign it, and then you'll have to modify it. I suggest you do some research and come back in a day or two."

Frustrated and disgruntled, you once again put on your hat and coat and depart for your office and your library. Clearly, a major question must be answered.

WHOSE STATEMENTS ARE THEY?

While the client may have doubts as to who is responsible for the content of his financial statements, the literature leaves no doubt. As far back as 1939, the American Institute of Accountants stated that "the function of the independent certified public accountant is to examine a concern's accounting records and supporting data, . . . to the extent necessary to enable him to form an opinion as to whether or not the financial statements *as submitted* present fairly. . . ." (Emphasis added.) *

It further stated that "management itself has the direct responsibility for the maintenance of an adequate and effective system of accounts, for the proper recording of transactions in the books of account. . . . It is also charged with the primary responsibility . . . for the substantial accuracy and adequacy of statements of position and operations. . . ." †

The above statements were issued by the AIA committee on auditing procedure. To further reinforce the concept that the financial statements were representations of management, the Institute committee on accounting procedure stated in 1939 that "underlying all committee opinions is the fact that the accounts of a company are primarily the responsibility of management. The responsibility of the auditor is to express his opinion concerning the financial statements. . . ." ‡

In its first codification of auditing procedures issued in 1951, the Institute stated that "the independent auditor's knowledge of them [the company's accounting transactions] is a secondary one, based on his examination. Accordingly, even though the form of the statements may show the influence of the accountant—it can do so only if the company accepts, and adopts, the form

---

* Statement on Auditing Procedure No. 1, *Extensions of Auditing Procedure* (New York: AIA, 1939), pp. 3–4.

† Ibid., p. 4.

‡ Accounting Research Bulletin No. 1 (New York: AIA, 1939). See also Accounting Research Bulletin No. 43 (New York: AICPA, 1953), Introduction, par. 11.

of disclosure advised by the accountant—the substance of the financial statements of necessity constitutes the representations of the company." *

While the above statements may appear to be directed to those companies with the human resources necessary to prepare financial statements, their implications are clear:

"In the case of some concerns the statements may, in fact, be prepared by the auditor from the books after giving effect to the results of his examination, in which event he will naturally discuss with the client any adjustments which may have been made in the figures as shown on the face of the books, and the form of presentation to be used. As to any such adjustments, the auditor will naturally seek to obtain concurrence of the client. In either event, the statements are regarded as the representations of the client. In the former event [prepared by company personnel] they are not only theoretically so but even physically so. In the latter event [prepared by company auditor] they are so because the client adopts them as his and decides whether they shall be promulgated." †

The Securities and Exchange Commission has taken an even more rigorous position than the accounting profession on management responsibility for the books and records and financial statements of the company. It considers the accountant's independence lost if he performs any bookkeeping services whatsoever. Thus, the commission has stated:

"The fundamental and primary responsibility for the accuracy of information filed with the Commission and disseminated among the investors rests upon management. Management does not discharge its obligations in this respect by the employment of independent public accountants, however reputable. Accountants' certificates are required not as a substitute for management's accounting of its stewardship, but as a check upon that accounting." ‡

The SEC and the accounting profession both have recognized the primacy of management's financial reporting obligations. The small or closely held business that retains an accountant to perform both auditing and accounting services must recognize that although the CPA may suggest adjusting entries and often prepare the financial statements, his knowledge of the transactions is a secondary one.

CLIENT'S WRITTEN REPRESENTATIONS

Before Statement on Auditing Standards No. 19, *Client Representations,* generally accepted auditing standards, with one exception, did not explicitly require the independent auditor to obtain written representations from management. This exception pertained to representations as to whether any events occurred subsequent to the date of the financial statements that would require

---

* *Codification of Statements on Auditing Procedure* (New York: AIA, 1951), p. 12.

† Walter A. Staub, *Auditing Developments During the Present Century* (Cambridge, Mass.: Harvard University Press, 1942), p. 68.

‡ *Interstate Hosiery Mills, Inc.,* 4 SEC 706, 721 (1939).

adjustment of or disclosure in the financial statements.* However, written representation letters were often used by auditors, particularly for client representations on inventories and liabilities. Thus, a pamphlet issued by the American Institute of Accountants in 1950 said:

"The CPA generally secures considerable information by discussing with officers and employees of the company various questions that arise during the audit. These inquiries generally involve points which are not completely clear from the records. . . . Not infrequently, the more important of these explanations are reduced to writing in a statement signed by responsible officers of the company." †

In 1941, Statement on Auditing Procedure No. 4 explained the need for client representations:

"Whether or not a written representation is required from the client, the information would necessarily have to be obtained where pertinent, and oral representations be made by the client. Reducing these to writing has the advantage of confirming the statements made and avoiding any misunderstanding regarding them. Moreover, they have the effect of reminding the client or the management of the client company that *the primary responsibility for the correctness of the statements rests with the client rather than the auditor and of insuring that the client realizes this primary responsibility.* . . . There seems to be little or no feeling that the representations of the client . . . reduce the examination the auditor should make or relieve him of his responsibility." (Emphasis added.) ‡

Thus, the practice of obtaining written client representations served the dual purpose of confirming management's oral representations and reinforcing the fact that the financial statements were in fact those of management.

AUDITOR INDEPENDENCE AND SAS NO. 19

SAS No. 19 requires the auditor to obtain certain specific written representations from the client including management's acknowledgement of its responsibility for the financial statements: "Management's refusal to furnish a written representation that the auditor believes is essential constitutes a limitation on the scope of the auditor's examination sufficient to preclude an unqualified opinion." //

Inherent in the audit function is the recognition that the financial statements are those of the one being audited. Management's acknowledgment of this fact is always essential.

---

* Statement on Auditing Standards No. 1, Codification of Auditing Standards and Procedures (New York: AICPA, 1973), Section 560.12(d). Also see SAP No. 47, Subsequent Events (1971); SAP No. 33, Auditing Standards and Procedures (a codification) (1963); and SAP No. 25, Events Subsequent to the Date of Financial Statements (1954).

† Audits by Certified Public Accountants (New York: AIA, 1950), p. 29.

‡ SAP No. 4, Clients' Written Representations Regarding Inventories, Liabilities, and Other Matters (New York: AIA, 1941), p. 26.

// Statement on Auditing Standards No. 19, par. 11.

There is a direct and significant relationship between client responsibility for the financial statements and auditor independence:

"A part of the rationale which underlies any rule on independence is that managerial and decision-making functions are the responsibility of the client and not of the independent accountant. It is felt that if the independent accountant were to perform functions of this nature, he would develop, or appear to develop, a mutuality of interest with his client which would differ only in degree, but not in kind, from that of an employee. And where this relationship appears to exist, it may be logically inferred that the accountant's professional judgment toward the particular client might be prejudiced in that he would, in effect, be auditing the results of his own work, thereby destroying the objectivity sought by shareholders [and credit grantors]. Consequently, the performance of such functions is fundamentally inconsistent with an impartial examination. *However, it is the role of the accountant to advise management and to offer professional advice on their problems. Therefore, the problem posed by this dilemma is to ascertain the point where advice ends and managerial responsibility begins.*" (Emphasis added.) *

One method of delineating the thin line between accounting services and managerial responsibility is to require management to acknowledge in writing its responsibility for the company's books and records and for the information developed from such records.

The conflict between independence and accounting services is a significant one in the relationship of the independent accountant with his small or closely held clients. The relationship is often closer than that which exists between the independent accountant and large, publicly held clients. For the small or closely held business, the independent accountant provides significant financial and accounting services and advice. Therefore, it is essential that the client recognize that although he receives and accepts accounting advice from his accountant, the responsibility for accepting such advice is his.

The AICPA code of professional ethics recognizes the close relationship between the independent accountant and the small or closely held client. In an interpretation of rule 101—the rule pertaining to independence—the code states: "The client must accept the responsibility for the financial statements as his own. A small client may not have anyone in his employ to maintain accounting records and may rely on the CPA for this purpose. Nevertheless, the client must be sufficiently knowledgeable of the enterprise's activities and financial condition and the applicable accounting principles so that he can reasonably *accept such responsibility, including, specifically, fairness of valuation and presentation and adequacy of disclosure. When necessary, the CPA must discuss accounting matters with the client to be sure that the client has the required degree of understanding.*" (Emphasis added.) †

---

* Accounting Series Release 126, "Guidelines and Examples of Situations Involving the Independence of Accountants" (Securities and Exchange Commission, July 1972).

† "Ethics By-laws Quality Control as of July 1, 1977," *AICPA Professional Standards*, vol. 2 (New York: AICPA, 1977), p. 4413.

The interpretation goes on to state that "the CPA, in making an examination of financial statements prepared from books and records which he has maintained completely or in part, *must conform to generally accepted auditing standards.*" (Emphasis added.) *

The independent accountant recommends, perhaps even decides, which generally accepted accounting principles should be applied; he indicates the method of recording certain transactions and, in some engagements, posts to the general ledger of the client. At the conclusion of his work, if he is to express an unqualified opinion on his client's financial statements, the accountant must establish his independence of the client. The client, by means of a written representation, must acknowledge responsibility for the fair presentation of its financial statements in conformity with generally accepted accounting principles. The client, however, may justifiably claim reliance on the accountant for such presentation and refuse to acknowledge his responsibility. The auditor has a duty to his client to educate the client on the nature and extent of the client's responsibility.

ENGAGEMENT LETTERS

It is especially important for the independent accountant to establish early in the engagement that the financial statements which he will report on are those of his client even though he will be the preparer. There is no better instrument for early clarification of this matter than the engagement letter.

Engagement letters are not required by generally accepted auditing standards; however, they are essential for the clear understanding of the services to be rendered by the independent accountant. In the past, they have been used sparingly by accountants with small or closely held clients; however, they are now used more often as accountants have become more aware of the hazards of litigation.

Engagement letters, if properly prepared and presented, improve client relations and avoid client misunderstandings. They enumerate the services to be performed and the responsibilities to be assumed by the independent accountant. They also cover the obligations and responsibilities of the client's accounting staff. However, engagement letters do not always indicate that the financial statements and the accounting principles underlying them are the sole responsibility of management.

Most engagement letters specify the inability of the accountant to uncover all frauds. They specify fee arrangements and terms of payment of such fees, and they indicate that the financial statements of the company will be examined by the accountant to express an opinion on such statements.

Because the engagement letter is the initial formalization of the terms of retention of the accountant by the client, it is suggested that a paragraph such as the following be added to the letter:

"Although we may prepare or help prepare the financial statements of XYZ Corp., these financial statements are solely the representations of management.

---

* Ibid., p. 4414.

Although we may advise as to which accounting principles should be applied to the financial statements and the method of application, the selection and method of application is a determination made solely by management."

The implications and ramifications of the above must be discussed with the client at the time of the signing of the engagement letter.

Although client responsibility for the financial statements must be established at the beginning of the engagement, it must not be allowed to stop at that point. Thus, during the year, as accounting decisions are made, the responsibility for such decisions must be noted and acknowledged.

PROCEDURES DURING THE YEAR

Many decisions about accounting principles are made during the year. Depreciation methods may be determined at the time assets are acquired; decisions to capitalize or to charge to income start-up and similar costs may be made when such costs are incurred; and the method of reporting long-term construction contracts may be determined at inception of the contract. All such decisions should be reviewed with the client, formalized in work sheets and acknowledged by the client. If the application of an accounting principle will have a material effect on the financial statements, it is suggested that the accountant write to the client explaining the principle and its effects and request a return written acknowledgment.

Before starting the engagement, the accountant should prepare a list of the accounting principles that were applied last year and that will be applied during the current year. This list and its implications should be reviewed with the client and his written acknowledgement obtained.

However, many decisions as to appropriate accounting principles are not made until the end of the year. The treatment of investment tax credits, the reporting of long-term leases and the valuation of inventories are examples of such decisions. Again, when these decisions are made, it is of utmost importance that they be acknowledged by the client.

As a final step in the acknowledgment procedure, it is suggested that at year-end a list be prepared of all significant accounting policies applied during the year. The partner in charge of the examination should review this with the client and present the effects of each principle's application. At the conclusion of this meeting, the partner should obtain from the client written acknowledgment that the client reviewed, understood and accepted such principles for application in his financial statements. Since disclosure of accounting policies is required in financial statements, this step can be combined with the review of the financial statements with the client.

DISCLOSURE OF ACCOUNTING PRINCIPLES

Accounting Principles Board Opinion No. 22, *Disclosure of Accounting Policies,* paragraph 8, states: "When financial statements are issued purporting to present fairly financial position, changes in financial position, and results of operations in accordance with generally accepted accounting principles, a description of all significant accounting policies of the reporting entity should be included as an integral part of the financial statements."

In paragraph 12, the opinion states that "disclosure of accounting policies should identify and describe the accounting principles followed by the reporting entity and the methods of applying those principles. . . ." It emphasizes who determines the accounting principles to be applied when, in paragraph 6, it states that "the *accounting policies* of a reporting entity are the specific accounting principles and the methods of applying those principles that are judged by the management of the entity to be the most appropriate in the circumstances to present fairly. . . ."

Thus, it can be seen that disclosure of accounting policies is an integral part of financial statements and that the determination of such accounting policies is the responsibility of management.

Opinion No. 22 merely reinforced that which has been stated in other authoritative literature—the financial statements, and the principles applied in their preparation, are the representations and responsibility of management. Requiring written acknowledgment of this by management merely reduces to writing that which is understood and accepted by most sophisticated users of financial statements. Thus, Opinion No. 22 presents no extra burden. It is a convenient way of assuring that the client reviews, understands and approves significant accounting policies.

THE OFFICIAL ANSWER TO
THE CLENT'S QUESTION

Both generally accepted auditing standards and generally accepted accounting principles recognize the primacy of management's responsibility for financial statements.

Paragraph 11 of the introduction to Accounting Rescearch Bulletin No. 43 emphasizes that underlying the development of all accounting principles is the fact that the accounts of the company and the financial statements it issues are the responsibility of management. Paragraph 6 of Opinion No. 22 acknowledges this concept of management responsibility by noting that accounting principles of a reporting entity are those judged by the management of that entity to be most appropriate in the circumstances. Thus, generally accepted accounting principles clearly establish the concept that financial statements are solely the representation and responsibility of the company.

Auditing literature acknowledges the accounting and advisory services performed by the independent accountant; it also recognizes the dichotomy of these services from its results—the financial statements of the enterprise. Thus, "it should be clearly understood that owners or management are responsible for the financial statements; the auditor is responsible for his report and opinion. . . . The auditor may assist, advise, and persuade management with respect to form and content of financial statements, but he cannot compel management to accept his recommendations." *

* Norman J. Lenhart and Philip L. Defliese, *Montgomery's Auditing*, 8th ed. (New York: The Ronald Press Company, 1957), p. 95. Reprinted by permission of John Wiley & Sons, Inc.

The independent accountant has the additional problem of establishing and maintaining his independence as interpreted under rule 101 of the code of professional ethics. Interpretation 101-3 states that, "with regard to accounting judgments, if third parties have confidence in a member's judgment in performing an audit, it is difficult to contend that they would have less confidence where the same judgment is applied in the process of preparing the underlying accounting records." *

The interpretation clearly recognizes and defends the important internal services provided by the independent accountant. Nonetheless, it emphasizes that the client must accept the responsibility for the financial statements. To obtain this acceptance, the independent accountant must "when necessary, . . . discuss accounting matters with the client to be sure that the client has the required degree of understanding." †

Thus, before expressing an opinion on financial statements, the auditor must formally establish his independence and his client's responsibility for those financial statements. The formal medium for establishing this condition is the client representation letter as described in SAS No. 19.

THE CLOSING CONFERENCE
WITH THE CLIENT

Having concluded your research, you are now ready to return to the client with the representation letter. However, you do recognize that, to some degree, you are at fault. During the year, you did not ascertain that your client had the required degree of understanding about accounting matters. Further, you did not discuss with him the adoption of accounting principles; you decided which principles to adopt. Therefore, you are now prepared to spend a significant amount of time reviewing with the client all significant accounting matters of the past year. You have now modified the client representation letter so that all significant accounting policies are enumerated. These will have to be explained to the client.

Your meeting has been set for late in the afternoon and, as you enter your client's office, you can see a clear desk; it is obvious he is prepared to devote his full attention to the problem at hand.

As you pull photocopies of articles and pronouncements from your briefcase, your client remarks, "I see you're well prepared. What did your research uncover?"

You report the results of your research, giving him copies of articles when appropriate. You conclude by acknowledging your error and handing him the modified representation letter.

The client reads it, pauses for a moment and says, "Okay, let's review it."

Three hours later, exhausted but with the signed representation letter in your briefcase, you prepare to leave. Your client says, "I'm sorry I put you through this, but you accountants created the problem. I always thought that

---

* *AICPA Professional Standards*, vol. 2, p. 4413.
† Ibid.

since you reviewed my records quarterly, maintained subsidiary records in your workpapers, prepared all tax returns and financial statements, and suggested appropriate accounting principles, my financial statements were your responsibility. I am willing to accept your rules, but I think your profession must reach out to people like me—the small business people—to explain to us in nontechnical terms exactly what it is you do and what it is you are responsible for. I assure you that in the future, if the financial statements are my responsibility, you and I will be spending more time together."

CONCLUSION

A long-established belief in practice and in law is that a company's financial statements are the responsibility of management. The AICPA code of professional ethics confronts the problem of auditor independence when accounting services as well as auditing services are provided. The client representation letter, as required by SAS No. 19, is the instrument by which management's responsibility for financial statements is acknowledged and auditor independence is firmly established. The letter gives management a final opportunity to consider the effects of its representations and its decisions on the financial statements. The accounting profession has not been sufficiently vocal in communicating to its major constituency—small business people—the importance and necessity of client representation letters.

It is suggested that the engagement letter, the initial formalization of the terms of retention of the accountant by the client, emphasize the client's responsibility for its financial statements. However, this emphasis is not enough. Throughout the year, it is essential that the accountant and his client discuss the choices of accounting principles and the effects of such choices on the financial statements. This constant communication should ultimately eliminate questions as to who is responsible for the statements. It is the client.[29]

1. Is it ethical for a CPA firm to place an advertisement in the newspapers? In the yellow pages? Are there any restrictions as to the frequency of placement, size, artwork, or type style?

2. Assume that you have a thriving tax practice. Would it be ethical for you to pay a small commission to any present client who refers a new client to you?

3. If you have particular expertise in SEC matters, could you ethically advertise this competence? Could you refer to yourself as a specialist in that area?

[29] Martin Benis, "The Small Client and Representation Letters," *Journal of Accountancy*, Sept. 1978, pp. 78–84. Copyright © 1978 by the American Institute of Certified Public Accountants, Inc.

4. Give six examples of advertising practices that would be prohibited under the AICPA Rules of Conduct.

5. What characteristics must a professional corporation have in order for it to be an acceptable form of practice under the AICPA Code of Ethics?

6. What is the responsibility of an internal professional with respect to management representation letters? What role should such an accounting professional play in connection with the "management report" advocated by the Commission on Auditors' Responsibilities (Cohen commission) and the Financial Executives Institute?

7. Could a CMA working as an internal professional ethically engage in another occupation? Should the CMA, for example, accept management consulting engagements apart from his regular employment?

8. If your firm were a member of the SEC Practice Section of the AICPA Division for Firms, what guidelines would you need to follow in providing executive recruiting services? Can you ethically accept an engagement to search for prospective candidates for managerial positions with your audit clients?

9. State the case for and against retaining management advisory services as an integral part of the public accounting profession. Is there any empirical evidence regarding the independence of an auditor whose firm also provides management advisory services?

10. Is it ethical to practice law and accounting concurrently? What is the view of the American Bar Association?

11. Are financial statements prepared for a small client the statements of management or of the auditor? What responsibility does the auditor have in this regard when dealing with small clients? What role does a client representation letter play?

12. What is an "engagement letter?" Discuss its desirability and usefulness.

SUGGESTED ADDITIONAL READINGS

American Institute of Certified Public Accountants, "Form of Practice and Name," *AICPA Professional Standards,* vol. 2, ET Section 505.

———, "Client Representations," *AICPA Professional Standards,* vol. 1, AU Section 333 (Statement on Auditing Standards No. 19).

"FEI Calls for 'Management Reports' in Annual Reports," *Journal of Accounting,* August 1978.

HOYLE, JOE, "Mandatory Auditor Rotation: The Arguments and an Alternative," *Journal of Accountancy,* May 1978.

OSTLUND, A. CLAYTON, "Advertising—in the Public Interest?" *Journal of of Accountancy,* January 1978.

Public Oversight Board, SEC Practice Section, Division for CPA Firms, *Scope of Services by CPA Firms* (New York: American Institute of Certified Public Accountants).

WOOD, THOMAS D., and DONALD A. BALL, "New Rule 502 and Effective Advertising by CPAs," *Journal of Accountancy,* June 1978.

Part Two

ACCOUNTANTS
AND
THE LAW

The foregoing chapters have been primarily concerned with professional ethics and with the professional responsibilities of members of the accounting profession. While there are some legal aspects to the matters previously discussed, the legal liability of accountants is usually predicated on principles and theories somewhat different than the Code of Professional Ethics. This second part of the text covers these legal aspects of the practice of accounting. In addition, it will be concerned with some of the rights of accountants which are founded on legal principles.

Chapter 7 deals with those aspects of the law of contracts that have special significance to the practicing accountant. It deals with the right of the accountant to be paid for extra services, as well as to be paid when the fee for services has not been agreed upon. It also covers agreements not to compete which may be a part of either an employment contract or articles of partnership between accountants. The legal aspects of exculpatory clauses and disclaimers of liability are also discussed.

No set of problems facing the accounting profession has a greater impact than those relating to malpractice suits. The amount of litigation against accountants has reached significant proportions. Most major accounting firms have been sued either by a client, a lender, or an investor.

The cost of malpractice insurance has skyrocketed in recent years. Chapters 8 and 9 deal with the various theories used by plaintiffs in malpractice litigation. Chapter 8 discusses common law tort theories, and chapter 9 deals with the liability created by the federal securities laws. These chapters emphasize the trend toward increased liability for accountants—liability which may exist even though generally accepted accounting principles have been followed.

In recent years, some accountants have been indicted and convicted of crimes in connection with the performance of their professional duties. Although the cases are relatively few in number, it is essential that all members of the profession recognize that the law has several so-called "white-collar" crimes that are directed at the accounting profession. Chapter 10 discusses the general principles applicable to criminal prosecutions of accountants.

Chapter 11 discusses the law of confidential and privileged communications as it relates to the accountant-client relationship. While there are many similarities between the attorney-client and the accountant-client relationships, the substantial differences in the functions of these professionals have caused the law to differentiate between them in regard to confidentiality with clients. This chapter attempts to create an awareness on the part of all accountants that they usually can be required to testify about matters which they have learned in the course of their professional services. Although a few states have enacted statutory accountant-client privileges, such privileges usually belong only to the client. As a result, they offer little, if any, protection to the accountant.

The last chapter in Part Two deals with a subject that often evokes a negative emotional reaction from members of the accounting profession. Nevertheless, this subject—the unauthorized practice of law by accountants —is of great importance to members of the accounting profession. A significant portion of the education and training of accountants is in the law. Practitioners are called upon daily to answer legal questions and to apply legal principles to the accounting function. This chapter discusses some of the limitations on the giving of legal advice by accountants. While it does not answer the infinite number of questions that may arise in this area, it seeks to create an awareness of the problem and the attitude of the courts when unauthorized practice of law issues are raised by clients and others in litigation.

As the chapters which follow are studied, it should be kept in mind that not all aspects of the topics have been covered. Rather, the attempt is made to illustrate the types of legal problems facing accountants and the accounting profession in today's highly complex litigious society.

Chapter

7

Accountants
and the Law
of Contracts

INTRODUCTION

The general principles of the law of contracts apply to the employment contract between the accountant and the client. Thus, the common law principles relating to offers, acceptances, and consideration determine the basic contract rights and duties of the parties. (The provisions of the Uniform Commercial Code are not applicable since the contract involves services rather than the sale of goods.) The provisions of the statute of frauds relating to contracts of long duration require that all employment contracts that are not possible of full performance within one year from the date of making must be evidenced in writing, the same as other employment contracts of long duration.

While the general principles of contract law govern the accountant-client relationship, there are certain contract problems that require special attention by the profession. In addition to discussing these matters, the chapter will cover the legality of licensing laws and of laws restricting the use of the CPA designation.

THE RIGHT TO COMPENSATION

As a general rule, the right of an accountant to be compensated for services rendered is predicated upon the contract of employment. The accountant will be paid the amount specified in the contract. However, many contracts do not specifically provide for the amount of the fee, and the accountant is frequently called upon to perform services beyond those called for in the original contract. In addition, on occasion, the accountant may withdraw prior to completion of performance. What recovery is available for accountants if no price is specified in their underlying contract for services? Are accountants entitled additional compensation if more work than was originally contemplated is necessary? What compensation is due if the auditor withdraws prior to completion of the work?

If an accountant performs services under a contract in which compensation is not specified, the accountant will not be precluded from recovering for the rendition of the services. The general rule regarding the failure of a contract for work or labor to fix the amount of compensation specifies that the absence of remunerative provisions does not invalidate the contract, since the law implies a promise to pay what the services are reasonably worth. The courts permit recovery on the basis of a theory known as *quantum meruit*. This theory provides that if one performs services for another which are knowingly and voluntarily accepted, and nothing else appears, the law implies a promise on the part of the recipient to pay the reasonable value of the services. Furthermore, where there is an agreement to pay, but the amount involved is unspecified, the person performing the services is entitled to recover on the same theory. One limitation of this theory is that it is not available if payment was not originally expected for the services which were performed. The import of this rule for accountants is that before *quantum meruit* becomes a viable theory of recovery, the accountants must dispel the notion that their services were being rendered gratuitously.

The recovery of compensation in addition to that which is provided by the original contract for services is permissible when the additional services are accepted by the offeree. The fact that a contract fixes compensation for specified services does not preclude recovery on the *quantum meruit* theory for the reasonable value of services rendered and accepted which are extra in the sense that they are not covered by the contract. A factor of vital significance to the determination that additional recovery is permissible is the acceptance by the offeree of the work upon which the plaintiff's demand for additional compensation is based.

In the absence of a voluntary acceptance of the benefits conferred by the performance of work not originally contemplated by the contract, there can be no recovery for extra work performed. Likewise, recovery is not available when the additional work performed was specifically precluded by a provision of the contract. The case which follows is typical of those allowing recovery for additional services, even though there was evidence of negligence by the accountants.

RYAN v. KANNE
170 N.W.2d 395 (Iowa) 1969

LARSON, J.

This action for accounting fees filed by plaintiff-accountants, . . . was tried to the court without a jury and resulted in a judgment against all defendants for accounting services in the sum of $3,434.67. . . .

Plaintiffs' petition, filed June 21, 1966, contained four counts, three of which are relevant to this appeal. In Division I it was alleged that the defendant James A. Kanne was liable to plaintiffs under an oral contract of employment. In Division II plaintiffs alleged the defendant Mid-States Enterprises, Inc., was liable to them as guarantor of the account; and in Division III plaintiffs based their claim against the Kanne Lumber and Supply, Inc. on *quantum meruit*. Defendants' answers denied all material allegations of plaintiffs' petition. . . .

It appears without serious controversy that James A. Kanne owned and operated certain businesses including lumber companies in Carroll and Breda, Iowa, that he had incurred considerable indebtedness in connection therewith, that his accounting procedures left much to be desired, and that he was in need of further financing. It further appears that at the instance of officers of a creditor, the Mid-States Enterprises, Inc., he sought the services of the plaintiffs, who were certified public accountants and directed them to consult Mr. Feldmann of Mid-States, who was also a C.P.A., as to what was necessary in the financial statement requested. Particular attention to the item of Accounts Payable-Trade was directed and became the critical part of plaintiffs' undertaking. Feldmann discussed with Ryan the procedure recommended to determine that item in the accounting, stating, "* * * we agreed that this would be the critical area, that we should do everything possible to find out what payables may exist." The witness Collison also testified, "* * * if I can correctly quote Bob Feldmann, he said, 'Use every conceivable means to determine the accounts payable.'" It appears Ryan agreed to follow the suggested investigative procedure to determine accounts payable, made some efforts to follow it, and guaranteed the accuracy of their statement as to that item within $5,000. He testified he felt very confident his balance sheet was correct within $5,000 at the time it was submitted.

Pursuant to these directions, plaintiffs spent considerable time and effort, as indicated in the itemized statement, Exhibit "A," attached to their petition, in preparing and submitting the contemplated financial statement. The rates charged for such services were admittedly fair and reasonable. . . .

There is substantial evidence to support a finding that Kanne employed the plaintiffs to make an examination for the purpose of preparing a balance sheet with special attention to Accounts Payable-Trade, that during the course of its preparation plaintiffs were advised that the purpose was to obtain additional capital or financing, that plaintiffs knew the balance sheet would be used to promote such financing through loans or incorporation and the sale of stock, that the balance sheet was to properly reflect the amount of the Accounts Payable-Trade, and under the direction of officers of Mid-States Enterprises, Inc., who guaranteed payment for such work, this sum was to be determined by contacting the payees of checks issued during a twelve month period from September 30, 1964, to September 30, 1965, that these services were performed at the instance and request of Kanne and Mid-States Enterprises, Inc., and for the benefit of Kanne Lumber and Supply, Inc., for which plaintiffs are entitled to reasonable compensation. The trial court found the services were rendered as alleged, that all defendants used the balance sheet to their advantage, and granted judgment in the sum of $3,434.67 against all defendants together with interest thereon as provided by law.

That there is substantial competent evidence in this record to sustain the findings as to the accounting claim is not denied, but the parties disagree as to whether the evidence in the record requires a finding that the accountants were so negligent in rendering their services as to make them valueless.

The itemized account introduced in evidence justifies the amount charged and verifies the time spent in performing the contract. Those items were not seriously attacked. Although the charge did substantially exceed the estimate of $500 to $750, plaintiffs were allowed to continue with the work after it became evident that the estimate was too low, and we are satisfied that the court, acting as a jury, did not err in finding plaintiffs' claim for services rendered under the contract was proven. It is also not denied that Kanne Lumber and Supply, Inc., used the plaintiffs' statement to form its corporate character and induce investors to buy stock therein.

In rejecting the valueless contention of defendants, the trial court apparently found the negligence of plaintiffs in investigating, preparing and submitting the financial statement caused no loss or damage to Kanne or Mid-States Enterprises, Inc., that no financial loss to them was claimed or shown, that in fact the audit was used to their advantage. The evidence shows that by the use of the audit Kanne sold his business as contemplated and Mid-States Enterprises, Inc. secured payment of its account against Kanne of $21,898.61. It would seem that as to these defendants the claim for services should not be denied, even though the negligence was greater than minor mistakes in the accounting.

We are well aware of the decisions holding that when it appears the accountants are so negligent in the reporting of facts of such a serious character that the accounting failed in a fundamental and essential particular, the accountants have not furnished the expert and faithful services contracted for and are entitled to no compensation under the contract. See Board of County Com'rs of Allen County v. Baker, 152 Kan. 164, 171, 102 P.2d 1006, 1011, and City of East Grand Forks v. Steele, 121 Minn. 296, 299, 141 N.W. 181, 182, 45 L.R.A., N.S., 205. Both of these cases are actions for damages for breach of contract, and the evidence was clear that the loss to plaintiff was only the accountant's fee. Both recognize minor errors or inaccuracies in the report will not avoid the fee, and that under some circumstances substantial value from the audit may remain in spite of its errors. The trial court concluded that was the situation in the instant case and we accept that determination here.

In any event, we are not inclined to hold as a matter of law that these services were under the circumstances so negligently performed as to be valueless. The trial court's judgment upon the accountants' claim for services rendered against Kanne, Mid-States Enterprises, Inc., and Kanne Lumber and Supply, Inc., is affirmed in the sum of $3,434.67 plus interest and costs. . . .

Withdrawal by accountants prior to the completion of services contracted for occurs from time to time. Withdrawal may result from the discovery of illegal acts by clients or from the discovery of irregularities in financial reports which the client refuses to correct. Accountants may withdraw because of the discovery of conflicts of interest or the discovery of other ethical problems. Finally, an accountant may withdraw simply because of problems arising between the accountant and the client.

The legal rights of an accountant who withdraws from an engagement depend upon the reasons for the withdrawal. If the withdrawal results from a breach of the contract by the client, then the accountant is entitled not only to payment for services rendered prior to the withdrawal, but to damages for the breach of contract. These damages would include the lost profit on the engagement or the unrealized gain which would have been realized from the completion of the engagement. In computing the unrealized gain on the engagement, the cost of performance, which is not required, is deducted from the gross amount due.

Withdrawal may result from conduct of the client which is not in violation of an express provision of the contract. Such conduct may be considered a violation of an implied provision of the contract or the withdrawal may be required by professional ethics. For example, there is an implied provision in every contract that the client will cooperate with the accountant. If the client fails to do so, there is a breach of this implied provision and the accountant is entitled to payment for work performed and to unrealized gains. If withdrawal is required by the ethics of the profession then the continued performance of the contract is contrary to public policy and the accountant is entitled to be paid for the services rendered to the date of the withdrawal. Unless it could be established that ethical considerations constitute a breach of contract by the client, the accountant is not entitled to unrealized gains when the withdrawal is for ethical reasons.

Sometimes continuance of the accountant-client relationship becomes undesirable, though not impossible or illegal. Personality conflicts and differences of opinion may arise which makes withdrawal a desirable alternative. In such cases mutual rescision of the contract should be sought by the accountant. If mutual rescision is obtained, the accountant is entitled to be paid for services rendered to the date of rescision, but neither party has any rights or liabilities after the rescision. All further obligations are cancelled. It is desirable that the engagement letter provides that either party has a right of mutual rescision.

If the client does not agree to mutual rescision and there is no breach of contract or ethically mandated withdrawal, then the accountant will have liability to the client for breach of contract upon withdrawal. This liability will be the additional cost to the client for hiring another accountant to finish the engagement.

In conclusion, it should be recognized that when an accountant agrees to perform various services, but no price is agreed upon, recovery is available under the theory of *quantum meruit* for the reasonable value of the services. If, during the performance of the work, the accountant's initial fee becomes unrealistic in light of various factors which were beyond his control, the accountant is entitled to additional compensation provided that the client voluntarily and knowingly accepts the extra services or permits the accountant to continue work while knowing of the added expense. Similarly, if an accountant is paid for services rendered and it later appears that the services were negligently performed, the client may recover not only the fee paid but actual damages as well. These matters, including negligent breach of contract, are discussed more fully in the next chapter.

AGREEMENTS NOT TO COMPETE

Individuals frequently enter into contracts that contain covenants not to compete. Such provisions are common to employment contracts and to shareholder or partnership buy and sell agreements. They are also found in leases and in contracts for the sale of a business. Employees of accounting firms may be required to sign such an agreement as a condition of employment. In the creation of a partnership, the partners may enter into a mutual agreement not to compete with the firm should a partner leave the practice.

Agreements not to compete are in partial restraint of trade, and thus, they may be illegal. Agreements not to compete must be a part of another contract and must be supported by consideration. A bare agreement by one party not to compete with another is against public policy. For example, if A threatens to open a practice to compete with B, and B offers A $1,000 to agree that he will not do so, such a contract would be illegal.

An agreement that is reasonably necessary for the protection of an accounting practice will be enforced provided the agreement (1) is reasonable in point of time, (2) is reasonable in the area of restraint, (3) is necessary to protect the goodwill of the firm, (4) does not place an undue burden on the covenantor, and (5) does not violate the public interest. The reasonableness of the agreement is determined as of the time the contract was entered into. Each agreement is examined by the court to see if it is reasonable to both parties and to the general public. In the employment situation, whether or not the public is being deprived of the person's skill is a factor to be considered.

The law looks with more favor on these contracts if they involve the partners than it does in the case of such a provision included in an employment contract. The reason courts are more likely to hold the agreements between partners valid as contrasted with employer-employee contracts is that in the former situations, there is more equality of bargaining power than in the latter. A partner could readily refuse to sign an agreement not to compete, whereas an employee seeking a job might feel obliged to sign almost anything in order to gain employment. In addition, it is evident that there is a goodwill factor involved; between partners, goodwill is an asset that deserves protection, whereas in employee-employer situations, it is less evident that the employee is able to create goodwill or take it with him upon termination of his employment.

A few states by statute or by their constitutions have declared agreements that restrict an employee's right to seek other employment to be illegal as a matter of public policy. Some states which allow such contracts except contracts involving professions from those that may be legal. The case which follows discusses the applicability of such statutes to CPAs and to other accountants.

BURKETT v. ADAMS
361 So.2d 1 (Ala.) 1978

JONES, J.

This appeal arises from a judgment holding that a contract containing a non-competition clause was valid and enforceable, and that payments were due pursuant to the agreement. We reverse and remand.

The undisputed facts, stipulated at trial, indicate that on February 1, 1973, Appellee, Bernard L. Adams, was employed by Appellant Ronald E. Burkett, as a public accountant. Thereafter, on March 14, 1973, Adams and Burkett entered into two agreements for the sale of Adams' accounting business and the sale and/or lease of several assets of that business, including its good will. Contained within one of these agreements was a provision that, upon Adams' termination of employment, he would not compete with Burkett and would recommend Burkett to his former clients. In consideration of this agreement, Burkett employed Adams and agreed to pay certain sums after termination of his employment. Burkett's contract to purchase certain of the physical assets of Adams' business is not in dispute.

Adams voluntarily terminated the employment effective August 11, 1973. Burkett, in compliance with the contract, paid several installments on the purchase price. After Adams prepared five 1974 income tax returns for former clients in the area, however, Burkett discontinued his payments. Adams received no payments for the returns he prepared and expects no such remuneration.

The peculiar posture of this action is apparent when it is understood that Adams filed suit to enforce the contract and recover sums due thereunder. It is Burkett who asserts the invalidity of the contract because it violates Tit. 9, 22, Code, and is void as a restraint on trade. In support of this contention, he argues that a public accountant is a professional and, as such, is not included within the exceptions stated in Tit. 9, 23, Code. Therefore, the contract would be covered by 22 and would be void.

The primary question which we must address, then, is whether the practice of "public accounting" is a "'profession" as that term is understood in the law. It appears this is a question of first impression and authorities from other jurisdictions are of little help because our statutes in this regard are, to a certain extent, unique.

It is well settled that contracts in restraint of trade are looked upon with disfavor. Furthermore, even a specific covenant not to compete in a profession, trade, or business is void except within the limitations imposed by Tit. 9, 23, and 24, Code. Because the term "profession" is not included within 23, and 24, a contract restraining the practice of a profession is void under 22. Thus, should we determine that the practice of public accounting is a profession, the contract presently under consideration must be held void.

We have previously held that the practice of accounting by a certified public accountant is a profession. This is not necessarily controlling here, however, because the question here presented concerns a "public accountant" not a C.P.A.

The record before us discloses no difference in the duties and capabilities between the two occupations.

Though several definitions of the term "profession" may be espoused, we can find no better definition than the following observation of the late Dean Roscoe Pound:

> "There is much more in a profession than a traditionally dignified calling.
> "The term refers to a group of men pursuing a learned art as a common calling in the spirit of public service—no less a public service because it may incidentally be a means of livelihood. Pursuit of the learned art is the purpose. Gaining a livelihood is incidental, whereas, in a business or trade it is the entire purpose. . . ."

Obviously, too, however, this definition is not dispositive.

In a case dealing with the revocation of a C.P.A.'s certification, we have previously stated:

"The rights of complainant in this case are unlike the rights of a physician, surgeon, dentist, lawyer, or school-teacher to practice their callings or professions. Under the law, they cannot practice without a certificate or license; and when their license or certificate is revoked, they are thereby prevented from practicing their profession at all. In the case of accountants, however, this is not true. They are not required to obtain a certificate or license to practice their calling, but obtaining the license or certificate is purely voluntary on their part. Nor does the revocation or cancellation of the license or certificate, when once issued, bar or deprive them from further or longer practicing their chosen calling. The license in their case is but a certificate of the board issuing it as to their competency and fitness. It is not at all a requisite to the practice of their calling, though it may be true, and doubtless is, that the certificate of license, being an authoritative recommendation or certification of a legally constituted board as to efficiency and qualifications, has some value."

Though not controlling, the above quote is instructive as to the distinction between a public accountant and a C.P.A. Certainly, a C.P.A. may be entitled, because of such status, to perform services not properly performed by a public accountant. But the close association and similarity of services performed by the two callings indicate that both could, and should, be considered together. Therefore, because we have previously held that the practice of accounting by a C.P.A. was a profession, we see no reason to prevent deeming public accounting likewise a profession. As such, the contract here under consideration, because it restricted Appellee's practice of his chosen profession, is void under Tit. 9, 22, Code. The Court will not interfere at the suit of either, but the parties are left where they have placed themselves.

Reversed and remanded.

In those states where agreements not to compete may be legal, a restrictive covenant that is unreasonable, is nevertheless illegal. The court in such cases leaves the parties where it finds them. In other words, the party who agreed not to compete is allowed to do so. However, if the restriction exceeds what is reasonably necessary, a few courts will reform the contract so as to make the restrictions reasonable.

In most states, if the covenant is silent in either the length of the restraint or on the area, the agreement is illegal. A few states will supply the missing element by prescribing a reasonable time or area however.

Covenants not to compete arise when a practice is sold also. Such agreements may cover the sale of a professional practice as well as the sale of a commercial business. The law makes little distinction between the agreements of professionals and those of tradesmen in the sale cases. Contracts for the sale of a practice are usually not subject to state laws declaring covenants not to compete to be illegal. Such statutes usually only cover employees and a seller's covenant is beyond the extent of the law.

The case which follows is typical of those in which an employee of an accounting firm has entered into an agreement not to compete with his employer.

FAW, CASSON & CO. v. CRANSTON
Del. Ch., 375 A.2d 463 (1977)

MARVEL, C.

This is an action for injunctive relief against a former employee in the form of a permanent injunction against such employee's alleged violation of a covenant not to compete with plaintiff prior to December 1, 1978 (such covenant being allegedly contained in defendant's employment contract), as well as for damages. . . .

Faw, Casson & Co. is a public accounting firm having offices in Dover, Salisbury, Easton and Ocean City, all on the Delmarva Peninsula. The defendant is a certified public accountant who was first employed by plaintiff as a staff accountant in November of 1971. In the latter part of November, 1975 defendant was offered a promotion from staff accountant to manager of plaintiff's office in Dover, a position of greater authority involving the organization of accounting work and the supervision of staff accountants. Defendant was informed that if he were to accept the promotion to manager, he would receive a salary increase of $2,000 per annum and would be required to sign an agreement not to compete against plaintiff in the business of accounting prior to December 1, 1978.

The defendant began to work in his new position as manager for the plaintiff on or about December 1, 1975, however, he did not sign the agreement not to compete until the end of January, 1976, at which time the agreement was back dated on December 1, 1975. During the interim, discussions apparently took place between the parties concerning the force and effect of the agreement not to compete after December, it being contended by defendant that he was told by Raymond D. Falconetti, a partner in the plaintiff firm, and who had reported the terms of his promotion to defendant, that the agreement was not enforceable.

Defendant left the employment of the plaintiff in October of 1976 when he resigned to open his own public accounting office in Dover, Delaware. Subsequently, a number of plaintiff's clients, who had been accustomed to consulting defendant for the most part as to their accounting problems, ceased doing business with the plaintiff and transferred their accounts from plaintiff to the defendant, resulting in the present litigation.

The agreement between the parties, which contains defendant's alleged covenant not to compete, takes the form of a letter addressed to the defendant and signed by Mr. Falconetti on behalf of the plaintiff. The text of the letter provides in its entirety:

"The Firm is pleased that you have accepted the position of Manager and we are proud to recognize your accomplishment.

"In discussing this position with you, we stated that the partnership would like to have an agreement from you stating you would refrain from practicing public accounting on the Delmarva Peninsula other than with Faw, Casson & Co. until December 1, 1978. Your signature on this letter will confirm our agreement."

Following the signature of Mr. Falconetti is a line to the effect . . . "* * The above terms are agreeable * * *", followed by a space for the signature of Mr. Cranston, which thereafter was affixed.

Plaintiff contends that the agreement of the defendant not to compete is an enforceable contractual provision, the breach of which entitles it to injunctive relief. Defendant's opposition to such contention is based on three basic arguments, made in the alternative, (1) that the letter in question does not constitute a binding contract; (2) that the agreement contained therein is unenforceable because of a failure of consideration; and (3) that the agreement is unreasonable. . . .

In general, an agreement by an employee not to follow his trade or business for a limited time and in a limited geographical area is not void as against public policy when the purpose of such agreement and its reasonable effect is to protect an employer from sustaining damages which an employee's subsequent competition may cause. However, such covenants are subject to somewhat greater scrutiny when contained in an employment contract as opposed to contracts for the sale of a business. . . .

The formal elements in an agreement not to compete are the same as those required for a contract in general, namely a mutual assent to the terms of the agreement by all parties and the existence of consideration. . . .

I conclude that defendant's act of signing the letter provided written confirmation of his agreement not to compete with the defendant for the period specified. Any other conclusion would directly contradict the two sentences which precede his signature. . . .

Defendant's argument that the letter in issue is ambiguous and does not represent a manifestation of mutual assent to definite terms is not persuasive.

Plaintiff's second argument namely that the agreement is unenforceable because of a failure of consideration is largely based upon the fact that the defendant began work as a manager on or about December 1, 1975, or about two months before he signed the letter agreement. Defendant urges that contracts not to compete entered into by an employee after he has already commenced work with an employer are not supported by consideration, citing . . . (a case) in which it was stated that:

"It is generally agreed that mutual promises of employer and employee furnish valuable considerations each to the other for the contract. However, when the relationship of employer and employee is already established without a restrictive covenant, any agreement thereafter not to compete must be in the nature of a new contract based upon a new consideration.

Therefore, the employer could not call for a covenant not to compete without compensating for it."

There also exists, however, a corollary to the principle enunciated in the cases upon which defendant relies, namely that a beneficial change in an employee's status may constitute sufficient consideration to support a restrictive covenant agreed to after the initial taking of employment.

Thus, it is clear that all of the terms of defendant's promotion were set forth fully at the time it was offered to him and the need for an agreement not to compete was not an afterthought sought to be imposed after the original proposal. Secondly, although the defendant began serving in the position of manager prior to the time when he signed the agreement not to compete, there is no evidence of a waiver on the part of the plaintiff of its right to a non-competition agreement as a condition precedent to promotion. Indeed, the plaintiff remained free to decline to accept such promotion. Moreover, there is evidence in the record of discussions between the plaintiff and defendant during the interim between the time when defendant began serving as manager and when he signed the letter of such a nature as to bring to defendant's attention that acceptance of the agreement was prerequisite to permanent retention of the position of manager. I therefore conclude that the agreement not to compete was an integral part of the overall promotion agreement and an element of consideration tendered by the defendant in exchange for his promotion to the position as manager and that a failure of consideration did not occur in the present case.

The third argument made by defendant is that the agreement is unenforceable in that any restraint of trade is generally held to be unreasonable if (a) it is greater than is required for the protection for which the restraint is imposed, or (b) it imposes undue hardship upon the restricted person, the modern rule being that a restrictive covenant should be enforced only to the extent that it is reasonable so to do.

Defendant argues that the covenant not to compete here in issue is excessively broad in that it restricts plaintiff from accepting rather than from actively soliciting former clients. However, I find such distinction to be without merit, one of the purposes of such a covenant being to protect the employer from loss of business arising out of an employee's profitable association with the former employer's clientele. Damages of this type occur as well whether an employer's clients are solicited or merely accepted by a former employee.

Defendant also argues that as a matter of public policy a restrictive covenant should be held per se unreasonable when applied to certified public accountants. On this point, defendant relies upon the New Jersey opinion of Dwyer v. Jung, 133 N.J.Super. 343 (Ch. Div.), (1975), in which the covenant involved had to do with the restricting of competition between former members of a law firm for a period of five years following such firm's dissolution. Such restrictive covenant was held to be void as against public policy. Defendant argues that this conclusion should be extended to similar covenants involving accountants.

While the opinion in Dwyer v. Jung, supra, speaks in general terms, the decision appears to be predicated on the provisions of DR2-108(A) of the

Disciplinary Rules of the Code of Professional Responsibility of the American Bar Association which expressly prohibits agreements between lawyers which restrict the right of a lawyer to practice law after the termination of an employment relationship. . . .

However, no comparable provision regulates the conduct of accountants. Indeed, testimony was adduced at trial to the effect that a substantial number of accounting firms utilize agreements such as the one in issue here and that such agreements are not considered to be unethical in the accounting profession.

Furthermore, several cases have upheld and enforced agreements not to compete when concerned with accountants. See Ebbeskotte v. Tyler, 127 Ind. App. 433, 142 N.E.2d 905 (1957), Scott v. Gillis, 197 N.C. 223, 148 S.E. 315 (1929), and Racine v. Bender, 141 Wash. 606, 252 P. 115 (1927). Each of these decisions recognizes that an accounting firm has a substantial interest in protecting its business from former employees who have gained knowledge of its clients and internal operations and who thereafter engaged in a competing practice. The policy underlying such decisions is well stated in the case of Ebbeskotte v. Tyler, supra, as follows:

"Courts scrutinize carefully all contracts limiting a man's natural right to follow any trade or profession anywhere he pleases and in any lawful manner. But it is just as important to protect the enjoyment of an establishment in trade or profession, which its possessor has built up by his own honest application to every day duty and the faithful performance of the tasks which every day imposes upon the ordinary man. What one creates by his own labor is his. Public policy does not intend that another than the producer shall reap the fruits of labor. Rather it gives to him who labors the right by every legitimate means to protect the fruits of his labor and secure the enjoyment of them to himself. 'Freedom to contract must not be unreasonably abridged. Neither must the right to protect by reasonable restrictions that which a man by industry, skill, and good judgment was built up, be denied.' "

Defendant next argues that the geographic area encompassed by the covenant in question, namely the Delmarva Peninsula, is unreasonably broad. As noted above, the plaintiff firm maintains offices in Easton, Salisbury and Ocean City, Maryland, and in Dover, Delaware. Thus, such offices are well dispersed throughout the peninsula, which contains virtually all of Delaware and the eastern shores of Maryland and Virginia rather than being concentrated in a section of such area. It may be assumed, therefore, that the plaintiff firm possesses the capability to serve clients throughout the area which is the subject matter of the agreement, and defendant has failed to prove that enforcement of the agreement of the Delmarva Peninsula would be an unreasonable restraint of trade in light of the nature of the business here involved.

However, determination of just where the northern border of the area to be protected lies is not without difficulty since the point at which a peninsula begins and ends is unclear. In this case I conclude that the agreement not to compete should not be enforced so as to prohibit business activities of the

defendant in competition with plaintiff taking place north of the Chesapeake
and Delaware Canal, such division line representing a practical division line
between northern Delaware and the Delmarva Peninsula.

Plaintiff's prayer for an order enjoining defendant from practicing public
accounting on the Delmarva Peninsula, as above defined, in competition with
plaintiff until December 1, 1978 will be granted and the case set down for a
hearing on the extent of plaintiff's damages.

An appropriate form of order may be submitted on notice.

What course of action should the employer follow in those instances
in which an employee who had signed a restrictive covenant nevertheless
competes directly or goes to work for a competitor? The employer, not
desiring the publicity and inconvenience of a lawsuit, may refrain from
taking action in the hope that the former employee's new activities will not
adversely affect his practice. If he ultimately finds that the employee's
competition is creating an adverse effect, he may decide to institute suit or
action against his former employee. If suit is instituted to enjoin the employee from this competitive activity, the employee may contend that by
failing to raise the issue promptly when the breach occurred, the employer
has waived his rights. The point may be a good one, since an employer
should not allow his former employee to expend money or otherwise materially alter his position by establishing a business or going to work for
another firm and then seek to prevent his action by attempting to enforce
the contract. The doctrines of estoppel and waiver can thus frequently be
used by an employee to prevent the use in equity of the contract rights to
which the employer would otherwise have been entitled. Equity does not
favor a party who "sleeps on his rights," and the failure to promptly seek
enforcement of the agreement may very well preclude its enforcement.

EXCULPATORY CLAUSES, DISCLAIMERS, AND QUALIFICATIONS

A party to a contract frequently includes a clause that provides that the
party has no tort liability even if at fault. Such a clause is commonly called
an exculpatory clause. For example, an accountant may attempt to negate
or limit his liability for negligence in the preparation of audit reports or
financial statements. These disclaimers of liability are not favored by the
law and are strictly construed against the party relying on them. They are
frequently declared to be illegal by courts as contrary to public policy.

Accountants may include an attempt to avoid tort liability in an employment contract, or they may preface their reports or statements with
disclaimers or other like qualifiers. What is the legal effect of such attempts?

Although there are no known cases testing the validity of exculpatory clauses contained in accountants' underlying contracts of employment, courts confronted with this issue would likely conclude that such clauses are against public policy and are therefore void. The general rule regarding the inclusion of exculpatory clauses in contracts is that private contracts exculpating one from the consequences of his own acts are looked upon with disfavor by the courts and will be enforced only when there is no vast disparity in the bargaining power between the parties and the intention to do so is expressed in clear and unequivocal language. Thus, even though most states have no statutory provisions covering accountant's exculpatory clauses, such clauses often will be invalidated because their enforcement would be contrary to public policy.

An exculpatory clause for an accountant engaged in the audit function will generally be found to contravene the public's interest because the profession is of the type generally thought suitable for public regulation and the party seeking exculpation is engaged in performing a service of great importance to the public. Moreover, because of the essential nature of the service, in the economic setting of the transaction, the party invoking exculpation possesses a decisive advantage when dealing with any member of the public who seeks his services. The client often must have an audit to comply with the law or the legitimate needs of the business community. If all accountants sought to contract upon the same terms, the client would be forced to agree to them. This inequality of bargaining power when coupled with the public interest aspect of the service eliminates freedom of contract and requires the court to set aside such provisions. This reasoning would certainly be applicable if the audit were required by the S.E.C.

Since exculpatory clauses are permissible except when statutory provisions or public policy provide otherwise, it is often argued that individual accountants who are self-employed and smaller accounting firms should be able to include exculpatory clauses in contracts for their services. Such an assertion is based on the fact that equality of bargaining power does exist. An analogous situation occurred when a federal district court upheld the validity of a clause that exempted a credit agency from liability for loss or injury caused by its negligence in procuring, compiling, collecting, interpreting, communicating or delivering information. The district court found that neither a special legal relationship existed nor was there any overriding public interest present, and the contract had been entered into voluntarily by competent parties.[1]

Obviously when an exculpatory clause is held to be void, it cannot be used to absolve accountants from liability to their clients or to third persons if the accountant owes a duty to that third party. A difficult issue arises

[1] Hong Kong Export Credit Ins. v. Dun & Bradstreet, 414 F. Supp. 153 (S.D.N.Y. 1975).

when it is found that the accountant owes duty of care to third persons, and the exculpatory clause between the accountant and the other contradicting party is considered to be valid. Whether or not the effects of the exculpatory clause extends to the third persons is contingent upon the theory used by the court for finding the accountant liable to the third party. If a third-party beneficiary to a contract approach is taken, then the beneficiary is subject to all the equities and defenses that would be available against the promisee. On the other hand, if the duty to the third person arose independently of the contract, the exculpatory clause should have no application with regard to the third party since, as a general rule, a person who is not named in a contract has not executed it, is not a party to the contract, and is therefore not bound by its terms.

The effectiveness of qualifications or disclaimers in accountants' certificates has generally been litigated in the context of injuries to third persons who relied on these certificates. The following is one of the leading cases on this issue. It left the effect of the disclaimer to the jury.

C.I.T. FINANCIAL CORPORATION v. GLOVER
224 F.2d 44 (1955)

CLARK, J.

The plaintiff, Commercial Investment Trust Financial Corporation (C.I.T.), sued the firm of Barrow, Wade, Guthrie & Co. (B.W.G.), certified public accountants, to recover for losses incurred by plaintiff through the bankruptcy of its debtor, Manufacturers Trading Corporation (M.T.C.), in October, 1948. In the course of its lending business plaintiff had lent M.T.C. some $1,440,000 on October 17, 1945, and failed to call in its loan thereafter, in alleged reliance on defendants' statements concerning the financial condition of M.T.C. The complaint stated five different causes of action, alleging negligence and gross negligence in pre-loan and post-loan audits, and also charging, in a fifth count, concealment of prior errors in each subsequent audit. Plaintiff's appeal does not contest the propriety of Judge Ryan's action in dismissing the first and fifth counts, but instead concentrates its attack on the jury verdict for the defendants on the remaining counts.

In response to special interrogatories, the jury found that plaintiff had established defendants' duty to it under the second and fourth counts relating to gross negligence, but not on the third count, which had charged ordinary negligence in the post-loan audits. On all three counts the jury further concluded that plaintiff had failed to prove defendants' representations false or misleading in any material respect. It is this latter finding which resulted in the defendants' verdict that the plaintiff particularly attacks on this appeal as erroneous in law and in fact.

The contentions of the parties as to the facts can be briefly summarized as follows. Plaintiff claimed that defendants' audits were fatally inadequate for failure to disclose overvaluation of M.T.C.'s loans to its debtors. Plaintiff argued that defendants should have pointed out the necessity for larger reserves due to the stagnancy of certain collateral, and due to its concentration in certain types of merchandise and in certain individual debtors, including Joseph Sachs, the brother of M.T.C.'s president, Alfred H. Sachs. This was the gist of the complaint, although reference was also made to alleged misclassification of particular items as accounts receivable, rather than as inventory loans.

The defense relied on the special nature of M.T.C.'s business and on plaintiff's knowledge of this. Defendants maintained that M.T.C. in its financial transactions had always relied primarily on the borrower's collateral, rather than on his general financial condition. Accurate appraisal of the value of such collateral in the event of the debtor's not infrequent insolvency and bankruptcy was always extremely difficult, and M.T.C.'s past income had resulted from Alfred H. Sachs' peculiar genius in such valuation. Defendants claimed that they had never asserted their own special competence to make such appraisals, but that they had inserted in their audit reports appropriate disclaimers qualifying their general assertions about M.T.C.'s financial stability. Further, they claimed that M.T.C.'s business was such that accountants had to rely to a great extent on management statements about the nature and the value of the collateral, and that, since the audit reports disclosed this reliance, defendants were not liable for whatever factual errors might have occurred. In addition, the defense asserted the factual correctness of the audits as made and claimed that plaintiff's inquiries of Sachs in response thereto showed adequate disclosure of M.T.C.'s weaknesses.

On all these points there was a sharp conflict of testimony. However we might ourselves have resolved this conflict, we cannot say that the jury's verdict was so clearly mistaken as to warrant reversal unless some error of law was committed.

In this connection the plaintiff strongly urges that the jury's verdict must have been based on the defendants' disclaimer, and that this issue should have been decided by the judge as a matter of law in plaintiff's favor. Each audit report had a disclaimer in these or similar words: "While it was not within our province to pass upon or assume responsibility for the legal or equitable title to the commercial receivables purchased by the companies or the valuation of any security thereto accepted and held by them, it was apparent from their books and records and by opinion of counsel, that their contractual and assignment forms are adequate for their legal protection in connection with the collection and liquidation of commercial receivables purchased." Plaintiff asserts that, as a matter of law, this disclaimer was limited to denying responsibility for the valuation of collateral and that, as a matter of law, defendants' responsibility for the valuation of receivables was unaffected by the disclaimer. But the jury could reasonably find that this dichotomy between face value and collateral was meaningless in the kind of transactions in which M.T.C. had been engaged, and that this fact had been adequately brought home to plaintiff, with the result that the disclaimer applied to the valuation of both collateral and receivables. With a proper charge, as given, the meaning of the disclaimer was therefore correctly left to the jury. . . .

Plaintiff argues vigorously the importance of this case in holding accountants to strict liability for their audits, and, in effect, for increasing that liability. But we do not believe we should attempt to go beyond the standards of the market place, as reflected in current judicial decisions. So when, after a fair and carefully conducted trial under existing law, a jury was found for the defendants, the function of the courts should be considered fulfilled.

Judgment affirmed.

In a similar case the courts of Georgia held that an accountant was not liable to third parties for negligence in the preparation and issuance of an uncertified financial statement, which contained an express disclaimer of opinion.[2] The disclaimer consisted of the following language:

> Disclaimer of Opinion. We are not independent with respect to Airway's Rent-A-Car of Atlanta, and the accompanying balance sheet as of March 31, 1970 and the related statement of income and accumulated deficit for the three months then ended were not audited by us; accordingly, we do not express an opinion on them.

However, courts have held that disclaimers under certain circumstances will not avoid liability.[3] For example, one court held that the fact that a public accounting firm issued only a qualified opinion as to the completeness and accuracy of its audit did not permit the firm to escape liability to a bank that had relied upon these negligently prepared audit reports in loaning money to the firm's client. When the accountants transmitted the financial statements to their client they wrote a covering letter expressing certain reservations about the "fairness of the accompanying statements." They further stated that "our examination included a general review of accounting procedures and such tests of accounting records as we were permitted to make." After it was established that this particular firm knew that the plaintiff would be relying on its report, the court stated that the qualifications to the audit report failed to indicate the true extent of knowledge and investigation by the accountants. Hence this attempted qualificaion could not be utilized to insulate the accountants from liability.

This case does not mean that qualifications are inadequate insulation against liability, but rather that qualifications can preclude liability only if

---

[2] MacNerland v. Barnes, 129 Ga.App. 367, 199 S.E.2d (1973).

[3] Rhode Island Hospital Trust Nat. Bank v. Swartz, Bresenoff, Yarner & Jacobs, 455 F.2d 847 (4th Cir. 1972).

certain criteria are met. If the accountants had conformed with the procedures enumerated in the AICPA Statement on Auditing Procedures No. 33 (1963) regarding the proper content of qualifications, they would probably have escaped liability.

The Supreme Court of another state took a harsher approach when it held that an accounting firm's arguments lacked merit.[4] The firm had argued that no liability to third parties should attach since the issued financial statement was not certified and since they affirmatively stated that "they expressed no opinion." The court concluded that liability must be dependent upon the accountants' undertaking, not their rejection of dependability. The court further held that the accountants could not escape liability for negligence by a general statement that they disclaimed liability.

From the foregoing we must conclude that there is no hard and fast rule controlling the validity of exculpatory clauses, disclaimers, and qualifications. In the absence of statutory provisions governing the result in a particular situation, courts will balance policy considerations. Generally, exculpatory clauses are not favored, especially when the party seeking to exclude liability maintains a superior bargaining position. Qualifications and disclaimers, if properly formulated, stand a chance of withstanding a plaintiff's challenge since they will sufficiently alert the relying party of particular deficiencies. On the other hand, the underlying purpose of the audit report or financial statement will be defeated if a person is told that he cannot reasonably rely on these materials. In those situations where accountants attempt to negate liability, important policy considerations must be weighed in determining the legality of such exculpatory clauses.

FIXING THE PRICE OF SERVICES

The U.S. economy is supposed to be a competitive one. In order to foster competition and to obtain the benefits of competition, Congress has enacted various statutes commonly referred to as the antitrust laws. The basic federal antitrust law is the Sherman Act which was passed in 1890. The Sherman Act prohibits contracts and conspiracies in restraint of trade or commerce. The most common example of such a contract or conspiracy is price-fixing or, in the case of accountants, agreements to fix fees.

The Sherman Act contains three legal sanctions of importance to accountants. First, it is a federal felony for any person or corporation to violate the act's provisions. An individual found guilty may be fined up to $100,000 and imprisoned up to three years. (A corporation found guilty may be fined up to a million dollars for each offense.) Second, the Sherman Act empowers courts to grant injunctions to prevent violations of

---

[4] Ryan v. Kanne, 170 N.W.2d 395 Iowa, 1969, supra, 193.

its provisions. The third and perhaps most important remedy affords relief to those persons who have been injured by another's violation of the act. Such victims are given the right, in a civil action, to collect three times the damages they have suffered, plus court costs and reasonable attorney's fees. The treble damage provision employs the remedy of damages as a means of both punishing the defendant for his wrongful act and compensating the plaintiff for his actual injury. The treble damage provision allows one's competitors as well as the injured members of the general public to enforce the law if government fails to do so.

Price-fixing or bid-rigging is said to be illegal *per se*. When an activity is illegal *per se*, proof that the activity is unreasonable or that it has anti-competitive effects is not required. Proof of the activity is proof of a violation. Since all price-fixing agreements are illegal *per se*, it is no defense that the prices fixed are fair or reasonable. It is no defense that price-fixing is engaged in by small competitors to allow them to compete with larger competitors. In addition, it is just as illegal to fix a low price as it is to fix a high price.

For many years it was argued that the Sherman Act covered only the sale of goods and that an agreement to fix the price of services was not covered by the law. That contention was rejected in the mid-1970s. Today, it is just as illegal to fix the price of services as it is to fix the price of goods. Price-fixing in the service sector has been engaged in by professional persons as well as by service occupations such as automobile and TV repair workers, barbers, and refuse collectors. For many years it was contended that there was a learned profession exception to the Sherman Act. The case which follows has ushered in a new era in the law of price-fixing as it relates to services. Although it establishes a rule for lawyers, the same arguments are applicable to other professions, including accounting.

GOLDFARB ET UX. v. VIRGINIA STATE BAR ET AL.
95 S.Ct. 2004 (1975)

BURGER, C. J.

We granted certiorari to decide whether a minimum fee schedule for lawyers published by the Fairfax County Bar Association and enforced by the Virginia State Bar violates § 1 of the Sherman Act, 15 U.S.C. § 1. The Court of Appeals held that, although the fee schedule and enforcement mechanism substantially restrained competition among lawyers, publication of the schedule by the County Bar was outside the scope of the Act because the practice of law is not "trade or commerce," and enforcement of the schedule by the State Bar was exempt from the Sherman Act as state action as defined in Parker v. Brown, 317 U.S. 341 (1943).

In 1971 petitioners, husband and wife, contracted to buy a home in Fairfax County, Virginia. The financing agency required them to secure title insurance; this required a title examinaton, and only a member of the Virginia State Bar could legally perform that service. Petitioners therefore contacted a lawyer who quoted them the precise fee suggested in a minimum fee schedule published by respondent Fairfax County Bar Association; the lawyer told them that it was his policy to keep his charges in line with the minimum fee schedule which provided for a fee of 1% of the value of the property involved. Petitioners then tried to find a lawyer who would examine the title for less than the fee fixed by the schedule. They sent letters to 36 other Fairfax County lawyers requesting their fees. Nineteen replied, and none indicated that he would charge less than the rate fixed by the schedule; several stated that they knew of no attorney who would do so.

The fee schedule the lawyers referred to is a list of recommended minimum prices for common legal services. Respondent Fairfax County Bar Association published the fee schedule although, as a purely voluntary association of attorneys, the County Bar has no formal power to enforce it. Enforcement has been provided by respondent Virginia State Bar which is the administrative agency through which the Virginia Supreme Court regulates the practice of law in that State; membership in the State Bar is required in order to practice in Virginia. Although the State Bar has never taken formal disciplinary action to compel adherence to any fee schedule, it has published reports condoning fee schedules, and has issued two ethical opinions indicating fee schedules cannot be ignored. The most recent opinion states that "evidence that an attorney *habitually* charges less than the suggested minimum fee schedule adopted by his local bar association raises a presumption that such lawyer is guilty of misconduct. . . ."

Because petitioners could not find a lawyer willing to charge a fee lower than the schedule dictated they had their title examined by the lawyer they had first contacted. They then brought this class action against the State Bar and the County Bar alleging that the operation of the minimum fee schedule, as applied to fees for legal services relating to residential real estate transactions, constitutes price fixing in violation of §1 of the Sherman Act. Practitioners sought both injunctive relief and damages. . . .

(The Court then reviewed the decisions of the lower courts which had resulted in a denial of relief to petitioners.)

We granted certiorari, and are thus confronted for the first time with the question of whether the Sherman Act applies to services performed by attorneys in examining titles in connection with financing the purchase of real estate.

Our inquiry can be divided into four steps: did respondents engage in price fixing? If so, are their activities in interstate commerce or do they affect interstate commerce? If so, are the activities exempt from the Sherman Act because they involve a "learned profession?" If not, are the activities "state action" within the meaning of Parker v. Brown and therefore exempt from the Sherman Act?

The County Bar argues that because the fee schedule is merely advisory, the schedule and its enforcement mechanism do not constitute price fixing. Its purpose, the argument continues, is only to provide legitimate information to aid member lawyers in complying with Virginia professional regulations. Moreover, the County Bar contends that in practice the schedule has not had the effect of producing fixed fees. The facts found by the trier belie these contentions, and nothing in the record suggests these findings lack support.

A purely advisory fee schedule issued to provide guidelines, or an exchange of price information without a showing of an actual restraint on trade, would present us with a different question. The record here, however, reveals a situation quite different from what would occur under a purely advisory fee schedule. Here a fixed, rigid price floor arose from respondents' activities: every lawyer who responded to petitioners' inquiries adhered to the fee schedule, and no lawyer asked for additional information in order to set an individualized fee. The price information disseminated did not concern past standards, but rather minimum fees to be charged in future transactions, and those minimum rates were increased over time. The fee schedule was enforced through the prospect of professional discipline from the State Bar, and the desire of attorneys to comply with announced professional norms, the motivation to conform was reinforced by the assurance that other lawyers would not compete by underbidding. This is not merely a case of an agreement that may be inferred from an exchange of price information, for here a naked agreement was clearly shown, and the effect on prices is plain.

Moreover, in terms of restraining competition and harming consumers like petitioners the price-fixing activities found here are unusually damaging. A title examination is indispensable in the process of financing a real estate purchase, and since only an attorney licensed to practice in Virginia may legally examine a title, consumers could not turn to alternative sources for the necessary service. All attorneys, of course, were practicing under the constraint of the fee schedule. . . . These factors coalesced to create a pricing system that consumers could not realistically escape. On this record respondent's activities constitute a classic illustration of price fixing.

The County Bar argues, as the Court of Appeals held, that any effect on interstate commerce caused by the fee schedule's restraint on legal services was incidental and remote. In its view the legal services, which are performed wholly intrastate, are essentially local in nature and therefore a restraint with respect to them can never substantially affect interstate commerce. Further, the County Bar maintains, there was no showing here that the fee schedule and its enforcement mechanism increased fees, and that even if they did there was no showing that such an increase deterred any prospective homeowner from buying in Fairfax County.

These arguments misconceive the nature of the transactions at issue and the place legal services play in those transactions. As the District Court found, "a significant portion of funds furnished for the purchasing of homes in Fairfax County comes from without the State of Virginia," and "significant amounts of loans on Fairfax County real estate are guaranteed by the United States Veterans Administration and Department of Housing and Urban Development, both headquartered in the District of Columbia." Thus in this class action the transactions which create the need for the particular legal services in question frequently are interstate transactions. The necessary connection between the interstate transactions and the restraints of trade provided by the minimum fee schedule is present because, in a particular sense, title examinations are necessary in real estate transactions to assure a lien on a valid title of the borrower. In financing realty purchases lenders require, "as a condition of making the loan, that the title to the property involved be examined. . . ." Thus a title examination is an integral part of an interstate transaction and this Court has long held that there is an obvious distinction to be drawn between a course of conduct wholly within a state and conduct which is an inseparable element of a larger program dependent for its success upon activity which affects commerce between the states. Given the substantial volume of commerce involved, and the inseparability of this particular legal service from the interstate aspects of real estate transactions we conclude that interstate commerce has been sufficiently affected.

The County Bar argues that Congress never intended to include the learned professions within the terms "trade or commerce" in § 1 of the Sherman Act, and therefore the sale of professional services is exempt from the Act. No explicit exemption or legislative history is provided to support this contention, rather the existence of state regulation seems to be its primary basis. Also, the County Bar maintains that competition is inconsistent with the practice of a profession because enhancing profit is not the goal of professional activities; the goal is to provide services necessary to the community. That, indeed, is the classic basis traditionally advanced to distinguish professions from trades, businesses, and other occupations, but it loses some of its force when used to support the fee control activities involved here.

In arguing that learned professions are not "trade or commerce" the County Bar seeks a total exclusion from antitrust regulation. Whether state regulation is active or dormant, real or theoretical, lawyers would be able to adopt anticompetitive practices with impunity. We cannot find support for the proposition that Congress intended any such sweeping exclusion. The nature of an occupation, standing alone, does not provide sanctuary from the Sherman Act, nor is the public service aspect of professional practice controlling in determining whether § 1 includes professions. Congress intended to strike as broadly as it could in § 1 of the Sherman Act, and to read into it so wide an exemption as that urged on us would be at odds with that purpose.

The language of § 1 of the Sherman Act, of course, contains no exception. "Language more comprehensive is difficult to conceive." And our cases have repeatedly established that there is a heavy presumption against implicit exemptions. Indeed, our cases have specifically included the sale of services within § 1. Whatever else it may be, the examination of a land title is a service; the exchange of such a service for money is "commerce" in the most common usage of that word. It is no disparagement of the practice of law as a profession to acknowledge that it has this business aspect, and § 1 of the Sherman Act [o]n its face shows a carefully studied attempt to bring within the Act every person engaged in business whose activities might restrain or monopolize commercial intercourse among the states. In the modern world it cannot be denied that the activities of lawyers play an important part in commercial intercourse, and that anticompetitive activities by lawyers may exert a restraint on commerce.

In Parker v. Brown, 317 U.S. 341 (1943), the Court held that an anti-competitive marketing program "which derived its authority and efficacy from the legislative command of the state" was not a violation of the Sherman Act because the Act was intended to regulate private practices and not to prohibit a State from imposing a restraint as an act of government. Respondent State Bar and respondent County Bar both seek to avail themselves of this so-called state action exemption. . . .

The threshold inquiry in determining if an anticompetitive activity is state action of the type the Sherman Act was not meant to proscribe is whether the activity is required by the State acting as soverign. Here we need not inquire further into the state action question because it cannot fairly be said that the State of Virginia through its Supreme Court Rules required the anticompetitive activities of either respondent. Respondents have pointed to no Virginia statute requiring their activities.

The fact that the State Bar is a state agency for some limited purposes does not create an antitrust shield that allows it to foster anticompetitive practices for the benefit of its members. The State Bar, by providing that deviation from County Bar minimum fees may lead to disciplinary action, has voluntarily joined in what is essentially a private anticompetitive activity, and in that posture cannot claim it is beyond the reach of the Sherman Act. Its activities resulted in a rigid floor from which petitioners, as consumers, could not escape if they wished to borrow money to buy a home.

We recognize that the States have a compelling interest in the practice of professions within their boundaries, and that as part of their power to protect the public health, safety, and other valid interests they have broad power to establish standards for licensing practitioners and regulating the practice of professions. We also recognize that in some instances the State may decide that victims of competition usual in the business world may be demoralizing to the ethics standards of a profession. The interest of the State in regulating lawyers is especially great since lawyers are essential to the primary governmental function of administering justice, and have historically been "officers of the courts." In holding that certain anticompetitive conduct by lawyers is within the reach of the Sherman Act we intend no diminution of the authority of the State to regulate its professions. Reversed and remanded.

After the foregoing decision, the courts in order to further encourage competition, held that professional persons have the right to advertise their services to the public. The traditional view that advertising by a professional was unethical was rejected because of the benefits of advertising to competition. This is not to say that all advertising is permissible or that professions may not regulate advertising. However, as a result of these fairly recent judicial decisions, competition is an important fact of life for the accounting profession.

PROFESSIONAL LICENSE

A personal service contract may be illegal if the party contracting to perform the service is not legally entitled to do so. Professions including that of certified public accountant require a license to practice. As a general rule, if the service that is rendered requires a license, the party receiving the benefit of the service can successfully refuse to pay for the service on the grounds the contract is illegal because the plaintiff has no license. This is true even if the person is licensed in a jurisdiction other than the one in which the services were rendered.

Each state has specific requirements for obtaining a license as a CPA. One of the more common requirements that causes difficulty in its application is the "practice" or "experience" requirement. The case which follows not only establishes the validity of such requirements but illustrates the strict application of them.

DUGGINS v. N.C. ST. BD. OF C.P.A. EXAMINERS
240 S.E.2d 406 (N.C.) 1978

Petitioner-appellant, James N. Duggins, Jr. (Duggins), graduated from the University of North Carolina School of Business in June 1965, with a major in accounting. In May 1965, he "passed satisfactorily" the examination given by the State Board of Certified Public Accountant Examiners (Board). However, in addition to passing this examination, N.C.Gen.Stats. § 93-12(5) also required that an applicant for a certificate of qualification to practice as a certified public accountant (CPA) "shall have had at least two years' experience on the field staff of a certified public accountant or a North Carolina public accountant in public practice, or shall have served two or more years as an internal revenue agent or special agent under a District Director of Internal Revenue or at least two years on the field staff of the North Carolina State Auditor under the direct supervision of a certified public accountant and shall have the endorsement of three certified public accountants as to his eligibility." Advanced degrees in economics or business administration may be substituted for one year of experience. The statute authorized the Board to permit persons otherwise eligible to take its examination and to withhold certificates until such persons shall have had the required experience.

In August 1965 the Board notified Duggins that his certification was being held "in suspense" until he had acquired the necessary experience and submitted proof thereof.

Duggins' file remained in suspense until 20 December 1972. In the meantime, Duggins graduated from the University of North Carolina Law School in the spring of 1968. In August 1968 he passed the North Carolina Bar examination and was licensed to practice law in this State. During the summer months of 1966 and 1967 he worked a total of 939 hours as a staff accountant for a firm of certified public accountants engaged in public practice in Durham, North Carolina. In the fall of 1968 Duggins joined the law firm of Smith, Moore, Smith, Schell & Hunter of Greensboro. There he worked under the direct supervision of one of the partners, Richard J. Tuggle, a lawyer and a CPA in good standing.

For more than four years Duggins spent over fifty percent of his time working on tax accounting matters under Tuggle's supervision. In this work he accumulated over 9,000 hours in the preparation of individual, corporate, and fiduciary income tax returns, state inheritance and federal estate tax returns, and in preparing tax protests; in making detailed analysis of financial information, verifications of financial transactions, books, accounts, and records; and in representing taxpayers at the agent level, conference level, and in the appellate division of the Internal Revenue Service.

On 20 December 1972 Duggins applied to the Board for his license as a CPA. His application, which recited his experience as detailed above was supported by an affidavit from Mr. Tuggle. Upon receiving notice that the Board intended to deny his application on the ground that he had not acquired the experience required by G.S. 93-12(5), Duggins requested a public hearing. At this hearing on 26 May 1973 Duggins testified to the facts summarized above. In a decision dated 21 August 1973, the Board denied Duggins' application. In addition to the facts set out above, the Board found as a fact "that the sole reason the Board rejected [petitioner's] application . . . is that he has been employed under the supervision of a lawyer who is also a CPA and not in the public practice of accountancy."

The Board concluded as a matter of law that "being an employee of a law firm [and] working under the supervision of a lawyer who is also a licensed certified public accountant not in the public practice of accountancy does not meet the experience requirements of the licensing statute and rules of the Board." Additionally, the Board noted that its administrative interpretation of G.S. § 93-12(5) had long been that "'employment by a licensed certified public accountant engaged in the practice of law is not experience which would qualify an applicant for licensing by the Board as a certified accountant." . . .

SHARP, J.

This appeal presents three questions: (1) Is Rule (9)(c)(1) of Section II of the Rules of the Board of Certified Public Accountant Examiners (Board) consistent with N.C.Gen.Stats. § 93-12(5) (1975) and thus within the Board's rule-making authority? (2) If so, are the statute and rule prima facie constitutional? (3) If so, have the statute and rule been discriminatively applied to appellant in violation of the due process and equal protection rights guaranteed him by the Fourteenth Amendment and by N.C.Const. art. I, § 19?

Pursuant to its rule-making authority, the Board promulgated Rule (9)(c) (1) to implement the alternative experience requirements of G.S. 93-12(5). The first alternative specified in the statute is proof by the applicant that he has had "at least two years' experience on the field staff of a certified public accountant or a North Carolina public accountant in public practice." It is this requirement which Duggins claims to have satisfied. As the Board construes this provision the phrase "in public practice" modifies both "a certified public accountant" and "a North Carolina public accountant." Under this construction therefore, whether an applicant's experience be acquired on the field staff of a certified public accountant (C.P.A.) or of a North Carolina public accountant, the accountant must have been in public practice.

It is Duggins' contention that G.S. 93-12(5) requires only "the North Carolina public accountant" (not the C.P.A.) under whom an applicant has worked for two years to be in public practice. Duggins does not contend that Mr. Richard J. Tuggle, the C.P.A. under whose supervision he had worked "more than 50% of his time" for over four years, is engaged in the public practice of accountancy. Mr. Tuggle, in addition to being a C.P.A. in good standing, is a lawyer and a partner in a large law firm engaged in the general practice of law. He, like Duggins, is an attorney specializing in tax matters. Their work for the firm "covers the full gamut of tax-related matters."

The first question we must consider, therefore, is whether the Board's Rule (9)(c)(1) enlarges the experience requirement of G.S. 93-12(5) in excess of its authority. We conclude that it does not. . . . (A)n applicant for certification who relies upon two years' experience on "the field staff" of a C.P.A. must have worked under a C.P.A. in public practice. . . .

A person is engaged in the "public practice of accountancy" who holds himself out to the public as an accountant and in consideration of compensation received or to be received offers to perform or does perform, for other persons, services which involve the auditing or verification of financial transactions, books, accounts, or records, or the preparation, verification or certification of financial, accounting and related statements intended for publication or renders professional services or assistance in or about any and all matters of principle or detail relating to accounting procedure and systems, or the recording, presentation or certification and the interpretation of such service through statements and reports. . . .

The requirement that an applicant's experience be on the "field staff" of a C.P.A. further evidences the legislative intent that the accountant under whom he serves his apprenticeship be in public practice. Although the term is not defined in the statute, "field staff" is a common expression understood alike by both laymen and accountants. The word *field* "has been defined as meaning the sphere of practical operation, as of an organization or enterprise; also the place or territory where direct contacts, as with a clientele, may be made or first-hand knowledge may be gained; sphere of action or place of contest, either literally or figuratively; hence, any scene of operations or opportunity for activity."

Duggins asserts that "it is manifestly obvious that the administrative differentiation between C.P.A. aspirants studying under Certified Public Accountants 'in public practice' and those not bears no reasonable, rational relationship to the one constitutionally permissible state objective of Chapter 93 . . . i.e., to insure the capability and fitness of an applicant to practice accountancy." Thus, he contends that a C.P.A. need not be in public practice for his "field staff" to obtain firsthand knowledge of "professional services or assistance in or about any and all matters of principle of detail relating to accounting procedure and systems. . . ."

The proposition that the range of experience contemplated by G.S. 93-12(5) will necessarily be acquired by one working with any C.P.A. regardless of the nature of his work or specialization is insupportable. . . . If Mr. Tuggle's activities as a lawyer–C.P.A. were limited entirely to tax litigation, no one would seriously contend that Duggins, by working with Tuggle or on his staff, would receive the type of experience which accomplished the purpose of the statute. For obvious reasons, when a profession or calling requires special skill or knowledge, and the General Assembly has specified certain qualifications, training, or experience as a condition precedent to the right to practice that profession or calling, the statutory specifications must be complied with strictly. The General Assembly discovered long ago that to allow the Board to accept "equivalent" experience or educational qualifications in lieu of those specified in the statute would not do. A provision permitting such acceptance, once in the law, was excised by 1951 N.C.Sess. Laws, Ch. 844. . . .

Suffice it to say that from the time the State first began to regulate the profession of accountancy, it has required that applicants for certification have several years' experience in the public practice. . . .

Duggins next argues that G.S. 93-12(5), as interpreted by the Board and the Court of Appeals, is unconstitutional on its face because, under the guise of promoting the general welfare, it imposes arbitrary and unnecessary restrictions upon his pursuit of a lawful occupation in violation of N.C.Const. art. I, § 19 and the "due process" and "equal protection" provisions of U.S. Const., amend. XIV.

Duggins bases his argument that he has been denied due process on two grounds. First, he contends that the experience requirement of the statute is invalid because it serves no legitimate public purpose; that it does nothing more than create a compulsory apprentice system by which applicants are forced to make their skills available, for a set period, to certified public accountants, North Carolina public accountants, and the other persons or entities mentioned in the statute. Secondly, Duggins argues that the requirement that an applicant's experience be received from a C.P.A. in public practice as opposed to any accountant who holds a certificate (e.g., a C.P.A. engaged in the practice of law) is not rationally related to the permissible legislative objective that only competent, moral, and experienced applicants receive certification.

After careful consideration we hold the requirement that an applicant for certification have two years' experience under the tutelage of an accountant engaged in the public practice of accountancy is rationally related to the legislative purpose of ensuring that only an applicant qualified and prepared to enter the public practice by himself be certified.

The General Assembly reasonably concluded that an applicant would be exposed to a wider range of experience and acquire more benefit therefrom while working under a C.P.A. in public practice than under one with a specialized practice. Since the regulatory statutes envision that most C.P.A.s will enter public practice it is logical that they require applicants to obtain experience in the public arena prior to certification. By clear implication the General Assembly has found that such experience and tutelage will provide, at least potentially, the everyday working knowledge so vital to the competent practice of the complex profession of accountancy. We cannot substitute our judgment for that of the legislature. . . .

We note . . . that North Carolina is not unique in requiring applicants for a C.P.A. certificate to have had supervised experience in the practice of public accounting. . . . More than half the states require one or more years of public accounting experience prior to certification. The Board asserts in its brief that "at least 33 states require from one to five years of accounting apprenticeship."

What we have previously said is also relevant to Duggins' contention that G.S. 93-12(5) is unconstitutional on its face because it violates the equal protection clauses of the federal and state constitutions. . . .

"The equal protection clauses of the United States and North Carolina Constitutions impose upon lawmaking bodies the requirement that any legislative classification 'be based on differences that are reasonably related to the purpose of the Act in which it is found.' . . . Such classifications will be upheld provided the classification is founded upon reasonable distinctions, affects all persons similarly situated or engaged in the same business without discrimination, and has some reasonable relation to the public peace, welfare and safety."

Applying these principles, we conclude that the classifications complained of are reasonably related to the purpose of the legislature and disclose no invidious discrimination. As we have heretofore pointed out, the purpose of Chapter 93 is to protect the public from unqualified accountants by ensuring that only knowledgeable, experienced applicants are issued certificates. An accountant seeks certification for the prestige it engenders and the confidence the public reposes in the designation "C.P.A." Ordinarily an accountant obtains certification for the purpose of holding himself out to the public as a C.P.A. It is logical, therefore, that experience in the "public practice" be deemed a prerequisite to certification. . . .

Affirmed.

While state licensing is required for the CPA designation, states may not prohibit unlicensed persons from performing the bookkeeping function. The public interest that prevents persons from presenting themselves as CPAs does not extend to services at this level. While it is important to limit the persons who may give professional opinions on financial statements, freedom of contract requires that anyone may claim to be qualified as an accountant or bookkeeper. Some states have limited the use of the word accountant under the police power, and the courts have upheld this limitation in the public interest. The states with such statutes do not limit the work a person may do any more than other states, but they prevent the representation of competency that comes from the use of the word *accountant*.

1. Assume that an accountant has agreed to perform an audit for a stated fee. During the course of the work, problems develop which necessitate significant increases in the amount of time and work required to perform the audit. Is the accountant entitled to be paid for these additional services? In the event of litigation, what legal theory will be used by a plaintiff-accountant? Explain.

2. A was paid $5,000 to conduct an audit of the XYZ company. Later it was discovered that A had failed to verify the receivables and the payables. As a result, the financial statements prepared by A were worthless. XYZ sues A to receive the audit fee. What result? Why?

3. A, B, & C form the ABC partnership to practice accounting in Los Angeles, California. As a part of the agreement, each partner agreed not to practice as a C.P.A. in the state of California for a period of ten years if the partner left the partnership for any reason. A resigned from the partnership and opened an office in a different building in Los Angeles. B and C brought suit to enjoin him from the practice of accounting in accordance with the agreement. What result? Why?

4. Assume that in question 3, A was not a partner but only an associate of the firm. To what extent would the legal principles applied to the case change? Explain.

5. Give the reasons that disclaimers of liability are not favored by the law and are frequently held to be illegal as contrary to public policy.

6. Give the reasons pro and con for enforcing disclaimers of liability by accountants in so far as third parties are concerned.

7. A community of 75,000 persons had seven firms of CPAs employing 55 accountants. Each month, the local chapter of CPAs had a meeting at which contemporary problems facing the profession were discussed. These discussions usually were conducted by one speaker with questions, answers and comments from the audience. X, who was responsible for the May meeting, selected the topic "The Need to Increase Professional Fees." As president of the organization, what steps should you take in regard to this topic? Explain.

8. X, a CPA in south Georgia, conducted an audit for a company in north Florida. X was not licensed in Florida. The company refused to pay X's fee, contending that the contract of employment was illegal. X sued to collect the fee. What result? Why?

9. Give the reasons that several states have an "experience" requirement in addition to the examination for awarding the license to practice as a CPA.

10. To what extent may a state regulate the bookkeeping function? Explain.

SUGGESTED ADDITIONAL READINGS

"Ads Start to Take Hold in the Professions," *Business Week,* July 24, 1978.
ANNOT. "Regulation of Accountants," 70 ALR 20 433, 1960.
"Competition Comes to Accounting," *Fortune,* July 17, 1978.
CORLEY, ROBERT N. and WILLIAM J. ROBERT, *Principles of Business Law,*
    11th ed. (Englewood Cliffs, N.J.: Prentice-Hall, Inc., 1979).
"Monopolies—Anticompetitive Covenants," 54 Am. Jur. 2nd, Section 511.
"Price-Fixing: Crackdown Underway," *Business Week,* June 2, 1975.

Chapter 8

Tort
Liability

INTRODUCTION

The term *tort* has been traditionally defined as a wrongful act against a person or his property, other than a breach of contract, for which a civil action may be brought for the injury sustained. A civil action for damages is allowed the victim, because the wrongdoer was "at fault." A tort is a private wrong or injury, as contrasted with a crime, which is a public wrong or injury. The same act may be both a crime and a tort. For example, a person who violates the criminal provisions of the securities laws may also be liable in dollar damages to those who suffered losses as a result of the criminal conduct.

Tort liability is predicated on two premises: (1) that in a civilized society, a person will not intentionally injure another person or his property, and (2) that all persons will exercise reasonable care and caution in the conduct of their affairs. The first premise has resulted in a group of torts usually labeled intentional torts. For purposes of the liability of accountants, fraud is the most common of these intentional torts. Intentional torts are given special treatment by the law. For example, a complaining party is entitled to exemplary or punitive damages in addition to the actual damages sustained. Intentional torts have this punitive aspect in order to discourage people from committing them. Furthermore, judgments obtained on a theory of intentional wrongdoing cannot usually be discharged in bankruptcy.

The second premise previously noted is the basis for the general field of tort liability known as *negligence*. Liability based on a theory of negligence is liability based on fault, just as in the case of an intentional tort. However, since the wrong is of a lesser degree, the theory of damages does not include any element of punishment. For simple negligence, a person is entitled to collect from the wrongdoer such a sum of money as will make him whole. He is not entitled to collect money to discourage the wrongdoer from repeating his wrong. In addition, simple negligence claims are dischargeable in bankruptcy.

Every person legally responsible is liable for his or her own torts. It is no defense that the wrongdoer is working under the direction of another. Such a fact may create liability on the part of the other person, but it is no defense for the wrongdoer. Thus, an accountant working for a firm has tort liability. In addition, the firm has liability if the tort is committed within the scope of the accountant's employment.

MALPRACTICE THEORIES

Suits against professional persons including accountants are commonly known as malpractice cases. An accountant's liability to clients and to those in privity of contract with them may be based on several theories. First, the liability may be based on a breach of contract theory. Under this theory, the accountant has liability for failing to perform contractual obligations as agreed. The use of this theory has several advantages. For example, contributory negligence on the part of the client usually would not be a defense, and the measure of damages would be the loss of the value of the benefit to be derived from the contract, rather than the loss sustained, as in the case of a tort. In addition, expert testimony is usually not required to prove a breach of contract, and the period of time designated by the statute of limitations for breach of a contract is usually longer than for a tort.

An accountant is also liable to clients for fraud and for negligence. These tort theories require proof of the elements of each tort, and claims are subject to the usual tort defenses. Negligence is usually at least one of the theories used in most malpractice cases. Negligence in such cases is defined as the failure to exercise the necessary care and caution that the professional calling requires. While professional persons do not guarantee that they will make no mistakes, they are required to meet the standards of their profession. While such suits involve standards of professional conduct, the issue of negligence is nevertheless submitted to a jury for a decision. In many cases, juries find that liability exists even though members of the profession contend that the services performed were all that could be reasonably expected under the circumstances.

The law has also developed some hybrid theories of liability. One of these combines contract and tort principles and is used when an accountant performs the contract as agreed but does so in a negligent manner. Such performance of a contract duty gives rise to a cause of action that may be considered either contractual or tortious. Confusion as to the basis of the litigation (tort or contract) frequently arises as a result of this distinction. The difference will be significant because (1) there are different periods of limitation for contract and tort cases, (2) each has its own theories of damages, and (3) the defenses available vary depending upon the theory. In order to take advantage of both theories, plaintiffs usually include a count in their lawsuits for breach of contract, one for negligence and one for negligent breach of contract. This allows courts to award the most liberal damages and to use the most liberal theory.

The discussion which follows covers these various theories. Later in this chapter, there will be a discussion of the extent to which persons other than clients are entitled to use each of the theories. All of the theories may be used by clients and by those in privity with them.

Before examining the legal principles of fraud and negligence, a basic understanding of admissibility of evidence, burden of proof, and expert testimony is helpful.

ADMISSIBILITY OF EVIDENCE
AND BURDEN OF PROOF

Laymen frequently fail to recognize the distinction between admissibility of evidence and conclusive proof of a fact in issue. The rules of evidence set forth the rules for determining what testimony or documents may be presented to the trier of fact (usually a jury) in an attempt to prove the truth or falsity of a matter in issue. Evidence is frequently conflicting, and the role of the fact-finder (judge or jury) is to determine where the truth lies. The fact that evidence is admissible does not mean that it will be accepted as the truth. The presence of evidence on an issue is not conclusive since it may be countered by conflicting evidence, or it may be open to more than one interpretation. For example, the mere fact that there is testimony that an auditor has conducted an audit in accordance with the standards of the profession does not conclusively establish a defense for the auditor. There could be testimony that the auditor had not met the standards of the profession, or more significantly, work as described in testimony might be viewed as inadequate by the jury exercising its independent judgment on the factual issue of negligence. This matter is discussed more fully in the next section.

Most lawsuits involve three types of questions: questions of fact, questions of law, and mixed questions of law and fact. In cases in which a jury demand is made by either party, the jury determines questions of fact and the court determines pure questions of law through jury instructions. While mixed questions create difficult problems, as a general rule they are determined by the jury. Issues of negligence are questions of fact so long as reasonable minds could differ on their interpretation. It is only when the evidence leads to but one conclusion that such issues become questions of law. Therefore, when there is conflicting evidence as to whether or not an auditor is at fault, that issue will be decided by the jury.

The term *burden of proof* has two meanings. First of all, it describes the party with the burden of coming forward with evidence to prove or disprove a relevant and material fact in dispute. In most cases, the plaintiff has the burden of coming forward with evidence to prove the essential allegations of the complaint, and the defendant has the burden of coming forth with evidence to prove affirmative defenses.

The second aspect of burden of proof involves the determination of the "quantum of proof" required for a favorable decision to be rendered on an issue. There are three generally recognized and distinct burdens of proof in this regard. First of all, there is the criminal burden of proof which is generally stated to be "beyond a reasonable doubt." Thus, before a person can be convicted of a crime, the prosecution must convince the trier of fact (usually a jury) that the defendant committed the crime alleged and such proof must be so positive that no reasonable doubt exists as to the defendant's guilt.

In most civil cases as contrasted with criminal cases, the burden of proof is said to be "by the greater weight of the evidence." Thus, all that is required for a party to prevail in a civil case is that the finder of fact believes that the evidence preponderates in favor of one party or that the manifest weight of the evidence favors one party. Negligence cases usually are subjected to this burden of proof.

The law has also developed a hybrid burden of proof between the heavy burden of the criminal law and the lighter burden in most civil cases. This burden of proof is usually known as "clear and convincing evidence." A matter to be proven by clear and convincing evidence requires greater proof than that the evidence merely favors one party but less than a proof that the matter is established beyond a reasonable doubt. Most states require that proof of fraud meet this standard.

EXPERT TESTIMONY

The evidence in most lawsuits against accountants includes expert testimony of CPAs other than the defendant. There are various views on the admissibility and conclusiveness of this testimony. Not unsurprisingly, most accountants and the AICPA often argue that professional standards (GAAP and GAAS) are conclusive. They argue that if the defendant-accountant complied with such standards, then there is no liability as a matter of law because the duty imposed by such standards has been met. By this view, expert testimony on custom in the profession is also conclusive, and a jury must accept the standards of the profession as the duty imposed. Accountants argue that courts cannot impose a higher standard than professional custom, because to do so would impose liability even if an accountant did everything that he had been taught to do.

The AICPA viewpoint has been objected to by plaintiff's lawyers because presumably custom and professional standards could establish too low standards of care. These lawyers, therefore, argue that professional standards and custom constitute only admissible evidence to be considered by the jury. Customary practice is only a factor to be considered in the overall decision of the jury.

The Securities and Exchange Commission also imposes an obligation on auditors beyond GAAP and GAAS professional standards. The SEC takes the position that auditors have a duty to effectively communicate material information. If following GAAP or GAAS does not result in such disclosure, the SEC takes the position that it has the power to promulgate additional standards and rules. Therefore, expert testimony on professional standards is not binding on the SEC.

Courts give greater weight to expert testimony in areas such as statistical sampling than they do in the communication of facts. Expert testimony on the latter is admissible and persuasive but not conclusive. Expert testimony in technical areas such as statistical sampling is treated as conclusive by most courts.

The prudent accountant should recognize that courts do not hesitate to require a higher standard than GAAP and GAAS where the facts warrant. Professional standards are not conclusive because a whole profession may lag in the adoption of new and viable concepts. A profession may not set its own tests of standards. In the final analysis, courts do so because there are precautions so imperative to the public welfare that their universal disregard does not excuse their omission.

In one case, the court expressed this concept in the following language:

> Much has been said by the parties about generally accepted accounting principles and the proper way for an accountant to report real estate transactions. We think this misses the point. Our inquiry is properly focused not on whether Laventhol's report satisfies esoteric accounting norms, comprehensible only to the initiate, but whether the report fairly presents the true financial position of Firestone, as of November 30, 1969, to the untutored eye of an ordinary investor.[1]

[1] Herzfeld v. Laventhol, Krerstein, Horwath & Horwath, CCH Fed. Sec. L. Rep. § 94,574 (S.D.N.Y. 1974).

FRAUD

INTRODUCTION

Lawsuits against accountants are frequently based on the theory of the intentional tort of fraud. The fraud theory is also used as a basis for avoiding contract liability. Victims of fraud are allowed to disaffirm contracts.

Although the elements of actionable fraud are stated differently from state to state, the following are generally required:

1. Scienter, or intention to mislead. This is knowledge of the falsity or statements made with such utter disregard and recklessness for the truth that knowledge is inferred.
2. A false representation or the concealment of a matter of fact material to the transaction.
3. Justifiable reliance on the false statement of concealment.
4. Injury as a consequence of the reliance.

Liability for fraud is not limited to persons with whom the accountant has contracted. An intentionally misrepresenting accountant is liable to all those persons whom he should reasonably have foreseen would be injured by the representation.

SCIENTER

The intent to mislead is often referred to by courts and writers as *scienter*. This Latin word means "knowingly." Scienter is present if the misrepresentation was willfully made. It exists if there has been a concealment of a material fact or a nondisclosure of such a fact. Intent may be and usually is inferred from conduct; of necessity, it must be proved by the statements or acts of the person whose act is being scrutinized, and ordinarily it can only be proved by circumstantial evidence. It includes anything calculated to deceive. Moreover, a statement that is partially or even literally true may be fraudulent in law if it was made in order to create a substantially false impression.

Intention to mislead may also be established by showing that a statement was made with such reckless disregard as to whether it is true or false that intention to mislead may be inferred. A party who makes a false statement, honestly believing it to be true but without reasonable grounds for such belief, has committed fraud. Negligent misrepresentation is equal to scienter and constitutes constructive fraud. An act or omission is constructive fraud because it violates a confidence justly reposed by the injured party. In other words, culpable ignorance of the truth or falsity will supply the intention to mislead. A false representation made without any belief as to its truth is the legal equivalent of one that is intentionally false, because it is made with gross negligence. For example, an accountant who certifies that financial statements accurately reflect the financial condition of a company may be guilty of fraud if he has no basis for the statement. Even though he may not actually intend to mislead, his statement is so reckless that the intention is inferred from the gross negligence as the case which follows illustrates.

STATE STREET TRUST CO. v. ERNST
15 N.E.2d 716 (1938)

FINCH, J.

Was the evidence introduced by plaintiff so inadequate that, resolving all contested issues and drawing all possible inferences in plaintiff's favor a jury could not find that defendants were guilty of gross negligence raising an inference of fraud, and that plaintiff relied upon the certified balance sheet prepared by defendants, thereby suffering damage?

The Pelz-Greenstein Company was organized in 1922 to engage in the business of financing wholesalers or mills. Its sole business was lending money, taking back, as collateral, inventory of the borrower and assignments of accounts receivable. Each borrower was referred to as a "department." Advances were made by Pelz-Greenstein to its borrowers to enable them to purchase or manufacture merchandise. Pelz-Greenstein was repaid in large part by the assignment of accounts receivable resulting from the sales of such merchandise. The collectibility of these advances thus depended in the first instance on the salability of the merchandise manufactured or purchased by the funds so advanced. If the merchandise failed to sell, not only was the repayment of the advances jeopardized, but likewise the income of Pelz-Greenstein, for its major item of income, to wit, commissions, was a percentage of the assigned accounts.

On January 19, 1929, the president of Pelz-Greenstein applied to plaintiff for a line of credit and a loan of $300,000. He presented an estimated balance sheet of the business as of December 31, 1928, and stated that defendants, a firm of accountants, were making an audit of the condition of the company as of that date and that a balance sheet certified by defendants would be submitted to plaintiff when it had been prepared. Plaintiff refused to grant the application of Pelz-Greenstein for a time loan until it had received the certified balance sheet of defendants and had found that it substantially corroborated the estimated balance sheet. Pending the receipt of the certified balance sheet of defendants plaintiff made a demand loan to Pelz-Greenstein of $300,000.

This certified balance sheet prepared by defendants was dated April 2, 1929, and issued in ten counterparts. The defendants admit that they knew it was to be used to obtain credit. On April 9 a copy was given by Pelz-Greenstein to plaintiff. Plaintiff found that the certified balance sheet substantially corroborated the estimated balance sheet. The demand note was then surrendered and a three months' time note taken in its place. This note was renewed for three month's periods, the last renewal being made January 9, 1930. Morgan, the lending officer of plaintiff, testifies that he relied upon this certified balance sheet in passing upon the application for the loan and in making the renewals. On April 26, 1930, Pelz-Greenstein was petitioned into bankruptcy. Plaintiff has received back only a portion of its loan and brings this action for the difference.

With the certified balance sheet defendants issued the following certificate: "We hereby certify that we examined the books of account and records pertinent to the assets and liabilities of Pelz-Greenstein Co., Inc., New York City, as of the close of business December 31, 1928, and, based on the records examined, information submitted to us, and subject to the foregoing notes [not here material], it is our opinion that the above condensed statement shows the financial condition of the company at the date stated and that the related income and surplus account is correct."

On May 9, 1929, a month after supplying ten copies of the balance sheet to be used, to the knowledge of the defendants, to obtain credit, defendants sent a letter to the Pelz-Greenstein Company containing comments on and explanations of the balance sheet. Apparently only one copy of this letter was sent, and it did not come to the attention of plaintiff nor, so far as the evidence shows, to any one else until after the bankruptcy of Pelz-Greenstein. This accompanying letter contained statements of facts discovered by defendants in the course of their audit, and, therefore, known to them when they prepared the original certified balance sheet, but which were not mentioned therein. One of the defendants testified before trial that the certified balance sheet was subject to the comments contained in the letter and the letter was sent for the purpose of trying to prevent any one from using this balance sheet without knowing the scope of the examination which was made.

At the close of plaintiff's case defendants moved to dismiss the complaint. The trial judge reserved decision. Defendants thereupon rested without calling any witnesses, although there would naturally be available the men who made the audit, those who prepared or supervised the preparation of the working papers or the certified balance sheet and experts to refute the testimony offered by the experts called by plaintiff. Defendants renewed their motion to dismiss and also moved for a directed verdict. The court reserved decision and submitted the case to the jury. After the jury rendered a verdict for plaintiff the trial judge denied the reversed motion to dismiss, but granted a motion to set aside the verdict, and directed a verdict for defendants. The Appellate Division has unanimously affirmed, and the appeal is here by permission of this court.

In the brief of respondents, Pelz and Greenstein are denominated as deliberately dishonest. It is there conceded that they made old and probably uncollectible accounts appear good by causing payments to be made to Pelz-Greenstein, Inc., by another corporation owned by themselves, which payments, credited to such old accounts, made it appear as if the debtors had been paying their debts. They induced one Saqui, who freely admitted his own dishonesty and testified on behalf of plaintiff, to furnish false inventories and to assign to

Pelz-Greenstein large numbers of false and fictitious accounts. In one account of $800,000 there were $300,000 of wholly fictitious sales. At the time Pelz-Greenstein was hopelessly insolvent.

To what extent may accountants be held liable for their failure to reveal this condition? We have held that in the absence of a contractual relationship or its equivalent, accountants cannot be held liable for ordinary negligence in preparing a certified balance sheet even though they are aware that the balance sheet will be used to obtain credit. Accountants, however, may be liable to third parties, even where there is lacking deliberate or active fraud. A representation certified as true to the knowledge of the accountants when knowledge there is none, a reckless misstatement, or an opinion based on grounds so flimsy as to lead to the conclusion that there was no genuine belief in its truth, are all sufficient upon which to base liability. A refusal to see the obvious, a failure to investigate the doubtful, if sufficiently gross, may furnish evidence leading to an inference of fraud so as to impose liability for losses suffered by those who rely on the balance sheet. In other words, heedlessness and reckless disregard of consequence may take the place of deliberate intention. . . .

The record is, indeed, replete with evidence, both oral and documentary, to make a prima facie case against the defendants. In the first place, we have these accountants guilty of an act which is the equivalent of active misrepresentation. On April 2, 1929, they sent to Pelz-Greenstein the certified balance sheet, with ten additional copies, knowing that it was to be used to obtain credit. . . . Not until thirty days later did the accountants send to Pelz-Greenstein a letter of explanation of this balance sheet, and then apparently only one copy. So important was this covering letter in the minds of defendants that, the balance sheet issued by the accountant, by its failure to point this out, contains, a misrepresentation. The very purpose of the bank in seeking the balance sheet prepared by the accountant is to check any possible fraud on the part of the person seeking the loan. Yet these accountants contend that they may accept as true a statement by the party whose books are being examined, make no check-up or investigation on their own part, and issue a statement omitting entirely any mention of the reason why investigation of the security was omitted.

We have explicit expert testimony, uncontradicted, that under these circumstances it was improper accounting practice for defendants to accept a letter from Pelz-Greenstein, and that they should have investigated these accounts very fully to ascertain whether the companies were still in business and to ascertain definitely and independently what security, if any, Pelz-Greenstein held for the payment of these accounts.

We next come to an item which is not as large as those which have gone before, but as to which there was obvious gross negligence. In the "Accounts Receivable" item of $3,200,000, protected only by a reserve of $15,000 was a group of accounts totaling over $72,000 denominated by defendants on their work sheet as "Ocean Bankrupt Accounts." Defendants stated that the failure to set up a reserve against this $72,000 of bankrupt accounts was justified because they were covered by policies of credit insurance. A mere cursory examination of the policies shows that over $32,000 of these accounts were not covered by the policies at all. Thus the reserve was shown to be inadequate by this one account alone. In addition, defendants' own work sheets showed that $14,000 of these bankrupt accounts had been with the insurance company from three years to fifteen months without action. There was expert testimony which a jury was at liberty to believe that a reserve of at least $46,000 should have been established against this account.

We find, also, a $10,000 demand note listed as part of the assets without reserve although it had been overdue and in the hands of an attorney, who had been unable to collect, for two years.

In connection with the foregoing items we have been concerned with evidence from which a jury might find that defendants had actual knowledge that the condition of the items in the balance sheet was not as represented. In the account of E. Heller & Bros., on the other hand, plaintiff contends that the evidence was sufficient to justify a jury in finding that there were circumstances appearing on the books which were so unusual and suspicious that proper accounting practice required defendants to make an investigation. The Heller account involved over $800,000 of the assets of Pelz-Greenstein. During the first eleven months of 1928 sales by the Heller Company never exceeded $191,000 a month, and averaged about $129,000. In December, just preceding the report of the accountants, sales were listed in the books as having jumped to $491,000. The amount included $300,000 of wholly fictitious sales. Plaintiff contends that this sudden increase of approximately $300,000 for the month should have put defendants on notice that something was wrong. Investigation was at least called for and would have disclosed the fictitious accounts.

We come now to evidence from which a jury could find that these defendants were at least heedless and reckless in purporting to reflect the condition of the books. We have an allowance of $101,000 for "doubtfuls" and "discounts," $86,000 of this $101,000 being for discounts and $15,000 for doubtfuls in the item of Accounts Receivable for $3,200,000. There was evidence that these figures for doubtfuls and discounts were arrived at, not by computation on the basis of business done during the year 1928, but by accepting the figures used for the year 1927. The working papers used by defendants for 1927 showed that in that year the amount of discounts had been based originally upon usual accounting practice, and was much larger than the final figure adopted by the accountants. Also, the original allowance for doubtfuls was greater than the final figure. On the basis of these higher figures, however, the profit for the year 1927 was less than the amount of dividends declared for that year. The reserves for discounts and for doubtfuls were then reduced so as to establish a profit in excess of the dividends for the year. The haphazard method used in arriving at these figures and the failure to follow usual accounting practice supports the contention urged by plaintiff, without answer or explanation upon this record, that defendants, in preparing this balance sheet, were negligent to such an extent as to amount to a reckless disregard for the accuracy necessary for a balance sheet to give the proper reflection of the condition of the business. . . .

The foregoing presents abundant evidence from which a jury could find that defendants knew facts which vitally affected the financial worth of Pelz-Greenstein, and which defendants totally suppressed on the certified balance sheet but disclosed to Pelz-Greenstein alone in the one copy of the covering letter sent thirty days later. The jury further could have found that the computation of reserves on the certified balance sheet was a misrepresentation which did not reflect the facts as known to defendants, and which they in good faith should have revealed. Where the record shows acts on the part of the accountants, as outlined above, we cannot say, as a matter of law, that plaintiff has failed to make out a case for the jury. . . .

The judgments should be reversed and a new trial granted, with costs in all courts to abide the event.

THE MISREPRESENTATIONS

An actual or implied false representation of a past or present fact is the essence of fraud. The misstatement of fact must be material. A fact is material if it is one to which a reasonable person would attach importance in determining his course of action in the transaction involved.

As a general rule, false statements of opinion as opposed to statements of fact are not actionable. This rule is an oversimplification, because an expression of opinion itself is a fact—the fact being the state of mind of the one expressing the opinion.

If a person has an opinion about something, it is a fact that he has that opinion. If he says his opinion is one thing when it actually is another, he has misstated a fact—what his opinion actually is. This concept is used when the person who is allegedly fraudulent is an expert, such as an accountant, or when the parties stand in a fiduciary relationship to each other. For example, assume that an accountant misstates his actual opinion as to the accuracy of financial statements. The accountant is guilty of fraud. He has misstated a fact—his professional opinion. Opinions of persons standing in a fiduciary relationship are actionable because of the high standard of conduct imposed by the relationship.

Misrepresentations of fact where the parties do not have equal knowledge of the facts or equal access to them are often found to be fraudulent. Whether a particular statement is one of fact or opinion is a matter for the jury to resolve.

The misstatement may in fact be true in part. A half-truth, or partial truth, that has the net effect of misleading may form the basis of fraud just as if it were entirely false. The untruth may be the result of a series of statements, the net result of which is to mislead. Although each statement taken alone may be true, there is fraud if all of them taken together tend to mislead the party to whom they are made. A partial truth in response to a request for information becomes an untruth whenever it creates a false impression and is designed to do so.

As a general rule, silence in the absence of a duty to speak does not constitute fraud. However, if there is a duty to speak, the concealment of a material fact is equivalent to fraudulent misrepresentation. There is a duty to speak when the parties stand in a fiduciary relationship. A fiduciary relationship is one of trust and confidence, such as exists between partners in a partnership, between a director and a corporation, or between an agent and a principal. Because such parties do not deal "at arm's length," there is the duty to speak and to make a full disclosure of all facts.

A duty to speak also arises when a person learns that a former statement was false. This duty to speak is in effect a duty to correct the prior impressions of the other party or parties as the case which follows illustrates.

FISCHER v. KLETZ
266 F.Supp. 180 (1967)

Plaintiff brought a class action suit against the defendant accountants, Peat, Marwick Mitchell & Co. (P.M.M.) asserting that defendants were liable for failure to correct financial statements when it discovered they were false. The defendants moved to dismiss the complaint for failure to state a claim upon which relief could be granted.

TYLER, J.

Sometime early in 1964, P.M.M., acting as an independent public accountant, undertook the job of auditing the financial statements that Yale Express System, Inc. ("Yale"), a national transportation concern, intended to include in the annual report to its stockholders for the year ending December 31, 1963. On March 31, 1964, P.M.M. certified the figures contained in these statements. On or about April 9, the annual report containing the certification was issued to the stockholders of Yale. Subsequently, on or about June 29, 1964, a Form 10-K Report, containing the same financial statements as the annual report, was filed with the SEC as required by that agency's rules and regulations.

At an unspecified date "early in 1964," probably shortly after the completion of the audit, Yale engaged P.M.M. to conduct so-called "special studies" of Yale's past and current income and expenses. In the course of this special assignment, sometime presumably before the end of 1964, P.M.M. discovered that the figures in the annual report were substantially false and misleading.

Not until May 5, 1965, however, when the results of the special studies were released, did P.M.M. disclose this finding to the exchanges on which Yale securities were traded, to the SEC or to the public at large. . . .

Plaintiffs attack P.M.M. for its silence and inaction after its employees discovered, during the special studies, that the audited and certified figures on the financial statements reflecting Yale's 1963 performance were grossly inaccurate. They contend that inasmuch as P.M.M. knew that its audit and certificate would be relied upon by the investing public, the accounting firm had a duty to alert the public in some way that the audited and certified statements were materially false and inaccurate. P.M.M. counters that there is no common law or statutory basis for imposing such a duty on it as a public accounting firm retained by the officers and directors of Yale.

Strict analysis leads to the conclusion that P.M.M. is attacked in the complaint because it wore two hats in conducting its business relations with Yale during the period in question. P.M.M. audited and certified the financial statements in the 1963 annual report and Form 10-K as a statutory "independent public accountant" whose responsibility is not only to the client who pays his fee, but also investors, creditors and others who may rely on the financial statements which he certifies. * * * The public accountant must report fairly on the facts as he finds them whether favorable or unfavorable to his client. His duty is to safeguard the public interest, not that of his client. Following the certification, P.M.M. switched its role to that of an accountant employed by Yale to undertake special studies which were necessitated by business demands rather than by statutory or regulatory requirements. In this sense, it can be seen that during the special studies P.M.M. was a "dependent public accountant" whose primary obligations, under normal circumstances, were to its client and not the public.

It was, of course, during the conduct of the special studies that the inaccuracies in the audited and certified statements were discovered. The time of this discovery makes the questions here involved difficult and unique. On the basis of the Commission's *Touche, Niven* opinion, an accountant has a duty to the investing public to certify only those statements which he deems accurate. This duty is not directly involved here, however, for the inaccuracies were discovered after the certification had been made and the 1963 annual report had been released. P.M.M. maintains, therefore, that any duty to the investing public terminated once it certified the relevant financial statements. Plaintiffs, of course, contend to the contrary. Thus, the serious question arises as to whether or not an obligation correlative to but conceptually different from the duty to audit and to certify with reasonable care and professional competence arose as a result of the circumstance that P.M.M. knew that investors were relying upon its certification of the financial statements in Yale's annual report. . . .

Plaintiff's claim is grounded in the common law action of deceit, albeit an unusual type in that most cases of deceit involve an affirmative misrepresentation by the defendant. Here, however, plaintiffs attack P.M.M.'s nondisclosure or silence.

It is Dean Prosser's view that in contrast with the issues raised when an affirmative misrepresentation is involved, "a much more difficult problem arises as to whether mere silence, or a passive failure to disclose facts of which the defendant has knowledge, can serve as the foundation of a deceit action." The law in this area is in a state of flux due to the inroads being made into the old doctrine of *caveat emptor*. Although the prevailing rule still seems to be that there is no liability for tacit nondisclosure, Dean Prosser adds the following important qualification: "to this general rule, if such it be, the courts have developed a number of expectations, some of which are as yet very ill-defined, and have no very definite boundaries." One of these exceptions is that one who has made a statement and subsequently acquires new information which makes it untrue or misleading, must disclose such information to any one whom he knows to be still acting on the basis of the original statement * * *

Section 551 of the First Restatement of Torts, which is couched in the specific terms of "a business transaction," is in substantial agreement with Dean Prosser. The Restatement position in Section 551(1) is that one who fails to disclose to another a thing which he knows may justifiably induce the other to act or refrain from acting in a business transaction is subject to the same liability to the other as though he had represented the nonexistence of the matter which he has failed to disclose, if, but only if, he is under a duty to the other to exercise reasonable care to disclose the matter in question.

Section 551(2) lists the instances when the requisite duty to disclose arises. For present purposes, the following portion from that subsection is important: One party to a business transaction is under a duty to exercise reasonable care to disclose to the other before the transaction is consummated * * * (b) any subsequently acquired information which he recognizes as making untrue or misleading a previous representation which when made was true or believed to be so. . . .

Generally speaking, I can see no reason why this duty to disclose should not be imposed upon an accounting firm which makes a representation it knows will be relied upon by investors. To be sure, certification of a financial statement does not create a formal business relationship between the accountant who certifies and the individual who relies upon the certificate for investment purposes. The act of certification, however, is similar in its effect to a representation made in a business transaction: both supply information which is naturally and justifiably relied upon by individuals for decisional purposes. Viewed in this context of the impact of nondisclosure on the injured party, it is difficult to conceive that a distinction between accountants and parties to a business transaction is warranted. The elements of "good faith and common honesty" which govern the businessman presumably should also apply to the statutory "independent public accountant." . . .

In cases involving affirmative misrepresentations, it is now the settled rule that a misrepresenter can be held liable, regardless of his interest in the transaction. . . .

In my view, accepting the pertinent allegations of the complaint to be true, P.M.M. must be regarded as bound at this preliminary stage of the litigation by this rule of law. Though concededly "disinterested" in the sense that it achieved no advantage by its silence, P.M.M. is charged in the complaint for losses realized by plaintiffs as a result of its nondisclosure. This is sufficient at least in the pleading sense, . . .

In light of the foregoing discussion, I find no sound reasons to justify barring plaintiffs from the opportunity to prove a common-law action of deceit against P.M.M. . . . The common law has long required that a person who has made a representation must correct that representation if it becomes false and if he knows people are relying on it. This duty to disclose is imposed regardless of the interest of defendant in the representation and subsequent nondisclosure. Plaintiffs have sufficiently alleged the elements of nondisclosure on the part of this "disinterested" defendant. Accordingly, they must be given an opportunity to prove those allegations.

To conclude thus is not to ignore the manifold difficulties that a final determination of liability on the part of public accountants for nondisclosure would create for professional firms and other business entities (and, indeed, individuals) similarly situated. Some obvious questions can be briefly set forth as examples of such potential problems. How long, for instance, does the duty to disclose after-acquired information last? To whom and how should disclosure be made? Does liability exist if the after-acquired knowledge is obtained from a source other than the original supplier of information? Is there a duty to disclose if an associate or employee of the accounting firm discovers that the financial statements are false but fails to report it to the firm members?

These and similar questions briefly indicate the potentially significant impact upon accountants, lawyers and business entities in the event that a precise rule or rules of liability for nondisclosure are fashioned and recognized in the law. On the other side of the coin, however, as the bulk of the discussion hereinbefore has shown, investors in publicly-held companies have a strong interest in being afforded some degree of protection by and from those professional and business persons whose representations are relied upon for decisional purposes. In my view, resolution of the issues posed by the complaint allegations here in question must be made with these important but conflicting interests in mind. Proper reconciliation of these interests or policy considerations, however, can only be made after full development of the facts of this case during the discovery process and at trial. . . .

So ordered.

JUSTIFIABLE RELIANCE

Before a false statement of fact can be considered fraudulent, the party to whom it has been made must reasonably believe it to be true, must act thereon to his damage, and in so acting must rely on the truth of the statement. If the party investigates the statement and its falsity is revealed, no action can be brought for fraud. The cases are somewhat in conflict as to the need to investigate. Some courts have indicated that if all the information is readily available for ascertaining the truth of statements, blind reliance upon the misrepresentation is not justified. In such a case, the party is said to be negligent in not taking advantage of the facilities available for confirming the statement.

In determining a person's negligence in relying upon the statements, courts will consider the education, intelligence, and experience of the party. The standard for justifiable reliance is not whether a reasonably prudent man would be justified in so relying, but whether the particular individual had the ability and a right to so rely. On the other hand, some courts have stated that one who has induced another to act to the other's prejudice by misrepresentation cannot impute negligence to the other merely because of his reliance on the misrepresentation. He cannot be heard to say, "You should not have believed me." A person has no duty to make inquiries or investigate unless he has knowledge of his own or of facts that should arouse suspicion and cast doubts on the truth of the statement made. Nor can a person relieve himself of liability for misrepresentations in advance by a disclaimer. Courts generally agree that reliance is justified when substantial effort or expense is required to determine the true facts. In any case, the issue as to whether or not the reliance is justified is for the jury to decide.

INJURY OR DAMAGE

In order to prevail, the party relying upon the misstatement must offer proof of resulting damage. Injury results when a party is not in as good a position as he would have been had the statements been true. Loans made on the basis of fraudulent financial statements to a bankrupt borrower result in injury equal to the loan.

In an action for damages for fraud involving the purchase of stock, the plaintiff may seek to recover damages on either of two theories. He may use the "benefit of the bargain" theory and seek the difference between the actual market value of what he received and the value if he had received what was represented. Or the plaintiff may use the "out of pocket" theory and collect the difference between the actual value and the purchase price. The market price may not be the actual value as illustrated by the following case.

TEICH v. ARTHUR ANDERSEN & CO.
263 N.Y.S.2d 932 (1965)

PER CURIAM.

The action is brought against the National Malleable and Steel Castings Company (National) and its auditors by a purchaser of its common stock. The plaintiff's causes of action are grounded upon the alleged fraudulent concealment or misrepresentations with respect to National's financial condition in the failure of disclosure in its 1950 and 1957 financial statements and in a stock listing agreement of substantial unfunded past pension obligations. On the theories of fraud and breach of warranty, the plaintiff alleges that he was induced by the concealment and misrepresentations to purchase for investment purposes in the market substantial quantities of the common stock, and he further alleges that the prices paid exceeded the value of the stock. . . . There are issues of fact as to whether or not plaintiff sustained any pecuniary loss. Injury is an essential element of a cause of action grounded in fraud; and the "true measure of damage is indemnity for the actual pecuniary loss sustained as the direct result of the wrong." The plaintiff claims pecuniary loss in "that the value of what he received was less than either the quotations or costs" of the stock which he purchased. The fact that the plaintiff paid no more for his stock than the market price thereof as reflected by tradings on a stock exchange is not necessarily decisive as to plaintiff's right of action. The market price is very cogent evidence as to the value of the stock but, upon the record here, the market quotations as of the days of plaintiff's purchases would not necessarily be controlling. Certainly, if it is established that the market price of the stock was inflated for a time by reason of the alleged wrongful concealment or misrepresentations in National's financial statements, the plaintiff should be entitled to show that, in paying the market price, he paid a price higher than the market price would have been except for the fraud.

Trial ordered on the above issues.

NEGLIGENCE

INTRODUCTION

The second premise of tort liability is that people should exercise reasonable care and caution in the conduct of their affairs. For professional persons, this means that they must exercise that degree of care and caution that their professional calling requires. Failure to meet these professional standards is negligence.

Negligence is usually expressed in terms of a breach of duty by one party which is the proximate cause of an injury to another. Negligence on the part of the party seeking damages (contributory negligence) is usually a bar to any recovery.

The duty owed by one party is usually expressed as the degree of care and caution that the wrongdoer is bound to exercise toward the other party by reason of the factual situation and their relationship. Generally, the greater the duty, the higher the standard of conduct. In other words, there are varying degrees of negligence usually labeled slight negligence, ordinary negligence, and gross negligence. These degrees are dependent upon the duty owed. The higher the duty, the lower the degree of negligence and vice versa. As noted in the preceding discussion on fraud, gross negligence will supply the essential element of scienter, whereas simple or slight negligence will not. The nature of the duty owed by one person to another is a question of law for the courts. The issue as to whether or not there has been a breach of the duty owed is almost always a question of fact for the jury. It is an issue of law for a court only when reasonable minds do not differ.

Negligence may consist of either an act or an omission—failure to act. The act or omission must be wrongful in the sense that another's legal right has been violated.

The right may arise from a contract or from the relationship of the parties. Many, if not most, cases of negligence involving accountants are based on omission as well as overt actions.

EXAMPLES OF NEGLIGENCE
BY ACCOUNTANTS

Negligence is usually defined in terms of a reasonable man. However, the definition of negligence for professionals is defined in terms of the knowledge, skill, and judgment usually possessed by members of the profession. A common explanation for this definition is:

> In all those employments where peculiar skill is requisite, if one offers his services, he is understood as holding himself out to the public as possessing the degree of skill commonly possessed by others in the same employment, and if his pretensions are unfounded, he commits a species of fraud upon every man who employs him in reliance on his public profession. But no man, whether skilled or unskilled, undertakes that the task he assumes shall be performed successfully, and without fault or error; he undertakes for good faith and integrity, but not for infallibility, and he is liable to his employer for negligence, bad faith, or dishonesty, but not for losses consequent upon mere errors of judgment.[2]

Negligence issues frequently arise when an auditor fails to discover fraud or embezzlement. Most courts have held that an auditor is not a fiduciary and that the auditor's duty is to act independently, objectively, and impartially and with the skills that were represented to the audior's clients. While an auditor is not a guarantor and, at least from a personal viewpoint, has no duty to discover fraud or embezzlement, auditors have been held liable when their negligence prevents the discovery of fraud. Negligence in these cases is usually based on a failure to adhere to specific auditing procedures which, if followed, would have disclosed the fraud or embezzlement. If proper performance of the audit would have disclosed the defalcation or other wrongful conduct, failure to perform is negligence.

---

[2] T. Cooley, *Torts* 335, 4th ed. (1932). The passage is quoted in Smith v. London Assurance Corp., 109 App. Div. 882, 96 N.Y.S. 820 (1905).

Failure to qualify financial statements is another example of negligence by an accountant. Since GAAS requires a clear indication of the auditor's examination, if any, and the degree of responsibility he is taking, failure to qualify allows a client to recover at least the cost of the audit if the financial statements are erroneous.

Negligence by accountants is often predicated upon the failure to adhere to common standards of honesty and loyalty. These standards are required even where no audit is conducted.

1136 TENANTS' CORP. v. MAX ROTHENBERG & CO.
319 N.Y.S.2d 1007 (1971)

PER CURIAM.

Judgment, Supreme Court, New York County, entered on July 1, 1970, in favor of plaintiff, after trial, based upon negligent performance of accounting services by defendant firm of certified public accountants, affirmed. . . .

The record amply supports the Trial Court's findings that defendant was engaged to audit and not merely "write-up" plaintiff's books and records and that the procedures performed by defendant were "incomplete, inadequate and improperly employed." One of defendant's senior partners admitted at the trial that defendant performed services for plaintiff which went beyond the scope of a "write-up" and that it actually performed some auditing procedures for plaintiff. Defendant's worksheets indicate that defendant did examine plaintiff's bank statement, invoices and bills and, in fact, one of the worksheets is entitled "Missing Invoices 1/1/63–12/31/63" (plaintiff's exhibit 16-B-6). That sheet alone indicates invoices missing from the records of Riker & Co. which totalled more than $44,000.

Utilization of the simplest audit procedures would have revealed Riker's defalcations. Moreover, even if defendant were hired to perform only "write-up" services, it is clear, beyond dispute, that it did become aware that material invoices purportedly paid by Riker were missing, and, accordingly, had a duty to at least inform plaintiff of this. But even this it failed to do. Defendant was not free to consider these and other suspicious circumstances as being of no significance and prepare its financial reports as if same did not exist.

Affirmed.

Another common activity that may result in liability on a theory of negligence is tax return preparation. An accountant is liable for penalties and interest if he negligently fails to file a return on time or fails to file a correct return. Liability for negligence may also arise from erroneous tax advice.

CONTRIBUTORY NEGLIGENCE

As a general rule, contributory negligence by a plaintiff usually bars a recovery on the theory of negligence. An early case in New York applied this doctrine to a client's suit against accountants. However, subsequent cases have noted that since accountants are employed to detect defalcations which the employer's negligence has made possible, contributory negligence should not prevent a recovery.

In one case, the court in rejecting contributory negligence as a defense observed:

> We are, therefore, not prepared to admit that accountants are immune from the consequences of their negligence because those who employ them have conducted their own business negligently. The situation in this respect is not unlike that of a workman injured by a dangerous condition which he has been employed to rectify. . . . Accountants, as we know, are commonly employed for the very purpose of detecting defalcations which the employer's negligence has made possible. Accordingly, we see no reason to hold that the accountant is not liable to his employer in such cases. Negligence of the employer is a defense only when it has contributed to the accountant's failure to perform his contract and to report the truth. Thus, by way of illustration, if it were found that the members of the firm of Halle & Stieglitz had been negligent in connection with the transfer of funds which occurred at about the time of each audit and that such negligence contributed to the defendants' false reports it would be a defense to the action for it could then be said that the defendants' failure to perform their contracts was attributable, in part at least, to the negligent conduct of the firm.[3]

A client may also be denied recovery if the auditor's negligence was not the proximate cause of the client's loss. Since the failure of the employer to exercise due care in supervising its employees is usually involved in embezzlement cases, a case can be made that the auditor's negligence was not the proximate cause of the client's loss. The damage in such a case does not flow directly from the accountant's negligence.

LIABILITY TO THIRD PARTIES—
THE ULTRAMARES DOCTRINE

As previously noted, an accountant is liable to his clients for breach of contract for fraud and for negligence. Liability for fraud also exists in favor of third parties. Liability for breach of contract exists if the third party is one for whose *direct benefit* the contract was made. Liability for

---

[3] National Surety Corp. v. Lybrand, 9 N.Y.S.2d 563 (1959).

breach of contract does not exist for persons who do not qualify as third-party beneficiaries of the contract.

Liability to third parties for negligence has caused a great deal of trouble for the courts. The case which follows is the leading case holding that there is no liability to third parties for simple negligence.

ULTRAMARES CORP. v. TOUCHE
255 N.Y. 170 (1931)

CARDOZO, J.

The Action is in tort for damages suffered through the misrepresentations of accountants, the first cause of action being for misrepresentations that were merely negligent and the second for misrepresentations charged to have been fraudulent.

In January, 1924, the defendants, a firm of public accountants, were employed by Fred Stern & Co., Inc., to prepare and certify a balance sheet exhibiting the condition of its business as of December 31, 1923. They had been employed at the end of each of the three years preceding to render a like service. Fred Stern & Co., Inc., which was in substance Stern himself, was engaged in the importation and sale of rubber. To finance its operations, it required extensive credit and borrowed large sums of money from banks and other lenders. All this was known to the defendants. The defendants knew also that in the usual course of business the balance sheet when certified would be exhibited by the Stern company to banks, creditors, stockholders, purchasers or sellers, according to the needs of the occasion, as the basis of financial dealings. Accordingly, when the balance sheet was made up, the defendants supplied the Stern company with thirty-two copies certified with serial numbers as counterpart originals. . . .

By February 26, 1924, the audit was finished and the balance sheet made up. It stated assets in the sum of $2,550,671.88 and liabilities other than capital and surplus in the sum of $1,479,956.62, thus showing a net worth of $1,070,715.26. Attached to the balance sheet was a certificate as follows:

TOUCHE, NIVEN & CO
Public Accountants
Eighty Maiden Lane
New York

February 26, 1924.

Certificate of Auditors

We have examined the accounts of Fred Stern & Co., Inc., for the year ending December 31, 1923, and hereby certify that the annexed balance sheet is in accordance therewith and with the information and explanations given us. We further certify that, subject to provision for federal taxes on income, the said statement, in our opinion, presents a true and correct view of the financial condition of Fred Stern & Co., Inc., as at December 31, 1923.

TOUCHE, NIVEN & CO.
Public Accountants

Capital and surplus were intact if the balance sheet was accurate. In reality both had been wiped out, and the corporation was insolvent. The books had been falsified by those in charge of the business so as to set forth accounts receivable and other assets which turned out to be fictitious. The plaintiff maintains that the certificate of audit was erroneous in both its branches. . . .

The plaintiff, a corporation engaged in business as a factor, was approached by Stern in March, 1924, with a request for loans of money to finance the sales of rubber. Up to that time the dealings between the two houses were on a cash basis and trifling in amount. As a condition of any loans the plaintiff insisted that it receive a balance sheet certified by public accountants, and in response to that demand it was given one of the certificates signed by the defendants and then in Stern's possession. On the faith of that certificate the plaintiff made a loan which was followed by many others. . . .

Nearly a year later, in December 1924, the house of cards collapsed. In that month, plaintiff made three loans to the Stern company, one of $100,000, a second of $25,000, and a third of $40,000. For some of these loans no security was received. For some of the earlier loans the security was inadequate. On January 2, 1925, the Stern company was declared a bankrupt.

This action, brought against the accountants in November 1926, to recover the loss suffered by the plaintiff in reliance upon the audit, was in its inception one of negligence. On the trial there was added a second cause of action asserting fraud also. . . . The verdict was in favor of the plaintiff for $187,576.32. . . .

The two causes of action will be considered in succession, first the one for negligence and second that for fraud.

(1) We think the evidence supports a finding that the audit was negligently made, though in so saying we put aside for the moment the question whether negligence, even if it existed, was a wrong to the plaintiff. To explain fully or adequately how the defendants were at fault would carry this opinion beyond reasonable bounds. A sketch, however, there must be, at least in respect of some features of the audit, for the nature of the fault, when understood, is helpful in defining the ambit of the duty.

We begin with the item of accounts receivable. At the start of the defendant's audit, there had been no posting of the general ledger since April, 1923. Siess, a junior accountant, was assigned by the defendants to the performance of that work. On Sunday, February 3, 1924, he had finished the task of posting, and was ready the next day to begin with his associates the preparation of the balance sheet and the audit of its items. The total of the accounts receivable for December, 1923, as thus posted by Siess from the entries in the journal, was $644,758.17. At some time on February 3, Romberg, an employee of the Stern company, who had general charge of its accounts, placed below that total another item to represent additional accounts receivable growing out of the transactions of the month. This new item, $706,843.07, Romberg entered in his own handwriting. The sales that it represented were, each and all, fictitious. Opposite the entry were placed other figures (12-29), indicating or supposed to indicate a reference to the journal. Siess when he resumed his work saw the entries thus added, and included the new item in making up his footings, with the result of an apparent increase of over $700,000 in the assets of the business. He says that in doing this he supposed the entries to be correct, and that his task at the moment being merely to post the books, he thought the work of audit or certification might come later, and put it off accordingly. . . .Verification, however, there never was either by Seiss or by his superiors, ... If any had been attempted, or any that was adequate, an examiner would have found that the entry in the ledger was not supported by any entry in the journal. If from the journal he had gone to the book from which the journal was made up, described as "the debit memo book," support would still have failed. Going farther, he would have found invoices, seventeen in number, which amounted in the aggregate to the interpolated item, but scrutiny of these invoices would have disclosed suspicious features in that they had no shipping number nor a customer's order number and varied in terms of credit and in other respects from those usual in the business. A mere glance reveals the difference.

The December entry of accounts receivable was not the only item that a careful and skillful auditor would have desired to investigate. There was ground for suspicion as to an item of $113,199.60, included in the accounts payable as due from the Baltic Corporation. As to this the defendants received an explanation, not very convincing, from Stern and Romberg. A cautious auditor might have been dissatisfied and have uncovered what was wrong. There was ground for suspicion also because of the inflation of the inventory. The inventory as it was given to the auditors, was totaled at $317,219.08. The defendants discovered errors in the sum of $303,863.20, and adjusted the balance sheet accordingly. Both the extent of the discrepancy and its causes might have been found to cast discredit upon the business and the books. There was ground for suspicion again in the record of assigned accounts. Inquiry of the creditors gave notice to the defendants that the same accounts had been pledged to two, three and four banks at the same time. The pledges did not diminish the value of the assets, but made in such circumstances they might well evoke a doubt as to the solvency of a business where such conduct was permitted. There was an explanation by Romberg which the defendants accepted as sufficient. Caution and diligence might have pressed investigation farther. . . .

We are brought to the question of duty, its origin and measure.

The defendants owed to their employer a duty imposed by law to make their certificate without fraud, and a duty growing out of contract to make it with the care and caution proper to their calling. Fraud includes the pretense of knowledge when knowledge there is none. To creditors and investors to whom the employer exhibited the certificate, the defendants owed a like duty to make it without fraud, since there was notice in the circumstances of its making that the employer did not intend to keep it to himself. A different question develops when we ask whether they owed a duty to these to make it without negligence. If liability for negligence exists, a thoughtless slip or blunder, the failure to detect a theft or forgery beneath the cover of deceptive entries, may expose accountants to a liability in an indeterminate amount for an indeterminate time to an indeterminate class. The hazards of a business conducted on these terms are so extreme as to enkindle doubt whether a flaw may not exist in the implication of a duty that exposes to those consequences. . . . The case was submitted to the jury and the verdict was returned upon the theory that even in the absence of a misstatement of a fact there is a liability . . . for erroneous opinion. The expression of an opinion is to be subject to a warranty implied by law. What, then, is the warranty, as yet unformulated, to be? Is it merely that the opinion is honestly conceived and that the preliminary inquiry has been honestly pursued, that a halt has not been made without a genuine belief that the search has been reasonably adequate to bring disclosure of the truth? Or does it go farther and involve the assumption of a liability for any blunder or inattention that could fairly be spoken of as negligence if the controversy were one between accountant and employer for breach of a contract to render services for pay?

The assault upon the citadel of privity is proceeding in these days apace. . . . In the field of the law of torts a manufacturer who is negligent in the manufacture of a chattel in circumstances pointing to an unreasonable risk of serious bodily harm to those using it thereafter may be liable for negligence though privity is lacking between manufacturer and user. A force or instrument of harm having been launched with potentialities of danger manifest to the eye of prudence, the one who launches it is under a duty to keep it within bounds. . . . However, what is released or set in motion is a physical force. We are now asked to say that a like liability attaches to the circulation of a thought or a release of the explosive power resident in words.

. . . (C)ases in this court are said by the plaintiff to have committed us to the doctrine that words, written or oral, if negligently published with the expectation that the reader or listener will transmit them to another, will lay a basis for liability though privity be lacking. . . .

In Glanzer v. Shepard the seller of beans requested the defendants, public weighers, to make return of the weight and furnish the buyer with a copy. This the defendants did. Their return, which was made out in duplicate, one copy to the seller and the other to the buyer, recites that it was made by order of the former for the use of the latter. The buyer paid the seller on the faith of the certificate which turned out to be erroneous. We held that the weighers were liable at the suit of the buyer for the moneys overpaid. Here was something more than the rendition of a service in the expectation that the one who ordered the certificate would use it thereafter in the operations of his business as occasion might require. Here was a case where the transmission of the certificate to another was not merely one possibility among many, but the "end and aim of the transaction," as certain and immediate and deliberately willed as if a husband were to order a gown to be delivered to his wife, or a telegraph company, contracting with the sender of a message, were to telegraph it wrongly to the damage of the person expected to receive it. The intimacy of the resulting nexus is attested by the fact that after stating the case in terms of legal duty, we went on to point out that . . . we could reach the same result by stating it in terms of contract. The bond was so close as to approach that of privity, if not completely one with it. Not so in the case at hand. No one would be likely to urge that there was a contractual relation, or even one approaching it, at the root of any duty that was owing from the defendants now before us to the indeterminate class of persons who, presently or in the future, might deal with the Stern company in reliance on the audit. In a word, the service rendered by the defendant in Glanzer v. Shepard was primarily for the information of a third person, in effect, if not in name, a party to the contract, and only incidentally for that of the formal promisee. In the case at hand, the service was primarily for the benefit of the Stern company, a convenient instrumentality for use in the development of the business, and only incidentally or collaterally for the use of those to whom Stern and his associates might exhibit it thereafter. Foresight of these possibilities may charge with liability for fraud. The conclusion does not follow that it will charge with liability for negligence. . . .

The antidote to . . . the over-use of the doctrine of liability for negligent misstatement may be found in Jaillet v. Cashman (235 N.Y. 511) and Courteen Seed Co. v. Hong Kong & Shanghai Banking P. Corp. (245 N.Y. 377). In the first of these cases the defendant supplying ticker service to brokers was held not liable in damages to one of the broker's customers for the consequences of reliance upon a report negligently published on the ticker. If liability had been upheld, the step would have been a short one to the declaration of a like liability on the part of proprietors of newspapers. In the second the principle was clearly stated by POUND, J., that "negligent words are not actionable unless they are uttered directly, with knowledge or notice that they will be acted on, to one to whom the speaker is bound by some relation of duty, arising out of public calling, contract or otherwise, to act with care if he acts at all."

From the foregoing analysis the conclusion is, we think, inevitable that nothing in our previous decisions commits us to a holding of liability for negligence in the circumstances of the case at hand, and that such liability, if recognized, will be an extension of the principle of those decisions to different conditions, even if more or less analogous. The question then is whether such an extension shall be made.

The extension, if made, will so expand the field of liability for negligent speech as to make it nearly, if not quite, coterminous with that of liability for fraud. Again and again, in decisions of this court, the bounds of this latter liability have been set up, with futility the fate of every endeavor to dislodge them. Scienter has been declared to be an indispensible element except where the representation has been put forward as true of one's own knowledge, or in circumstances where the expression of opinion was a dishonorable pretense. Even an opinion, especially an opinion by an expert, may be found to be fraudulent if the grounds supporting it are so flimsy as to lead to the conclusion that there was no genuine belief back of it. Further than that this court has never gone. . . . This has not meant, to be sure, that negligence may not be evidence from which a trier of the facts may draw an inference of fraud but merely that if that inference is rejected, or, in the light of all the circumstances, is found to be unreasonable, negligence alone is not a substitute for fraud. . . .

We have said that the duty to refrain from negligent representation would become coincident or nearly so with the duty to refrain from fraud if this action could be maintained. A representation even though knowingly false does not constitute ground for an action of deceit unless made with the intent to be communicated to the persons or class of persons who act upon it to their prejudice. Affirmance of this judgment would require us to hold that all or nearly all the persons so situated would suffer an impairment of an interest legally protected if the representation had been negligent. . . .

Liability for negligence if adjudged in this case will extend to many callings other than an auditor's. Lawyers who certify their opinion as to the validity of municipal or corporate bonds with knowledge that the opinion will be brought to the notice of the public, will become liable to the investors, if they have overlooked a statute or a decision, to the same extent as if the controversy were one between client and adviser. Title companies insuring titles to a tract of land, with knowledge that at an approaching auction the fact that they have insured will be stated to the bidders, will become liable to purchasers who may wish the benefit of a policy without payment of a premium. These illustrations may seem to be extreme, but they go little, if any, farther than we are invited to go now. Negligence, moreover, will have one standard when viewed in relation to the employer, and another and at times a stricter standard when viewed in relation to the public. Explanations that might seem plausible, omissions that might be reasonable, if the duty is confined to the employer, conducting a business that presumably at least is not a fraud upon his creditors, might wear another aspect if an independent duty to be suspicious even of one's principal is owing to investors. "Everyone making a promise having the quality of a contract will be under a duty to the promisee by virtue of the promise, but under another duty, apart from contract, to an indefinite number of potential beneficiaries when performance has begun. The assumption of one relation will mean the involuntary assumption of a series of new relations, inescapably hooked together." "The law does not spread its protection so far."

Our holding does not emancipate accountants from the consequences of fraud. It does not relieve them if their audit has been so negligent as to justify a finding that they had no genuine belief in its adequacy, for this again is fraud. It does no more than say that if less than this is proved, if there has been neither reckless misstatement nor insincere profession of an opinion, but only honest blunder, the ensuing liability for negligence is one that is bounded by the contract, and is to be enforced between the parties by whom the contract has been made. We doubt whether the average businessman receiving a certificate without paying for it and receiving it merely as one among a multitude of possible investors would look for anything more.

(2) The second cause of action is yet to be considered.

The defendants certified as a fact, true to their own knowledge, that the balance sheet was in accordance with the books of account. If their statement was false, they are not to be exonerated because they believed it to be true. We think the triers of the facts might hold it to be false. . . .

In this connection we are to bear in mind the principle already stated in the course of this opinion that negligence or blindness, even when not equivalent to fraud, is none the less evidence to sustain an inference of fraud. At least this is so if the negligence is gross. . . .

We conclude, to sum up the situation, that in certifying to the correspondence between balance sheet and accounts the defendants made a statement as true to their own knowledge, when they had, as a jury might find, no knowledge on the subject. If that is so, they may also be found to have acted without information leading to a sincere or genuine belief when they certified to an opinion that the balance sheet faithfully reflected the condition of the business.

(The court then held that the cause of action for negligence was to be dismissed and that a new trial would be held on the cause of action for fraud.)

The *Ultramares* case recognizes that an auditor may be liable to a third party for negligence when the duties performed were for the *primary* benefit of the identified third party. This is consistent with third-party liability for breach of contract. For example, if an auditor is hired to prepare financial statements for the primary benefit of a known third party, the third party may collect its damages from a negligent accountant. The case also held that there is no liability for simple negligence to other third parties.

MODIFICATIONS OF
THE *ULTRAMARES* DOCTRINE

Courts in recent years have tended to modify and, in some cases, overrule the *Ultramares* decision. While it is still the law in many states, it is not the law in many others, and the trend of the cases is away from the reasoning of Justice Cardozo in *Ultramares*.

Some courts have expanded the liability by liberalizing the third-party beneficiary concept. These courts have not required that the accountant's services be for the primary benefit of the third party. All they have required is that the auditor know that the reports are for the benefit of a third party and that the third party be identified. It should be noted that some courts have refused to extend liability to all known persons who benefit from the services and have retained the primary benefit test.

Section 522 of the *Restatement of Torts, Second* contains provisions creating liability for negligence to third persons. That provision was used as part of the reasoning in the case which follows:

RUSCH FACTORS, INC. v. LEVIN
284 F.Supp. 85 (1968)

PETTINE, J.

In late 1963 and early 1964 a Rhode Island corporation sought financing from the plaintiff. To measure the financial stability of the corporation the plaintiff requested certified financial statements. The defendant accountant prepared the statements which represented the corporation to be solvent by a substantial amount. In fact, the corporation was insolvent. On or before February 10, 1964, the corporation submitted the statements to the plaintiff. The plaintiff relied upon the statements and loaned the corporation a sum in excess of $337,000.00. Subsequently, the corporation went into receivership, and the plaintiff has been able to recover only a portion of the amount loaned to the corporation.

The plaintiff complains that it has been injured in an amount in excess of $121,000.00 as a result of its reliance upon the fraudulent or negligent misrepresentations in the financial statements certified by the defendant accountant. The defendant has moved to dismiss . . . on the ground . . . that the absence of privity of contract between the defendant accountant and the plaintiff reliant party is a complete defense. . . .

Privity of contract is clearly no defense in a fraud action. An intentionally misrepresenting accountant is liable to all those persons whom he should reasonably have foreseen would be injured by his misrepresentation. Neither active knowledge by the accountant of the third person's reliance nor quantitative limitation of the class of reliant persons is requisite to recovery for fraud.

The same broad perimeter prevails if the misrepresenter's conduct is heedless enough to permit an inference of fraud. There are several reasons which support the broad rule of liability for fraudulent misrepresentation. First, liability should extend at least as far in fraud, an intentional tort, as it does in negligence cases resulting in personal injury or property damage. Second, the risk of loss for intentional wrongdoing should invariably be placed on the wrongdoer who caused the harm, rather than on the innocent victim of the harm. Finally, a broad rule of liability may deter future misconduct. The Court determines, for the above stated reasons, that the plaintiff's complaint is sufficient insofar as it alleges fraud.

No appellate court, English or American, has ever held an accountant liable in negligence to reliant parties not in privity.

The reluctance of the courts to hold the accounting profession to an obligation of care which extends to all reasonably foreseeable reliant parties is predicated upon the social utility rationale first articulated by Judge Cardozo in the *Ultramares* case. . . .

The wisdom of the decision in *Ultramares* has been doubted and this Court shares the doubt. Why should an innocent reliant party be forced to carry the weighty burden of an accountant's professional malpractice? Isn't the risk of loss more easily distributed and fairly spread by imposing it on the accounting profession which can pass the cost of insuring against the risk onto its customers, who can in turn pass the cost onto the entire consuming public? Finally, wouldn't a rule of foreseeability elevate the cautionary techniques of the accounting profession? For these reasons it appears to this Court that the decision in *Ultramares* constitutes an unwarranted inroad upon the principle that "(t)he risk reasonably to be perceived defines the duty to be obeyed. . . ."

This Court need not overrule the *Ultramares* decision, . . . for the case at bar is qualitatively distinguishable from *Ultramares*. There, the plaintiff was a member of an undefined, unlimited class of remote lenders and potential equity holders not actually foreseen but only foreseeable. Here the plaintiff is a single party whose reliance was actually foreseen by the defendant. The case at bar is, in fact, far more akin to the case of Glanzer v. Shephard, 233 N.Y. 236, another Cardozo opinion and the first case to extend to persons not in privity, liability for negligent misrepresentation causing pecuniary loss. In fact, the Glanzer principle has been applied to accountants. The tentative drafts of the Restatement (Second) of Torts §552 states the rule of law as follows:

(1) One who, in the course of his business, profession or employment, or in a transaction in which he has a pecuniary interest, supplies false information for the guidance of others in their business transactions, is subject to liability for pecuniary loss caused to them by their justifiable reliance upon the information, if he fails to exercise reasonable care or competence in obtaining or communicating the information.

(2) Except as stated in subsection (3), the liability stated in subsection (1) is limited to loss suffered

    (a) by the person or one of the persons for whose benefit and guidance he intends to supply the information, or knows that the recipient intends to supply it; and

    (b) through reliance upon it in a transaction which he intends the information to influence, or knows that the recipient so intends, or in a substantially similar transaction.

(3) The liability of one who is under a public duty to give the information extends to loss suffered by any of the class of persons for whose benefit the duty is created, in any of the transactions in which it is intended to protect them.

With respect, then to the plaintiff's negligence theory, this Court holds that an accountant should be liable in negligence for careless financial misrepresentations relied upon by actually foreseen and limited classes of persons. According to the plaintiff's complaint in the instant case, the defendant knew that his certification was to be used for, and had as its very aim and purpose, the reliance of potential financiers of the Rhode Island corporation. The defendant's motion is, therefore, denied.

In 1971 the Court of Civil Appeals in Texas adopted the modern approach including the *Restatement of Torts* viewpoint in the case of

Shatterproof Glass Corporation v. *James*, 466 S.W.2d 873. The court in that case said in part:

> With respect to the fraudulent or dishonest aspect of appellees' argument, it is sufficient to say that when misrepresentations are made, it is immaterial whether they be made innocently or deliberately or whether they be made with a fraudulent or dishonest intent.
>
> As is evident from recent decisions involving investors and other persons who extend credit to corporations, the courts have replaced "privity" and "primary benefit" with the concepts of "good faith" and "common honesty." . . .
>
> We believe that the Restatement (Second), Torts, § 552 (Tent. Draft No. 12, 1966) should be adopted in Texas for application to cases of this nature. . . .
>
> We find and hold that within the scope defined in Restatement, Second, Torts, § 552 (Tent. Draft No. 12, 1966), an accountant may be held liable to third parties who rely upon financial statements, audits, etc., prepared by the accountant in cases where the latter fails to exercise ordinary care in the preparation of such statement, audits, etc., and the third party because of such reliance suffers financial loss or damage.

The draftsmen of the *Restatement (Second)* provided the following hypothetical illustrations to help clarify its provisions:

2. A is negotiating with the X Bank for a credit of $50,000. The Bank requires an audit by certified public accountants. A employs B & Company, a firm of accountants, to make the audit, telling them that it is to meet the requirements of the X Bank. B & Company agree to make the audit, with express understanding that it is for transmission to X Bank only. The X Bank fails, and A without any further communication with B & Company submits their certification to the Y Bank, which in reliance upon it extends a credit of $50,000 to A. The audit is so carelessly made as greatly to overstate the financial resources of A, and in consequence the Y Bank suffers pecuniary loss through its extension of credit. B & Company is not liable to Y Bank.

3. The same facts as in Illustration 2, except that nothing is said about supplying the information for the guidance of X Bank only, and A merely informs B & Company that he expects to negotiate a bank loan, and has the X Bank in mind. B & Company is subject to liability to Y Bank.

4. The same facts as in Illustration 2, except that A informs B & Company he expects to negotiate a bank loan, but does not mention the name of any bank. B & Company is subject to liability to Y Bank. . . .

7. A, a certified public accountant, is employed by B Company to prepare and certify a balance sheet for the corporation. A is not informed of any intended use of the balance sheet, but A knows that such certificates are customarily used in a wide variety of financial transactions with the corporation, and that it may be relied upon by

lenders, investors, shareholders, creditors, purchasers, and the like, in numerous possible kinds of transactions. In fact, B Company uses the certified balance sheet to obtain a loan from X Bank. Because of A's negligence the balance sheet presents an inaccurate picture of the finances of B Company, and through reliance upon it X Bank suffers pecuniary loss. A is not liable to X Bank."

The *Restatement (Second)* also takes the position that the maker of the misrepresentation is liable for those transactions or substantially similar transactions which he intends to influence or knows that the recipient intends to influence. It notes:

Thus accountants who negligently make an audit of the books of the A Corporation, which they are told is to be used only for the purpose of obtaining a particular line of banking credit, are not subject to liability to a wholesale merchant whom the corporation induces to supply it with goods on credit by showing him the audit and the certification. On the other hand, it is not necessary that the transaction in which the negligent audit is relied on shall be identical in all of its minutest details with the one intended. It is enough that it is substantially the same transaction, or one substantially similar. Thus, in the situation above stated, if the corporation, finding that at the moment it does not need the credit to obtain which the audit was procured, uses it a month later to obtain the same credit from the same bank, the accountants will remain subject to liability to the bank for the loss resulting from its extension of credit, unless the financial condition of the corporation has materially changed in the interim, or so much time has elapsed that the bank cannot justifiably rely upon the audit.

There may be many minor differences which do not affect the essential character of the transaction. The question may be one of the extent of the departure which the maker of the representation understands is to be expected. If he is informed that the information which he supplies is to be used in applying to a particular bank for a loan of $10,000, the fact that the loan is made by that bank for $15,000 will not necessarily mean that the transaction is a different one. But if the loan is for $500,000, and secured by an issue of bonds, the very difference in amount, with the type of security not usually contemplated on a loan, would lead the ordinary borrower or lender to regard it as a different kind of loan. The ordinary practices and attitudes of the business world are to be taken into account; and the question becomes one of whether the departure from the contemplated transaction is so major, and so significant, that it cannot be regarded as essentially the same transaction. It is also possible, of course, that more than one kind of transaction may be understood as intended.

The following hypothetical illustrations are also provided by the restatement to clarify the foregoing.

9. A, a certified accountant, negligently certifies a balance sheet for B Corporation, which shows it to be in a favorable financial condition

although it is in fact insolvent. A knows that B Corporation intends to exhibit the balance sheet to C Corporation as a basis for applying for credit for the purchase of goods. In reliance upon the balance sheet, C Corporation buys the controlling interest in the stock of B Corporation, and as a result suffers pecuniary loss. A is not liable to C Corporation.

10. The same facts as in Illustration 9, except that A expects that C Corporation will be asked to extend credit for the purchase of washing machines, and credit is extended instead for the purchase of electric refrigerators. A is subject to liability to C Corporation.

As a result of the foregoing and other cases, many jurisdictions today hold accountants liable for ordinary negligence to foreseeable third parties. This liability has even been extended to incomplete unaudited workpapers and adjusting entries when completed financial statements were not prepared. Since a primary function of the audit is to supply information to third parties, there are substantial numbers of foreseen third parties. There is a definite trend toward increased responsibility and liability and away from *Ultramares*.

CONCLUSION

Accountants have common law liability to clients and to third parties in certain situations. The liability of an accountant to his client may be based on the theory of breach of contract or on the tort theories of fraud and negligence in the performance of his duties. The breach of contract theory is used when an accountant fails to perform certain tasks that he was engaged by the client to perform.

Liability for fraud requires proof of the usual elements of fraud. However, the element of scienter (intention to mislead) may be supplied by gross negligence. As a result, a statement made with a reckless disregard as to its accuracy or truthfulness may be the basis of a tort action of deceit. The scienter requirement may be met by proving that the party making the statement lacked actual knowledge as to whether or not it was true or false. This type of statement is usually described as reckless or grossly negligent. Liability for fraud extends to third parties as well as to clients.

A suit against an accountant on the theory of negligence is a malpractice action predicated on the failure of the accountant to perform his duties with that standard of care, skill, and competence required of members of the profession. Every professional accountant owes a duty to his client to perform the services with reasonable care. While professional persons cannot guarantee that they will make no mistakes, they are required to meet the standards of their profession and sometimes even higher standards. In the event that negligence is established, the accountant's liability will be for all damages approximately caused by the failure to exercise the requisite degree of care.

The law is not uniform or entirely clear as it relates to liability to third parties for negligence. Many states follow the *Ultramares* rule and hold that there is no liability in the absence of privity of contract or where the primary purpose of the services was to benefit the third party. However, many states have overruled or abandoned this rule and hold that an accountant is liable for negligence in the performance of his services to those persons whose reliance on the financial representations was actually foreseen by the accountant. The *Restatement of Torts (Second)* extends the liability of the accountant to those persons, of whom the accountant is aware, to whom his client intends to supply the product of the accountant's services. For example, if an accountant knows that his financial statements are to be furnished to banks as part of the loan process, the accountant has liability to the bank for negligence in the preparation of the financial statements. As a general rule, the accountant is liable for negligence to the limited class of third persons who come within the description "actually foreseen."

Even in the states that have abandoned *Ultramares,* an accountant is not liable on a theory of general negligence to unforeseen third persons. This result is based on the requirement of privity of contract. There is no liability to unforeseen third parties even though the accountant knows that some third party may rely on his work product.

Accountants also have liability created by statutes. That liability is discussed in the next chapter. The common law liabilities are summarized in the following chart.

THE TORT LIABILITY OF ACCOUNTANTS

Theories of Liability	Liability to Clients	Liability to Those in Privity and to Primary Beneficiaries	Liability to Known Third Parties	Liability to Unknown Third Parties
1. Common Law Fraud	Yes	Yes	Yes	Yes
2. Gross Negligence— Reckless Statements	Yes	Yes	Yes	Yes
3. Breach of Contract	Yes	Yes	No	No
4. Negligence in Those States Following *Ultramares*	Yes	Yes	No	No
5. Negligence in Those States Following Section 552 of the *Restatement of Torts, Second*	Yes	Yes	Yes	No

1. Intentional torts have punitive aspects. What are they? Why are these aspects so significant in malpractice cases?

2. Describe three malpractice theories. To what extent do they overlap?

3. Define negligence, gross negligence, and contributory negligence. Give three examples of negligence by accountants and two of gross negligence.

4. X, an accountant, is sued for malpractice by a client. Another accountant testifies that X had followed generally accepted accounting principles in the performance of his duties. Does this evidence entitle X to a verdict in his favor? Why or why not?

5. What are the elements of actionable fraud?

6. X, an accountant, conducted an audit for ABC Company. Due to a time limitation, X did not verify the accuracy of the closing inventory but rather accepted the president of ABC's statement that the inventory was correct. Unknown to both X and the president, the inventory was overstated by 33⅓% due to theft by employees. A bank which loaned money to ABC upon the strength of the financial statements sued X on a theory of fraud. X defended, denying any intention to mislead. What result? Why?

7. Under what circumstances will a misstatement of an opinion constitute grounds for an action of fraud and deceit? Explain.

8. Under what circumstances will silence by an accountant constitute a misrepresentation for purposes of an action for fraud and deceit? Explain.

9. Compare the "benefit of the bargain" theory of damages with the "out of pocket" theory.

10. What was the rationale of the *Ultramares* doctrine holding that accountants do not have liability to third persons for simple negligence?

11. Why have the courts of many states and the *Restatement of Torts, Second* overruled the *Ultramares* doctrine and held that accountants do have liability to foreseen third parties for simple negligence?

12. Contrast the liability of accountants to their clients with their liability to known and unknown third parties.

SUGGESTED ADDITIONAL READINGS

"Accountants Are Liable to Third Parties . . . ," *Drake Law Review,* January 1971.

"Accountant's Liabilities for False and Misleading Financial Statements," *Columbia Law Review,* December 1967.

"Accountants' Liabilities to Third Parties under Common Law and Federal

Securities Law," *Boston College Industrial and Commercial Law Review,* Fall 1967.

American Jurisprudence Legal Forms 2d vol. 1, chap. 5, "Accountants," New York: Lawyers Co-operative Publishing Co., 1971.

American Jurisprudence Pleading and Practice Forms Annotated, rev. ed., vol. 1, "Accountants," New York: Lawyers Co-operative Publishing Co., 1967.

ANNOT., "Liability of one preparing income tax return for another, for losses or penalties resulting from errors in return." 47 *A.L.R.*3d 1286, 1973.

ANNOT., "Liability of Public Accountant." 54 *A.L.R.*2d 324, 1957.

ANNOT., "Liability of Public Accountant to Third Parties." 46 *A.L.R.*3d 979, 1972.

"Auditors' Responsibility for Misrepresentation: Inadequate Protection for Users of Financial Statements," *Washington Law Review,* 1968–1969.

BYRD, KENNETH F., "Accountancy and the Onslaught of Case Law in North America," *Accountant,* July 8, 1967.

Comment, "Evidence—Privileged Communications—Accountant and Client." *North Carolina Law Review,* 1968.

LEVY, SAUL, *Accountants' Legal Responsibility,* New York: American Institute of Accountants, 1954.

MARINELLI, ARTHUR J., JR., "The Expanding Scope of Accountants' Liability to Third Parties," *Case Western Reserve Law Review,* November 1971.

"Privileged Communications—Accountants and Accounting," *Michigan Law Review,* April 1968.

PROSSER, WILLIAM L., *Law of Torts* (4th ed.). St. Paul, Minnesota: West Publishing Co., 1971. "Misrepresentation and Third Persons," *Vanderbilt Law Review,* March 1966.

RICH, WILEY DANIEL, *Legal Responsibilities and Rights of Public Accountants,* New York: American Institute Publishing Co., 1955.

SIMPSON, LAURENCE P., *Contracts* (2nd ed.). St. Paul, Minnesota: West Publishing Co., 1965.

WISE, T. A., "The Very Private World of Peat, Marwick, Mitchell," *Fortune,* July 1, 1966.

ADDITIONAL CASES

Aluma Kraft Manufacturing Co. v. Elmer Fox & Co., 403 S.W.2d 378, (Md.) 1973.

Bonhiver v. Graff, 248 N.W.2d 291 (Minn.) 1976.

Bunge Corporation v. Eide, 372 F.Supp. 1058 (1974).

Canaveral Capital Corporation v. Bruce, 214 So.2d 505 (Fla.) 1968.

Craig v. Anyon, 211 App.Div. 55 (1925).

Delmar Vineyard v. Timmons, 486 S.W.2d 914 (Tenn.) 1972.

Donovan Construction Company of Minn. v. Woosley, 358 F.Supp. 375 (1973).

Duro Sportswear v. Cogen, 131 N.Y.S.2d 20 (1954).

Franklin Supply Comany v. Tolman, 454 F.2d 1059 (1972).

Gammel v. Ernst & Ernst, 72 N.W.2d 364 (Minn.) 1955.

Investment Corporation of Florida v. Buchman, 208 So.2d 291 (Fla.) 1968.

Landell v. Lybrand, 107 A.783 (Pa.) 1919.

Lindner v. Barlow, Davis & Wood, 27 Cal. Rptr. 101 (1963).

MacNerland v. Barnes, 199 S.E.2d 564 (Ga.) 1973.

Milliner v. Elmer Fox and Co., 529 P.2d 806 (Utah) 1974.

National Surety Corp. v. Lybrand, 256 App.Div. 226 (1939).

Rassieur v. Charles, 188 S.W.2d 317 (Mo.) 1945.

R.I. Hosp. Tr. Nat. Bk. v. Swartz, Bresenoff, Yanver & Jacobs, 455 F.2d 847 (1972).

Ryan v. Kanne, 170 N.W.2d 395 (Iowa) 1969.

Stephens Industries, Inc. v. Haskins and Sells, 438 F.2d 357 (1971).

William Iselin, Etc. v. Muhlstock, Elowitz & Co., 382 N.Y.S.2d 83 (1976).

Chapter 9

Statutory Liability

INTRODUCTION

Since the Great Depression of the early 1930s, government at both the federal and state levels has been involved in the regulation of the sale of securities. Numerous statutes have been enacted not only to protect the investing public but to impose liability on anyone—including accountants —assisting in the sale of securities in violation of the law. These liabilities are both civil and criminal. The civil liabilities are discussed in this chapter, the criminal liabilities in the next.

The responsibility for administering the federal securities law is primarily vested in the Securities and Exchange Commission. The SEC exercises vast quasi-legislative and quasi-judicial powers. In order to prevent fraudulent sales of securities, the agency has adopted rules and regulations relating to financial and other information which must be included in the documents filed with the commission as well as those given to potential investors. It also regulates the various stock exchanges, utility holding companies, investment trusts, and investment advisors. Many of the rules and regulations of the SEC have a direct and significant impact on the accounting profession, especially upon the liability of accountants. This chapter will discuss the various aspects of this liability.

In order to understand the various provisions of the securities laws which impose liability upon accountants, the scope of such laws and the definition of the term *security* must be understood. Since the objective of the securities laws is to protect innocent persons from investing their money in speculative enterprises over which they have little or no control, the laws are paternalistic in character and are liberally construed to protect the investing public. The securities laws therefore cover not only stocks and bonds but every kind of investment in which one person invests money and looks to others for the success of the venture. The laws are applicable to every investment contract in which a person receives some evidence of indebtedness or a certificate of interest or participation in a profit-sharing agreement. As a result, sales of oil well interests, whiskey receipts, interests in limited partnerships, and even savings and loan investments have been held to come within the scope of the securities laws. In addition, cases have held that purchases such as an interest in an orange grove or a self-improvement course are securities. Thus, the term *security* is broadly defined to include any investment in which a person turns his money or property over to another to manage for profit. The accountant must recognize that any time financial statements are prepared for the purpose of raising money from investors, potential liability under the securities laws exists.

THE SECURITIES ACT OF 1933

COVERAGE

The Securities Act of 1933 was enacted by Congress under its power to regulate "commerce among the several states." Its provisions declare that it is unlawful to use the mails or any interstate means of communication or transportation in violation of the act. The 1933 law may be thought of as a disclosure law. It requires that securities subject to its provisions be registered and that a prospectus be furnished each investor. The prospectus must supply the investor with sufficient facts, including financial information, to enable him to make an intelligent investment decision. The law does not prohibit the sale of worthless securities. It only requires that certain factual information be furnished potential investors.

The information contained in the prospectus must not be untrue or even misleading. The SEC has adopted rules relating to the detailed requirements of the prospectus. The major requirements concern facts about the issuer and the financial statements, including balance sheet and statements of operation of the issuer.

The law exempts certain transactions from its coverage. The provisions that exempt certain transactions have the effect of limiting the application of the law to transactions in which a security is sold to the general public by the issuer, an underwriter, or a controlling person. (A *controlling person* is one who controls or is controlled by the issuer, such as the major stockholder of a corporation.)

The law also exempts certain securities from its coverage. These are securities subject to regulation by governmental agencies other than the SEC, such as securities of banks and savings and loan institutions. The law also exempts intrastate offerings. The intrastate exemption covers securities that are offered and sold only to persons who reside within the state of incorporation: If the issuer is unincorporated, the purchasers must reside within the state of its residence and place of business. If the sale is to a resident with the intention that it will be resold to a nonresident, the intrastate state exemption is lost. The same is true if the mails or interstate systems of communication are used to sell the security. It should be remembered that even if the sale is exempt under federal law, it is probably subject to a similar state law.

The 1933 Act contains a provision declaring that it is unlawful to commit fraud in the offer of sale of any securities. While a civil cause of action may be based on this provision, most cases use the fraud remedy of the 1934 Act which will be discussed later. It is also a crime to violate this section, and criminal prosecutions are often based on these antifraud provisions. (The provisions of the law relating to fraud in the sale of a security are applicable to exempt transactions as well as to those covered by it.)

LIABILITY UNDER THE 1933 ACT

The 1933 Securities Act imposes both civil and criminal liability for violation of its provisions. There are civil liability provisions relating to registration statements (Section 11 of the Act) and others relating to prospectuses and oral and written communications (Section 12 of the Act). The civil liability provisions relating to registration statements impose liability on the following persons in favor of purchasers of securities:

a. Every person who signed the registration statement
b. Every director of the corporation or partner in the partnership issuing the security
c. Every person who with his consent is named in the registration statement as about to become a director or partner
d. Every *accountant,* engineer, or appraiser who has with his consent been named as having prepared or certified any part of the registration statement or as having prepared or certified any report or

valuation which is used in connection with the registration statement. (Emphasis added.)

For purposes of civil liability in connection with a registration statement, liability is imposed if the registration statement (1) contains an untrue statement of a material fact, or (2) omits to state a material fact required to be stated in order that the facts as stated are not misleading. This latter situation describes the factual situation of a statement containing a half-truth which has the net effect of misleading the reader. The test of accuracy and materiality is operative as of the date the registration statement becomes effective.

The separate provision relating to liability arising in connection with prospectuses and communications imposes liability on sellers who fail to comply with the registration requirements of the act. This liability is imposed irrespective of wrongful intent or conduct on those who fail to comply with the law. It also imposes liability on sellers who use a prospectus or make communications (by mail, telephone or other instrumentalities of interstate commerce) that contain an untrue statement of material facts required to be stated or necessary to make the statements not misleading. The purchasers of such securities may sue for their actual damages or to rescind the purchase and obtain a refund of the price. Used when the purchaser still owns the security, this latter remedy requires privity of contract. There is no liability for aiding and abetting someone who violates Section 12.

A defendant to an action under Section 12 may assert as a defense that he did not know and in the exercise of reasonable care could not have known of the untruth or omission. In other words, the seller has the burden of proof to establish a due diligence defense.

The case which follows is typical of those imposing liability under Section 11 of the 1933 Act.

ESCOTT v. BARCHRIS CONSTRUCTION CORPORATION
283 F.Supp. 643 (1968)

McLEAN, J.

This is an action by purchasers of 5½ per cent convertible subordinated fifteen year debentures of BarChris Construction Corporation (BarChris). Plaintiffs purport to sue on their own behalf and "on behalf of all other and present and former holders" of the debentures. . . .

The action is brought under Section 11 of the Securities Act of 1933. Plaintiffs allege that the registration statement with respect to these debentures filed with the Securities and Exchange Commission, which became effective on May 16, 1961, contained material false statements and material omissions.

Defendants fall into three categories: (1) the persons who signed the registration statement; (2) the underwriters, consisting of eight investment banking firms, and (3) BarChris's auditors, Peat, Marwick, Mitchell & Co. (Peat, Marwick). . . .

Defendants, in addition to denying that the registration statement was false, have pleaded the defenses open to them under Section 11 of the Act, plus certain additional defenses, including the statute of limitations. . . . On the main issue of liability, the questions to be decided are (1) did the registration statement contain false statements of fact, or did it omit to state facts which should have been stated in order to prevent it from being misleading; (2) if so, were the facts which were falsely stated or omitted "material" within the meaning of the Act; (3) if so, have defendants established their affirmative defenses? . . .

At the time relevant here, BarChris was engaged primarily in the construction of bowling alleys, somewhat euphemistically referred to as "bowling centers." These were rather elaborate affairs. They contained not only a number of alleys or "lanes," but also, in most cases, bar and restaurant facilities. . . . It is estimated that in 1960 BarChris installed approximately three percent of all lanes built in the United States. It was thus a significant factor in the industry, although two large established companies, American Machine & Foundry Company and Brunswick, were much larger factors. . . .

BarChris's sales increased dramatically from 1956 to 1960. According to the prospectus, net sales, in round figures, in 1956 were some $800,000, in 1957 $1,300,000, in 1958 $1,700,000. In 1959 they increased to over $3,300,-000, and by 1960 they had leaped to over $9,165,000. . . .

In general, BarChris's method of operation was to enter into a contract with a customer, receive from him at that time a comparatively small down payment on the purchase price, and proceed to construct and equip the bowling alley. When the work was finished and the building delivered, the customer paid the balance of the contract price in notes, payable in installments over a period of years. BarChris discounted these notes with a factor and received part of their face amount in cash. The factor held back part as a reserve.

In 1960 BarChris began a practice which has been referred to throughout this case as the "alternative method of financing." In substance this was a sale and leaseback arrangement. . . .

Under either financing method, BarChris was compelled to expend considerable sums in defraying the cost of construction before it received reimbursement. As a consequence, BarChris sold 560,000 shares of common stock to the public at $3.00 per share. This issue was underwritten by Peter Morgan & Company, one of the present defendants.

By early 1961, BarChris needed additional working capital. The proceeds of the sale of the debentures involved in this action were to be devoted, in part at least, to fill that need.

The registration statement of the debentures, in preliminary form, was filed with the Securities and Exchange Commission on March 30, 1961. A first amendment was filed on May 11 and a second on May 16. The registration statement became effective on May 16. The closing of the financing took place on May 24. On that day BarChris received the proceeds of the financing.

By that time BarChris was experiencing difficulties in collecting amounts due from some of its customers. Some of them were in arrears in payments due to factors on their discounted notes. As time went on those difficulties increased. Although BarChris continued to build alleys in 1961 and 1962, it became increasingly apparent that the industry was overbuilt. Operators of alleys, often inadequately financed, began to fail. Precisely when the tide turned is a matter of dispute, but at any rate, it was painfully apparent in 1962. . . .

. . . In October 1962 BarChris came to the end of the road. On October 29, 1962, it filed in this court a petition for an arrangement under Chapter XI of the Bankruptcy Act. BarChris defaulted in the payment of the interest due on November 1, 1962 on the debentures.

THE DEBENTURE REGISTRATION STATEMENT

. . . Peat, Marwick, BarChris's auditors, who had previously audited BarChris's annual balance sheet and earnings figures for 1958 and 1959, did the same for 1960. These figures were set forth in the registration statement. In addition, Peat, Marwick undertook a so-called "S-1 review," the proper scope of which is one of the matters debated here.

The registration statement in its final form contained a prospectus as well as other information. Plaintiffs' claims of falsities and omissions pertain solely to the prospectus, not to the additional data.

The prospectus contained, among other things, a description of BarChris's business, a description of its real property, some material pertaining to certain of its subsidiaries, and remarks about various other aspects of its affairs. It also contained financial information. It included a consolidated balance sheet as of December 31, 1960, with elaborate explanatory notes. These figures had been audited by Peat, Marwick. It also contained unaudited figures as to net sales, gross profit and net earnings for the first quarter ended March 31, 1961, as compared with the similar quarter for 1960. In addition, it set forth figures as to the company's backlog of unfilled orders as of March 31, 1961, as compared with March 31, 1960, and figures as to BarChris's contingent liability, as of April 30, 1961, on customers' notes discounted and its contingent liability under the so-called alternative method of financing.

Plaintiffs challenge the accuracy of a number of these figures. They also charge that the text of the prospectus, apart from the figures, was false in a number of respects, and that material information was omitted. . . . (The court then reviewed each allegation relative to the financial statements and summarized the various falsities and omissions as follows:)

1. 1960 Earnings

    (a) Sales

As per prospectus	$9,165,320
Correct figure	8,511,420
Overstatement	$ 653,900

(b) Net Operating Income

As per prospectus	$1,742,801
Correct figure	1,496,196
Overstatement	$ 246,605

(c) Earnings per Share

As per prospectus	$ .75
Correct figure	.65
Overstatement	$ .10

2. 1960 Balance Sheet

Current Assets

As per prospectus	$4,524,021
Correct figure	3,914,332
Overstatement	$ 609,689

3. Contingent Liabilities as of December 31, 1960 on Alternative Method of Financing

As per prospectus	$ 750,000
Correct figure	1,125,795
Understatement	$ 375,795
Capitol Lanes should have been shown as a direct liability	$ 325,000

4. Contingent Liabilities as of April 30, 1961

As per prospectus	$ 825,000
Correct figure	1,443,853
Understatement	$ 618,853
Capitol Lanes should have been shown as a direct liability	$ 314,166

5. Earnings Figures for Quarter ending March 31, 1961

(a) Sales

As per prospectus	$2,138,455
Correct figure	1,618,645
Overstatement	$ 519,810

(b) Gross Profit

As per prospectus	$ 483,121
Correct figure	252,366
Overstatement	$ 230,755

6. Backlog as of March 31, 1961

As per prospectus	$6,905,000
Correct figure	2,415,000
Overstatement	$4,490,000

7. Failure to Disclose Officers' Loans
Outstanding and Unpaid on May
16, 1961 $ 386,615

8. Failure to Disclose Use of Proceeds
in Manner not Revealed in Prospectus

Approximately $1,160,000

9. Failure to Disclose Customers'
Delinquencies in May 1961 and
BarChris's Potential Liability with
Respect Thereto

Overstatement $1,350,000

10. Failure to Disclose the Fact that
BarChris was Already Engaged, and
was about to be More Heavily Engaged,
in the Operation of Bowling Alleys

MATERIALITY

It is a prerequisite to liability under Section 11 of the Act that the fact which is falsely stated in a registration statement, or the fact that is omitted when it should have been stated to avoid misleading, be "material." The regulations of the Securities and Exchange Commission pertaining to the registration of securities define the word as follows (17 C.F.R. § 230.405 (*1*)):

The term "material," when used to qualify a requirement for the furnishing of information as to any subject, limits the information required to those matters as to which an average prudent investor ought reasonably to be informed before purchasing the security registered.

What are "matters as to which an average prudent investor ought reasonably to be informed"? It seems obvious that they are matters which such an investor needs to know before he can make an intelligent, informed decision whether or not to buy the security.

Early in the history of the Act, a definition of materiality was given in Matter of Charles A. Howard, 1 S.E.C. 6, 8 (1934), which is still valid today. A material fact was there defined as:

* * * a fact which if it has been correctly stated or disclosed would have deterred or tendered to deter the average prudent investor from purchasing the securities in question.

The average prudent investor is not concerned with minor inaccuracies or with errors as to matters which are of no interest to him. The facts which tend to deter him from purchasing a security are facts which have an important bearing upon the nature or condition of the issuing corporation or its business.

Judged by this test, there is no doubt that many of the misstatements and omissions in this prospectus were material. This is true of all of them which relate to the state of affairs in 1961, i.e., the overstatement of sales and gross profit for the first quarter, the understatement of contingent liabilities as of April 30, the overstatement of orders on hand and the failure to disclose the true facts with respect to officers' loans, customers' delinquencies, application of proceeds and the prospective operation of several alleys.

The misstatements and omissions pertaining to BarChris's status as of December 31, 1960, however, present a much closer question. The 1960 earnings figures, the 1960 balance sheet and the contingent liabilities as of December 31, 1960 were not nearly as erroneous as plaintiffs have claimed. But they were wrong to some extent, as we have seen. Would it have deterred the average prudent investor from purchasing these debentures if he had been informed that the 1960 sales were $8,511,420 rather than $9,165,320, that the net operating income was $1,496,196 rather than $1,742,801 and that the earnings per share in 1960 were approximately 65¢ rather than 75¢? . . .

These debentures were rated "B" by the investment rating services. They were thus characterized as speculative, as any prudent investor must have realized. It would seem that anyone interested in buying these convertible debentures would have been attracted primarily by the conversion feature, by the growth potential of the stock. The growth which the company enjoyed in 1960 over prior years was striking, even on the correct figures. It is hard to see how a prospective purchaser of this type of investment would have been deterred from buying if he had been advised of these comparatively minor errors in reporting 1960 sales and earnings.

Since no one knows what moves or does not move the mythical "average prudent investor," it comes down to a question of judgment, to be exercised by the trier of the fact as best he can in the light of all the circumstances. It is my best judgment that the average prudent investor would not have cared about these errors in the 1960 sales and earnings figures, regrettable though they may be. I therefore find that they were not material within the meaning of Section 11. . . .

This leaves for consideration the errors in the 1960 balance sheet figures . . . Current assets were overstated by approximately $600,000. Liabilities were understated by approximately $325,000. . . .

As per balance sheet, cash was $285,482. In fact, $145,000 of this had been borrowed temporarily from Talcott and was to be returned by January 16, 1961 so that realistically, cash was only $140,482. Trade accounts receivable were overstated by $150,000 by including Howard Lanes Annex, an alley which was not sold to an outside buyer.

As per balance sheet, total current assets were $4,524,021, and total current liabilities were $2,413,867, a ratio of approximately 1.9 to 1. This was bad enough, but on the true facts, the ratio was worse. As corrected, current assets, as near as one can tell, were approximately $3,924,000, and current liabilities approximately $2,478,000, a ratio of approximately 1.6 to 1.

Would it have made any difference if a prospective purchaser of these debentures had been advised of these facts? There must be some point at which errors in disclosing a company's balance sheet position become material, even to a growth-oriented investor. On all the evidence I find that these balance sheet errors were material within the meaning of Section 11.

Since there was an abundance of material misstatements pertaining to 1961 affairs, whether or not the errors in the 1960 figures were material does not affect the outcome of this case except to the extent that it bears upon the liability of Peat, Marwick. . . .

THE "DUE DILIGENCE" DEFENSES

Section 11(b) provides:

"Notwithstanding the provisions of subsection (a) no person * * * shall be liable as provided therein who shall sustain the burden of proof—
* * *
"(3) that * * * (B) as regards any part of the registration statement purporting to be made upon his authority as an expert * * * (i) he had, after reasonable investigation, reasonable ground to believe and did believe, at the time such part of the registration statement became effective, that the statements therein were true and that there was no omission to state a material fact required to be stated therein or necessary to make the statements therein not misleading * * *."

This defines the due diligence defense for an expert. Peat, Marwick has pleaded it.

The part of the registration statement purporting to be made upon the authority of Peat, Marwick as an expert was, as we have seen the 1960 figures. But because the statute requires the court to determine Peat, Marwick's belief, and the grounds thereof, "at the time such part of the registration statement became effective," for the purposes of this affirmative defense, the matter must be viewed as of May 16, 1961, and the question is whether at that time Peat, Marwick, after reasonable investigation, had reasonable ground to believe and did believe that the 1960 figures were true and that no material fact had been omitted from the registration statement which should have been included in order to make the 1960 figures not misleading. In deciding this issue, the court must consider not only what Peat, Marwick did in its 1960 audit, but also what it did in its subsequent "S-1 review." The proper scope of that review must also be determined. . . .

THE 1960 AUDIT

Peat, Marwick's work was in general charge of a member of the firm, Cummings, and more immediately in charge of Peat, Marwick's manager, Logan. Most of the actual work was performed by a senior accountant, Berardi, who had junior assistants, one of whom was Kennedy.

Berardi was then about thirty years old. He was not yet a C.P.A. He had had no previous experience with the bowling industry. This was his first job as a senior accountant. He could hardly have been given a more difficult assignment.

After obtaining a little background in formation on BarChris by talking to Logan and reviewing Peat, Marwick's work papers on its 1959 audit, Berardi examined the results of test checks of BarChris's accounting procedures which one of the junior accountants had made, and he prepared an "internal control questionnaire" and an "audit program." Thereafter, for a few days subsequent to December 30, 1960, he inspected BarChris's inventories and examined certain alley construction. Finally, on January 13, 1961, he began his auditing work which he carried on substantially continuously until it was completed on February 24, 1961. Toward the close of the work, Logan reviewed it and made various comments and suggestions to Berardi.

It is unnecessary to recount everything that Berardi did in the course of the audit. We are concerned only with the evidence relating to what Berardi did or did not do with respect to those items which I have found to have been incorrectly reported in the 1960 figures in the prospectus. More narrowly, we are directly concerned only with such of those items as I have found to be material. . . . [The court then reviewed the evidence and found that:

1. Berardi failed to discover that one facility listed as sold was actually leased to a subsidiary of the corporation. This error affected both the sales figure and the liability side of the balance sheet.
2. Berardi treated financing revenues as current assets when it was obvious that most of them would not be released within one year.
3. Berardi erred in computing the contingent liability on leaseback transactions at 25 percent. The contracts established this liability at 100 percent.]

THE S-1 REVIEW

The purpose of reviewing events subsequent to the date of a certified balance sheet (referred to as an S-1 review when made with reference to a registration statement) is to ascertain whether any material change has occurred in the company's fiancial position which should be disclosed in order to prevent the balance sheet figures from being misleading. The scope of such a review, under generally accepted auditing standards, is limited. It does not amount to a complete audit.

Peat, Marwick prepared a written program for such a review. I find that this program conformed to generally accepted auditing standards. Among other things, it required the following:

1. Review minutes of stockholders, directors and committees.* * *
2. Review latest interim financial statements and compare with corresponding statements of preceding year. Inquire regarding significant variations and changes.

* * *

4. Review the more important financial records and inquire regarding material transactions not in the ordinary course of business and any other significant items.

* * *

6. Inquire as to changes in material contracts * * *.

* * *

10. Inquire as to any significant bad debts or accounts in dispute for which provision has not been made.

* * *

14. Inquire as to * * * newly discovered liabilities, direct or contingent * * *.

Berardi made the S-1 review in May 1961. He devoted a little over two days to it, a total of 20½ hours. He did not discover any of the errors or omissions pertaining to the state of affairs in 1961. . . . The question is whether, despite his failure to find out anything, his investigation was reasonable within the meaning of the statute.

What Berardi did was to look at a consolidating trial balance as of March 31, 1961 which had been prepared by BarChris, compare it with the audited December 31, 1960 figures, discuss with Trilling certain unfavorable developments which the comparison disclosed, and read certain minutes. He did not examine any "important financial records" other than the trial balance. As to minutes, he read only what minutes Birnbaum gave him, which consisted only of the board of directors' minutes of BarChris. He did not read such minutes as there were of the executive committee. He did not know that there was an executive committee, hence he did not discover that Kircher had notes of executive committee minutes which had not been written up. He did not read the minutes of any subsidiary.

In substance, . . . Berardi . . . asked questions, he got answers which he considered satisfactory, and he did nothing to verify them. For example, he obtained from Trilling a list of contracts. The list included Yonkers and Bridge. Since Berardi did not read the minutes of subsidiaries, he did not learn that Yonkers and Bridge were intercompany sales. The list also included Woonsocket and the six T-Bowl jobs, Moravia Road, Milford, Groton, North Attleboro, Odenton and Severna Park. Since Berardi did not look at any contract documents, and since he was unaware of the executive committee minutes of March 18, 1961 (at that time embodied only in Kircher's notes), he did not learn that BarChris had no contracts for these jobs. Trilling's list did not set forth contract prices for them, although it did for Yonkers, Bridge, and certain others. This did not arouse Berardi's suspicion.

Berardi noticed that there had been an increase in notes payable by BarChris. Trilling admitted to him that BarChris was "a bit slow" in paying its bills. Berardi recorded in his notes of his review that BarChris was in a "tight cash position." Trilling's explanation was that BarChris was experiencing "some temporary difficulty."

Berardi had no conception of how tight the cash position was. He did not discover that BarChris was holding up checks in substantial amounts because there was no money in the bank to cover them. He did not know of the loan from Manufacturers Trust Company or of the officers' loans. Since he never read the prospectus, he was not even aware that there had ever been any problem about loans from officers.

During the 1960 audit Berardi had obtained some information from factors, not sufficiently detailed even then, as to delinquent notes. He made no inquiry of factors about this in his S-1 review. Since he knew nothing about Kircher's notes of the executive committee meetings, he did not learn that the delinquency situation had grown worse. He was content with Trilling's assurance that no liability theretofore contingent had become direct. . . .

There had been a material change for the worse in BarChris's financial position. That change was sufficiently serious so that the failure to disclose it made the 1960 figures misleading. Berardi did not discover it. As far as results were concerned, his S-1 review was useless.

Accountants should not be held to a standard higher than that recognized in their profession. I do not do so here. Berardi's review did not come up to that standard. He did not take some of the steps which Peat, Marwick's written program prescribed. He did not spend an adequate amount of time on a task of this magnitude. Most important of all, he was too easily satisfied with glib answers to his inquiries.

This is not to say that he should have made a complete audit. But there were enough danger signals in the materials which he did examine to require some further investigation on his part. Generally accepted accounting standards required such further investigation under these circumstances. It is not always sufficient merely to ask questions.

Here again, the burden of proof is on Peat, Marwick. I find that that burden has not been satisfied. I conclude that Peat, Marwick has not established its due diligence defense. . . .

Pursuant to Rule 52(a), this opinion constitutes the court's findings of fact and conclusions of law with respect to the issues determined herein.

So ordered.

As a result of the statute and cases such as the foregoing, liability under the 1933 Act extends to clients and to third parties. Privity of contract is not required. Liability of accountants is based on false statements or misleading omissions in the financial statements. Proof of negligence or fraud is not required, neither is proof of reliance or causal connection between the act of the accountant and the loss sustained. However, due diligence is a defense which can be established by proof of lack of fraud and freedom from negligence. The accountant has the burden of proof on this and other defenses which are discussed further in the next section.

DEFENSES

The 1933 Securities Law recognizes several defenses that may be used in an attempt to avoid liability. Since the law imposes liability upon proof that the portion of registration statement attributable to the accountant contains an untrue statement of a *material fact* or omits a *material fact* necessary to prevent the statements made from being misleading, lack of materiality is a common defense. Determining whether or not a particular fact is material depends on the facts and the parties involved. For the average investor, minor inaccuracies do not create liability. A material fact is one that would either deter or encourage a purchase because it had an important bearing on the nature or condition of the issuing corporation.

A plaintiff-purchaser need not prove reliance on the registration statement in order to recover, but actual knowledge on his part of falsity is a defense. Scienter is not an element of proof, but except for the issuer, reliance on an expert such as an accountant is a defense. Thus, other defendants will often seek to avoid liability by proof of reliance on the accountants. Such attempts increase the need for honesty and due diligence by accountants.

The statute of limitations is a defense for both civil and criminal liability. The basic period is one year. The statute does not become effective until the discovery of the untrue statement or omission or from the time such discovery would have been made with reasonable diligence. In no event may a suit be brought more than three years after the sale.

A defense similar to the statute of limitations is also provided. The statute provides that if the person acquiring the security does so after the issuer has made generally available an earnings statement covering at least twelve months after the effective date of the registration statement, then this person must prove actual reliance on the registration statement. However, this defense has little applicability in most cases.

Another defense available to the accountant is that he had, after reasonable investigation, reasonable grounds to believe and did believe that the statements contained in the registration statement were true and that there was no omission to state a material fact required or necessary to make the statements not misleading. In other words, "due diligence" is a defense. In determining whether or not an accountant has made a reasonable investigation, the law provides that the standard of reasonableness is that required of a prudent man in the management of his own property. This due diligence defense was raised in the BarChris case, the details of which are discussed there.

THE SECURITIES EXCHANGE ACT OF 1934

COVERAGE

The 1933 Securities Act deals with all aspects of original offerings. The 1934 Securities Exchange Act, as the title implies, is concerned with security exchanges and with the trading of securities after the primary offering stage. In addition to creating the SEC, the 1934 Act contains provisions regulating the various stock exchanges. It regulates brokers and dealers in securities and contains numerous provisions relating to such matters as proxy solicitation and insider transactions.

The Securities Exchange Act prohibits the sale of a security on a national exchange unless a registration is effective for the security. Registration under the 1934 Act is somewhat different from registration under the 1933 Act. Registration under the Securities Exchange Act requires the filing of prescribed forms with the applicable stock exchange and with the SEC. As a general rule, all equity securities that are held by five hundred or more owners must be registered if the issuer has more than $1 million in gross assets. This rule picks up issues that are traded over the counter, and it applies to securities that might have qualified under one of the exemptions under the 1933 Act.

Issuers of registered securities are required by the 1934 Act to file periodic reports with the SEC, as well as to report any significant development. The SEC rules on proxies apply to all securities registered under the act. These rules regulate all aspects of proxy solicitation in great detail and also regulate insider transactions.

In order to comply with the provisions of the 1934 Act, firms must use the services of CPAs. The responsibility of public accountants in certifying financial statements used to comply with the law is not only to the client who pays the fees but also to investors, creditors, and all others who may rely on the statements. As a result, accountants must report fairly on the facts as found, whether favorable or unfavorable to the client. The accountant's duty is to safeguard the public interest and not that of the client. Under this statute, the accountant has a duty to certify only those financial statements which are accurate.

LIABILITY UNDER SECTION 18

Two major statutory provisions impose civil liability under the 1934 Securities Exchange Act. These are Section 18 and Section 10b. Section 18 of the act imposes liability for false and misleading statements of material fact in any application, report, or document filed under the act. The section provides:

Any person who shall make or cause to be made any statement in any application, report, or document filed pursuant to this title or any rule or regulation thereunder . . . , which statement was at the time and in the light of the circumstances under which it was made false or misleading with respect to any material fact, shall be liable to any person (not knowing that such statement was false or misleading) when in reliance upon such statement, shall have purchased or sold a security at a price which was affected by such statement, for damages caused by such reliance, unless the person sued shall prove that *he acted in good faith and had no knowledge that such statement was false or misleading.* [Emphasis added.]

Liability under Section 18 for fraud extends to both purchasers and sellers. Plaintiffs under this section must prove scienter, reliance on the false or misleading statement, and damage. It is a defense that the person sued acted in good faith and without knowledge that the statement was false and misleading. In other words, freedom from fraud is a defense under an action predicated on Section 18. There is no liability under this section for simple negligence. Gross negligence can supply the element of intent however.

Section 18 is little more than a codification of common law fraud. It does require proof that some document or registration statement was filed with the SEC and that the plaintiff purchased or sold the security in reliance on it. Documents which are filed with the SEC for information only are exempted from the coverage of Section 18.

LIABILITY UNDER SECTION 10b
AND RULE 10b-5

Most of the litigation under the 1934 Act is brought under Section 10b and Rule 10b-5 of the SEC. These provisions are concerned with manipulative and deceptive devices and contrivances. Rule 10b-5 declares that it is unlawful to use the mails or any instrumentality of interstate commerce or any national securities exchange to defraud any person in connection with the purchase or sale of any security. As a result of judicial interpretation, this section and the rules promulgated under it provide a private civil remedy for defrauded investors, including purchasers and sellers of securities. This remedy may be invoked against "any person" who indulges in fraudulent practices in connection with the purchase or sale of securities.

In actual practice, defendants in Section 10b and Rule 10b-5 cases have tended to fall into four general categories: (1) insiders, (2) broker-dealers, (3) corporations whose stock is purchased or sold by plaintiffs, and (4) those who "aid and abet" or conspire with a party who falls into one of the first three categories. Accountants usually fall into the fourth category. Silence may constitute aiding and abetting. While there is no general duty on the part of all persons with knowledge of improper activities to report them, a duty to disclose may arise from the fact of a special relationship or set of circumstances such as an accountant certifying financial statements.

The application of Section 10b and Rule 10b-5 is not limited to securities subject to the act. It applies to all sales of any security if the requisite fraud exists and the interstate aspect is established. The rule requires that those standing in a fiduciary relationship disclose all material facts before entering into transactions. This means that an officer, a director, or a controlling shareholder has a duty to disclose all material facts. Failure to do so is a violation and, in effect, fraudulent. Privity of contract is not required for a violation, and lack of privity of contract is no defense.

Liability under Rule 10b-5 may be imposed even though the accountant performs only an unaudited write-up. An accountant is liable for errors in financial statements contained in a prospectus or other filed report even though unaudited if there are errors which he knew or should have known. Even when performing an unaudited write-up, an accountant is obligated to undertake at least a minimal investigation into the figures supplied to him, and is not free to disregard suspicious circumstances.

Section 10b and Rule 10b-5 are usually referred to as the antifraud provisions of the act. A plaintiff seeking damages under the provisions must establish (1) the existence of a material misrepresentation or omission made in connection with the purchase or sale of a security, (2) the culpable state of mind of the defendant, (3) his reliance and due diligence, and (4) damage as a result of the reliance. These elements are discussed in the sections which follow.

MATERIAL MISREPRESENTATION

The antifraud provisions are designed to protect the investing public by promoting disclosure and the free flow of information. They do not attempt to create violations out of misstatements or omissions of a trivial nature. Therefore, the materiality of the misstatements or omissions is a critical element of proof.

Material facts are those which reasonable investors would deem important in making a decision to buy a security. The element of materiality is measured by an objective test which asks whether a reasonable man would attach importance to the fact misrepresented in determining his choice of action in the transaction in question.

In determining whether the financial reports and statements are materially misleading, courts do not consider whether they comply with accounting norms, but whether the reports and statements fairly present the true financial position of the issuer to the untutored eye of an ordinary investor. Conformity with generally accepted accounting principles is not determinative of liability under the antifraud provisions of the Securities Exchange Act of 1934.

As previously noted, the concept of fraud encompasses not only untrue statements of material facts but the omission of material facts necessary to prevent the statements actually made from being misleading. In other words, a half-truth that misleads is fraudulent. Finally, a failure to correct a misleading impression left by statements already made or silence where there is a duty to speak gives rise to a violation of Rule 10b-5. As a result, an accountant has a duty to disclose subsequently acquired information if prior reports prepared for reliance by investors are false.

SCIENTER

Suits by investors under the antifraud provisions require proof of intent to defraud or scienter. However, the cases take the modern view of scienter and hold that either actual knowledge or a reckless disregard for the truth equivalent to actual knowledge supply proof of this element. However, proof of negligence does not supply this element, as the following case illustrates. In addition, an accountant may be liable as an aider and abettor of someone else who is violating Rule 10b-5. In cases concerning aiding and abetting, actual knowledge of the falsity is required for liability. A negligent failure to inquire and disclose is an insufficient basis to impose liability for aiding and abetting another to violate the securities laws.

ERNST & ERNST v. HOCHFELDER ET AL.
96 S.Ct. 1375 (1976)

POWELL, J.

The issue in this case is whether an action for civil damages may lie under § 10(b) of the Securities Exchange Act of 1934 (1934 Act) and Securities and Exchange Commission Rule 10b-5 in the absence of an allegation of intent to deceive, manipulate, or defraud on the part of the defendant. Petitioner, Ernst & Ernst, is an accounting firm. From 1946 through 1967 it was retained by First Securities Company of Chicago (First Securities), a small brokerage firm and member of the Midwest Stock Exchange and of the National Association of Securities Dealers, to perform periodic audits of the firm's books and records. In connection with these audits Ernst & Ernst prepared for filing with the Securities and Exchange Commission (the Commission) the annual reports required of First Securities under § 17(a) of the 1934 Act. It also prepared for First Securities responses to the financial questionnaires of the Midwest Stock Exchange (the Exchange).

Respondents were customers of First Securities who invested in a fraudulent securities scheme perpetrated by Lestor B. Nay, president of the firm and owner of 92% of its stock. Nay induced the respondents to invest funds in "escrow" accounts that he represented would yield a high rate of return. Respondents did so from 1942 through 1966, with the majority of the transactions occurring in the 1950's. In fact, there were no escrow accounts as Nay converted respondent's funds to his own use immediately upon receipt. These transactions were not in the customary form of dealings between First Securities and its customers. The respondents drew their personal checks payable to Nay or a designated bank for his account. No such escrow accounts were reflected on the books and records of First Securities, and none was shown on its periodic accounting to respondents in connection with their other investments. Nor were they included in First Securities' filings with the Commission or the Exchange.

This fraud came to light in 1968 when Nay committed suicide, leaving a note that described First Securities as bankrupt and the escrow accounts as "spurious." Respondents subsequently filed this action for damages against Ernst & Ernst . . . under § 10(b) of the 1934 Act. The complaint charged that Nay's escrow scheme violated § 10(b) and Commission Rule 10b-5, and that Ernst & Ernst had "aided and abetted" Nay's violations by its "failure" to conduct proper audits of First Securities. As revealed through discovery, respondents' cause of action rested on a theory of negligent nonfeasance. The premise was that Ernst & Ernst had failed to utilize "appropriate auditing procedures" in its audits of First Securities, thereby failing to discover internal practices of the firm said to prevent an effective audit. The practice principally relied on was Nay's rule that only he could open mail addressed to him at First Securities or addressed to First Securities to his attention, even if it arrived in his absence. Respondents contended that if Ernst & Ernst had conducted a proper audit, it would have discovered this "mail rule." The existence of the rule then would have been disclosed in reports to the Exchange and to the Commission by Ernst & Ernst as an irregular procedure that prevented an effective audit. This would have led to an investigation of Nay that would have revealed the fraudulent scheme. Respondents specifically disclaimed the existence of fraud or intentional misconduct on the part of Ernst & Ernst.

After extensive discovery the District Court granted Ernst & Ernst's motion for summary judgment and dismissed the action. . . .

The Court of Appeals of the Seventh Circuit reversed and remanded, holding that one who breaches a duty of inquiry and disclosure owed another is liable in damages for aiding and abetting a third party's violation of Rule 10b-5 if the fraud would have been discovered or prevented but for the breach. . . .

We granted certiorari to resolve the question whether a private cause of action for damages will lie under § 10(b) and Rule 10b-5 in the absence of any allegation of "scienter"—intent to deceive, manipulate, or defraud. We conclude that it will not and therefore we reverse.

Federal regulation of transactions in securities emerged as part of the aftermath of the market crash in 1929. The Securities Act of 1933 (1933 Act) was designed to provide investors with full disclosure of material information concerning public offerings of securities in commerce, to protect investors against fraud and, through the imposition of specified civil liabilities, to promote ethical standards of honesty and fair dealing. The 1934 Act was intended principally to protect investors against manipulation of stock prices through regulation of transactions upon securities exchanges and in over-the-counter markets, and to impose regular reporting requirements on companies whose stock is listed on national securities exchanges. Although the Acts contain numerous carefully drawn express civil remedies and criminal penalties, Congress recognized that efficient regulation of securities trading could not be accomplished under a rigid statutory program. As part of the 1934 Act Congress created the Commission, which is provided with an arsenal of flexible enforcement powers.

Section 10 of the 1934 Act makes it "unlawful for any person . . . (b) [t]o use or employ, in connection with the purchase or sale of any security . . . any manipulative or deceptive device or contrivance in contravention of such rules and regulations as the Commission may perceive as necessary or appropriate in the public interest or for the protection of investors." In 1942, acting pursuant to the power conferred by § 10(b), the Commission promulgated Rule 10b-5, which now provides:

Employment of manipulative and deceptive devices.

It shall be unlawful for any person, directly or indirectly, by the use of any means or instrumentality of interstate commerce, or of the mails, or of any facility of any national securities exchange.

1. To employ any device, scheme, or artifice to defraud,
2. To make any untrue statement of a material fact or to omit to state a material fact necessary in order to make the statements made, in the light of the circumstances under which they were made, not misleading, or
3. To engage in any act, practice, or course of business which operates or would operate as a fraud or deceit upon any person, in connection with the purchase or sale of any security.

Although § 10(b) does not by its terms create an express civil remedy for its violation . . . the existence of a private cause of action for violations of the statute and the rule is now well established. During the 30-year period since a private cause of action was first implied under § 10(b) and Rule 10b-5, a substantial body of case law and commentary has developed as to its elements. Courts and commentators long have differed with regard to whether scienter is a necessary element of such a cause of action, or whether negligent conduct alone is sufficient. In addressing this question, we turn first to the language of § 10(b), for "[t]he starting point in every case involving construction of a statute is the language itself."

Section 10(b) makes unlawful the use of employment of "any manipulative or deceptive device or contrivance" in contravention of Commission rules. The words "manipulative or deceptive" used in conjunction with "device or contrivance" strongly suggest that § 10(b) was intended to proscribe knowing or intentional misconduct.

In its *amicus curiae* brief, however, the Commission contends that nothing in the language "manipulative or deceptive device or contrivance" limits its operation to knowing or intentional practices. In support of its view, the Commission cites the overall congressional purpose in the 1933 and 1934 Act to protect investors against false and deceptive practices that might injure them.

The Commission then reasons that since the "effect" upon investors of given conduct is the same regardless of whether the conduct is negligent or intentional, Congress must have intended to bar all such practices and not just those done knowingly or intentionally. . . . The argument simply ignores the use of the words "manipulative," "device," and "contrivance," terms that make unmistakable a congressional intent to proscribe a type of conduct quite different from negligence. Use of the word "manipulative" is especially significant. It is and was virtually a term of art when used in connection with securities markets. It connotes intentional or willful conduct designed to deceive or defraud investors by controlling or artificially affecting the price of securities. . . .

. . . When a statute speaks so specifically in terms of manipulation and deception, and of implementing devices and contrivances—the commonly understood terminology of intentional wrongdoing—and when its history reflects no more expansive intent, we are quite unwilling to extend the scope of the statute to negligent conduct.

Reversed.

RELIANCE AND DUE DILIGENCE

The law requires that the investor be justified in relying upon the matter that is allegedly false. In effect, there must be a causal connection between the misstatement or nondisclosure and the loss suffered. While causation is an essential element of a private action for damages, there is no requirement that plaintiff establish sole reliance or even primary reliance upon audit or financial statements. A plaintiff must only prove that they were a "substantial factor" in his decision.

The element of due diligence in civil suits requires that the plaintiff act with the caution expected of a reasonable person in his position, that is, due diligence requires plaintiff to demonstrate that whatever actual reliance he claims is well founded. The duty to investigate facts surrounding a securities transaction which attaches to the sophisticated investor is greater than the corresponding duty of a novice.

Sophisticated investors who possess either special expertise or resources available to draw upon expertise may be deemed to have knowledge of certain investments and their attendant risks, whether in fact they do or not and irrespective of whether material information was actually disclosed.

Likewise, persons with vast business experience are similarly charged with a high degree of knowledge. When, however, there is neither access to critical information nor opportunity to discover the fraud, even the sophisticated investor can be defrauded.

While reliance is an element of a cause of action, direct proof of reliance is not required. All that is required is that the facts misrepresented are material in the sense that a reasonable investor might have considered them important in making the investment decisions. The law does not require proof of inducement.

In nondisclosure actions, no significant showing of reliance is required; the materiality of the statement presupposes reliance, and a causation in fact test is substituted for positive proof of causation. In such cases, the test of causation is whether the plaintiff would have been influenced to act differently than he did if the defendant had disclosed the undisclosed fact.

The case which follows discusses the extent to which "reliance" is required in suits under 10b-5. It also discusses the language of that statute which requires that the fraud be "in connection with the purchase or sale" of a security.

COMPETITIVE ASSOCIATES, INC. v. LAVENTHOL, KREKSTEIN, HORWATH & HORWATH
516 F.2d 811 (1975)

HAYS, J.

This is an appeal by plaintiff Competitive Associates, a publicly held mutual fund, from summary judgment entered . . . in favor of defendants Laventhol, Krekstein, Horwath and Horwath, an accounting firm, and Morton Dear, Robert E. Bier, and Thomas Martino, Jr., three individual employees of that firm. The action is based variously on section 19(b) of the Securities Exchange Act of 1934, SEC Rule 10b-5, section 17(a) of the Securities Act of 1933, sections 206(1) and 206(2) of the Investment Advisers Act of 1940, common law fraud and breach of fiduciary duty. Plaintiff alleges that defendants, in furtherance of fraudulent scheme to induce plaintiff to retain one Akiyoshi Yamada and his company, Takara Asset Management Corporation, to manage a portion of its portfolio, knowingly certified false and misleading financial statements of Takara Partners, a private investment fund managed by Yamada. As a result, plaintiff avers, it subsequently lost several million dollars from purchases and sales of securities which Yamada in his capacity as advisor, unlawfully caused it to make. Specifically, plaintiff contends that the investment performance of Takara Partners was generally regarded as the primary measure of Yamada's expertise as an investment adviser, that the statements for the period ended December 31, 1969, certified by Laventhol, Krekstein were materially false and misleading with respect to the size and quality of the partnership's assets and its profit and loss performance, that Laventhol, Krekstein knowingly and with intent to defraud certified these statements in order to facilitate, aid and abet Yamada's scheme to attract a showcase of investors to Takara, inflate his reputation as a successful investment advisor, and thereby create a dumping ground for securities which he was manipulating. An examination of the record convinces us that under the circumstances of this case, summary judgment was inappropriate; we therefore reverse and remand for trial.

I.

Competitive Associates retained defendant Yamada and his company Takara Asset Management Corporation as one of its portfolio managers on October 9, 1970. Prior to his retention, Yamada's credentials were investigated by Competitive Associates. Jerome Randolph, then president of Competitive Capital, the fund manager for Competitive Associates, was responsible for conducting the investigation. In the course of his investigation, Randolph interviewed various people in the securities industry. In addition he received a letter from Yamada dated June 12, 1970, which included a list of Takara's general and limited partners, and set forth certain financial information concerning Takara Partners, although it did not refer to the financial statements audited by the accounting defendants. Randolph also examined "portfolio sheets" for Takara Partners consisting of lists of stocks owned and their respective market values. Randolph prepared a summary description of Yamada and the funds he was then managing together with a description of other potential portfolio managers for Competitive Associates and presented this material to its Board of Directors who thereupon approved Yamada as one of the portfolio managers. This choice was subsequently ratified by the shareholders of Competitive Associates. Yamada served as adviser until May 14, 1971, at which time his contract was terminated. During this period, Competitive Associates suffered substantial losses as a result of purchases and sales of securities made by Yamada on its behalf.

The district court granted defendants motion for summary judgment on the theory that proof of direct reliance on the financial statements of Takara was an indispensable element of plaintiff's cause of action. Relying on excerpts from testimony given by Randolph before the SEC on May 10, 1971 asserting that he, Randolph, had not seen the Takara financial statements prior to that date, the admissibility of which evidence plaintiff vigorously contests, the courts concluded that plaintiff would be unable to prove the necessary reliance at trial. The court further held that even if the Takara financial statements did constitute an inducement to plaintiff to hire Yamada as its investment adviser, the connection between the fraudulent acts and omissions of the accounting defendants and the purchase or sale of securities which is required to support a claim under the federal securities laws was lacking. We disagree.

II.

As a matter of law, the district court erred in its determination that plaintiff could not prevail unless it could prove direct reliance on the false financial statements certified by defendants. The Supreme Court specifically rejected such a restrictive reading of section 10(b) and Rule 10b-5 in Affiliated Ute Citizens v. United States, 406 U.S. 128 (1972). In that case, members of a large class of stockholders alleged that two employees of a bank in which their shares were deposited had, contrary to Rule 10b-5, arranged for sales of this stock without disclosing to plaintiffs facts regarding the role of the bank and its employees as "market makers" or the true value of the stock. In reversing the Court of Appeals, which had held that section 10(b) and Rule 10b-5 necessitated showing of reliance for recovery, the Supreme Court stated that

> [u]nder the circumstances of this case, involving primarily a failure to disclose, positive proof of reliance is not a prerequisite to recovery. All that is necessary is that the facts withheld be material in the sense that a reasonable investor might have considered them important in the making of this decision. (Citations omitted.) This obligation to disclose and this withholding of a material fact establish the requisite element of causation in fact.

This Court has also expressed the view that a plaintiff need not prove that nondisclosure of material facts induced its purchases, but need only allege that it would not have acted as it did had it known of the information withheld by defendants. "To the extent that reliance is necessary for a finding of a 10b-5 violation in a non-disclosure case . . . the test is properly one of tort 'causation in fact.' "

Defendants . . . submit that the instant case involves allegations of misrepresentation as opposed to nondisclosure and that therefore plaintiff must show reliance in addition to causation in fact. However, a showing of reliance is not required where a comprehensive scheme to defraud which includes not only omissions and misrepresentations, but substantial collateral conduct as well, is alleged. Not every violation of the anti-fraud provisions of the federal securities law can be, or should be, forced into a category headed "misrepresentations" or "nondisclosures." Fraudulent devices, practices, schemes, artifices and courses of business are also interdicted by the securities laws. In the case before us, plaintiff has charged the accounting defendants not only with affirmative misrepresentations in the financial statements, but also with a failure to disclose the true financial condition of Takara Partners and the alleged receipt of payoffs in return for its certification; furthermore, both misrepresentations and omissions are alleged to be only one aspect of an elaborate scheme to defraud. Under the circumstances, plaintiff need only show causation in fact: in order to do so plaintiff should have the opportunity to prove, but is not required to prove, that it saw, or directly relied upon, the financial statements certified by the accounting defendants.

III.

The finding of the district court that the auditing and certification activities of defendants was not conduct "in connection with the purchase or sale" of a security involving plaintiffs within the meaning of section 10(b) and Rule 10b-5 is error. The "in connection with" requirement has been broadly interpreted by the Supreme Court to require only that plaintiff shall have "suffered an injury as a result of deceptive practices touching its sale of securities as an investor."

The broad "touch" test . . . is certainly met by plaintiff's allegations that the very purpose of defendants' certification of Takara's financial statement was to aid in placing Yamada in a position where he could manipulate securities prices and sell these securities to investors attracted by Yamada's reputation and performance.

Defendants attempt to characterize the purchases and sales of securities before us here as fortuitous transactions unrelated to their auditing and certification of the Takara Partners' financial statements. They rely upon a number of cases relieving accountants from liability on the ground that the "in connection with" requirement was not satisfied. We find these cases to be inapposite. In each case, the court premised the result on a finding that the accountants involved did not know or expect their reports to be relied upon by anyone other than the members of the entity for which the reports were specifically prepared and therefore were not reasonably calculated to influence the investing public. In contrast, plaintiff here alleges that the accountants accepted payoffs and otherwise actively collaborated with Yamada for the specific purpose of influencing investors to authorize Yamada to carry out security transactions on its behalf. [We do not] think it sound to dismiss a complaint merely because the alleged scheme does not involve the type of fraud that is "usually associated with the sale or purchase of securities." We believe that § 10(b) and Rule 10b-5 prohibit *all* fraudulent schemes in connection with the purchase or sale of securities, whether the artifices employed involved a garden type variety of fraud, or present a unique form of deception. Novel or atypical methods should not provide immunity from the securities laws.

Plaintiff has alleged a fraudulent scheme the accomplishment of which is directly related to the trading process. We think that the district court was premature in denying it an opportunity to prove its claims. The record before us gives rise to conflicting inferences of active fraudulent conduct on the part of defendant accountants which should be resolved at trial rather than on a motion for summary judgment. Accordingly, the judgment of the district court is reversed and we remand for trial.

DAMAGES

A plaintiff in a suit under Rule 10b-5 must prove damages. The damages of a defrauded purchaser are usually "out-of-pocket" losses or the excess of "what was paid" over the value of "what was received." Courts in a few cases have used the "benefit of the bargain" measure of damages and awarded the buyer the difference between what he paid and what the security was represented to be worth. A buyer's damages are measured at the time of purchase.

The computation of a defrauded seller's damages is more difficult. A defrauding purchaser usually benefits from an increase in the value of the securities, while the plaintiff seller loses this increase. Courts do not allow defrauding buyers to keep these increases in value. Therefore, the measure of the seller's damages is the difference between the fair value of all that the seller received and the fair value of what he would have received had there been no fraud, except where the defendant received more than the seller's loss. In this latter case, the seller is entitled to the defendant's profit. As a result, defendants lose all profits flowing from the fraudulent conduct.

Plaintiffs under Rule 10b-5 are also entitled to consequential damages. These include lost dividends, brokerage fees and taxes. In addition, courts may order the payment of interest on the funds. Punitive damages are not permitted as they are in cases of common law fraud based on state laws. This distinction results from the language of the statute which limits recoveries to "actual damages."

As a general rule, attorney's fees are not recoverable. This is consistent with the rule in most litigation. However, in class action suits, the attorneys are allowed to collect their fees out of the recovery. These fees in a class action suit will often exceed the usual hourly rate and will often be close to or equal to the contingent fee rate (one-third of the recovery).

CONCLUSION

There are numerous federal statutory provisions which may be used to impose liability upon accountants. These are in addition to the common law theories discussed in the previous chapters. The most frequently used section of the securities laws is Section 10b of the Securities Act of 1934 with its SEC Rule 10b-5. This section requires scienter and cannot be predicated upon mere negligence. It compliments Section 18 of the same act which codifies common law fraud.

Liability may also be imposed under section 11 of the Securities Act of 1933. This section creates liability for false registration statements. Liability may be avoided by proof that the accountant reasonably believed the statements after making a reasonable investigation. The 1933 Act also creates a cause of action against sellers for false statements in a prospectus or in a communication, whether oral or written, that is a part of the sale of a security.

The law recognizes several defenses which may be used to avoid liability. While the "due diligence" defense previously noted is the most obvious, the burden of proof in that issue is upon the accountant and the decision on that point is usually question of fact for the jury.

1. Define the term *security* as used in the state and federal laws regulating the sale of securities.

2. What is the basic purpose of the Securities Act of 1933? How does it seek to accomplish this purpose? Explain.

3. Give an example of (1) an exempt transaction, and (2) an exempt security under the Securities Act of 1933.

4. What are the elements of proof required of a plaintiff seeking to impose liability on an accountant under Section 11 of the Securities Act of 1933?

5. X, an accountant, is sued by Y, a client who alleges a violation of Section 11 of the Securities Act of 1933. X contends that he has exercised "due diligence" in the performance of his professional duties, while Y contends that X failed to do so. Is "due diligence" a defense that will allow X to avoid liability? Who has the burden of proof on the issue? Explain.

6. List four defenses in addition to "due diligence" which may be asserted by a defendant-accountant who has allegedly violated the Securities Act of 1933.

7. Compare the coverage of the Securities Act of 1933 with the Securities Exchange Act of 1934.

8. What are the elements of a course of action or claim under Section 10b and Rule 10b-5 of the Securities Exchange Act of 1934?

9. Discuss the extent to which the federal securities laws require an accountant to investigate suspicious circumstances and the extent to which silence may provide a basis for holding accountants liable to investors.

10. Define the following terms as used in cases involving the federal securities laws: material facts, aiding and abetting, reliance, and consequential damages.

11. Discuss the difference in the concept of reliance by the average person with the concept as it relates to sophisticated investors.

SUGGESTED ADDITIONAL READINGS

BLOOMENTHAL, HAROLD S., *Securities and Federal Corporate Law,* vols. 3 and 3A. New York: Clark Boardman Company, Ltd., 1974.

COHEN, MILTON H., "Truth in Securities Revisited," *Harvard Law Review,* May 1966.

ISBELL, DAVID B., "An Overview of Accountants' Duties and Liabilities Under the Federal Securities Laws and A Closer Look at Whistle-Blowing," *Ohio State Law Journal,* 1974.

JACOBS, ARNOLD S., *The Impact of Rule 10b-5,* vols. 5 and 5A. New York: Clark Boardman Company, Ltd., 1974.

LEVY, S., "Liability to Third Parties—By Statute," *C.P.A. Handbook,* ed. Robert L. Kane. New York: American Institute of Certified Public Accountants, 1952.

LIGGIO, C., "The Ernst Ruling—Expansion of a Trend," *The New York Law Journal,* April 14–15, 1976.

LOSS, LOUIS, *Securities Regulation* (2nd ed.), vols. 1, 2, and 3. Boston: Little, Brown and Co., 1961.

———, *Securities Regulation: Supplement to Second Edition,* vols. 4, 5, and 6. Boston: Little, Brown and Co., 1969.

MATHEWS, ARTHUR R., "SEC Enforcement in 1974: Despite Criticism a Vigorous, Expanding Program Proceeds," *New York Law Journal,* December 1974.

RAPPAPORT, LOUIS H., *SEC Accounting Practice and Procedure* (3rd ed.), New York: Ronald Press Co., 1972.

REILING, HENRY B., and RUSSELL A. TAUSSIG, "Recent Liability Cases— Implications for Accountants," *Journal of Accountacy,* September 1970.

REININGA, WARREN, "The Unknown Materiality Concept," *Journal of Accountancy,* January 1970.

"Responsibilities and Liabilities of Auditors and Accountants," *Business Lawyer,* March 1975.

RUDER, DAVID S., "Multiple Defendants in Securities Law Fraud Cases: Aiding and Abetting, Conspiracy, *in Pari Delicito,* Indemnification, and Contribution," *University of Pennsylvania Law Review,* April 1972.

"Symposium on Accounting and the Federal Securities Laws," *Vanderbilt Law Review,* January 1975.

ADDITIONAL CASES

SEC v. Texas Gulf Sulphur Co., 401 F.2d 833 (2d Cir. 1968).

Heit v. Weitzen, 402 F.2d 909 (2d Cir. 1968), cert. denied, 395 U.S. 903 (1969).

SEC v. First Securities, 463 F.2d 981 (7th Cir. 1972).

Gerstle v. Gamble-Skogmo, MC 47 F.2d 1281 (2d Cir. 1973).

Chris-Craft Industries, Inc. v. Piper Aircraft Corp., 480 F.2d 341 (2d Cir. 1973).

Koch Industries, Inc. v. Vosko, 494 F.2d 713 (1974).

Norteck, Inc. v. Alexander Grant & Co., 532 F.2d 1013 (1976).

Fischer v. Kletz, 266 F.Supp. 180 (S.D.N.Y. 1967).

Krake v. Thor Power Tool Co., 282 F.Supp. 94 (N.D.Ill. 1967).

Gordon v. Lipoff, 320 F.Supp. 255 (1972).

Blakely v. Lisac, 357 F.Supp. 255 (1972).

Gold v. DCL Incorporated, 399 F.Supp. 1123 (1973).

Katz v. Realty Equities Corp. of New York, 406 F.Supp. 802 (1976).

Rich v. Touche Ross & Co., 415 F.Supp. 95 (1976).

McLean v. Alexander, 420 F.Supp. 1057 (1976).

Coleco Industries, Inc. v. Berman, 423 F.Supp. 275 (1976).

Berkowitz v. Baron, 428 F.Supp. 1190 (1977).

Chapter 10

Criminal Liability

INTRODUCTION

The previous chapters have been devoted to the civil liability of accountants. However, accountants may also be charged with criminal conduct in the performance of their professional duties. There are several so-called white-collar crimes that are significant to the accounting profession.

A crime is a wrong committed against society. Every crime must include certain elements before a defendant can be found guilty of a violation. Criminal cases differ from civil cases in the amount of proof required to convict. In a civil case, the plaintiff is entitled to a verdict if the evidence preponderates in his favor. In other words, if when weighing the evidence the scales tip even slightly in favor of the plaintiff, the plaintiff wins. However, in a criminal case, the people or the prosecution must prove the defendant's guilt beyond a reasonable doubt. Note that the law does not require proof "beyond the shadow of a doubt" or proof that is susceptible of only one conclusion. It does require proof to the extent that a reasonable man viewing the evidence would have no reasonable doubt about the guilt of the defendant.

As a general rule, a crime involves a combination of act and criminal intent. Criminal intent without an overt act to carry it out is not considered a crime. Some act toward carrying out this intent is necessary for the intent to be criminal. A legislature may declare an act to be a crime without intent, but crimes lacking intent are rare. A wrongful act committed without the requisite criminal intent is not a crime. Criminal intent may be supplied by negligence to the degree that it equals intent. Criminal intent is not synonymous with motive. Motive is not an element of a crime. Proof of motive may help to establish guilt, but it is not an essential element of a crime.

There is a presumption of intention in most criminal cases. The intent may be implied from the facts. In other words, the criminal act implies the criminal intent. (The accused may rebut this presumption, however.) The accused is presumed to intend the natural and probable consequences of his acts. Thus, if a person's actions cause a result that the criminal law is designed to prevent, that person is legally responsible even though the actual result was not intended. The subject of intent as it relates to crimes involving accountants will be discussed further in this chapter.

While state laws often declare that certain conduct by accountants is criminal, most cases are prosecuted under federal law. Therefore, the sections that follow are concerned with federal laws.

SECURITIES ACT OF 1933—SECTION 24

Section 24 of the Securities Act of 1933 declares that willful violations of its provisions constitute a crime. It provides:

> Any person who *willfully* violates any of the provisions of this title, or the rules and regulations promulgated by the Commission under authority thereof, or any person who *willfully*, in a *registration statement* filed under this title, *makes any untrue statement of a material fact or omits to state any material fact* required to be stated therein or necessary to make the statements therein *not misleading*, shall upon conviction be fined not more than $5000 or imprisoned not more than five years, or both. [Emphasis added.]

As a result of the foregoing statute, an accountant may have criminal liability for fraud in *any* offer or sale of securities. The penalty is a $5000 fine, five years in prison, or both. Fraud in the sale of an exempt security is still a criminal violation if the mail is used or if an instrumentality of interstate commerce has been used.

Accountants sometimes use the words *pro forma* on financial statements. The use of such a label will not prevent a criminal conviction. If an accountant prepares false financial statements with the requisite criminal intent, the label *pro forma* will not eliminate the intent to defraud required to convict.

The most important aspect of this section is the requirement that the accountant's conduct be a willful violation. "Willful" means with intent to defraud. The government can meet its burden by proving that a defendant deliberately closed his eyes to facts he had a duty to see or recklessly stated as facts things of which he was ignorant. The willfulness requirement can be satisfied by mere "proof of representation which due diligence would have shown to be untrue." In discussing the accountant's state of mind required for a criminal violation one court observed:

> In our complex society the accountant's certificate and the lawyer's opinion can be instruments for inflicting pecuniary loss more potent than the chisel or the crowbar. Of course, Congress did not mean that any mistake of law or misstatement of fact should subject an attorney or an accountant to criminal liability simply because more skillful practitioners would not have made them. But Congress equally could not have intended that men holding themselves out as members of these ancient professions should be able to escape criminal liability on a plea of ignorance when they have shut their eyes to what was plainly to be seen or have represented a knowledge they knew they did not possess.

SECURITIES EXCHANGE ACT OF 1934— SECTION 32(a)

The 1934 Act also provides for criminal sanctions for false and misleading statements. Section 32(a) of that law provides:

> Any person who willfully violates any provisions of this title, or any rule or regulation thereunder the violation of which is made unlawful or the observance of which is required under the terms of this title, or any person who *willfully* and *knowingly* makes, or causes to be made, any statement in any application, report, or document required to be filed under this title or any rule or regulation thereunder or any undertaking contained in a registration statement . . . which statement was false or misleading with respect to any material fact, shall upon conviction be fined not more than $10,000, or imprisoned not more than two years, or both, . . . *but no person shall be subject to imprisonment under this section for the violation of any rule or regulation if he proves that he had no knowledge of such rule or regulation.* [Emphasis added.]

The *Continental Vending* case which follows is the leading case interpreting this section. The case imposes upon accountants a duty to disclose what they know when they have reason to believe that to a material extent, a corporation (or client's business) is being operated not to carry out its business in the interest of all stockholders, but for the private benefit of its management. It also establishes that compliance with generally accepted acounting principles is not an absolute defense in a criminal case.

UNITED STATES v. SIMON
425 F.2d 796 (1969)

FRIENDLY, J.

Defendant Carl Simon was a senior partner, Robert Kaiser a junior partner, and Melvin Fishman a senior associate in the internationally known accounting firm of Lybrand, Ross Bros. & Montgomery. They stand convicted under three counts of an indictment charging them with drawing up and certifying a false or misleading financial statement of Continental Vending Machine Corporation (hereafter Continental) for the year ending September 30, 1962. . . . The judge fined Simon $7,000 and Kaiser and Fishman $5,000 each.

Count One of the indictment was for conspiracy to violate 18 U.S.C. §§ 1001 and 1341 and § 32 of the Securities Exchange Act of 1934, 15 U.S.C. § 78ff. Section 1001 provides:

> Whoever, in any matter within the jurisdiction of any department or agency of the United States knowingly and willfully falsifies, conceals or covers up by any trick, scheme, or device a material fact, or makes any false, fictitious or fraudulent statements or representations, or makes or uses any false writing or document knowing the same to contain any false, fictitious or fraudulent statement or entry, shall be fined not more than $10,000 or imprisoned not more than five years, or both.

Section 1341 makes criminal the use of the mails in aid of "any scheme or artifice to defraud." Section 32 of the Securities Exchange Act renders criminal the willful and knowing making of a statement in any required report which is false or misleading with respect to any material fact. Counts Three and Six charged mailings of the statement in violation of 18 U.S.C. § 1341. Nothing turns on the different phrasings of the test of criminality in the three statutes. The Government concedes it had the burden of offering proof allowing a reasonable jury to be convinced beyond a reasonable doubt not merely that the financial statement was false or misleading in a material respect but that defendants knew it to be and deliberately sought to mislead.

While every criminal conviction is important to the defendant, there is a special poignancy and a corresponding responsibility on reviewing judges when, as here, the defendants have been men of blameless lives and respected members of a learned profession. This is no less true because the trial judge, wisely in our view, imposed no prison sentences. On the other hand, . . . our office is limited to determining whether the evidence was sufficient for submission to the jury and, if so, whether errors prejudicial to the defendants occurred at the trial.

I.

The trial hinged on transactions between Continental and an affiliate, Valley Commercial Corporation (hereafter "Valley"). The dominant figure in both was Harold Roth, who was president of Continental, supervised the day-to-day operations of Valley, and owned about 25% of the stock of each company.

Valley, which was run by Roth out of a single office on Continental's premises, was engaged in lending money at interest to Continental and others in the vending machine business. Continental would issue negotiable notes to Valley, which would endorse these in blank and use them as collateral for drawing on two lines of credit, of $1 million each, at Franklin National Bank ("Franklin") and Meadowbrook National Bank ("Meadowbrook"), and would then transfer to Continental the discounted amount of the notes. These transactions, beginning as early as 1956, gave rise to what is called "the Valley payable." By the end of fiscal 1962, the amount of this was $1,029,475, of which $543,345 was due within the year.

In addition to the Valley payable, there was what is known as the "Valley receivable," which resulted from Continental loans to Valley. Most of these stemmed from Roth's custom, dating from mid-1957, of using Continental and Valley as sources of cash to finance his transactions in the stock market. At the end of fiscal 1962, the amount of the Valley receivable was $3.5 million, and by February 15, 1963, the date of certification, it had risen to $3.9 million. The Valley payable could not be offset, or "netted," against the Valley receivable since, as stated, Continental's obligations to Valley were in the form of negotiable notes which Valley had endorsed in blank to the two banks and used as collateral to obtain the cash which it then lent to Continental.

By the certification date, the auditors had learned that Valley was not in a position to repay its debt, and it was accordingly arranged that collateral would be posted. Roth and members of his family transferred their equity in certain securities to Arthur Field, Continental's counsel, as trustee to secure Roth's debt to Valley and Valley's debt to Continental. Some 80% of these securities consisted of Continental stock and convertible debentures.

The 1962 financial statements of Continental, which were dismal by any standard, reported the status of the Valley transactions as follows:

ASSETS

Current Assets:

* * * * * * * *

Accounts and notes receivable:

* * * * * * * *

Valley Commercial Corp., affiliate
(Note 2) $2,143,335

* * * * * * * *

Noncurrent accounts and notes receivable:
Valley Commercial Corp., affiliate
(Note 2)   1,400,000

* * * * * * * *

LIABILITIES

Current Liabilities:

* * * * * * * *

Long-term debt,
portion due within one year $8,203,788

* * * * * * * *

Long-term debt (Note 7)

* * * * * * * *

Valley Commercial Corp., affiliate
(Note 2)   486,130

* * * * * * * *

NOTES TO CONSOLIDATED
FINANCIAL STATEMENTS

2. The amount receivable from Valley Commercial Corp. (an affiliated company of which Mr. Harold Roth is an officer, director and stockholder) bears interest at 12% a year. Such amount, less the balance of the notes payable to that company, is secured by the assignment to the Company of Valley's equity in certain marketable securities. As of February 15, 1963, the amount of such equity at current market quotations exceeded the net amount receivable.

7. * * * The amounts of long-term debt, including the portion due within one year, on which interest is payable currently or has been discounted in advance, are as follows:

* * * * * * * *

Valley Commercial Corp., affiliate $1,029,475

The case against the defendants can be best encapsulated by comparing what Note 2 stated and what the Government claims it would have stated if defendants had included what they knew:

2. The amount receivable from Valley Commercial Corp. (an affiliated company of which Mr. Harold Roth is an officer, director and stockholder), which bears interest at 12% a year, was uncollectable at September 30, 1962, since Valley had loaned approximately the same amount to Mr. Roth who was unable to pay. Since that date Mr. Roth and others have pledged as security for the repayment of his obligation to Valley and its obligation to Continental (now $3,900,000, against which Continental's liability to Valley cannot be offset) securities which, as of February 15, 1963, had a market value of $2,978,000. Approximately 80% of such securities are stock and convertible debentures of the Company.

Striking as the difference is, the later version does not reflect the Government's further contention that in fact the market value of the pledged securities on

292

February 15, 1963, was $1,978,000 rather than $2,978,000 due to liens of James Talcott, Inc. and Franklin for indebtedness other than Roth's of which defendants knew or should have known.

II.

Although the facts set forth up to this point were uncontroverted, there were some sharp disagreements concerning just what defendants knew and when they learned it. Issues of credibility, however, were for the jury, and we have set forth what the jury could permissibly have found the further facts to be.

Roth engaged the Lybrand firm as Continental's auditors in 1956. George Shegog was the partner in charge: Simon was "second partner" but had no responsibility save for the review of SEC filings. Upon Shegog's death, early in 1960, Simon became the partner in charge. Kaiser was first assigned to the Continental audit as "audit manager" for the 1961 audit. Fishman had been assigned to the Continental audit in 1957 as a young junior accountant; in 1962 he was promoted to be manager of the Continental audit for that year and Kaiser was retained as "second partner." The day-to-day supervision of the audit was the responsibility of Richard McDevitt. As is usual, the structure was pyramidal in terms of time spent.

The Valley receivable had attracted attention early in Lybrand's engagement. In the late fall of 1958, Yoder, who was then manager of the Continental audit, discussed it with Roth. In a memorandum which was read by Fishman at the time and remained in the Lybrand audit files, Yoder recorded that during fiscal 1958 Continental had made net cash payments to Valley of $1,185,790, which "appeared to be for no other purpose than to provide Valley with cash." He recorded also that since September 30 Continental had made additional payments to Valley of $824,752 which was used "to finance the acquisition of capital stock of U.S. Hoffman Machine Corporation by Mr. Roth, or for loans by Valley to U.S. Hoffman." He also stated that he was informed that the receivable should be applied to notes of Continental and its subsidiaries which represented the Valley payable, and that he had agreed provided that the notes, which Valley had pledged as collateral for its borrowings from Franklin and Meadowbrook, were surrendered and made available for Lybrand's inspection. In a memorandum to Simon in November 1960, Yoder again discussed the Valley receivable, noting that the payments were frequent, in round amounts, and unaccompanied by written explanations. He observed that during the 1960 fiscal year the receivable had ranged from $695,000 in October 1959 to $398,000 in September 1960 with a high of $1,583,000 in April 1960.

In 1961 and 1962, the cash payments giving rise to the Valley receivable continued to be frequent, in round amounts, and without written explanation. Moreover, the balance in the Valley receivable account characteristically was parabolic, rising after the end of one fiscal year and falling prior to the end of the next. The payments and repayments and the year-end balance for 1958–1962 are shown by the following table:

Year	Advances to Valley	Repayments by Valley	Receivable at Year-End
1958	$3,356,239	$2,583,172	$ –0–
1959	4,586,000	3,510,451	384,402
1960	2,511,000	2,670,500	397,996
1961	2,390,674	1,520,000	848,006
1962	4,708,000	1,986,500	3,543,335

Although the figure for the end of 1961 was more than double that at the end of the two preceding years, and had increased to about $2 million by December 31, 1961, prior to the certification date, the 1961 financial statement made no comment on the receivable, and none of the defendants asked whether Continental's directors had been informed of the transactions. Simon merely warned Roth that an examination of Valley's books would be required if the receivable at the end of fiscal 1962 was as large as at the end of 1961.

When Fishman visited Continental's office in early September 1962 in preparation for that year's audit, he was told that as of July 31 the Valley receivable had reached $3.6 million. He was told also that Continental was operating a check float in excess of $500,000 daily, that cash was "tighter than ever," and that Continental's Assistant Comptroller had spent most of July and August "juggling cash." Fishman reported this to Simon and Kaiser, noting that "all in all, it promises to be an 'interesting' audit."

The cash audit, conducted in early October 1962, showed how stringent cash had become. The $286,000 in hand on September 30 resulted only from thirty-day loans of $1.5 million from Franklin and Meadowbrook four days earlier. The Valley receivable was found to be around $3.5 million and Fishman told Roth in late October that this was so large that "there could be a problem with the year end audit." In answer to a question by Fishman in November why Valley needed so much money, Kalan, Continental's Assistant Comptroller, said that "Roth needed the money to maintain the margin accounts on the U.S. Hoffman stock and bonds and the Continental stock and bonds."

Early in November Fishman met with Kaiser and reviewed the history of the Valley receivable. A memorandum of November 12 from Fishman to Kaiser, with a copy to Simon, "anticipated that September 30, 1962, Continental's balance sheet will show a net receivable from Valley of approximately $1,000,000 representing the excess of cash transfers to Valley over notes issued to Valley" and stated an intention to review the collectibility of the "net receivable" by examining "the latest available financial statements of Valley and other documentation."

In December Fishman phoned Simon that the Valley receivable as of September 30 was about $3.5 million. Simon instructed Fishman to tell Roth that Lybrand would need the financial statements of Valley in order to evaluate the receivable's collectibility. Roth called Simon and said that Valley's audit was not yet finished and that the statements would be made available when it was. There were similar conversations during January 1963.

Meanwhile, according to Roth, he had contacted Simon in December and said that although Valley had a net worth of $2 million, it was not in a position to repay its $3.5 million debt to Continental as it had lent him approximately the same amount which he was unable to repay. He suggested that he secure the indebtedness with his equity in stocks, bonds and other securities of Continental and Hoffman International if this would be acceptable. Roth called Simon some ten days later and received the latter's assent. On December 31 Roth placed Arthur Field, counsel for Continental, in charge of preparing the assignments.

Late in January 1963 Fishman visited Roth and showed him a draft of Note 2 substantially identical with the final form; he told Roth that Simon wanted to see him. They met in the Lybrand office on February 6. Defendants concede that at this meeting Roth informed Simon that Valley could not repay Continental and offered to post securities for the Valley receivable, and also to post as collateral a mortgage on his house and furnishings. Simon agreed that if adequate collateral were posted, a satisfactory legal opinion were obtained, and Continental's board approved the transactions, Lybrand could certify Continental's statements without reviewing Valley's, which still were not available. There was also a discussion of verification procedures. Simon determined that Roth, with a Lybrand employee listening on an extension phone, would call the various banks and brokers then holding Roth's securities to confirm the "amount of securities pledged and the amount due to them."

On February 12, Roth told Simon that Field had the collateral ready for verification. Simon instructed Kaiser to go to Field's office. Finding that Field had made the proposed assignments run to Valley, Kaiser called this "ridiculous" and asked, "If the securities or if the cash equity gets back into Valley Commercial Corporation, what is to stop Harold Roth from taking the money out again as he did before?" On Kaiser's direction Field made the assignments run to himself as trustee for Valley and Continental. Field also discussed the available collateral and exhibited to Kaiser some handwritten notes prepared by Field and Miss Gans, secretary to Roth. These showed that the bulk of the collateral would consist of an equity in Continental stock and debentures. Kaiser made a number of calls having reference to this information and prepared notes of them which he later showed Simon; as developed in section V of this opinion, the Government alleges these demonstrated a complete encumbrance of all of Roth's securities held by Franklin, Meadowbrook and James Talcott, Inc. ("Talcott"). At Kaiser's request Field prepared a letter stating that $3.5 million in collateral was being posted and outlining the mechanics of the collateralization. On the following business day, Simon called to request that Field amend the letter to include an opinion that the collateral adequately secured the Valley receivable; the amended letter was sent on February 15 or 18. Meanwhile Field had informed Simon and Kaiser on February 13 that Continental's board of directors had disapproved of the loans to Valley.

On Friday, February 15, Kaiser assigned James Harris, a supervisor who had no previous connection with the Continental audit, to confirm the collateral. Kaiser explained the agreed procedure and introduced him to Roth and Miss Gans, but did not warn him of the possibility of encumbrances at Franklin,

Meadowbrook and Talcott. The telephone calls began around 10 A.M. and continued until later afternoon when Miss Gans "started having difficulty in reaching some of the people at some of these financial institutions." The calls ended, and Harris totalled the then quoted market price of the confirmed securities, subtracted the indebtedness disclosed over the telephone, and arrived at an equity interest of some $3.1 million, this including an equity of $1.2 million in stock held at Franklin, Meadowbrook and Talcott. He telephoned Kaiser the results. Meanwhile Roth removed some $100,000 in odd securities from an office safe and offered them if Harris didn't have enough. The offer was declined. The schedule was then delivered to McDevitt, who applied the closing market quotations of February 15; these reduced the value to $2,978,000.

The three defendants met at Continental's plant on Saturday, February 16, and prepared a printer's draft of the financial statements. Simon telephoned Roth and discussed the proposed statement, including Note 2. In the course of the conversation he requested payment of some $13,000 still owing for the 1961 audit. On Roth's instructions Kalan gave Simon a check, saying "This is going to bounce."

On Monday, February 18, Simon reviewed a printer's proof of the statements. At that time, for reasons which were not developed at trial but are now conceded to be proper, he moved from noncurrent into current assets $1,433,104, representing a receivable from the sale of certain vending routes. At the same time, he dropped from current assets to noncurrent assets some $1,400,000 of the Valley receivable, which Roth caused to be refinanced by Valley's issuance of long-term notes in that amount. Although Simon testified that he made this change solely because of the issuance of the notes, in which he had no part, Roth testified that Simon had earlier told him that some of the $3.5 million Valley receivable would have to go "below the line"—i.e., into noncurrent assets.

The financial statements were mailed as part of Continental's annual report on February 20. By that time the market value of the collateral had declined some $270,000 from its February 15 value. The value of the collateral fell an additional $640,000 on February 21. When the market reopened on February 25 after the long Washington's birthday recess, it fell another $2 million and was worth only $395,000. The same day a Continental check to the Internal Revenue Service bounced. Two days later the Government padlocked the plant and the American Stock Exchange suspended trading in Continental stock. Investigations by the SEC and bankruptcy rapidly ensued.

III.

The defendants called eight expert independent accountants, an impressive array of leaders of the profession. They testified generally that, except for the error with respect to netting, the treatment of the Valley receivable in Note 2 was in no way inconsistent with generally accepted accounting principles or generally accepted auditing standards, since it made all the informative disclosures reasonably necessary for fair presentation of the financial position of Continental as of the close of the 1962 fiscal year. Specifically, they testified that neither generally accepted accounting principles nor generally accepted auditing standards required disclosure of the make-up of the collateral or of the increase of the receivable after the closing date of the balance sheet, although three of the eight stated that in light of hindsight they would have preferred that the make-up of the collateral be disclosed. The witnesses likewise testified that disclosure of the Roth borrowings from Valley was not required, and seven of the eight were of the opinion that such disclosure would be inappropriate. The principal reason given for this last view was that the balance sheet was concerned solely with presenting the financial position of the company under audit; since the Valley receivable was adequately secured in the opinion of the auditors and was broken out and shown separately as a loan to an affiliate with the nature of the affiliation disclosed, this was all that the auditors were required to do. To go further and reveal what Valley had done with the money would be to put into the balance sheet things that did not properly belong there; moreover, it would create a precedent which would imply that it was the duty of an auditor to investigate each loan to an affiliate to determine whether the money had found its way into the pockets of an officer of the company under audit, an investigation that would ordinarily be unduly wasteful of time and money. With due respect to the Government's accounting witnesses, an SEC staff accountant, and, in rebuttal, its chief accountant, who took a contrary view, we are bound to say that they hardly compared with defendants' witnesses in aggregate auditing experience or professional eminence.

Defendants asked for two instructions which, in substance, would have told the jury that a defendant could be found guilty only if, according to generally accepted accounting principles the financial statements as a whole did not fairly present the financial condition of Continental at September 30, 1962, and then only if his departure from accepted standards was due to willful disregard of those standards with knowledge of the falsity of the statements and an intent to deceive. The judge declined to give these instructions. Dealing with the subject in the course of his charge, he said that the "critical test" was whether the financial statements as a whole "fairly presented the financial position of Continental as of September 30, 1962, and whether it accurately reported the operations for fiscal 1962." If they did not, the basic issue became whether defendants acted in good faith. Proof of compliance with generally accepted standards was "evidence which may be very persuasive but not necessarily conclusive that he acted in good faith, and that the facts as certified were not materially false or misleading." "The weight and credibility to be extended by you to such proof, and its persuasiveness, must depend, among other things, on how authoritative you find the precedents and the teachings relied upon by the parties to be, the extent to which they contemplate, deal with, and apply to the type of circumstances found by you to have existed here, and the weight you give to expert opinion evidence offered by the parties. Those may depend on the credibility extended by you to expert witnesses, the definiteness with which they testified, the reasons given for their opinions, and all the other facts affecting credibility, * * *"

Defendants contend that the charge and refusal to charge constituted error. We think the judge was right in refusing to make the accountants' testimony so nearly a complete defense. The critical test according to the charge was the same as that which the accountants testified was critical. We do not think the jury was also required to accept the accountants' evaluation whether a given fact was material to overall fair presentation, at least not when the accountants' testimony was not based on specific rules or prohibitions to which they could point, but only on the need for the auditor to make an honest judgment and their conclusion that nothing in the financial statements themselves negated the conclusion that an honest judgment had been made. Such evidence may be highly persuasive, but it is not conclusive, and so the trial judge correctly charged.

Defendants next contend that, particularly in light of the expert testimony, the evidence was insufficient to allow the jury to consider the failure to disclose Roth's borrowings from Valley, the make-up of the collateral, or the post-balance sheet increase in the Valley receivable. They concentrate their fire on what they characterize as the "primary, predominant and pervasive" issue, namely the failure to disclose that Continental's loans to Valley were not for a proper business purpose but to assist Roth in his personal financial problems. It was "primary, predominant and pervasive" not only because it was most featured by the prosecution but because defendants' knowledge of Roth's diversion of corporate funds colored everything else. We join defendants' counsel in assuming that the mere fact that a company has made advances to an affiliate does not ordinarily impose a duty on an accountant to investigate what the affiliate has done with them or even to disclose that the affiliate has made a loan to a common officer if this has come to his attention. But it simply cannot be true that an accountant is under no duty to disclose what he knows when he has reason to believe that, to a material extent, a corporation is being operated not to carry out its business in the interest of all the stockholders but for the private benefit of its president. For a court to say that all this is immaterial as a matter of law if only such loans are thought to be collectible would be to say that independent accountants have no responsibility to reveal known dishonesty by a high corporate officer. If certification does not at least imply that the corporation has not been looted by insiders so far as the accountants know, or, if it has been, that the diversion has been made good beyond peradventure (or adequately reserved against) and effective steps taken to prevent a recurrence, it would mean nothing, and the reliance placed on it by the public would be a snare and a delusion. Generally accepted accounting principles instruct an accountant what to do in the usual case where he has no reason to doubt that the affairs of the corporation are being honestly conducted. Once he has reason to believe that this basic assumption is false, an entirely different situation confronts him. Then, as the Lybrand firm stated in its letter accepting the Continental engagement, he must "extend his procedures to determine whether or not such suspicions are justified." If as a result of such an extension or, as here, without it, he finds his suspicions to be confirmed, full disclosure must be the rule, unless he has made sure the wrong has been righted and procedures to avoid a repetition have been established. At least this must be true when the dishonesty he has discovered is not some minor peccadillo but a diversion so large as to imperil if not destroy the very solvency of the enterprise.

On this dominating issue of Roth's diverting corporate funds we do not have a case where the question is whether accountants may be subjected to criminal sanction for closing their eyes to what was plainly to be seen. Fishman was proved to have known what was going on since 1958, Simon must have had a good idea about it from the spring of 1960 when Roth informed him that he had borrowed $1,000,000 from investment bankers to make a repayment to Valley, and the jury could infer that Kaiser also was not unaware. If Roth's testimony was believed, the defendants knew almost all the facts from December 1962. In any event they concede knowledge prior to the certification. Beyond what we have said, Field testified that at a meeting in February 1963 before the statements were certified, he, Simon and Kaiser discussed "how was it possible for a man like Harold Roth * * * for a man like that to go wrong and to take out this money through the circuitous method of having it first go into Valley and then to withdraw it immediately by himself * * *." The jury could reasonably have wondered how accountants who were really seeking to tell the truth could have constructed a footnote so well designed to conceal the shocking facts. This was not simply by the lack of affirmative disclosure but by the failure to describe the securities under circumstances crying for a disclosure and the failure to press Roth for a mortgage on his house and furnishings, description of which in the footnote would necessarily have indicated the source of the collateral and thus evoked inquiry where the money advanced to Valley had gone. . . .

We are likewise unimpressed with the argument that defendants cannot be charged with criminality for failure to disclose the known increase in the Valley receivable from $3.4 to $3.9 million. The jury was . . . entitled to infer that the failure to reveal the increase in the Valley receivable was part of an effort to create an appearance of collectibility which defendants knew to be false. Indeed one of the defense experts agreed that the increase in the receivable was a material event that required disclosure in the absence of sufficient collateral. Moreover, this issue, like the others, must be considered in context. The jury could find that failure to reveal the known increase in the Valley receivable, rather than being motivated by adherence to accepted accounting principles, was due to fear that revelation of the increase would arouse inquiry why a company in the desperate condition of Continental would go on advancing money to an affiliate and thus lead to discovery of Roth's looting.

IV.

Defendants properly make much of the alleged absence of proof of motivation. . . .

Even if there were no satisfactory showing of motive, we think the Government produced sufficient evidence of criminal intent. Its burden was not to show that defendants were wicked men with designs on anyone's purse, which they obviously were not, but rather that they had certified a statement knowing it to be false. As Judge Hough said for us long ago, "while there is no allowable inference of knowledge from the mere fact of falsity, there are many cases where from the actor's special situation and continuity of conduct an inference that he did know the untruth of what he said or wrote may legitimately be drawn." Moreover, so far as criminal intent is concerned, the various deficiencies in the footnote should not be considered in isolation. Evidence that defendants knowingly suppressed one fact permitted, although it surely did not compel, an inference that their suppression of another was likewise knowing and willful. . . .

The Government furnished added evidence of criminal intent in the shape of conflicting statements by the defendants and contradictions by other witnesses. Simon and Fishman had testified before the Referee in Continental's bankruptcy proceedings that they had discussed, together with Kaiser, whether disclosure need be made of the nature of the collateral, and had rejected this as unnecessary. Yet Simon testified at trial that no consideration had been given to this and Fishman could not recall any discussion. Simon and Fishman swore to the Referee that they had not known of Roth's borrowings from Valley until March 1963. On the other hand, Fishman admitted before the grand jury that he had known of them as early as 1958; Roth testified to telling Simon about them in December 1962; all the defendants now admit they were fully informed before the certification in February 1963; and counsel for Continental's trustee testified that Simon had admitted knowing the facts "a long time" before that. When we add the delay in getting at the critical matter of the Valley receivable, the failure to follow up Roth's offer of a mortgage on his house and furniture, and the last minute changes in the balance sheet, we find it impossible to say that a reasonable jury could not be convinced beyond a reasonable doubt that the striking difference between what Note 2 said and what it needed to say in order to reveal the truth resulted not from mere carelessness but from design. That some other jury might have taken a more lenient view, as the trial judge said he would have done, is a misfortune for the defendants but not one within our power to remedy. . . .

We have carefully reviewed the few other arguments made by the defendants but do not consider them of sufficient importance to justify prolonging this already long opinion. This was a trial bitterly but honorably fought, by exceedingly capable and well-prepared counsel, before an able judge experienced in complicated litigation and a highly intelligent jury. Finding that the evidence was sufficient for submission to the jury and that no legal errors were committed, we must let the verdict stand.

Affirmed.

CRIMINAL INTENT

Lack of criminal intent is the defense usually asserted by accountants charged with a crime. They usually admit mistakes or even negligence but deny any criminal wrongdoing. Intent is sometimes easily established as it was in the so-called *Equity Funding* case.[1] In other cases, it is not so clearly established.

[1] United States v. Weiner, U.S.D.C.C.D. of Calif. (Case No. CR13390-JWC).

In the leading case of *United States* v. *Natelli,* 527 F.2d 311 (1975), the United States Court of Appeals for the Second Circuit had occasion to discuss the element of criminal intent and the role of the jury in deciding if it exists. It noted that the failure to follow sound accounting practice is evidence that may prove criminal intent. It said in part:

> It is hard to probe the intent of a defendant. Circumstantial evidence, particularly with proof of motive, where available, is often sufficient to convince a reasonable man of criminal intent beyond a reasonable doubt. When we deal with a defendant who is a professional accountant, it is even harder, at times, to distinguish between simple errors of judgment and errors made with sufficient criminal intent to support a conviction, especially when there is no financial gain to the accountant other than his legitimate fee. . . .
>
> The arguments Natelli makes in this court as evidence of his innocent intent were made to the jury and presented fairly. There is no contention that Judge Tyler improperly excluded any factual evidence offered. While there is substance to some of Natelli's factual contentions for jury consideration, we cannot find, on the totality of the evidence, that he was improperly convicted.
>
> The original action of Natelli in permitting the booking of unbilled sales after the close of the fiscal period in an amount sufficient to convert a loss into a profit was contrary to sound accounting practice, particularly when the cost of sales based on time spent by account executives in the fiscal period was a mere guess. When the uncollectibility, and indeed, the nonexistence of these large receivables was established in 1969, the revelation stood to cause Natelli severe criticism and possible liability. He had a motive, therefore, intentionally to conceal the write-offs that had to be made.
>
> Whether or not the deferred tax item was properly converted to a tax credit, the jury had a right to infer that "netting" the extraordinary item against ordinary earnings on the books in a special journal entry was, in the circumstances, motivated by a desire to conceal. . . .
>
> We reject the argument of insufficiency as to Natelli, our function being limited to determining whether the evidence was sufficient for submission to the jury. We hold that it was.
>
> There are points in favor of Natelli, to be sure, but these were presented to the jury and rejected.

From the foregoing, it is clear that great deference is given to the findings of fact by the jury in criminal cases. As a result, the instructions given to the jury by the court are quite important. In the *Natelli* case, the court discussed a jury instruction on knowledge and its effect on the intent of the defendant. The instruction was as follows:

While I have stated that negligence or mistake do not constitute guilty knowledge or intent, nevertheless, ladies and gentlemen, you are entitled to consider in determining whether a defendant acted with such intent if he deliberately closed his eyes to the obvious or to the facts that certainly would be observed or ascertained in the course of his accounting work or whether he recklessly stated as facts matters of which he knew he was ignorant.

If you find such reckless deliberate indifference to or disregard for truth or falsity on the part of a given defendant, the law entitles you to infer therefrom that the defendant willfully and knowingly filed or caused to be filed false financial information of a material nature with the SEC.

The reviewing court in discussing this instruction observed:

The thrust of appellant's argument, as we understand it, is that the judge charged that each appellant could be convicted "if (his) failure to discover the falsity of (Marketing's) financial statements was the result of some form of gross negligence." We do not read the charge that way. It followed the charge of Judge Mansfield which was sustained in United States v. Simon.

It was a balanced charge which made it clear that negligence or mistake could be insufficient to constitute guilty knowledge. Judge Tyler also carefully instructed the jury that "good faith, an honest belief in the truth of the data set forth in the footnote and entries in the proxy statement would constitute a complete defense here." On the other hand, "Congress equally could not have intended that men holding themselves out as members of these ancient professions (law and accounting) should be able to escape criminal liability on a plea of ignorance when they have shut their eyes to what was plainly to be seen or have represented a knowledge they knew they did not possess."

One of the bases for attack on the charge is that in charging "reckless disregard for the truth or falsity" or "closing his eyes," there must also be an instruction like "and with a conscious purpose to avoid learning the truth.

It is true that we have favored this charge in false statement cases, while noting that both phrases "'mean essentially the same thing,'" and in cases involving knowledge that goods were stolen. The dual instruction is not necessarily required however, when the defendant is under a specific duty to discover the true facts, the facts tendered are suspect, and he does nothing to correct them. In United States v. Benjamin, 328 F.2d at 862, this court said, regarding an accountant, that "the Government can meet its burden by proving that a defendant deliberately closed his eyes to facts he had a duty to see."

TAX RETURN PREPARATION

Criminal sanctions are applicable to accountants for their participation in falsifying tax returns. Tax crimes for which accountants may be held liable are contained in both the Internal Revenue Code (IRC) and the United States Criminal Code (Title 18). The IRC provision that imposes criminal liability on accountants is § 7206(2) which provides that

> any person who . . . willfully aids or assists in, or procures, counsels, or advises the preparation or presentation under, or in connection with any matter arising under, the internal revenue laws, of a return, affidavit, claim, or other document, which is fraudulent or is false as to any material matter, . . . shall be guilty of a felony and upon conviction thereof, shall be fined not more than $5,000 or imprisoned not more than three years, or both, together with the costs of prosecution.

This provision subjects accountants to penal sanctions for misconduct in the preparation of tax returns. For example, in *Couch* v. *United States,* 409 U.S. 322 (1973), the Supreme Court noted that the accountant risks criminal prosecution if he willfully assists in the preparation of a false return.

It should always be kept in mind that whether or not the falsity or fraud is committed with the knowledge or consent of the client involved is irrelevant. Additionally, tax return preparers may be found guilty of assisting in the preparation of a false return when they utilize information furnished by the taxpayer that they know is false.

Certain conduct by accountants and others in the preparation of tax returns is proscribed by the United States Criminal Code (Title 18). More specifically, it authorizes criminal penalties for anyone who conspires either to commit an offense against the United States or to defraud the United States, or any agency thereof. The penalty for a violation of this section includes a maximum fine of $10,000 and/or a maximum term of five years of imprisonment. The case which follows is typical of those charging an accountant with violations of the U.S. code.

UNITED STATES v. WARDEN
545 F.2d 32 (1976)

CAMPBELL, J.

Defendant Warden and one Melvin Greenberg were charged in a 24 count indictment with one count of conspiracy (18 U.S.C. § 371) and 23 substantive violations of 26 U.S.C. § 7206(2). Each of the substantive counts concerned the false preparation and filing of specific income tax returns for the years 1969 through 1972. Prior to trial, Greenberg entered a plea of nolo contendere to one count of the indictment, and was sentenced to probation for a term of one year.

Warden was found guilty of the conspiracy count and on eleven of the thirteen substantive counts which were considered by the jury. He was sentenced to a four year term of probation, the first ninety days of which were to be spent at the Chicago Community Treatment Center under psychiatric care. We affirm.

The evidence disclosed that Warden was a certified public accountant doing business as Warden and Company in Chicago, Illinois. Individually, and in conspiracy with Greenberg and others in his employ, he fraudulently prepared false income tax returns for various clients. The evidence revealed a pattern and practice whereby Warden would "plug-in" either inflated or totally fabricated figures for various expenses used to calculate certain deductions. These deductions included (1) unreimbursed business expenses; (2) unreimbursed use of auto; (3) cash contributions; (4) contributions other than cash; (5) medical and medical related expenses; (6) stock portfolio expenses, and (7) business expenses.

In calculating deductions for unreimbursed business use of auto, for example, Warden would typically plug-in an expense for garaging the taxpayer's car at an annual cost of $180.00. On returns involved in six of the counts upon which he was convicted, this item and figure appeared even though the taxpayer did not provide that figure and, in certain cases, either did not own a garage or owned one but used it only for storage. Similarly, when calculating the "contributions—other than cash" deduction, Warden would fabricate a list of clothes which allegedly had been donated to charity, together with a valuation schedule. In some cases rather than preparing a separate clothing schedule for each taxpayer, Warden made several copies of the same schedule and merely inserted them in various returns. As a result, one taxpayer, whose returns were challenged in counts 5 and 6, listed virtually the same clothing in his 1968 amended return as in his 1971 return. According to another return prepared by Warden, the very same clothing was also donated by a different taxpayer whose 1971 return formed the basis for count 21. As testimony of Warden employee D'Amico, Lazarini, and co-conspirator Greenberg revealed, the monetary figure for these deductions was totally unsubstantiated.

To justify the unreimbursed business expense deductions, Warden would use, in some instances, a fabricated letter from the taxpayer's employer delineating certain business expenses which were not reimbursed. The evidence showed that on other occasions, he would note on the schedules that the deductions were "per substantiating detail" even though such detail existed in neither Warden's nor the taxpayer's file.

It also appears that Warden's clients were unaware of his activities since they were required by Warden to sign their returns either in blank or, if signed when completed, without the falsified schedules attached. Warden's fee was contingent upon the amount of the refund.

On appeal. Warden asserts (. . . the following) grounds for reversal:

1. That there existed a fatal variance between the indictment and proof.

2. That the trial judge erred in refusing to enforce a subpoena *duces tecum* served upon the Internal Revenue Service for certain materials which appellant contends were both relevant and capable of being compiled from the computer files of the Internal Revenue Service.

3. That whether the allegedly false statements in the income tax returns were "material" is a question of fact to be submitted to the jury under an appropriate instruction. . . .

Warden first contends that there existed substantial and fatal variances between the charges in the indictment and the proof adduced at trial. He argues that some counts of the indictment allege deductions in excess of the actual deductions contained in the tax returns, and that in other instances, the indictment alleges a specific item deduction which does not correspond to any individual item appearing on the return. In other instances, he argues, the amounts set forth in the indictment are less than those on the return, even though the indictment figures purport to correspond to identifiable entries appearing on the returns.

The government responds that the amounts listed in the indictment under "Amounts Per Return," while occasionally corresponding to the amount ultimately taken as a deduction, were intended to represent the total dollar amounts being challenged as materially false for each expense category listed under "Claim Per Return." Each deduction or expense category was comprised of one or more specific expenditures or expense items. The challenged expense items were then totalled for each category of deductions and the total was set forth in the indictment. The government contends that more often than not the amount in the indictment was only a portion of the amount claimed on the return because not every line entry or expenditure within each category was challenged.

It is well settled that in order for a variance between indictment and proof to be fatal, the evidence offered must prove facts materially different from those alleged in the indictment; a variance will not be deemed fatal where the defendant is so informed of the charges against him that he is protected against a second prosecution for the same offense and is able to adequately prepare his defense against the charges set forth in the indictment. In the instant case, we are satisfied that no fatal variance occurred. In a prosecution charging the filing of false tax returns, the government is not obliged to prove the exact amount alleged in the indictment.

Warden next contends that the district court's quashing of his subpoena *duces tecum* was error, arguing that the materials requested in the subpoena were relevant and could have easily been procured from the computer files of the Internal Revenue Service. In support of his contention, Warden states that the government had at least three computer programs at its disposal, by means of which the materials requested existence easily could have been procured. The alleged existence of these programs and the alleged case with which the desired materials could have been obtained, were not presented by defendant to the district judge, who granted the government's motion to quash the sub-poena on the ground that "defendant's demand could place an impossible burden on the government." . . .

We deem it unnecessary to resolve whether production of the requested materials would have been easy, cumbersome, diffifficult or impossible. In ruling on the government's motion to quash the subpoena, Judge McLaren gave due consideration to the government's argument that copies of the materials in question—all tax returns prepared by Warden between 1972 and 1974—were already in his possession. Moreover, the district judge offered a compromise solution under which defendant would produce a list of persons whose returns he desired to review, and the government in turn would identify whether the corresponding tax returns were prepared by Warden, whether an audit was conducted by the IRS and whether the IRS ultimately challenged the tax deduc-tions claimed therein. The defendant did not pursue this suggestion.

On the basis of the facts before the district court, we find that Judge McLaren did not abuse his discretion in granting the government's motion to quash the subpoena *duces tecum*.

Warden next contends that his Sixth Amendment right to a trial by jury was violated by one of the trial judge's instructions to the jury. In instructing the jury on the elements necessary to establish a violation of 26 U.S.C. § 7206(2), the judge stated:

Three essential elements are required to be proved in order to establish the offense charged in these counts of the indictment. First the act or acts of aiding and/or assisting in procuring, counseling, advising in the preparation or the presentation of an income tax return false or fraudulent as to a material matter, (second) doing such act or acts with the knowledge that the income tax return in question was false or fraudulent as to a material matter as charged, and (third) doing such act or acts willfully.

After explaining various elements of the offense, the judge then ex-plained the term "deduction" and described the various deductions involved in the instant case. He concluded with the following sentence:

I instruct you that the deductions I have just described are material matters as that term is used in the indictment.

It is Warden's contention that the above instruction took the entire issue of materiality, which the judge had just described as an essential element of the offense, away from the jury. We do not agree.

The test of materiality with respect to a false return case is whether a particular item must be reported "in order that the taxpayer estimate and compute his tax correctly." Since deductions are subtracted from gross income or adjusted gross income to reduce the ultimate tax liability, they are material to the contents of the return. Stated otherwise, the deduction will invariably affect the taxpayer's liability. Thus, when Judge McLaren instructed the jury that the deductions were material matters as that term is used in the indictment he did no more than state the obvious fact that deductions affect the computation of tax liability.

In this connection, it is important to note that the jury was also instructed:

> The evidence need not establish beyond a reasonable doubt that the deductions totalled the exact amount alleged in the indictment, or that the deductions were overstated in the exact amount alleged, but only that the accused willfully overstated or caused to be overstated *in some substantial amount* the deductions as charged in the indictment. (Emphasis added.)

The jury, therefore, was required to find that the deductions, whcih invariably affect the ultimate determination of tax liability, were substantially overstated. We find no error with respect to the materiality instruction challenged by appellant. . . .

For the foregoing reasons, the conviction is affirmed.

Affirmed.

The United States Code also proscribes falsely swearing to the truth of any testimony or document for which a law of the United States authorizes an oath to be administered. The penalty for a violation of this section is a fine of not more than $2,000 or five years' imprisonment or both. This code is supplemented by a penalty for falsely verifying any statement which is within the purview of the tax law, IRC § 7206(1). Thus, in effect, an accountant who perjures himself in the preparation of a tax return is subject to the sanctions of both of the foregoing provisions.

In summary, it should be recognized by all who participate in the preparation of tax returns and any related documents that criminal liability may be imposed for conduct which violates either the Internal Revenue Code or the United States Criminal Code. Accountants are prohibited from willfully assisting any one in falsifying tax returns or claims. Furthermore, it is illegal for accountants to participate in conspiracies for the purpose of tax evasion. Additionally, false information given under oath may subject accountants to punishment on the grounds of perjury.

OTHER CRIMINAL STATUTES

There are other federal criminal statutes under which accountants are sometimes indicted. For example, the Federal Mail Fraud Statute, Section 1341, imposes criminal sanctions for using the mail to defraud.

> Whoever, having devised or intending to devise any scheme or artifice to defraud, or for obtaining money or property by means of false or

fraudulent pretenses, representations, or promises, or to sell, dispose of, loan, exchange, alter, give away, distribute, supply, or furnish or procure for unlawful use any counterfeit or spurious coin, obligation, security, or other article, or anything represented to be or intimated or held out to be such counterfeit or spurious article, for the purpose of executing such scheme or artifice or attempting so to do, places in any post office or authorized depository for mail matter, any matter or thing whatever to be sent or delivered by the Postal Service, or takes or receives therefrom, any such matter or thing, or knowingly causes to be delivered by mail according to the direction thereon, or at the place at which it is directed to be delivered by the person to whom it is addressed, any such matter or thing, shall be fined not more than $1,000 or imprisoned not more than five years, or both.

The Federal False Statements Statutes, Section 1001, imposes criminal sanctions for false statements made in matters within a federal department jurisdiction such as the SEC. It provides:

Whoever, in any matter within the jurisdiction of any department or agency of the United States *knowingly* and *willfully* falsifies, conceals or covers up by any trick, scheme, or device a material fact, or makes any false, fictitious or fraudulent statements or representations, or makes or uses any false writing or document *knowing* the same to contain any false, fictitious or fraudulent statement or entry, shall be fined not more than $10,000 or imprisoned not more than five years, or both. (Emphasis added.)

The ease of obtaining convictions under the above statutes is fairly obvious. The use of the mails is so common that proof of its use adds little to the burden of the prosecution in such cases.

1. Distinguish a tort from a crime.

2. X, an accountant charged with a criminal violation of the securities laws, is found to be "not guilty" by a jury. Later, Y, the investor upon whose testimony the criminal case was brought filed a civil action against X seeking dollar damages. X sought to have the case dismissed because of the acquittal in the criminal case. Will the court do so? Why?

3. List four statutes that may be used as the basis of a criminal indictment of an accountant. What are the elements of each crime which must be alleged and proven?

4. Is proof of negligence sufficient to sustain a conviction under Section 24 of the Securities Act of 1933? Explain.

5. Is compliance with generally accepted accounting principles an absolute defense to a criminal prosecution? Why?

6. Describe the deference given to the verdict of the jury in a criminal case.

7. To what extent is proof of motive required in a criminal prosecution? Explain.

8. Assume that a defendant accountant had deliberately closed his eyes to material facts which affected the financial statements of a company being audited. Will this evidence supply the criminal intent required to convict under the securities laws? Explain.

9. Give three examples of practices or activities that may result in the criminal conviction of one engaged in the preparation of income tax returns.

10. What is the test of "materiality" in determining if an accountant is guilty of violating the law in the preparation of income tax returns? Who decides if the errors on the returns were material? Why?

SUGGESTED ADDITIONAL READINGS

ANDREWS, F., "Why Didn't Auditors Find Something Wrong With Equity Funding?" in *Perspectives in Auditing,* ed. D. R. Carmichael and J. Willingham. New York: McGraw-Hill, 1975.

DUNFEE, THOMAS W., and IRVIN N. GLEIM, "Criminal Liability of Accountants: Sources and Policies," *American Business Law Journal,* Spring 1971.

"Federal Criminal and Administrative Controls for Auditors: The Need for a Consistent Standard," *Washington University Law Quarterly,* Spring 1969.

ISBELL, DAVID B., "The Continental Vending Case: Lessons for the Profession," *Journal of Accountancy,* August 1970.

"The Criminal Liability of Public Accountants: A Study of United States v. Simon," *Notre Dame Lawyer,* Spring 1971.

ADDITIONAL CASES

United States v. Benjamin, 328 F.2d 854 (2d cir. 1964).

United States v. Natelli, 527 F.2d 311 (1975).

United States v. Weiner, United States District Court, Central District of California (Case No. CR 13390-JWC).

United States v. Goldblum, CCH Fed. Sec. L. Rep. § 94,700 (Equity Funding).

United States v. Clark, CCA Fed. Sec. L. Rep. § 93,745 (S.D.N.Y., 1972) (Four Season Case).

Chapter 11

Privileged
and Confidential
Communications

INTRODUCTION

The subject of privileged and confidential communications between an accountant and a client is extremely complex. Issues relating to privileged and confidential communications frequently arise in tax litigation and in criminal cases such as embezzlement. However, they may also arise in civil matters such as collection suits or even divorce cases. While issues of privilege and confidentiality may arise in suits directly involving accountants, they most frequently arise in litigation to which the client is a party-litigant.

Questions of privilege also arise when an accountant is required to report to an employer or to a government agency. Although such matters are often derogatory to another person and may be considered defamatory, the law of privilege protects the accountant from a suit for libel or slander as a result of such reports.

The contention that a communication by a client to an accountant is privileged and thus not subject to either testimony by the accountant or to discovery raises difficult policy questions. Those who would assert the need for a privilege and who would thus bar the testimony of an accountant are, in effect, hindering the search for truth. This suppression of truth frequently involves matters directly affecting the public interest. On the other hand, total and accurate communication of information by clients to accounts may be directly affected if the subject matter of such communications is not in fact confidential.

The problem of privileged communications is highlighted by the Code of Professional Ethics which states that an accountant should not violate the confidential relationship between himself and his client. While a voluntary disclosure of confidential communications would violate the code, testimony pursuant to court order (involuntary disclosure) would not be an ethical violation. Moreover, courts have no duty to enforce the Code of Professional Ethics since it is not a law.

The complexity of the problem is increased by the fact that lawyers frequently employ accountants to assist in the legal function and by the fact that many accountants are also lawyers. The attorney-client privilege must therefore be considered in addition to the accountant-client privilege. Issues of compulsory self-incrimination as protected by the Fifth Amendment to the Constitution of the United States are also frequently interwoven with these privileges. This chapter will discuss the extent to which communications to an accountant are in fact confidential and not subject to discovery by judicial process or to testimony by accountants in litigation. It will also discuss the attorney-client privilege and its relationship to the accounting profession.

AN OVERVIEW OF
PRIVILEGED COMMUNICATIONS

In litigation, evidence may be inadmissible under two different theories. Some evidence is automatically excluded by courts. For example, a typical rule of exclusion prevents hearsay evidence. On the other hand, some evidence is admissible unless a valid reason is provided for denying its admissibility. The law relating to the admissibility of privileged communications comes under this category. Therefore, a privilege may be claimed or waived at a party's discretion. Communications that may be privileged against disclosure are admissible as evidence unless the person claiming the privilege objects to its admission as evidence or to its discovery if the question is not asked in open court.

Privileged communications arise as the result of a special relationship between the parties. Such relationships are often inherently confidential and frequently include fiduciary elements. The secrecy that is protected by a privilege arises because of the special relationship of the parties and the duty of other parties to protect this relationship.

Important privileged communications include those between husband and wife, attorney and client, physician and patient, and priest and penitent. Each of these privileges is based upon important public policy considerations. For example, communications to an attorney are privileged in order that clients will fully inform their attorneys of all matters that may affect the relationship. The attorney-client privilege developed in early Roman law and was carried over into the English system at an early date. Barristers have taken an oath not to disclose the secrets of their clients since Elizabethan times. It is felt that the cost to justice by silencing the lawyer's lips is outweighed by the benefits to justice from a full disclosure to the lawyer by the client.

Historically, privileges were created by judges. In recent years, statutes have frequently created new privileged communications. For example, most states have created by statute a privilege for communications between a penitent and a priest. Courts have extended the concept of privilege by creating the right of privacy, used in recent years to prevent official snooping into the private lives of individuals. Courts have attempted to broaden this right on a case-by-case basis.

Privileged communications by their very nature create difficult problems for courts. These problems arise because of the inherent conflict between the search for truth and protecting the interest asserted by the privilege. For example, communications between a husband and wife are privileged in order to preserve the marital relationship by encouraging trust and confidence. Yet if the marriage has been dissolved by divorce, should the former spouse be allowed to testify? One of the more difficult aspects of privileged communications arises when an eavesdropper is called to testify about matters learned by eavesdropping. The alleged confidential communication was not in fact confidential. Should the eavesdropper be allowed to testify? Courts frequently side with the search for truth and allow such testimony.

Difficult side issues often arise when a party asserts a privilege and prevents the use of evidence. For example, does a jury tend to draw an adverse inference from the assertion of the privilege? Many courts have held that if evidence which is material is excluded from consideration because of the assertion of a personal privilege, the claim of privilege may be referred to in argument and considered by the jury as an indication that the evidence, if received, would be prejudicial. The courts have held that such an inference cannot be used in relation to the privilege against compulsory self-incrimination, but many courts have not extended that view to other privileges such as the one between attorney and client.

Insofar as the law of libel and slander is concerned, some communications are absolutely privileged. For example, statements by members of Congress on the floor cannot be the basis of a defamation case, even if they are maliciously false. Likewise, pleadings in a lawsuit and evidence given in open court cannot be used as the basis for a tort action of defamation. The need for open and free debate in Congress and for witnesses to speak freely in court is so important that the law will not allow the possibility of a lawsuit to act even as a slight deterrent to them. On the other hand, some communications are only protected by a limited privilege in libel and slander litigation. These statements are privileged unless made with malice. An auditor's report would be an example of a communication which is clothed with the limited privilege insofar as the law of defamation is concerned. An accountant would not be liable for defamatory statements unless they were made with actual malice.

THE ATTORNEY-CLIENT PRIVILEGE

This privilege is perhaps the oldest one. The reasons for it are obvious, especially in criminal law. An attorney cannot give his best advice without the knowledge of all pertinent facts, which the client would not openly give if the attorney could be forced to testify against his client. Thus, this privilege belongs to the client, and only the client can waive it. These aspects are important to keep in mind because those who seek to establish a similar privilege for the accountant-client relationship frequently seek it for the accountant and not for the client.

The attorney-client privilege extends to civil litigation as well as to criminal cases. Complete candor between an attorney and a client will not only aid in the settlement of disputes but will often prevent unfounded litigation. While the reasons for the privilege in civil litigation are not so obvious, it is so deeply ingrained in the legal profession that its elimination is probably impossible.

The attorney-client privilege is based on the confidentiality of the communication. However, the mere existence of the relationship does not mean that all communications are privileged. The communication must be made by someone seeking legal advice from a lawyer in that capacity. Thus, if an attorney is performing another function, such as keeping books of account, no privilege would attach to the client's communications. Business advice would fall into the same category, but if the advice involves the law to any degree at all, the communication will be considered privileged.

Communications are privileged even though the lawyer does not accept the client's case. If a communication is made with a view toward the relationship, it is privileged. Likewise, the client need not pay a fee for the privilege to exist.

As previously noted, the communication must in fact be confidential. If overheard by someone, then that person may testify. However, the protection extends to prevent testimony by secretaries and clerks who may be present during a confidential communication or who may transcribe a recording of it. The law takes a realistic approach and recognizes that an attorney may have someone take notes or actually transcribe the record of confidential communications between an attorney and his client.

The attorney-client privilege only protects communications. It does not prevent the attorney from testifying about observable facts, such as the color of a client's suit. In addition, any documents that may be obtained from the client may be obtained from the attorney. Books and records are not given additional protection by turning them over to an attorney.

THE ACCOUNTANT-CLIENT PRIVILEGE

INTRODUCTION

The common law recognizes no accountant-client privilege. Therefore, if one is to exist, it must be created by statute. Several states have adopted such statutes, but Congress has not. The applicability of a state statute in a given case depends upon whether the litigation is in a state or federal court and whether it involves state or federal laws. Before examining some state statutes, a brief discussion relative to the jurisdiction of courts and to the substantive law used by them to decide cases is essential.

THE JURISDICTION OF FEDERAL COURTS

The judicial system of the United States is a dual system consisting of state courts and federal courts. The federal courts are created by Congress, but their jurisdiction is limited by the Constitution. The Constitution creates the Supreme Court and authorizes such inferior courts as the Congress may from time to time establish.

The district courts are the trial courts of the federal judicial system. They have original jurisdiction, exclusive of the courts of the states, over all federal crimes, that is, all offenses against the laws of the United States. The accused is entitled to a trial by jury in the state and district where the crime was committed.

In civil actions, the district courts have jurisdiction only when the matter in controversy exceeds the sum or value of $10,000, exclusive of costs and interest, and is based on either diversity of citizenship or a federal question. Diversity of citizenship exists in suits between (1) citizens of different states, (2) a citizen of a state and a citizen of a foreign country, and (3) a state and citizens of another state. The plaintiff or plaintiffs must be citizens of a different state than any one of the defendants for diversity of citizenship to exist. Diversity of citizenship does not prevent the plaintiff from bringing his suit in a state court, but if the defendant is a citizen of another state, the defendant has the right to have the case removed to a federal court. A defendant, by having the case removed to the federal court, can have a jury selected from a larger area than the county where the cause arose, thus hopefully avoiding the possibility of jurors prejudicial to the plaintiff.

For the purpose of suit in a federal court, a corporation is considered a "citizen" of the state where it is incorporated and of the state in which it has its principal place of business. As a result, there is no federal jurisdiction in many cases in which one of the parties is a corporation. If any one of the parties on the other side of the case is a citizen either of the state in which the corporation is chartered or is doing its principal business, there is no diversity of citizenship and thus no federal jurisdiction.

Federal jurisdiction based on a federal question exists if the lawsuit arises out of rights granted by the Constitution, laws, or treaties of the United States. The federal courts have jurisdiction of federal question cases if $10,000 or more is involved or if the case involves personal rights without reference to money value of the controversy. For example, the amount of the controversy is not a jurisdictional question when the suit is brought by the United States or a federal officer and arises under the Constitution or federal laws and treaties. These civil actions may involve matters such as bankruptcy or setting aside orders of administrative agencies such as the Securities and Exchange Commission. Other federal question cases that do not require the $10,000 limit are suits based on patents, copyrights, trademarks, taxes, elections, the rights guaranteed by the Bill of Rights, and those rights secured to individual citizens by the Fourteenth Amendment.

THE LAW IN FEDERAL QUESTION CASES

Law may be classified as *substantive law* or *procedural law*. Substantive law defines the rights and duties of citizens and is the result of legislative or judicial action. Procedural law specifies the method and means by which the substantive law is made, enforced, and administered. Procedural rules define the methods by which courts apply substantive law to resolve conflicts. Substantive rights have no value unless there are procedures that provide a means for establishing and enforcing them. As a general proposition, each court system uses its own rules of procedure. Thus, in the federal courts, the federal rules of procedure (both civil and criminal) are followed. For state court proceedings, each state has adopted applicable rules of procedure.

The problem as to the applicable substantive law is far more complex. In federal criminal cases, federal courts use federal law and there is no accountant-client privilege. In civil federal question cases, the controlling statutes and judicial decisions are those of the federal courts also. As the following case illustrates, a state statute dealing with an accountant privilege does not apply when the federal courts exercise federal question jurisdiction.

BAYLOR v. MADING-DUGAN DRUG COMPANY
57 F.R.D. 509 (1972)

BAUER, J.

This case comes on a motion by defendant Mading-Dugan Drug Company (Mading-Dugan) to quash a subpoena duces tecum served upon the accounting firm of Lybrand, Ross Brothers, and Montgomery (Lybrand). The plaintiff has had a subpoena duces tecum issued for the taking of a deposition in Texas in order to aid a deposition notice filed with the Clerk of this court. This subpoena requires Lybrand and one or more of its "officers, directors, or agents" to produce documents relating to the June 1969 financial statement of Mading-Dugan and its subsidiaries. Lybrand was the accountant for Mading-Dugan during the period in question in the instant litigation.

The defendant based its motion to quash the subpoena on the Illinois accountant privilege pursuant to Ch. 110½, sec. 51 of the Illinois Revised Statutes. Lybrand in an affidavit submitted to this Court by J. Eugene Clement, Attorney for Lybrand, has joined in Mading-Dugan's motion to invoke the accountant privilege.

The plaintiff contends in opposition to the motion to quash:

1. The Illinois statute is not applicable to communications between accountants and their clients in a state other than Illinois. It is limited solely to Illinois "public accountants."

2. Where its jurisdiction is based on alleged violation of Federal law, this court should not enforce a statutory privilege specially created by Illinois.

It is the opinion of this Court that the Illinois accountant privilege is not applicable in this case.

A state statute dealing with an accountant privilege does not apply where the district court is exercising federal question jurisdiction.

Federal courts dealing with the issue of privileged communications in diversity cases have generally applied state privilege statutes and followed state case law. However, even in diversity cases some courts have failed to apply state privilege statutes.

The instant action is based on the alleged boot-strap acquisition of an insurance company in violation of the Federal Securities laws. . . . Thus jurisdiction in the instant action is not based on diversity of citizenship but on the violation of a federal statute.

It is the court's opinion that, as a matter of policy, states should not be permitted to decide for federal courts when they must refrain from hearing useful testimony in matters involving federal law. There is a significant difference between the application of such privilege in diversity actions as opposed to application of such privilege in cases involving a federally created right. State legislatures create privileges because a particular relationship is considered so valuable to society that it should be fostered by preserving the confidentiality of the relationship even though evidence which might aid in the quest for truth will be lost. The states' efforts to encourage these relationships are thwarted if the secrets which were privileged by a state statute are allowed to be disclosed in a federal diversity action merely because litigants happen to be citizens of different states. In a diversity case, the litigation is based on a state created right in which there is no justification for federal interference with the state's decision that a specific relationship is more important than the litigation. Federal courts have refused to honor state privileges in actions involving enforcement of rights created under federal law. More specifically, federal courts in cases involving the violation of federal laws have refused to apply an accountant privilege.

In federal question cases, there may be compelling reasons for ignoring a state privilege statute and following an independent federal rule. One such compelling reason occurs where there are clear indications of a federal policy toward uniformity and no significant state policy would be served by absorption of the state law into the federal proceeding.

It is this Court's opinion that a federal district court may no longer apply a state created accountant privilege in federal question cases. This opinion is based upon the federal policy announced in the Federal Rules of Evidence and the necessity for uniformity in the litigation of federal questions. . . .

Thus it is the opinion of this court that the Illinois accountant privilege is not applicable in federal question cases.

Accordingly, it is hereby ordered that the defendant's motion to quash the subpoena duces tecum is denied.

THE LAW IN DIVERSITY CASES

Federal courts in diversity of citizenship cases are just another court of the state in which they sit. As such, they apply the substantive law, including conflict of law principles, of that state in cases before them. Federal courts in such cases use the rules of federal procedure.

Prior to 1975, federal courts in diversity of citizenship cases were confronted with difficult issues when the application of state statutes on the accountant-client privilege was raised. The law of privilege as law of evidence was essentially procedural. If treated as such, then state privilege statutes would not be followed in diversity of citizenship cases. Courts, however, frequently found reasons to allow the privilege as the following case illustrates.

LUKEE ENTERPRISES, INC. v. NEW YORK LIFE INSURANCE CO.
52 F.R.D. 21 (1971)

BRATTON, J.

Plaintiffs bring this action against three defendant insurance companies to collect on certain insurance policies. Federal jurisdiction is based solely on grounds of diversity of citizenship.

Presently at issue is plaintiffs' Motion for an order striking notice of deposition of William B. Bonds, C.P.A.; for an order quashing the subpoena served upon him which would compel his attendance at deposition proceedings; and for a protective order prohibiting further attempts to obtain his deposition.

Plaintiffs seek this order because Bonds is a certified public accountant and it is claimed that any knowledge or information which he has relating to Charles M. Preston or Lukee Enterprises, Inc. was supplied to him by privileged communications from them. It is contended these communications are privileged by operation of New Mexico's accountant-client privilege statutes.

Plaintiffs contend that Bonds will not be called as a witness, and that their claim does not put the "financial aspects and dealing of plaintiffs" into issue. Defendants, however, claim full discovery is necessary to their defense. They also maintain the Plaintiffs have waived any privilege they may have by bringing the action.

The specific question presented is whether a federal court, in a diversity case, should accord an accountant-client privilege granted by state statute.

(1) Federal courts in such matters of privilege in diversity cases generally follow state statutes and decisional law. Although some courts and the proposed Rules of Evidence for the United States District Courts and Magistrates disregard state law in diversity cases, the weight of authority favors application of state law in such cases. In so applying state privilege statutes some courts have based their decision on the premise that under the Erie doctrine a privilege confers a substantive right which is beyond regulation by the Federal Rules of Civil Procedure. Many other courts, while giving effect to the state-created privileges, both in terms of admission of evidence under Rule 43(a) and in terms of discovery under Rule 26(b), have not placed the result on the compulsion of Erie. They relied either upon the reference to state law in Rule 43(a) and the practice in the federal courts prior to the adoption of the federal rules, or on the principal of accommodating the policy of the state.

(2) It is not necessary to select among the various grounds cited for application of state statutory privileges in a diversity case to conclude that the privilege claimed by plaintiffs in this case should be recognized and accorded. . . .

Plaintiff's Motion for an order striking notice of deposition of William B. Bonds and for an order quashing the subpoena served on Bonds will be granted.

While several decisions similar to the preceding case have been decided, some courts concluded that state privilege statutes would not be followed in diversity of citizenship cases. These decisions occurred prior to 1975 and were based upon a federal rule which in effect provided that if evidence were admissible under either the federal or state rule of evidence, it was admissible. Since there was no accountant-client privilege under the federal rules, testimony of the accountant was held to be admissible. In 1975 new federal rules of evidence were adopted. Rule 501 provides as follows:

> Rule 501. *General Rule*
> Except as otherwise required by the Constitution of the United States or provided by Act of Congress or in rules prescribed by the Supreme Court pursuant to statutory authority, the privilege of a witness, person, government, State, or political subdivision thereof shall be governed by the principles of the common law as they may be interpreted by the courts of the United States in the light of reason and experience. However, in civil actions and proceedings, with respect to an element of a claim or defense as to which State law supplies the rule of decision, the privilege of a witness, person, government, State, or political subdivision thereof shall be determined in accordance with State law.

Rule 501 means that state privilege laws will be applied in civil actions if the decision in the case is based on state law. Thus, if a state has an accountant privilege statute, the federal courts will use it in diversity of citizenship cases involving issues to be decided by state law. Rule 501 in no way changes the law for federal criminal cases or federal question cases.

AN OVERVIEW OF STATE STATUTES

Fifteen states and Puerto Rico have passed statutes on the subject of the accountant-client privilege. Although these statutes have a common purpose, they employ such a variety of approaches to the problem that there is almost no uniformity among them. Most create the privilege for the client, but a few create it for the accountant. In those cases in which courts have been called upon to decide whether the privilege belongs to the accountant or to the client, the decision usually is that it belongs to the client. This is especially true when the client seeks to have the accountant disclose evidence.

Courts have held that the privilege is personal to the client because the conditions of social policy usually present in privileged communication cases are not present when a client seeks the testimony of an accountant. These conditions usually include that (1) the communication originated in confidence, (2) confidentiality must be maintained for the relationship of the parties to continue, and (3) the injury that would result to the relationship by the disclosure is greater than the benefits to be gained by disclosure of the evidence. Courts have concluded that a privilege in the hands of accountants not only would tend to insulate them from their responsibilities, but it would foster incompetence and irresponsibility.

While the welfare of the client may be served by a zone of privacy relating to communications between the client and the accountant, this zone must be controlled by the client. The fundamental purpose of the privilege would be thwarted if accountants were unilaterally allowed to suppress evidence to the detriment of their clients. Those decisions holding that the privilege belongs to the client are consistent with the AICPA Code of Ethics provisions which prohibit disclosure of confidential information attained in the course of a professional engagement except with the consent of the client.

Some states exempt criminal and bankruptcy cases from the application of the privilege laws. In these states, accountants may be required to testify if the client is accused of crime or is involved in bankruptcy proceedings. The legislatures in these states apparently felt that the search for truth in criminal cases and bankruptcy proceedings was more important than the need for confidentiality between an accountant and his client.

Some states exempt criminal and bankruptcy cases from the application employees. Other states extend the privilege to all public accountants. In these states, the privilege would not extend to internal accountants. Two states exclude the audit function from the privilege. For example, the Pennsylvania statute provides:

> Except by permission of the client or person or firm or corporation engaging him, or the heirs, successors or personal representatives of such client or person, or firm or corporation, a certified public accountant or a public accountant, or a person employed by a certified public accountant or a public accountant shall not be required to and shall not voluntarily disclose or divulge information of which he may become possessed, relative to and in connection with any professional services as a certified public accountant or a public accountant. The information derived from as the result of such professional services shall be deemed confidential and privileged: Provided, however, that nothing herein shall be construed as prohibiting a certified public accountant or a public accountant from disclosing any data which he believes should be disclosed by the standards of the profession in rendering an opinion on the presentation of financial statements, or in making disclosure where said financial statements, or professional services of the accountant pertaining thereto are contested.

An argument can be made that the privilege should extend to the audit function notwithstanding the fact that one primary beneficiary of the product of the function is the public. Whether it does or not is up to the legislature.

When an accountant performs a public audit, he is often called upon to examine data relevant to a variety of complex financial, tax, and management problems. To do so properly, the accountant should have access to the details of his client's operations, many of which his client may consider confidential. If the privilege enables the accountant to obtain more complete information, then the public benefits from the privilege as well. To the extent that an accountant-client privilege can assure audited concerns that financial data revealed to accountants will not be disclosed in court, it promotes the public interest in having accurate financial statements. However, the fact that thirty-five states have no statute at all on the subject realistically means that it does not exist for accountants serving publicly held businesses engaged in interstate commerce or doing business in several states.

Assuming that the accountant-client privilege has the capacity to promote increased disclosure and that this outweighs the adverse effect upon the fact-finding process, it can be argued that the privilege still results in a sacrifice of the public's right to inquire into the information used by the accountant in preparing his audit. If members of the public cannot examine such information when they suspect fraud or negligence, they may be less willing to rely on certified financial statements. Considered in this light, the accountant-client privilege may well serve to undermine the utility of certified financial statements. Thus, if the privilege is to become universal, safeguards may be required, and the privilege may be held not to apply in cases involving fraud or negligence by the accountant.

STATE STATUTES—INTERPRETATIVE CASES

Since state statutes creating the accountant-client privilege are only applicable in litigation that does not involve federal law, there are few cases interpreting them. In one Colorado case, the Colorado courts held that an accountant could be required to testify (notwithstanding the statute) in a case brought by a shareholder against a corporate client of the accountant. The court stated in part:

> Certified Public Accountants hired by a corporation are hired for the benefit of all its shareholders and such employment forbids concealment from the stockholders of information given the accountant by the corporation.

The court also held that the privilege applied to noncertified work. It noted:

> Nowhere does the statute distinguish between communications made for the purpose of preparing *certified* reports and those made for the

purpose of preparing non-certified works. . . . Accordingly, we hold that any confidential communication made by a client to a licensed certified public accountant in the course of his professional employment falls within the statutory privilege whether or not they are made for the purpose of preparing *certified* reports.

Several cases have held that the privilege has been waived by the client. Waiver frequently occurs when a party seeks to use an audit or a tax return to support his case. The introduction of such evidence by a party constitutes a waiver of any privilege, and the other party may question the accountant without interference by the assertion of the privilege.

PRIVATE COMMUNICATIONS BEFORE ADMINISTRATIVE AGENCIES

Accountants are frequently called upon to testify and to deliver documents to federal governmental agencies. The Internal Revenue Code authorizes the subpoena of records from an accountant or anyone else in possession of them. The Securities and Exchange Commission frequently seeks evidence from accountants. Since the matters before these agencies are based on federal laws, state statutes creating privileges are not applicable, and no privilege exists on behalf of accountants in these proceedings.

Bankruptcy proceedings create a special problem. They are in the nature of a judicial proceeding, yet much of our bankruptcy law is based upon state statutes. However, all of the rights of the bankrupt pass to the trustee in bankruptcy, and the trustee is in a position to waive any privilege the client may have had based on state law. As a result, it is not likely that an accountant can avoid testimony in bankruptcy proceedings.

OTHER PRIVILEGED COMMUNICATIONS AND ACCOUNTANTS

INTRODUCTION

There are several other privileges which affect the accountant-client relationship. For example, the privilege against compulsory self-incrimination found in the Fifth Amendment frequently may be involved when government seeks documents or the testimony of the accountant. As previously noted, the attorney-client privilege may include under its protection an accountant hired by a lawyer, as well as one who is also a lawyer. The following sections will discuss these privileges as they relate to the accounting function.

PRIVILEGES BASED ON THE BILL OF RIGHTS

The Fourth Amendment to the Constitution of the United States protects individuals from unreasonable searches and seizures. Its purpose is to protect individuals and their private property from unwarranted intrusions. Among the protections found in the Fifth Amendment is the protection against compulsory self-incrimination. Each of these protections has been made applicable to the states by the Fourteenth Amendment.

Accountants are frequently asked to protect their clients' interests by raising Fourth and Fifth Amendment objections to summonses and subpoenas directed at them, as well as to questions asked of them during investigations and litigation concerning the clients. Cases interpreting these amendments have generally held that accountants cannot assert these constitutional guarantees in order to protect their clients. Of course, they could be asserted by accountants to protect themselves. As the case which follows illustrates, the constitutional protections of these amendments are personal to the client.

COUCH v. UNITED STATES
93 S.Ct. 611 (1973)

Petitioner operates a restaurant, and since 1955 she had given her financial records to her accountant, Shafer, for the purpose of preparing her income tax returns. During an IRS audit, the auditor believed that there was a substantial understatement of gross income and reported the matter to the Intelligence Division of the IRS. A special agent of the Intelligence Division contacted Shafer to go over the records, and his request was refused. A summons was then delivered to Shafer, who at petitioner's request, delivered all of the records to petitioner's attorney. An action was then commenced in the District Court to enforce the summons for the records. Petitioner then asserted her Fifth Amendment privilege against compulsory self-incrimination. The lower court held that the records were not privileged and ordered them delivered to the IRS.

POWELL, J.

. . . The question is whether the taxpayer may invoke her Fifth Amendment privilege against compulsory self-incrimination to prevent the production of her business and tax records in the possession of her accountant. . . . The importance of preserving inviolate the privilege against compulsory self-incrimination has often been stated by this Court and need not be elaborated. By its very nature, the privilege is an intimate and personal one. It respects a private inner sanctum of individual feeling and thought and proscribes state intrusion to extract self-condemnation. Historically, the privilege sprang from an abhorrence of governmental assault against the single individual accused of crime and the temptation on the part of the State to resort to the expedient of compelling incriminating evidence from one's own mouth.

In *Murphy v. Waterfront Commission of New York Harbor*, 378 U.S. 52, 55 (1964), the Court articulated the policies and purposes of the privilege:

. . . our unwillingness to subject those suspected of crime to the cruel trilemma of self-accusation, perjury or contempt; our preference for an accusatorial rather than an inquisitorial system of criminal justice; our fear that self-incriminating statements will be elicited by inhumane treatment and abuses; our sense of fair play which dictates "a fair state-individual balance by requiring the government . . . in its contest with the individual to shoulder the entire load," . . . our respect for the inviolability of the human personality and of the right of each individual "to a private enclave where he may lead a private life." . . .

It is important to reiterate that the Fifth Amendment privilege is a personal privilege; it adheres basically to the person, not to information which may incriminate him. As Mr. Justice Holmes put it: "A party is privileged from producing the evidence, but not from its production." The Constitution explicitly prohibits compelling an accused to bear witness "against himself," it necessarily did not proscribe incriminating statements elicited from another. Compulsion upon the person asserting it is an important element of the privilege, and "prohibition of compelling a man . . . to be witness against himself is a prohibition of the use of physical or moral compulsion to extort communication from him." It is extortion of information from the accused himself that offends our sense of justice.

In the case before us the ingredient of personal compulsion against an accused is lacking. The summons and the order of the District Court enforcing it are directed against the accountant. He, not the taxpayer, is the only one compelled to do anything. And the accountant makes no claim that he may tend to be incriminated by the production. Inquisitorial pressure of coercion against a potentially accused person compelling her, against her will, to utter self-condemning words or produce incriminating documents is absent. In the present case, no "shadow of testimonial compulsion upon or enforced communications by the accused" is involved.

The divulgence of potentially incriminating evidence against petitioner is naturally unwelcomed. But petitioner's distress would be not less if the divulgence came not from her accountant but from some other third party with whom she was connected and who possessed substantially equivalent knowledge of her business affairs. The basic complaint of petitioner stems from the fact of divulgence of the possible incriminating information, not from the manner in which or the person from whom it was extracted. Yet such divulgence, where it did not coerce the accused herself, is a necessary part of the process of law enforcement and tax investigation. . . .

Petitioner further argues that the confidential nature of the accountant-client relationship and her resulting expectation of privacy in delivering the records protect her under the Fourth and Fifth Amendments, from the production.

Although not in itself controlling, we note that no confidential accountant-client privilege exists under federal law, and no state-created privilege has been recognized in federal cases. . . . Nor is there justification for such a privilege where records relevant to income tax returns are involved in a criminal investigation or prosecution. . . . The criterion for Fifth Amendment immunity remains not the ownership of property, but the "physical or moral compulsion exerted." We hold today that no Fourth or Fifth Amendment claim can prevail where as in this case, there exist no legitimate expectation of privacy and no semblance of governmental compulsion against the person of the accused. It is important, in applying constitutional principles, to interpret them in light of the fundamental interest of personal liberty they were meant to serve. Respect for these principles is eroded when they leap their proper bounds to interfere with the legitimate interest of society in enforcement of its laws and collection of the revenues. . . .

Affirmed.

THE UMBRELLA OF
THE ATTORNEY-CLIENT PRIVILEGE

Accountants may come under the protection of the attorney-client privilege in certain factual situations. For example, if an attorney hires an accountant to assist in giving legal advice to a client, the accountant is within the scope of the privilege. This rule recognizes that accounting concepts are foreign to many lawyers. Therefore, the assistance of an accountant is often highly valuable and even essential for a lawyer to effectively serve a client. The accountant is in a status similar to a legal secretary or law clerk for purposes of confidential communications.

UNITED STATES v. SCHMIDT
360 F.Supp. 339 (1973)

SHERIDAN, J.

Petitioners, the United States of America and James W. Meade, Jr., Special Agent of the Internal Revenue Service, seek judicial enforcement of an Internal Revenue summons. . . . The purpose of the summons is to elicit testimony from J. Donald Schmidt, a Certified Public Accountant, with respect to the tax liabilities of Vincent C. McCue for the taxable years 1966 through 1969, and regarding the preparation of the 1969 income tax return of Vincent C. and Elizabeth A. McCue. . . .

On or about July 31, 1969, Vincent McCue retained the law firm of Shumaker, Williams and Placey of Harrisburg, Pennsylvania, in order to obtain legal advice regarding certain unspecified business transactions and income tax matters. Thereafter, counsel decided that the services of an accountant were necessary to allow them to properly advise their client. Accordingly, on April 1, 1970, they retained Schmidt, Nenninger & Company, an accounting firm, to assist them in the accumulation of business and financial information required to provide accurate and complete legal advice to Vincent McCue.

The agreement between the law firm and the accounting firm provided, inter alia, that accounting services were to be performed at the written request of counsel; that, except as otherwise directed, the accountants were to bill the law firm monthly for services rendered during the preceding month; and that information obtained by the accountants while performing the services contemplated by the agreement was to be confidential.

In November 1970, Special Agent Meade was assigned to a preliminary investigation of the tax liability of Vincent McCue. Since Schmidt possesses information relevant thereto, Meade issued a summons requiring him to appear and to testify. At the appointed time and place, Schmidt appeared with counsel and testified to a limited extent; he also set forth the legal bases of his refusal to be more expansive. This proceeding followed.

Respondents, in opposing enforcement of the summons, rely upon Schmidt's alleged right to assert . . . the attorney-client privilege. . . .

Since questions of privilege arising in an action for judicial enforcement of an Internal Revenue summons should be resolved pursuant to federal law, neither Pennsylvania's accountant-client privilege nor any other privilege recognized in federal court allows Schmidt to refuse to testify in his role as accountant. However, there are circumstances in which an accountant may be within the scope of the attorney-client privilege, the elements of which are set forth as follows:

(1) Where legal advice of any kind is sought (2) from a professional legal adviser in his capacity as such, (3) the communications relating to that purpose, (4) made in confidence, (5) by the client, (6) are at his instance permanently protected (7) from disclosure by himself or by the legal adviser, (8) except the protection be waived. 8 Wigmore, Evidence § 2292 (McNaughton rev. 1961).

The burden of establishing the foregoing rests on the claimant against disclosure, and the operative rule of construction is that the privilege ought to be confined within the narrowest limits consistent with its policy to promote freedom of consultation of legal advisers by clients.

One corollary of the prerequisite that a professional legal adviser be consulted in his capacity as such is that the privilege does not apply when a person who merely happens to be an attorney translates his activities into those of an accountant.

Similarly, what is vital to the assertion of the privilege by an accountant employed by an attorney is that he assist in providing legal advice rather than merely rendering accounting services; and the specific nature of the proponent's burden is to establish that the accountant's role is essentially consultative.

The significant facts are undisputed. Vincent McCue retained Shumaker, Williams & Placey in 1969 to obtain a legal opinion regarding certain business and tax matters. Approximately eight months later, the attorneys employed Schmidt's firm to assist them in accumulating the business and financial information necessary to allow them to provide complete legal advice to McCue.

Under the circumstances, it is immaterial that the particular information sought pertains to preparation of the McCues' 1969 income tax return. Preparation of a return by an attorney pursuant to a bona fide attorney-client relationship is sufficiently within his professional legal competence to be subsumed by the privilege; any attempt to limit the protection of the privilege along functional lines to account for Schmidt's participation in the process would distort the interactional realities of the relationship, i.e., to the extent that preparation of a return requires the exercise of legal judgment the adequate formulation of which itself is contingent upon prior consultative accounting, a legal process is involved within which related accounting services legitimately are included.

However, the privilege extends only to confidential communications made by a client within the context of the relationship, not to the relationship itself.

Therefore, the inquiry presently before the court is whether, under all the circumstances, a responsive answer to each question might threaten disclosure of information communicated in professional confidence.

Questions 7B–7I, 8D-2, 8E, 8F, 16A, 16B and 16D, insofar as they inquire into the identities of persons who prepared various portions of the 1969 return, and whether Schmidt's firm prepared any other returns for McCue, the nature of them, and upon whose authority they were prepared, must be answered. . . . Neither the identity of any of the parties nor the fact that legal services are performed is privileged from disclosure.

Questions 9B–9H and 10B–10F attempt to ascertain, respectively, from where the books and records used to secure information compiled on the return came; who instructed members of Schmidt's firm in their use; when the instructions were given; how the meeting at which they were given was arranged; who arranged it; what disposition was made of them after use by Schmidt's firm; their present location; the disposition made of accounting workpapers compiled during preparation of the 1969 return; their present location; whether they are available for Internal Revenue Service review; and, if no, why not.

This information relates to peripheral matters which are not confidential within the meaning of the attorney-client privilege.

In 17A, Schmidt is asked the amount of the fee charged by his firm for preparation of the McCues' 1969 individual income tax return. . . .

Amounts paid for legal services ordinarily are not protected by the attorney-client privilege, and there is no evidence from which to infer that such an estimate might threaten disclosure of a confidential communication. . . .

Question 11 inquires whether Schmidt was given instructions during preparation of the 1969 return; by who they were given; and the nature of them. The reply indicates that the firm was given specific instructions by Shumaker, Williams & Placey, but he refuses to reveal their substance. Because of the likelihood that disclosure of the instructions would provide a basis for inference of the tenor of information communicated in confidence by the McCues, the question need not be answered.

The same principle applies, *mutatis mutandis,* to questions 14 and 15A, in which petitioners ask, respectively, why a specific question on page one of the 1969 return was not answered, and why no pre-paid taxes were listed on line 19–22, inclusive.

Questions 7C-7, 8A-2, 8B, 8C, 8C-1 and 15B seek substantive information related to that which appears on the return. Each threatens the disclosure of confidential communications, either directly or by inference.

However, as previously noted, the substance of information acquired from sources other than the clients or their agents is not privileged. Therefore, Schmidt will be directed to reveal from whom the information requested in 7C-7 and 15B came. Upon compliance, he need only disclose its content to the extent that it is derived form sources without the protection of the privilege.

Similar considerations are dispositive of question 10A, in which Schmidt is requested to describe in detail all workpapers, memoranda and notations compiled during preparation of the 1969 return. The workpapers should be protected insofar as they record clients' confidential communications; but much of the information contained in them may have come from unprotected sources, and a blanket claim of testimonial immunity arising from a consultative employment relationship falls short of meeting respondents' burden to establish that the specific information they desire to withhold is within the scope of the privilege.

Accordingly, Schmidt must disclose the sources of information contained in his workpapers; to the extent that they are unprotected, the substance of it must be revealed.

For the reason given, and in the manner indicated, Schmidt will be directed to respond to all questions except 11, 14 and 15A.

This memorandum shall constitute findings of fact and conclusions of law in accordance with Rule 52(a) of the Federal Rules of Civil Procedure.

If the work of the accountant is performed before retention of the attorney, the attorney-client privilege cannot cover the work–product of the accountant. This prevents a client facing legal problems from simply hiring a lawyer, turning all of the accountant's papers and records over to the attorney, thus clothing them with the privilege. For documents prepared by an accountant to be covered by the attorney-client privilege, they must be prepared for the purpose of legal advice.

UNITED STATES v. BROWN
478 F.2d 1038 (1973)

SPRECHER, J.

On September 11, 1972, the district court for the Northern District of Illinois, . . . ruled that the accounting firm of Arthur Andersen & Company was required to comply with a summons issued by the Internal Revenue Service to produce certain documents concerning its client, Delbert Coleman. Coleman . . . appealed the court's order requiring production of the Andersen documents. . . .

This action began with an Internal Revenue Service investigation of Coleman for the years 1965 through 1969. Pursuant to 26 U.S.C. § 7602 a summons was served on Arthur Andersen & Company, demanding all records pertaining to Coleman. A second summons was issued on the firm on May 26, 1971, after Andersen refused to produce a portion of these records. Andersen thereafter formally protested that some of the required documents were protected by the attorney-client privilege. . . . This appeal concerns . . . two . . . documents.

The first of these (Document 7) is a three-page memorandum, dated October 7, 1969, prepared by David N. Hurwitz, an attorney and member of the law firm of Marshall, Bratter, Greene, Allison & Tucker, which represented Coleman, as well as a cover letter regarding the memorandum. The memorandum summarizes notes and legal judgments made by attorney Hurwitz at a meeting attended by Mr. Seiden, an aide to Coleman, Mr. Ruther, an associate to Arthur Andersen, and Hurwitz, on October 2, 1968.

The second (Document 8) consists of six pages of handwritten notes prepared by Andersen's Ruther at the October 2, 1968 meeting concerning the accounting assistance rendered by Ruther at that meeting.

The purpose of the October meeting was to discuss the tax consequences of a potential Coleman business transaction. The IRS states as its reason for seeking the documents a need to gain a full understanding of the details of this transaction and thereby to ascertain whether Coleman properly reported the tax consequences.

The classic statement of the attorney-client privilege is the formulation in 8 Wigmore, Evidence § 2292:

> (1) Where legal advice of any kind is sought (2) from a professional legal adviser in his capacity as such, (3) the communications relating to that purpose, (4) made in confidence (5) by the client, (6) are at his instance permanently protected (7) from disclosure by himself or by the legal adviser, (8) except the protection be waived.

It is clear from this definition that neither document is protected by the privilege. In regard to the handwritten notes taken by accountant Ruther concerning accounting assistance, although the attorney-client privilege may in some instances extend to communications to accountants providing assistance to an attorney, "(w)hat is vital to the privilege is that the communication be made in *confidence* for the purpose of obtaining *legal* advice *from the lawyer.* If what is sought is not legal advice but only accounting service, . . . or if the advice sought is the accountant's rather than the lawyer's, no privilege exists." In this case the accounting firm was retained by the taxpayer and not the attorney and the accountant's presence at the October meeting was requested by the taxpayer's assistant and not by the attorney. We agree with the district court that "(n)otes taken by an accountant at such a meeting should not be considered privileged simply because an attorney is present at the meeting." We also agree that there has been an insufficient showing that these notes reflect communications between an attorney and his client.

Nor is Document 7 covered by the attorney-client privilege. In the first place, there is severe doubt that his document, held in the files of the accountant and not in those of the attorney, retained any confidential nature. . . . There can be little expectation of privacy where records are handed to an accountant, knowing that mandatory disclosure of much of the information therein is required in an income tax return. Furthermore, the Supreme Court held in Hickman v. Taylor, 329 U.S. 495, (1947), that the privilege did not attach to "memoranda, briefs, communications and other writings prepared by counsel for his own use in prosecuting his client's case; and it is equally unrelated to writings which reflect an attorney's mental impressions, conclusions, opinions or legal theories." The district court found that the document in question summarized attorney Hurwitz' notes and legal judgments made at the October meeting. Our agreement with that conclusion disposes of this question. . . .

Affirmed.

THE WORK-PRODUCT PRIVILEGE
OF ATTORNEYS

The law grants attorneys a special privilege called the "work-product" privilege. This privilege was created in order to limit the discovery process. The discovery process before a trial is designed to ensure that each side has the opportunity to be fully advised of all evidence likely to be presented at the trial. The process includes taking depositions, serving written interrogatories, requiring parties to submit to compulsory physical examinations, and requiring a party to produce documents, photographs, or other exhibits for copying or reproduction. The use of discovery procedures is a means of encouraging settlement as well as taking the surprise element out of lawsuits.

The law recognizes that it is possible for one side to take unfair advantage of the other by excessive utilization of the discovery techniques. For example, one side might interview all of the witnesses in preparation for trial while the other side did nothing except to seek copies of the record of the other's interviews. In order to prevent such unfairness, courts have held that an attorney's "work product" is not subject to discovery. This in effect creates a privilege for papers and documents prepared in preparation for trial. The work-product privilege aids the diligent attorney.

The concept of an attorney's work product may include documents and records prepared by an accountant for the attorney's use at the trial. If the books and records used by the accountant are available to the other side (usually the IRS), then the work product of the accountant should not be subject to discovery any more than the work product of the attorney. Thus, work performed for an attorney in preparation for trial is protected in the same way as confidential communications by a client.

THE FUTURE OF
THE ACCOUNTANT-CLIENT PRIVILEGE

It is not likely that the accountant-client privilege will be expanded for the audit function in many states. The auditor's function is to serve the public as well as the client. This public duty contradicts the confidential relationship which is the foundation of the attorney-client and most other privileged relationships. In addition, an auditor's independence might be lost if communications by the client were the subject of a legally enforced privilege. This is not to say that accountants should be able to disclose trade secrets and other detailed confidential matters learned in the course of the audit function. However, objective opinions relating to financial statements would be much more difficult if the client could assert that matters communicated to the auditor were privileged. Moreover, the client's need for protection here is probably outweighed by the interest of the public in full disclosure of all pertinent facts affecting financial statements.

Even if a privilege were created for the audit function, courts would likely hold that it had been waived. The waiver would result from the fact that there was an intent to disclose the matter to the general public because that was the function of the audit and of the certification of the financial reports.

The tax function of the accountant is a different matter, since tax advice is per se legal advice, and the tax accountant's duty is essentially to his client. While truthfulness and integrity are required, doubtful issues may be resolved in the client's favor as long as there is a reasonable basis to do so. A tax accountant does not have the same requirement of independence as does an auditor. While a tax attorney need not disclose weaknesses in his client's tax position, an auditor would be required to disclose weaknesses in financial statements. Therefore, a case can be made for creating and enforcing a tax accountant-client privilege coextensive with the attorney-client privilege in the tax field. The IRS recognizes that accountants may practice before the Treasury Department in the same way as lawyers. Both are giving legal advice involving the same interests of their clients. The purpose of the privilege would be to insure an atmosphere wherein the client will transmit all relevant information to his accountant without fear of any future disclosure. Without this atmosphere of confidentiality, the client might withhold facts he considers unfavorable to this situation, thus rendering the accountant powerless to adequately perform his job.

There would seem to be no logical or legal basis for extending the privilege to management services. This function is not professional in the same sense that the audit or tax function is. Moreover, there is probably no need for the matters communicated in this function to be confidential. Such things as trade secrets and customer lists which need to be protected are already protected by other rules of law.

The trend in the federal law is toward less confidentiality and fewer privileges. The Freedom of Information Act has resulted in disclosure of many matters heretofore thought to be private and secret. Therefore, it is not likely that Congress will create an accountant-client privilege for cases involving federal laws.

1. Give five examples or situations in which the issue of privileged communications between an accountant and a client may arise.

2. Why are communications between an attorney and a client privileged?

3. X, an attorney, is questioning Y, his client, about the facts relating to a criminal case pending against Y. Unknown to X and to Y, Z, a cleaning person in an adjoining room, overhears the conversation. Z reports the conversation to the prosecutor who calls Z as a witness against Y. X objects asserting the attorney-client privilege. Is the evidence admissible? Why?

4. Assume the same facts as in question 3 except that Z is X's secretary. Is the evidence admissible? Why?

5. Over what types of cases do the federal courts have jurisdiction?

6. For diversity of citizenship purposes, a corporation is a citizen of two states. Name them.

7. A case is in the federal courts based on the presence of a question of federal law. The state in which the court sits has a state statute creating an accountant-client privilege. Is this privilege applicable to this case? Why?

8. A case is in the federal courts based on diversity of citizenship. The state in which the court sits has a state statute creating an accountant-client privilege. Is this privilege applicable to this case? Why?

9. A state enacts a statute creating an accountant-client privilege. A client sues his accountant alleging negligence in the performance of an audit. The attorney for the client calls the accountant to the witness stand to cross-examine him about certain conversations with the client in which the accountant admitted to deviations from generally accepted account-

ing principles. The attorney for the accountant objected to the questioning on the basis of the statutory privilege. Is the evidence admissible? Why?

SUGGESTED ADDITIONAL READINGS

CLEARY, *McCormick on Evidence* (2nd ed.), West Publishing Company, 1972, title 5, chapters 8 & 10.

DONNELLY, "The Law of Evidence: Privacy and Disclosure," 14 *Louisiana Law Review* 361 (1954).

FALKNOR, "Extrinsic Policies Affecting Admissibility," 10 *Rutgers Law Review* 574 (1956).

8 Wigmore, Evidence (McNaughton rev. 1961).

NOTE, "Privileged Communications—Accountants and Accounting," 66 *Michigan Law Review* 1264 (1968).

Chapter 12

Unauthorized Practice of Law

INTRODUCTION

This chapter will discuss a subject that is confusing, complex, and unsettled, as well as extremely frustrating for accountants. It will attempt to create an understanding of the many difficult questions that exist as a result of the close connection between accounting and law, especially in the tax area. Accountants have a significant amount of law-related education; in fact, 25 percent of the CPA examination is in the legal area. This chapter will focus on the extent to which accountants may properly utilize their knowledge of the law. It will also illustrate the sanctions that may be used if someone is guilty of unauthorized practice of law.

The extent to which an accountant may properly utilize legal knowledge depends to a significant degree upon the service being performed. The knowledge and skill of the person involved appears to be a factor in some cases, but it is not as important a variable as one might think.

Issues relating to unauthorized practice of law by accountant may arise in a variety of legal proceedings. First of all, it is a crime to practice law without a license in most states, and conceivably an accountant could be charged with criminal conduct. Second, most states have statutes prohibiting such practice and a suit could be brought either to enjoin such activity or to hold one violating such a statute in contempt of court. Finally, a client may raise the issue in a suit by an accountant to collect fees for services rendered.

AN OVERVIEW OF THE PRACTICE OF LAW— STATE STATUTES

In most states, the power to regulate the practice of law is essentially a judicial function and not a legislative function. The doctrine of separation of powers prevents one branch of government from encroaching upon the functions of the others. If the legislative branch were allowed to determine the qualifications to practice law or to deny the judiciary this power, the general view is that such action would be unconstitutional as a violation of separation of powers. This is not to say, however, that legislatures may not pass laws under the police power to *aid* the judiciary in regulating the practice of law. Thus, while the licensing of attorneys and admission to practice law is governed by the courts, all states have legislation on the subject as well. The purpose of these statutes is to establish minimum standards for the practice of law.

Some state statutes provide for an integrated bar by limiting the practice of law to members of the state bar association. A majority of states have an integrated bar either by legislation or court rules.

The statutes of several states attempt to define "the practice of law." Most statutes include three activities within the definition: (1) representation of others before courts or administrative agencies, (2) drafting legal instruments, and (3) giving legal advice. The latter activity causes the most difficulty in determining the scope of the limitation. The real issue as to what is included within the definition is left to the courts to decide on a case-by-case basis.

In a case decided in Georgia, an accountant advised a defendant in an income tax evasion case to plead "guilty" even though the client professed his innocence. The accountant gave the advice on the theory that if the client pled guilty, a similar indictment against the client's daughter would be dismissed. The court, in a case by the client against the accountant for refund of the fee paid, held that giving this advice amounted to unauthorized practice of law. The court stated that the practice of law includes not only representation of litigants in court but also giving legal advice about judicial proceedings. The accountant was required to refund the fee.

Some states limit the practice of law to cases in which a fee is charged for services, but this is not the usual view. Charging a fee is not a test of the practice of law. One court observed that attorneys frequently represent indigents in court without a fee and that such activities are clearly the practice of law. Just as a surgeon who performs an operation without a charge is practicing medicine, so also a person may practice law without charging for the service. Thus, compensation does not usually determine whether or not the person is engaged in the practice of law.

STATUTORY EXCEPTIONS

The law in most states has provided some exceptions to the prohibition against practicing law without a license. The most common exception allows persons to represent themselves, known as appearing in court *pro se.* This exception does not allow corporate officers to represent a corporation in litigation. It applies only to individual persons.

Several states have also created exceptions that apply to justice of the peace courts or small claim courts. Some states have created exceptions for practice before certain administrative agencies such as worker's compensation boards.

Statutes authorizing the practice by laymen before administrative agencies have sometimes been held to be unconstitutional. For example, one judge in reviewing such a statute simply concluded, "The legislature cannot authorize laymen to engage in the practice of law." Notwithstanding these decisions, several statutes authorized practice before unemployment compensation boards and worker's compensation boards. The usual statute says that a person may be represented by counsel or other duly authorized agent.

DEFINING THE SUBJECT MATTER

As previously noted, most definitions of the practice of law include three activities. The easiest to identify is participation in litigation for someone else. Of course, the practice of law includes all aspects of litigation. However, the practice of law is not limited to cases conducted in court. The major portion of the private practice of law consists of work done out of court. Therefore, any definition of the practice of law includes the rendering of services requiring the use of legal skill or knowledge such as preparing wills, contracts, or other documents, the legal effect of which must be carefully determined. For example, the preparation of an application for a corporate charter by a nonlawyer constitutes unauthorized practice of law. The following case is typical of those prohibiting the drafting of legal documents which are not a part of a judicial proceeding. A petition to review a tax decision is a legal document which must be prepared by a lawyer because of its complexity. Note that the case was a contempt proceeding. If the defendant continued his activities after the decision, a jail term was a likely punishment.

KENTUCKY STATE BAR ASSOCIATION v. BAILEY
409 S.W.2d 531 (Ky.) 1966

PER CURIAM.

This is an original contempt proceeding in this Court against respondent, an accountant, for allegedly engaging in the practice of law. . . .

For many years respondent has been filing for clients with the Kentucky Board of Tax Appeals petitions for review of adverse rulings entered by the Department of Revenue. These petitions have raised questions of statutory interpretation and constitutional law. They pertained principally to legal issues rather than accounting problems. We have no doubt . . . that the nature of the work performed by respondent for his clients, in the matters upon which the complaint was based, constituted the unauthorized practice of law under Rule 3.020 of this Court. That Rule provides:

> "The practice of law" is any service rendered involving legal knowledge or legal advice, whether of representation, counsel, or advocacy in or out of court, rendered in respect to the rights, duties, obligations, liabilities, or business relations of one requiring the services. But nothing herein shall prevent any person not holding himself out as a practicing attorney from drawing any instrument to which he is a party without consideration unto himself therefor.

Respondent is apparently so impressed with his legal ability that he not only failed to employ his own counsel in this proceeding but declined to have counsel appointed for him. His brief in this Court constitutes an attack on the legal profession and purports to raise legal questions which properly should be presented by a person licensed to practice law.

The special commissioner was of the opinion that respondent was innocent of the charges against him because he did not know he was engaging in the unauthorized practice of the law. Our review of the record convinces us that his continuing conduct did not so much stem from lack of knowledge as from his forthright determination to attend to all matters in which he felt himself qualified, regardless of whether he was engaging in legal controversies which actually constituted the practice of law. We do not think a simple notice would sufficiently impress respondent with the unauthorized nature of his conduct.

Respondent, Espy Bailey, is hereby adjudged in contempt of court for the unauthorized practice of law and a fine of $100 is hereby imposed, but the payment of said fine is suspended until further order of this Court. Respondent shall pay the costs of this proceeding.

The third part of the usual definition of the practice of law is giving legal advice. This portion causes the most confusion to laymen. It is easy for anyone to give advice. Advice is often personal opinion based on experience as well as education. When does advice become legal advice and thus the giving of it illegal? The sections which follow will attempt to answer this question as it applies to accountants. Before examining the cases directly related to accountants, a look at the underlying reasoning for prohibiting the practice of law by laymen provides helpful background understanding.

REASONS FOR PROHIBITING
THE UNAUTHORIZED PRACTICE OF LAW

Courts grant licenses to practice law only to individuals who have been proven to possess two general characteristics. First of all, they must have general knowledge and special qualifications in regard to the law. Secondly, they must be of good moral character. The courts retain the right to revoke a license if an attorney does not continue to meet either of these qualifications. Attorneys owe a duty both to their clients and to the courts. These duties are found in the Canons of Professional Ethics, and these canons are enforced by the courts.

Lack of training alone is a sufficient reason for preventing the practice of law by laymen in court proceedings. Even a lawyer who represents himself in litigation is said to have "a fool for a client." In cases in which the individual allegedly practicing law without a license has either attempted to prepare legal documents or give legal advice, the reasoning is less obvious. While the giving of legal advice and the preparation of legal instruments is not directly connected with judicial proceedings, they are always subject to subsequent involvement in litigation. They require a high degree of legal skill to adapt the law to difficult and complex situations. Therefore, these activities which may have a profound effect on the administration of justice can only be performed by a licensed attorney. It is of great importance to the general public that legal services be performed only by persons with adequate learning and skill and of sound moral character, acting at all times under the supervision of the courts.

The importance of the licensing statutes and of the control over conduct by the courts is apparent in the rules that prohibit attorneys licensed in one state from practicing in other states. Such persons are at least prima facie qualified to practice law. Yet the fact that they would not be subject to the same control as licensed attorneys is a sufficient basis for denying them the right to practice law in the unlicensed state. Courts sometimes allow attorneys to appear in litigation under special grants of authority, but even here it is usually required that they associate themselves with resident attorneys.

THEORIES USED IN DECIDING CASES

INTRODUCTION

Numerous theories are used by the courts to decide unauthorized practice issues. Some courts recognize the futility of attempting to define the subject and simply include all activities "commonly understood" to be the practice of law. In drawing the line between legal and illegal activities by laymen, these courts simply follow custom. If the acts—whether performed in a court or in a law office—are those customarily performed by lawyers, they constitute the practice of law. The phrase "commonly understood" is the rationale behind such cases.

It has been previously noted that whether or not a fee is charged is not determinative of the issue. Neither is the knowledge or ability of the one performing the service. There is no exception for lay specialists. In one case involving an accountant, the court stated:

> The interest of the public is not protected by the narrow specialization of an individual who lacks the perspective and the orientation which only comes from a thorough knowledge and understanding of basic legal concepts, of legal processes, and of the interrelation of the law in all its branches.

Courts sometimes examine the facts and circumstances and simply reach a conclusion on a case-by-case basis. These courts admit that the line of demarcation between permissible activities by laymen and unauthorized practice of law is often unclear. The courts in making decisions on a case-by-case basis are heavily influenced by the reasons for preventing unauthorized practice and by the special facts of each case. The following case discusses the development of the prohibition against unauthorized practice of law and some of the theories used to decide issues relating to it.

GARDNER v. CONWAY
48 N.W.2d 788 (Minn.) 1951

MATSON, J.

Defendant appeals from an order denying his motion for a new trial.

This action, to have the defendant perpetually enjoined from further engaging in the unauthorized practice of law and to have him adjudged in contempt of court therefor, was brought by the plaintiffs in their own behalf as licensed lawyers and in a representative capacity in behalf of every other licensed lawyer in Minnesota, as well as in behalf of the courts and the public.

Defendant, who is possessed of only a grade-school education, has never been admitted to the practice of law in Minnesota or elsewhere. During a two-year period immediately prior to the time of trial, he followed the occupation of a public accountant. Prior thereto, he served for three years as a United States deputy collector of internal revenue. Before that, he had worked for six years as the credit manager of a hardware company, about five years as the operator of a collection agency, and for four years as an insurance solicitor and risk inspector.

At and prior to the time which we are concerned, defendant held himself out to the public by newspaper advertisements and by other advertising media as an "Income Tax Expert," duly qualified to give advice, aid, and assistance to the public generally in the discharge of a taxpayer's duty to make accurate returns of income to the federal government. Defendant alleges that he is thoroughly familiar with income tax rules and regulations. He has used a business card on which he describes himself as a "Tax Consultant" and prominently calls attention thereon to the fact that he was a former deputy collector of internal revenue.

On or about March 4, 1948, Cecil G. Germain, a private investigator employed by plaintiffs to obtain information as to whether defendant was engaged in the practice of law, went to the office of defendant under the assumed name and identity of an alleged taxpayer, George Heinl. Germain, as George Heinl, informed defendant that he operated a truck farm, that he had come to have his income tax return prepared, and that he needed help with certain questions. For a cash consideration, defendant prepared the income tax return and gave Germain professional advice for the determination of the following questions:

(a) Whether the taxpayer, who himself had exclusive control of the operation of the truck farm, was in partnership with his wife, who had contributed one-half of the purchase price, who helped with the work, and who received one-half the profits.

(b) Whether the taxpayer was entitled to claim his wife as an exemption, since he had never been ceremonially married, though maintaining a common-law marriage status.

(c) Whether the taxpayer should file his separate return and advise his so-called common-law wife to file a separate return.

(d) Whether certain money expended on improvements of buildings on the truck farm was deductible from his earnings.

(e) Whether a certain product loss sustained by frost and subsequent flood was a deductible item. . . .

A proceeding to adjudge a person in contempt of court for the unauthorized practice of law—whether such unauthorized practice occurred within or outside the presence of the court—is punitive and criminal in its nature and is primarily brought in the public interest to vindicate the authority of the court and to deter other like derelictions. Although a prosecution for the unauthorized practice of law, as an offense against society, inures incidentally to the individual benefit of properly licensed lawyers, the criminal nature of the proceding is unaffected. . . .

Was defendant, however, practicing law when, as a preliminary to and as part of his preparation of an income tax return, he advised the purported taxpayer (on the answers to the foregoing questions) . . .

Much of what is law practice is conducted outside the courtroom, and as to that field of activity we have said: "* * * The line between what is and what is not the practice of law cannot be drawn with precision. Lawyers should be the first to recognize wherein much of what lawyers do every day in their practice may also be done by others without wrongful invasion of the lawyers' field."

Although it is difficult to draw any precise dividing line, the task is ours to find some criterion for distinguishing that which is from that which is not law practice. The development of any practical criterion, as well as its subsequent application, must be closely related to the purpose for which lawyers are licensed as the exclusive occupants of their field. That purpose is to protect the public from the intolerable evils which are brought upon people by those who assume to practice law without having the proper qualifications. The need for public protection is not of new origin. As early as 1292, the problem was recognized when Edward I, by royal ordinance, limited the number of attorneys and directed his justices "to provide for every county a sufficient number of attornies and apprentices from among the best, the most lawful and the most teachable, so that king and people might be well served." The limitation and selection of lawyers, without strict regulation, proved inadequate.

"* * * The evil finally became so great that in the year 1402 Parliament this time took cognizance of it and enacted the now famous statute, 4 Henry IV, Ch. 18, which provided that all attorneys should be examined by the justices, and in their discretion, only those found to be good and virtuous, and of good fame, learned and sworn to do their duty, be allowed to be put upon the roll and all others put out." These early English statutes illustrate that a licensed bar subject to the supervision of the courts originated with a public demand for the exclusion of those who assumed to practice without being qualified therefor.

The protection of the public, as the purpose of confining law practice to a licensed bar, ancient as it is in its origin, is of vital importance today. Any criterion for distinguishing law practice from that which belongs to other fields can be properly geared to the public welfare only if we keep in mind the manner in which the licensing of lawyers serves its purpose. The law practice franchise or privilege is based upon the threefold requirements of ability, character, and responsible supervision. The public welfare is safeguarded not merely by limiting law practice to individuals who are possessed of the requisite ability and character, but also by the further requirement that such practitioners shall thenceforth be officers of the court and subject to its supervision. In consequence, lawyers are not merely bound by a high code of professional ethics, but as officers of the court they are subject to its inherent supervisory jurisdiction, which embraces the power to remove from the profession those practitioners who are unfaithful or incompetent in the discharge of their trust. This is in itself an important reason why law practice should be confined to members of the bar. Protection of the public is set at naught if laymen who are not subject to court supervision are permitted to practice law. Although professional standards for safeguarding the public interest must be sufficiently flexible to allow for adaptation to changes in conditions, they must in any event be of such stability and permanence as to protect the individual practitioner in the enjoyment of his professional franchise; otherwise men of ability and character will find no inducement to undergo the years of training necessary to qualify them as lawyers. This principle, as a part of the public weal, is applicable to any profession which demands of its members high skill and proficiency based upon years of intensive preparatory training.

If we bear in mind that any choice of criterion must find its ultimate justification in the interest of the public and not in that of advantage for either lawyer or nonlawyer, we soon cease to look for an answer in any rule of thumb such as that based upon a distinction between the incidental and the primary. Any rule which holds that a layman who prepares legal papers or furnishes other services of a legal nature is not practicing law when such services are incidental to another business or profession completely ignores the public welfare. A service performed by one individual for another, even though it be incidental to some other occupation, may entail a difficult question of law which requires a determination by a trained legal mind. Are we to say that a real estate broker who examines an abstract of title and furnishes an opinion thereon may not be held to practice law merely because the examination of a title is ancillary to a sale and purchase of real estate? Can we say that a lawyer employed to bring a suit for damages for personal injuries is competent to diagnose the nature of his client's injuries and that he is not practicing medicine merely because such diagnosis is incidental to a proper presentation of his client's case? The drawing of a simple instrument or the application of an elementary legal principle is one thing in the incidental classification, but it is wholly another when such incidental act or service requires professional skill. The incidental test has no value except in the negative sense that if the furnishing of the legal service is the primary business of the actor such activity is the practice of law, even though such service is of an elementary nature. In other words, a layman's legal service activities are the practice of law unless they are incidental to his regular calling; but the mere fact that they are incidental is by no means decisive. In a positive sense, the incidental test ignores the interest of the public as the controlling determinant.

In rejecting the incidental test, it follows that the distinction between law practice and that which is not may be determined only from a consideration of the nature of the acts of service performed in each case. No difficulty arises where such service is the primary business of the actor. We then have law practice. Difficulty comes, however, when the service furnished is incidental to the performance of other service of a nonlegal character in the pursuit of another calling such as that of accounting. In the field of income taxation, as in the instant case, we have an overlapping of both law and accounting. An accountant must adapt his accounting skill to the requirements of tax law, and therefore he must have a workable knowledge of law as applied to his field. By the same token, a lawyer must have some understanding of accounting. In the income tax area, they occupy much common ground where the skills of both professions may be required and where it is difficult to draw a precise line to separate their respective functions. The public interest does not permit an obliteration of all lines of demarcation. We cannot escape reality by hiding behind a facade of nomenclature and assume that "taxation," though composed of both law and accounting is something sui generis and apart from the law. If taxation is a hybrid of law and accounting, it does not follow that it is so wholly without the law that its legal activities may be pursued without proper qualifications and without court supervision. The interest of the public is not protected by the narrow specialization of an individual who lacks the perspective and the orientation which comes only from a thorough knowledge and understanding of basic legal concepts, of legal processes, and of the interrelation of the law in all its branches. Generally speaking, whenever, as incidental to another transaction or calling, a layman, as part of his regular course of conduct, resolves legal questions for another—at the latter's request and for a consideration—by giving him advice or by taking action for and in his behalf, he is practicing law if difficult or doubtful legal questions are involved which, to safeguard the public, reasonably demand the application of a trained legal mind. What is a difficult or doubtful question of law is not to be measured by the comprehension of a trained legal mind, but by the understanding thereof which is possessed by a reasonably intelligent layman who is reasonably familiar with similar transactions. A criterion which designates the determination of a difficult or complex question of law as law practice, and the application of an elementary or simple legal principle as not, may indeed be criticized for uncertainty if a rule of thumb is sought which can be applied with mechanical precision, to all cases. Any rule of law which purports to reflect the needs of the public welfare in a changing society, by reason of its essential and inherent flexibility, will, however, be as variable in operation as the particular facts to which it is applied.

In restraining laymen from improper activity, the difficult question of law criterion is to be applied in a common-sense way which will protect primarily the interest of the public and not hamper or burden that interest with impractical and technical restrictions which have no reasonable justification. We are therefore not concerned with a technical application which would ban the giving of any and all legal advice or the taking of any and all action for another. Whether a difficult or doubtful question of law is resolved by the giving of advice to, or the doing of an act for, another must in each case depend upon the nature of the problem involved. As applied to the preparation of income tax returns, it has been well said: "* * * Federal income taxation is founded on statute, elaborated and interpreted by administrative regulations and interpreted by administrative regulations and rulings, and construed by court decisions. Matters in this field, as in other statutory subjects, will at times involve difficult questions of interpretation of statute or court decision, and the validity of regulations or statute; they will also involve doubtful questions of nontax law on which the tax issues may depend, and questions of liability for criminal or civil penalties or of statutes of limitation or of liability as transferee for the taxes of another. Such questions, in general, are the kind for which lawyers are equipped by training and practice.

When an accountant or other layman who is employed to prepare an income tax return is faced with difficult or doubtful questions of the interpretation or application of statutes, administrative regulations and rulings, court decisions, or general law, it is his duty to leave the determination of such questions to a lawyer. In so holding that the determination of difficult or doubtful questions is the practice of law, it does not follow that the entire income tax field has been preempted by lawyers to the exclusion of accountants. The work of an accountant disassociated from the resolving of difficult or doubtful questions of law is not law practice. In the determination of income—the subject of taxation—difficult accounting problems may arise by presenting "such aspects as inventory pricing methods (last-in–first-out, first-in–first-out, retail method, cost determination, actual costs, standards costs, cost of in-process merchandise, market price valuation, etc.), accrual and installment accounting, carryover and carryback of net operating losses, depreciation, depletion and corporate distributions. The taxation of such income may involve such concepts as consolidated returns, taxable years of less than twelve months, invested capital, etc. All of these are concepts of accounting, * * * ."

Where difficult accounting questions arise, the careful lawyer will naturally advise his client to enlist the aid of an accountant. In the income tax field, the lawyer and the accountant each has a function to perform in the interest of the public.

In the instant case, the evidence sustains the trial court's findings and conclusions that defendant was engaged in the practice of law. For a consideration, and as part of his regular income tax work, defendant advised and determined for the taxpayer whether the latter had attained the status of a lawful marriage with a woman with whom he had been living but to whom he had never been ceremonially married. He further gave advice as to whether such taxpayer and his consort should file separate or joint returns. The purported taxpayer was likewise uncertain as to whether he occupied the status of a partner with his so-called common-law wife in the operation of a truck farm, over which he himself exercised exclusive control but in which the latter shared equally in the labor, investment, and profit. This question, the answer to which obviously required legal training, he also resolved. We do not here have the case of a taxpayer whose legal status was established or known beforehand. In addition, defendant gave advice as to the deductions which the taxpayer might claim for certain farm improvements and for certain produce loss by frost and subsequent flood. Although the preparation of the income tax return was not of itself the practice of law, defendant, incidental to such preparation, resolved certain difficult legal questions which, taken as a whole, constituted the practice of law.

In further confirmation of the conclusion that defendant was practicing law, the evidence establishes that he advertised and held himself out as a "Tax Consultant," which by reasonable implication advised the public that he was competent to give legal advice on the law of taxation. A layman, whether he is or is not an accountant, may not hold himself out to the public as a tax consultant or a tax expert, or describe himself by any similar phrase which implies that he has a knowledge of tax law. . . .

Affirmed.

To what extent the lack of ability and training of the defendant influenced the court in the preceding case we will never know. If the defendant had been a CPA who did not claim to be a "tax expert," the chances are that the case would not have been brought in the first place.

THE COMPLEXITY TEST

One theory that frequently arises in cases such as the foregoing is known as the complexity theory. If the legal issue on which the layman gives advice is considered difficult or complex, then the advice is held to be legal advice. On the other hand, if the issue is simple, the advice may be legally given. The case which follows is another of the early leading cases following the complexity theory.

AGRAN v. SHAPIRO
273 P.2d 619 (Cal.) 1954

Plaintiff, a CPA, sued the defendant, his client, to recover $2,000 for accounting services rendered. Plaintiff, in addition to preparing the defendant's income tax return, prepared "an application for a tentative carry-back adjustment" of excess loss from 1948 to the preceding two years. If the application was approved by the Internal Revenue, the taxpayers would have received a refund.

Plaintiff met with a treasury agent to discuss the loss "carry-back" and whether or not it qualified as an "operating loss." Plaintiff testified that at these conferences he cited numerous cases to the treasury agent and that he had spent five days in the county law library researching the matter.

Plaintiff's bill to the defendant stated that it was for research of the problems involved and the preparation of arguments as well as the conference with the revenue agent.

PATROSSO, J.

While courts have experienced difficulty in formulating a precise and all-embracing definition as to what constitutes the practice of law, the one generally accepted is as follows: "As the term is generally understood, the practice of the law is the doing and performing services in a court of justice, in any matter depending therein, throughout its various stages, and in conformity to the adopted rules of procedure. *But in a larger sense it includes legal advice and counsel, and the preparation of legal instruments and contracts by which legal rights are secured although such matter may or may not be depending in court.*" (Emphasis added.) However, whether a particular activity falls within this general definition is frequently a question of considerable difficulty, and particularly is this true in the field of taxation where questions of law and accounting are frequently inextricably intermingled as a result of which doubt arises as to where the functions of one profession end and those of the other begin. Specifically, whether practice before an administrative tribunal in tax matters constitutes the practice of law has been the subject of decisions elsewhere which appear to be in some conflict. The question, under the circumstances here, is a particularly perplexing one, and we acknowledge the aid and assistance which has been afforded us in our efforts to resolve it by the excellent briefs filed by counsel as amici curiae on behalf of the State Bar of California and the California Society of Certified Public Accountants, respectively.

It appears to be generally conceded that it is within the proper function of a public accountant, although not a member of the bar, to prepare federal income tax returns, except perhaps in those instances where substantial questions of law arise which may competently be determined only by a lawyer. In the case at hand we find no real difficulty in concluding that in the preparation of the income tax returns in question plaintiff did not engage in the practice of law. They are of such a simple character that an ordinary layman without legal or accounting training might have prepared them in the first instance. . . .

A different and more serious question arises, however, with respect to the services rendered by the plaintiff in preparing the applications for a carry back adjustment and refund of taxes paid for the previous two years. At this stage no question of accounting was involved. Neither the fact that the loss had been sustained nor the manner in which it arose was questioned. The only question was whether, under the admitted facts, the loss was one which could be "carried back," the answer to which depended upon whether or not it was a loss "attributable to the operation of a trade or business regularly carried on by the taxpayer" within the meaning of that phrase as used in the Internal Revenue Code. We see no escape from the conclusion that under the circumstances this question was purely one of law. . . .

Not only was the question which arose here one of law but a difficult and doubtful one as well, as evidenced by the many occasions upon which the courts and the Treasury Department have had occasion to consider it. Moreover, it is evident that the plaintiff himself fully appreciated this. He not only testified that "in his opinion it was a tough case because it was an isolated one" but he detailed at length the extensive research of the legal authorities which he was required to make in order to support his position that the loss was one which qualified as a "net operating loss" under a proper interpretation of the statutory definition. . . .

[The court then reviewed the New York decision in the Bercu case (page 352 of this text) and the Minnesota decision in the Conway case (page 340 of this text.)]

We are confirmed in our conclusion that the activities of the plaintiff which we have detailed fall within the domain of the lawyer by a consideration of The Statement of Principles Relating to Practice in the Field of Federal Income Taxation, which was recommended by the National Conference of Lawyers and Certified Public Accountants and approved by The Council of the American Institute of Accountants May 8, 1951, wherein it is stated (par. 3, 6, 8):

"3. *Ascertainment of probable tax effects of transactions* * * *) The ascertainment of probable tax effects of transactions frequently is within the function of either a certified public accountant or a lawyer. However, in many instances, problems arise which require the attention of a member of one or the other profession, or members of both. When such ascertainment raises uncertainties as to the interpretation of law (both tax law and general law), or uncertainties as to the application of law to the transaction involved, the certified public accountant should advise the taxpayer to enlist the services of a lawyer. When such ascertainment involves difficult questions of classifying and summarizing the transaction in a significant manner and in terms of money, or interpreting the financial results thereof, the lawyer should advise the taxpayer to enlist the services of a certified public accountant. * * *

"6. *Representation of taxpayers before Treasury Department.* Under Treasury Department regulations lawyers and certified public accountants are authorized, upon a showing of their professional status, and subject to certain limitations as defined in the Treasury Rules, to represent taxpayers in proceedings before that Department. If, in the course of such proceedings, questions arise involving the application of legal principles, a lawyer should be retained, and if, in the course of such proceedings accounting questions arise, a certified public accountant should be retained. * * *

"8. *Claims for refund.* * * * Claims for refund may be prepared by lawyers or certified public accountants, provided, however, that where a controversial legal issue is involved or where the claim is to be made the basis of litigation, the services of a lawyer should be obtained."

From what has been said, it appears that plaintiff undertook to determine the "tax effect of defendant's transaction with Pritchard, the ascertainment of which involved uncertainties both as to the interpretation of the taxing statute as well as the application thereof to the transaction in question." It is likewise evident from the plaintiff's testimony that at the time of preparing the application for carry back adjustment and refund he realized that a "controversial legal issue" was involved with respect to which the Treasury Department might take a contrary view, for he assigned this as a reason why he could not then advise defendants as to what his fee in the matter would be. And when he finally submits his bill we find that, in detailing therein the services covered thereby, no mention is made of accounting work or that involved in the preparation of the returns, but rather he describes the same as consisting of "conferences with revenue agent(s)" and "research of the problems involved and preparation of arguments to overcome" the proposed additional assessments, the only basis for which could be the Treasury Department's claim that the Pritchard loss did not constitute a "net operating loss" under section 122. Surely the solution of this "problem" did not involve or depend upon the application of accounting principles or procedure, but of legal principles and precedents. These were the subject of plaintiff's "research" and these alone could serve as the foundation for his "arguments" addressed to the representatives of the Treasury Department in resisting the "proposed assessments."

From what has been said, we . . . have but little hesitance in concluding that the services rendered by plaintiff other than those involved in the preparation of the income tax returns and possibly others of an accounting character constitute the practice of law as that term has been judicially defined in this State. . . .

Thus we conclude that, as indicated, the judgment in favor of plaintiff includes the award for services which constituted the practice of law, for which, not being a member of the bar he was not entitled to recover.

Judges sometimes reject this simple vs. complex distinction with the observation that if it is necessary for a person to obtain advice or assistance, the problem is obviously not a simple one. Complex issues are simple to the skilled, while simple ones are complex to the inexperienced.

The "difficult or doubtful" legal question test is apt to be resolved in favor of the accountant if legal research is not required. The extensive use of precedent and the citing of cases by an accountant is evidence of the presence of a difficult legal question. The absence of such cases may convince the court that the accountant is not guilty of unauthorized practice of law as happened in the following case.

ZELKIN v. CARUSO DISCOUNT CORPORATION
9 Cal. Rptr. 220 (1961)

FOX, J.

Defendants appeal from a judgment in favor of plaintiff in the amount of $19,500 for services rendered pursuant to the terms of a written agreement. The agreement was executed by defendant Caruso Discount Corporation on November 9, 1957, and provided that plaintiff was employed "to represent this Company and its afflicted Companies in connection with their current Federal tax examination." Compensation for these services was stated to be $32,500; a retainer of $3,000 having already been paid "leaving a balance of $29,500.00 payable when signed agreements with the Federal Government have been executed." Plaintiff is a certified public accountant who maintains no office but works out of his home. He is a graduate of a law school and is a certified public accountant in both California and New York. His primary business is representing taxpayers in negotiating with the Internal Revenue Service concerning tax liabilities. In September or October, 1957, he was introduced to defendant H. J. Caruso, who told him that the Treasury Department was conducting an audit of the various Caruso enterprises and had proposed large deficiency assessments, principally upon monies held by Commercial Credit Corporation as reserves on conditional sales contracts sold to Commercial Credit Corporation by Caruso Discount Corporation. Other deficiency assessments were proposed which related to the amounts paid certain officers as salaries and to certain amounts deducted as travel and entertainment expenses. At a later meeting with defendant H. J. Caruso, plaintiff indicated that he would undertake further consideration of the matter for a retainer of $3,000 which Caruso paid him. Following discussions with the revenue agent, representatives of Commercial Credit Corporation and the auditor for Caruso Discount Corporation, plaintiff, on November 9, 1957, met with defendant H. J. Caruso and submitted a proposed contract calling for the payment of $45,000 for his services in representing the various Caruso enterprises in an attempt to reach an equitable settlement of the proposed deficiency assessments. Insofar as here material, the parties finally agreed upon a fee of $32,500. Prior to the execution of this latter agreement, all of the defendants had executed powers of attorney by which plaintiff was appointed their lawful representative before the Treasury Department. Following the signing of the November 9 agreement, plaintiff had several meetings with representatives of Commercial Credit Corporation, and also met with the Treasury agent 8 or 10 times. As a result of plaintiff's efforts a tentative agreement was reached with the Treasury Department that the amount of the deficiency assessment against Caruso Discount Corporation, which involved the reserves held by Commercial Credit Corporation, would be set at about $240,000. In January, 1958, the Treasury Department sent certain documents entitled "Waiver of Restrictions on Assessments and Collection of Deficiencies in Tax and Acceptance of Overassessment" (Treasury Form 870) to plaintiff, who transferred them to defendants, and these forms were subsequently executed by defendants. Following the signing of the "Waivers" plaintiff sought payments of his fee and was subsequently paid a total of $10,000 reducing the outstanding balance to $19,500. The judgment herein awards plaintiff the amount of $19,500 the outstanding balance, and defendants have appealed.

During the course of the trial defendants attempted to prove that the services rendered by plaintiff constituted the practice of law and entailed no accounting services exclusively and did not constitute the practice of law. Defendants contend on appeal that the uncontroverted evidence demonstrates conclusively that plaintiff's services were entirely legal in nature and that, therefore, the contract was illegal, and plaintiff was entitled to recover nothing. While acknowledging the settled rule on appeal that all evidence and inferences from the evidence must be construed in the light most favorable to the prevailing party, defendants have set forth at length the testimony of plaintiff which they claim demonstrates that his services were, in fact, legal services and not accounting services. They correctly point out that plaintiff testified that he did "research" at two separate law libraries and that he "reviewed" the original reserve agreement between Commercial Credit Corporation and Caruso Discount Corporation. However, plaintiff also testified that his "research" was directed exclusively toward a determination of the accounting methods employed by other companies which had been involved in similar tax problems. He consistently and repeatedly denied that he had read any cases to determine the applicable law; that he was completely disinterested in the results of the cases which he reviewed and was searching only for the proper methods of accounting which had been employed.

However, defendants strongly argue that by the very nature of the question involved in the dispute between defendants and the Treasury Department, only a question of law was involved. Simply stated, the determination of the amount of the deficiencies which should be assessed against Caruso Discount Corporation involved the amount of the reserve which Commercial Credit Corporation could legitimately withhold as security for the conditional sales contracts which it had purchased from Caruso Discount Corporation. The question resolved itself to a consideration of what percentage of the total paper held by the Commercial Credit Corporation it could legitimately retain as a reserve based upon the quality of the paper held, market conditions, and general business activity. Any amounts retained by it over and above the permissible percentage would be available to Caruso Discount Corporation upon demand and would, therefore, be taxable income. (Caruso Discount Corporation was in the years here pertinent on a cash basis for tax purposes.) Thus, defendants argue, a legal question is presented as to the availability of the reserves to Caruso Discount Corporation upon their demand. Plaintiff, on the other hand, contends that all that was involved was a question of fact; i.e., what percentage of the total paper held could be properly held in reserve against Caruso Discount Corporation's demand? It clearly appears from the evidence that the original reserve agreement between Commercial Credit Corporation and Caruso Discount Corporation, which called for a 5 percent reserve, had ceased to control prior to the Government's interest in the reserves, at least as far as the percentage thereof was concerned. There is evidence that this percentage clause was modified orally and that the parties acted upon the oral modification for during the taxable periods here in question, in excess of 11 percent was being retained. Clearly, the only question involved in plaintiff's negotiations with the Treasury Department concerning this reserve was the percentage retention allowable to Commercial Credit Corporation to properly secure it against the contingent liabilities inherent in the conditional sales contracts which it had purchased from Caruso Discount Corporation. While it might be true that decisional precedent could play a major role in such a consideration, at least in relation to the factual question posed, yet there is no evidence to indicate that this was the case. We cannot say, as a matter of law, that plaintiff did, in fact, negotiate with the Treasury Department on the basis of decided cases similar on their facts; but rather, we must conclude that the trial court's determination that he did not practice law, which is based upon his uncontradicted testimony, is fully supported by the evidence. Defendants cite *Agran v. Shapiro,* 127 Cal. App. 2d Supp. 807, as being controlling in this case and argue that it requires a finding that plaintiff's services constituted the illegal practice of law. The Agran case is, however, clearly distinguishable from the instant matter, for the accountant there testified that he cited numerous cases to the Internal Revenue agent and that he "spent approximately four days in reading and reviewing over one hundred cases on the proposition of law involved." In this case plaintiff testified that he read no law nor did he cite any to the Internal Revenue agent, thus he could be said to have been practicing law only if on the face of the problem which he was negotiating no discussion of that problem would be possible without reference to legal issues and no persuasive argument could be made which did not include a discussion of legal principles. However, no such inescapable conclusion is apparent on the face of "the availability of reserves" question which plaintiff negotiated with the Treasury Department. Therefore, defendants' contention that the undisputed facts show conclusively that plaintiff was illegally practicing law is without merit.

Affirmed.

Note that in the preceding case, the fact that the plaintiff was a law school graduate was not raised. Apparently, since he was not licensed to practice law in California, his education was immaterial.

This case was an attempt to avoid an otherwise valid contract by one party. It was not an attempt by a bar association or government official to stop the plaintiff's activities. Moreover, the plaintiff may have understood the *Agran* precedent and thus limited his activities as he saw them to insure that he did not come within its approach to the problem. A detailed cross-examination of plaintiff might have established facts with the *Agran* case doctrine.

ADDITIONAL APPROACHES TO
THE TAX PROBLEM

Accountants must utilize knowledge of tax law in the preparation of tax returns. Laymen, including CPAs, are allowed to decide questions of law in the process of preparing tax returns. They are also allowed to use legal knowledge in preparing books and records and as a part of the audit function. But what if an accountant gives tax advice without being involved in the preparation of tax returns or in the preparation of financial records? The following case, commonly known as the *Bercu* case, is one court's answer to that question.

IN RE NEW YORK COUNTY LAWYERS ASSOC.
78 N.Y.S.2d 209 (1951)

PECT, J.

The New York County Lawyers Association brought this proceeding to punish respondent for contempt and to enjoin him from pursuing certain activities which petitioner claims constitute the practice of law. The substantive question is whether the professional practice in which respondent is admittedly engaged constitutes the practice of law. . . .

Respondent is an accountant. He gave certain advice to the Croft Company on a tax question. He was not the auditor for the company, nor did he do any work of any kind on the books of the company. He did not prepare the tax return. . . .

For his services respondent submitted a bill for $500, describing the services as follows: "Consultations in re deductibility in current taxable year of N.Y. City excise taxes for prior years" and "Memorandum in re above."

The charge was at the rate of about $50 an hour for his time. Respondent admitted that his work was not an isolated instance of its kind and that he often gave advice of the character which he gave to the Croft Company, without examining books or preparing tax returns. . . .

We shall not dwell on the adequacy or accuracy of the advice given, or discuss the applicable law, for the decision in a case of this kind should not turn on the quality of the advice given. The decision must rest on the nature of the services rendered and on whether they were inherently legal or accounting services.

Petitioner acknowledges that tax law enters into accounting and accounting into tax law and that it is a proper function of an accountant to prepare tax returns, which work requires a knowledge and application of the law, but contends that giving advice with respect to the tax law, unconnected with work on the books or tax returns, is giving legal advice and practicing law. . . .

The case is not an easy one because of the overlapping of law and accounting. An accountant must be familiar to a considerable extent with tax law and must employ his knowledge of the law in his accounting practice. By the same token, a tax lawyer must have an understanding of accounting. It is difficult, therefore, to draw a precise line in the tax area between the field of the accountant and the field of the lawyer. Unless we are to say, however, that because common ground exists between the lawyer and accountant in the tax area no bounds may be recognized between them, some line of demarcation must be observed. We believe that the line has not been altogether obliterated, and with due regard to the latitude which should be given to the accountant, a majority of this court is quite clear in its mind that respondent's services in this matter were well into the field of the law and outside of the field of accounting. To hold otherwise would be tantamount to saying that an accountant may practice tax law.

The accountant serves in setting up or auditing books, or advising with respect to the keeping of books and records, the making of entries therein, the handling of transactions for tax purposes and the preparation of tax returns. Naturally his work and advice must take cognizance of the law and conform with the law, particularly the tax law. The application of legal knowledge in such work, however, is only incidental to the accounting functions. It is not expected or permitted of the accountant, despite his knowledge or use of the law, to give legal advice which is unconnected with accounting work. That is exactly what this respondent did. He was doing no accounting work for the Croft Company within the ordinary or proper conception of an accountant's work. He had nothing to do with the Croft Company's books or its tax return. . . . In short, legal advice was sought and given on a question of law. . . .

We are told in behalf of respondent that the basis of the tax law is accounting and that the tax subject upon which respondent gave his advice is a matter of proper accounting practice. We are also told that the administration of the tax subject upon which respondent gave his advice is a matter of proper accounting practice. We are also told that the administration of the tax law in the Treasury Department and other agencies of government is mainly in the hands of accountants, and that taxation is a particular specialty of accountants in which they are more expert than lawyers.

Fortunately the tax law conforms largely with accepted principles of accounting, as most law conforms with business customs and practices. One need only thumb through the Internal Revenue Code relating to income taxes, however, or listen to the criticism leveled at the tax laws and decisions by some writers on accountancy, to note the many respects in which tax law is at variance with usual accounting principles. And it is certainly contrary to fact to view the advice which respondent gave in this case as following accounting principles. . . .

An accountant may know more about the tax law than some law practitioners, just as a labor relations adviser, trust officer or customs broker may know more about the law relating to their businesses than many lawyers not specialist in the law relating to such business. A layman may know a lot of law about a particular subject, upon the knowledge of which he may rely at his own risk in his own business. He may not, however, set himself up as a public consultant on the law of his specialty. If the services of a specialist in some particular branch of the law are required, the public must still turn to the bar, for all the reasons of public protection for which the bar and bar standards are maintained. The law specialist offers more and much more is required of him for admission to practice than knowledge of his specialty. He must have a grounding in the law and a legal education and training, must pass examinations in the law and attain and maintain standards which are imposed by the Bench and Bar for the protection of the public.

The law includes many specialties, perhaps as diverse as specialties in medicine, but they are all related and integrated in the common body of the law, much the same as specialties in medicine are linked in the whole body of medicine. One might become informed, and even expert, in some narrow specialty of medicine without the general training, preparation and experience required for admission to practice medicine. Yet we know that only the generally trained doctor, grounded in medicine as a whole, has the understanding requisite to practice medicine in any of its branches, albeit the laboratories, so intimately and vitally connected with medical service, are staffed by technicians who are not medical doctors.

Similarly, the law specialist should be trained and grounded in the law. A thorough knowledge and understanding of basic legal concepts, legal processes and the interrelation of the law in its parts are quite essential to the practice of law in any of its branches. Technicians are needed to serve in bureaus and agencies and in numerous nonlegal capacities, but the counselor licensed and trusted to advise the public with respect to the law must be a duly qualified and admitted lawyer. We are unable, therefore, to regard the admission of accountants, subject to certain qualifications and regulations of the Treasury Department and the Tax Court, to practice before those agencies, as an authorization to accountants to practice tax law at large or as an eradication of the distinction between the lawyer's and the accountant's function in the tax field.

It is much too narrow a view, and one revealing inadequate perception, to regard the tax law as mainly a matter of accounting. More than most specialties in the law, tax law is drawn from and involved with many branches of law. It bridges and is intimately connected, for example, with corporation law, partnership law, property law, the law of sales, trusts and frequently constitutional law. Quite obviously, one trained only in accounting, regardless of specific tax knowledge, does not have the orientation even in tax law to qualify as a tax lawyer. Equally obvious, as a matter of administration, he may not practice any phase of tax law, regardless of what might be his subjective qualifications for the particular undertaking. Inquiry cannot be made in each case as to whether the particular accountant or accountants generally are sufficiently familiar with the law on a particular tax question to be qualified to answer it. An objective line must be drawn, and the point at which it must be drawn, at very least, is where the accountant or nonlawyer undertakes to pass upon a legal question apart from the regular pursuit of his calling. . . .

This does not mean, of course, that many or most questions which may arise in preparing a tax return may not be answered by an accountant handling such work. But if the question is such a problem that an outside consultant, besides the regular accountant preparing the tax return, must be called in to do legal research of the kind which was necessary in this case and to advise as to the none too clear, if not obscure, law, that consultant must be a lawyer.

When such problems arise who is to say how much "general" law is involved? Essential to the solution of any problem is recognizing all the elements of the problem. It is a fair question whether respondent recognized all the elements in this case. Will anyone but the generally trained lawyer be competent to analyze difficult tax problems, which are beyond the regular accountant's ken, and be able to say what other law besides tax law is involved? And when confronted with any question of whether an accountant, acting as a tax consultant, is practicing law, are we to decide it upon the basis of determining whether any law besides tax law is involved in the matter upon which he was consulted?

Any attempt at such delineation and control would be wholly impractical. We must either admit frankly that taxation is a hybrid of law and accounting and, as a matter of practical administration, permit accountants to practice tax law, or, also as a matter of practical administration, while allowing the accountant jurisdiction of incidental questions of law which may arise in connection with auditing books or preparing tax returns, deny him the right as a consultant to give legal advice. We are of the opinion that the latter alternative accords to the accountant all necessary and desirable latitude and that nothing less would accord to the public the protection that is necessary when it seeks legal advice.

Respondent is most persuasive when he challenges the consistency of recognizing an accountant's right to prepare income tax returns while denying him the right to give income tax advice. As respondent says, precisely the same question may at one time arise during the preparation of an income tax return and at another time serve as the subject of a request for advice by a client. The difference is that in the one case the accountant is dealing with a question of law which is only incidental to preparing a tax return and in the other case he is addressing himself to a question of law alone.

The preparation of an income tax return is not primarily a matter of law and generally and mainly is not a matter of law. It may usually be prepared by one having no legal knowledge, from instruction prepared for lay consumption, or by one having only incidental legal knowledge. A taxpayer should not be required, therefore, and is not required, to go to a lawyer to have a tax return prepared. It is a practical, reasonable and proper accommodation to business men and the accounting profession not only to permit accountants to prepare tax returns but to permit them, despite the risks involved, to assume jurisdiction of the incidental legal questions that may arise in connection with preparing tax returns. It is quite another thing to say that apart from preparing a tax return and from doing the accounting work in connection with the return an accountant should be permitted as an independent consultant to pass upon specific questions which are questions of law, especially when the occasion for such consultation is apt to be, as it was in this case, a particularly knotty question of law. The distinction is altogether valid and desirable. The law here, as elsewhere, is a rational and practical adjustment of conflicting interests, objectively calculated to be of the greatest public benefit. . . .

A taxpayer may, if he wishes, leave the entire preparation of the tax return to his accountant, legal incidents included, without the necessity of engaging a lawyer.

When . . . a taxpayer is confronted with a tax question so involved and difficult that it must go beyond its regular accountant and seek outside tax law advice, the considerations of convenience and economy in favor of letting its accountant handle the matter no longer apply, and considerations of public protection require that such advice be sought from a qualified lawyer. At that point, at least, the line must be drawn. The line does not impinge upon any of the business or public interests which respondent cites or oust the accountant from the tax field or prejudice him in any way in the pursuit of his profession or create any monopoly in the tax field in favor of the legal profession. It allows the accountant maximum freedom of action within the field which might be called "tax accounting" and is the minimum of control necessary to give the public protection when it seeks advice as to tax law.

The order appealed from should be reversed, respondent adjudged in contempt and fined $50 and an injunction as prayed for issued.

The foregoing New York case has been frequently asserted as authority for limiting the role of accountants. However, its value as precedent is limited to the facts of the case, and its holding would not cover advice given as an incident of the accounting function. Moreover, its principles are probably not applicable if the accountant is licensed by the Treasury Department. The effect of licensing by the Treasury Department is discussed in the next two sections. The case which follows illustrates a different result from the *Bercu* case and the effect of federal law on the issue.

GRACE v. ALLEN
407 S.W.2d 321 (Tex.) 1966

BATEMAN, J.

There is a suit to recover the value of accountants' services performed. The appellees, residents of New York, rendered the services in New York to the appellants, who were then residents of New York but who subsquently moved to Dallas, Texas, where they were sued. Appellants pled, inter alia, that appellees, were not entitled to recover because their alleged services constituted the unauthorized practice of law. The jury fixed the value of the services at $8,400 and found that appellees were also entitled to a reasonable attorney's fee in the sum of $4,200. . . .

[Appellants contend] that the court erred in holding as a matter of law that the services rendered by appellees did not constitute the practice of law. Appellants assert that under the circumstances New York law should control in the determination of that question. Appellees contend that their services in question did not constitute the practice, even under the New York law, and that in any event such services were within the purview of the federal law and Treasury Department regulations; that although not members of the Bar, they were licensed to practice before the Treasury Department, that everything they did was pursuant to and in accordance with that license, and that if their services were prescribed under New York law they were fully authorized by the federal law and Treasury regulations and, therefore, lawful. The defense in question was on motion kept from the jury, and the court resolved it in favor of appellees as a matter of law.

There is no substantial dispute as to the facts. Appellees were both licensed public accountants, one of them being certified, and both were admitted to practice before the Treasury Department, although neither of them was a lawyer. Both of them had been employed by the Internal Revenue Service for a number of years before entering private practice. Although the appellees had not prepared the appellants' income tax returns for the years 1955, 1956, 1957 and 1958, when the Internal Revenue Service assessed additional taxes for those years they were employed to work with appellants' attorneys in New York City in the preparation and presentation of a protest of such assessment. They did so, and it is these services which appellants say constituted the unauthorized practice of law, pointing out that one of the appellees testified that "complicated issues" were involved, that the protest cited numerous cases as authority for the position they were taking, some of which cases had been discussed with the lawyers but some of which had been found as a result of research by the appellee Brown. Appellees had prepared in their office several Forms 872, "Consent to

Extension of the Statute of Limitations," also memoranda used and presented in various conferences, with representatives of the Internal Revenue Service. Appellees conferred frequently with appellants' attorneys and kept them advised by telephone and mail as to audits by the Internal Revenue Service and the preparation of the protest. The attorneys participated and cooperated in the preparation of the protest and in conferences with the Internal Revenue Service examining agent and conference coordinator. Appellees also prepared a power of attorney authorizing the attorneys to act for appellees in connection with audits of appellants' tax returns. Appellants employed appellees to prepare and file their Federal and New York State income tax returns for 1960 and their declarations of estimated income tax (Federal and State) for 1961; also to maintain appellants' proper books and records therefor.

To support their position that under New York law the work done by appellees constituted unauthorized law practice, appellants rely wholly on the case of In the Matter of New York County Lawyers Association (Bernard Bercu, Respondent), 273 App. Div. 524; 78 N.Y.S.2d 209, 9 A.L.R.2d 787. In that case the Association sought to punish Bercu, an accountant, for contempt and to enjoin him from practicing law. It was shown that Croft Steel Products, Inc. had sought and obtained his advice in connection with its liability for certain New York City taxes and federal income taxes. Bercu was not the auditor for the company, nor did he prepare its tax returns or do any work of any kind on its books; all he did was render a written opinion on the legal question of tax liability. He admitted that this was not an isolated instance of its kind and that he often gave advice of the same character without examining books or preparing tax returns. The court pointed out that the decision was made difficult because of the overlapping of law and accounting, that an accountant must be familiar to a considerable extent with tax law and must employ his knowledge of the law in his accounting practice, and that a tax lawyer must have an understanding of accounting. The court recognized that an accountant employed to keep a taxpayer's books or prepare his tax returns would be expected and permitted to answer legal questions arising out of an incidental to the accounting work. The court also recognized that the matter of taxation, "which permeates almost every phase of modern life, is as inextricably interwoven with nearly every branch of law that one could hardly pick any tax problem and say this is a question of pure taxation or pure tax law wholly unconnected with other legal principles, incidents or ramifications." Recognizing the necessity of drawing a line of demarcation between the work of the tax lawyer and that of the tax accountant, the court said, "* * * the point at which it must be drawn, at very least, is where the accountant or non-lawyer undertakes to pass upon a legal question apart from the regular pursuit of his calling." Since Bercu's advice concerning the law was not incidental to any accounting work done by him for Croft Steel Products, Inc., it was held that he was unlawfully practicing law.

However, in the case at bar it is not shown that appellants consulted appellees or sought or obtained their opinion on any legal subject that was not incidental to their accounting work. Appellees were preparing the appellants' 1960 income tax returns and were the regular accountants for appellants. They were also doing accounting work in reviewing and classifying the great volume of papers and records of appellants necessary to the preparation of the protest of the tax assessment and to enable them to discuss with the Revenue Agents the asserted tax liability. It is true that in the preparation of the protest appellees cited numerous cases in support of their position, but this was necessary and incidental to the preparation and presentation of the protest. Moreover, appellees consulted the appellants' attorneys concerning these authorities and other aspects of the work being done and kept them informed as the work progressed.

Both parties agree that the Bercu case correctly announces the New York law on the subject. A careful reading of that opinion demonstrates the dissimilarity between it and the case at bar. It is clear from the record before us that the work performed by appellees, which appellants assert constituted the unauthorized practice of law, was only incidental to their accounting work and was therefore permissible and not unlawful under New York law.

Appellees assert, and appellants do not deny, that the work done by appellees was all within the purview of their licenses to practice before the Treasury Department. It was agreed on the trial that the court might take judicial notice of the federal law and Treasury regulations on the subject. One of those regulations, in part, provides:

> Practice before the Internal Revenue Service comprehends all matters connected with presentations to the Internal Revenue Service or any of its officers or employees relating to a client's rights, privileges, or liabilities under laws or regulations administered by the Internal Revenue Service. Such presentations include the preparation and filing of necessary documents, correspondence with, and communications to the Internal Revenue Service, and the representation of a client at conferences, hearings, and meetings.

Appellees take the position that if there is a conflict between the state law and the federal law, the former must yield, and that, since the regulations referred to were promulgated under sanction of the federal law, they have the force and effect of law. We agree with appellees. The rights conferred by the admission to practice before the Treasury Department are federal rights which cannot be impinged upon by the states in their praiseworthy efforts to protect their citizens from unskilled and unethical practitioners of the law.

This is not to say that the states have surrendered their right to regulate and control the practice of law within their respective boundaries, as was done in the Bercu case. In fact, one of the Treasury regulations referred to (§ 10.39) contains this proviso: "And provided further: That nothing in the regulations in this part shall be construed as authorizing persons not members of the bar to practice law."

Finding no error requiring reversal, we affirm the judgment of the trial court.

Affirmed.

FEDERAL LICENSING AND STATE LAWS

INTRODUCTION

A person may obtain a license to practice before the IRS, and the Tax Court also grants licenses to practice before it. These licenses are based on federal law. As the Texas case (*Grace* v. *Allen*) noted, it is frequently contended that the federal licensing provisions preempt the state statutes on unauthorized practice of law, an argument based on the supremacy clause of the United States Constitution.

To date, there has been no decision by the Supreme Court holding that persons licensed to practice before the IRS or the Tax Court are immune from state statutes dealing with unauthorized practice of law. However, the Supreme Court has held that such statutes must yield to federal legislation regulating the practice of patent law. The court in the patent law case stated that a state may not deny to those failing to meet its qualifications, the right to perform functions within the scope of federal authority. It held that a state may not overrule a federal determination that a person is qualified to perform a certain function, and a state may not impose additional conditions not contemplated by Congress upon the performance of an activity sanctioned by federal license. While similar reasoning was used in the Texas case, the actual relationship between federal licensing and unauthorized practice has not been passed upon by the Supreme Court.

The following sections discuss these licensing requirements. It should be kept in mind that federal licensing does not purport to cover state and local tax practice or the factual situation described in the *Bercu* case.

PRACTICE BEFORE THE IRS

The Treasury Department has adopted rules regulating practice before the IRS. An attorney in good standing as a member of the bar can represent others before the IRS by filing a written declaration setting forth his qualifications and authority. Similar rules apply to a CPA in good standing. As members in good standing of their respective professions, attorneys and CPAs are allowed to represent clients before the IRS without enrollment.

The rules also allow persons who do not qualify as attorneys or CPAs to represent others by qualifying as an enrolled agent. A person may become an enrolled agent by demonstrating special competencies in tax matters on written examinations administered by the IRS. Enrollment may also be based on former employment by the IRS (at least five years prior service is required).

The rules also provide for limited practice without enrollment in certain situations. Individuals may appear on their own behalf and may also represent partnerships in which they are a member. In addition, corporations may be represented by officers or regular full-time employees. Trusts and estates may be represented by their trustees or personal representatives, and governmental agencies may be represented by persons performing their official duties. Moreover, a person who signs a return that he has prepared may appear without enrollment as the taxpayer's representative before revenue agents and examining officers conducting audits with respect to the tax liability for the period covered by that return. Such appearances require proper authorization from the taxpayer. This limited appearance does not extend to district conferences in a district director's office.

The duties which may be performed by one authorized to practice before the IRS include the representation of clients at conferences, hearings, and meetings, as well as representation through correspondence. As a general rule, both nonlawyers and lawyers can handle all matters connected with the presentation of a client's interest to the Treasury Department. However, the nonlawyer should not prepare any written instrument transferring title to property in order to affect taxes, nor give advice as to the legal sufficiency of such an instrument.

PRACTICE BEFORE THE TAX COURT

No one can represent a taxpayer before the Tax Court without a license to practice before the court. An exception is that an individual may represent himself before that court. In addition, a corporation may be represented by an officer, and an estate or trust may appear by its fiduciary. Authorization to practice before the IRS does not carry with it the right to practice before the Tax Court.

Attorneys in good standing are admitted to practice before the Tax Court by filing an application and paying a nominal fee. All other applicants for authority to practice must take a written examination, and a further oral examination may be required. Each applicant must be sponsored by at least three persons allowed to practice before the court. The examination includes the following subjects: (1) the Rules of Practice and Procedure of the court; (2) the practice before the court, including the preparation of pleadings, motions, and briefs; (3) the rules of evidence applicable in the court; (4) the principles of legal ethics; (5) the structure and history of the Internal Revenue Code, the various revenue laws and their interpretation by the courts; and (6) the constitutional and general substantive law involved in cases coming before the court.

In the event someone appears before the Tax Court on behalf of another without authority, the Tax Court decision may not be collaterally attacked. Moreover, a person's Sixth Amendment rights are not violated because of improper representation before the Tax Court. The Sixth Amendment protection is limited to criminal prosecutions.

A further illustration of the complexity of the problem is found when a non-CPA lawyer is employed full time by a CPA firm. In 1968, the American Bar Association adopted an ethics opinion which concluded that a lawyer so employed may not ethically represent clients of the CPA firm in tax matters either before the IRS or the Tax Court. It was the American Bar Association's conclusion that to do so would be to allow CPA firms to practice law. It reasoned that CPA firms should not be able to do indirectly, by hiring lawyers, what they were prohibited from doing directly. This informal opinion, which is not binding as precedent, has been strongly criticized even by the Justice Department for its obviously anticompetitive implications. The Justice Department is advocating that lawyers hired by CPA firms should be entitled to perform any service that other lawyers might perform. Such is not now the case, however.

CONCLUSION

A significant problem as to what constitutes unauthorized practice of law by accountants does exist. It is clear that there are activities that are prohibited to accountants. In addition to appearing in court (other than the Tax Court) on behalf of a client, an accountant is prohibited from drafting legal documents and from giving advice relating to litigation. However, there are many activities closely connected with the law that may be properly performed by accountants, most of which exist in the tax field. Between activities that are clearly proper and those that constitute the unauthorized practice of law lies a "grey" area of considerable width. This grey area is probably reduced in size for CPAs who are licensed by the IRS and is even smaller for persons licensed to practice before the Tax Court. Yet even for these persons, some doubt as to the proper scope of their activities still exists due to the lack of a definitive decision on the matter by the Supreme Court.

In seeking to define the boundary between proper accounting services and unauthorized practice of law, it should be recognized that the cases have not been consistent in their holdings. Distinctions have been made between tax advice and the preparation of tax returns, as well as between simple and difficult legal issues. Courts have held that there are activities related to the field of taxation which are the sole domain of lawyers, but no exact definition of these activities exists. The issue is most likely to be raised in cases involving the collection of fees by accountants, and the issues will be decided on a case-by-case basis. It should be expected that whenever a

CPA sues a client for a fee that the unauthorized practice defense may be raised.

Many of the cases set forth in this chapter are not rigidly followed today. Many, if not most, accounting firms are engaged in almost every aspect of tax practice. There are few challenges to the common practice of accountants giving specific advice involving legal considerations. In recent years, lawyers and accountants, especially CPAs, have generally recognized the desirability of both groups giving advice and suggestions to their mutual clients. There has in effect been a truce insofar as the issues of unauthorized practice of law are concerned. The accountant usually qualifies his advice with the admonition to the client to check with his attorney. This truce is largely the result of an agreement between the American Bar Association and the American Institute of Certified Public Accountants as approved by the National Conference of Lawyers and Certified Public Accountants. This 1951 statement of principles is set forth in Appendix 9 of this text. In addition, no one has been anxious to have a test case decided by the Supreme Court because of the unpredictability of the outcome.

Most unauthorized practice of law cases make reference to the public interest theory and will continue to do so. Laymen still view these cases as attempts by the legal profession to either maintain a monopoly or to protect their own financial interests. Lawyers and judges will continue to argue that it is solely an attempt to protect the public. Undoubtedly, both views have some merit. Protecting the public interest is a factor in many decisions, while financial considerations are a motivation in enforcing the ban on unauthorized practice. Federal licensing will continue to be a major source of regulation and will tend to limit the practice of "tax law" to those accountants shown to possess the necessary minimum level of training and competence.

The public interest is probably best served by a continuation of the truce, by continuing efforts to further define the proper scope of activity for both professions, and by the maximum amount of cooperation between lawyers and accountants. The purpose of this chapter will be achieved if those performing the accounting function are aware of the problem, and if they recognize that these are activities which can only be performed by licensed attorneys. The frustration that comes from not knowing the exact nature and scope of such activities is the price paid for the close relationship between accounting and the law. Both professions are better served by unauthorized practice cases directed at unlicensed "tax experts" who lack the training and professional commitment of accountants and attorneys, than by cases directed at CPAs.

1. What are the three legal sanctions that may be used to prevent the unauthorized practice of law?

2. Which branch of government has the power to license attorneys and to regulate the practice of law?

3. Give examples of activities by accountants which may bring about the contention that an accountant is engaged in the unauthorized practice of law.

4. Why is it difficult to define those activities which constitute the practice of law? Explain.

5. List the reasons given for prohibiting the unauthorized practice of law?

6. Describe three theories used to determine whether an activity does or does not constitute the unauthorized practice of law.

7. Is it a defense to a charge of unauthorized practice of law that no fee was required for the advice or service? Why?

8. Give the arguments "pro" and "con" for using the complexity test in deciding whether or not a specific aspect of tax practice constitutes unauthorized practice of law.

9. Give reasons why the *Bercu* case should not be considered a valid precedent today.

10. Assuming that the *Bercu* case is a valid precedent, what steps can be taken by an accountant to avoid its application? Explain.

11. Summarize the effect of federal licensing statutes on state laws regulating the practice of law.

SUGGESTED ADDITIONAL READINGS

ALAND, "Relations between Lawyers and Certified Public Accountants in Federal Tax Practice," 15 *Ala. L. Rev.* 517 (1963).

BITTKER, B. I., "Does Tax Practice by Accountant Constitute the Unauthorized Practice of Law?" 25 *Journal of Taxation* 184 (1966).

BURKE, H. G., "Dueling over the Dual Practice," 27 *Md. Law Rev.* 142 (1967).

CAREY, "AIA's Carey Holds Treasury Interpretation Protects CPAs in Treasury Practice," 5 *Journal of Taxation* 42 (1956).

———, "Ethics, 'Unauthorized Practice,' and Federal Income Taxation—an Accountant's Viewpoint," 25 *Rocky Mt. L. Rev.* 435 (1953).

DONNELL, G. R., "More Light than Heat on the Lawyers' Paradox: Dual Practice," 18 *Mercer L. Rev.* 309 (1967).

GRAY, "Lawyers and Accountants in Tax Practice—A Challenge to the Bar," 15 *Journal of Taxation* 100 (1961); 27 *U.P.N.* 243 (No. 3, 1961).

GRISWOLD, "Lawyers, Accounts, and Taxes," 99 *Journal of Accountancy* 33 (No. 4, 1955); 2 *Journal of Taxation* 130 (1955); 10 *Record* 52 (1955); 18 *Tex. B.J.* 109, 137, 157, 178 (1955); 21 *U.P.N.* 3 (No. 2, 1955).

MURPHY, "Practice of Law by Attorney – Accountant," 70 *W. Va. L. Rev.* 388 (1968).

SHAW, "Scope and Limitation of Tax Practice," 104 *Journal of Accountancy* 37 (No. 5, 1957).

Part Three

APPENDIXES

Appendix

1

Rules of Conduct
and Interpretations of
Rules of Conduct[1]

ET SECTION 91

Definitions

.01 The following definitions of terminology are applicable wherever such terminology is used in the Rules and Interpretations.

.02 Client. The person(s) or entity which retains a member or his firm, engaged in the practice of public accounting, for the performance of professional services.

.03 Council. The Council of the American Institute of Certified Public Accountants.

.04 Enterprise. Any person(s) or entity, whether organized for profit or not, for which a CPA provides services.

.05 Firm. A proprietorship, partnership, or professional corporation or association engaged in the practice of public accounting, including individual partners or shareholders thereof.

[1] Code of Professional Ethics, *AICPA Professional Standards,* vol. 1, ET Sections 91, 92, 101, 102, 201, 202, 203, 204, 301, 302, 501, 502, 503, 504, and 505. Copyright © by the American Institute of Certified Public Accountants, Inc.

.06 Financial statements. Statements and footnotes related thereto that purport to show financial position which relates to a point in time or changes in financial position which relate to a period of time, and statements which use a cash or other incomplete basis of accounting. Balance sheets, statements of income, statements of retained earnings, statements of changes in financial position, and statements of changes in owners' equity are financial statements.

.07 Incidental financial data included in management advisory services reports to support recommendations to a client and tax returns and supporting schedules do not, for this purpose, constitute financial statements; and the statement, affidavit, or signature of preparers required on tax returns neither constitutes an opinion on financial statements nor requires a disclaimer of such opinion.

.08 Institute. The American Institute of Certified Public Accountants.

.09 Interpretations of Rules of Conduct. Pronouncements issued by the division of professional ethics to provide guidelines concerning the scope and application of the Rules of Conduct.

.10 Member. A member, associate member, or international associate of the American Institute of Certified Public Accountants.

.11 Practice of public accounting. Holding out to be a CPA or public accountant and at the same time performing for a client one or more types of services rendered by public accountants. The term shall not be limited by a more restrictive definition which might be found in the accountancy law under which a member practices.

.12 Professional services. One or more types of services performed in the practice of public accounting.

ET SECTION 92

Applicability of Rules

.01 The Institute's Code of Professional Ethics derives its authority from the bylaws of the Institute which provide that the Trial Board may, after a hearing, admonish, suspend, or expel a member who is found guilty of infringing any of the bylaws or any provisions of the Rules of Conduct.

.02 The Rules of Conduct which follow apply to all services performed in the practice of public accounting including tax and management advisory services except (a) where the wording of the rule indicates otherwise and (b) that a member who is practicing outside the United States will not be subject to discipline for departing from any of the rules stated herein so long as his conduct is in accord with the rules of the organized accounting profession in the country in which he is practicing. However, where a member's name is associated with financial statements in such a manner as to imply that he is acting as an independent public accountant and under circumstances that would entitle the reader to assume that United States practices were followed, he must comply with the requirements of Rules 202 and 203.

.03 A member may be held responsible for compliance with the Rules of Conduct by all persons associated with him in the practice of public accounting who are either under his supervision or are his partners or shareholders in the practice.

.04 A member engaged in the practice of public accounting must observe all the Rules of Conduct. A member not engaged in the practice of public accounting must observe only Rules 102 and 501 since all other Rules of Conduct relate solely to the practice of public accounting.

.05 A member shall not permit others to carry out on his behalf, either with or without compensation, acts which, if carried out by the member, would place him in violation of the Rules of Conduct.

ET SECTION 101

Independence

.01 **Rule 101—Independence.** A member or a firm of which he is a partner or shareholder shall not express an opinion on financial statements of an enterprise unless he and his firm are independent with respect to such enterprise. Independence will be considered to be impaired if, for example:

A. During the period of his professional engagement, or at the time of expressing his opinion, he or his firm

1. (a) Had or was committed to acquire any direct or material indirect financial interest in the enterprise; or
   (b) Was a trustee of any trust or executor or administrator of any estate if such trust or estate had or was committed to acquire any direct or material indirect financial interest in the enterprise; or
2. Had any joint closely held business investment with the enterprise or any officer, director, or principal stockholder thereof which was material in relation to his or his firm's net worth; or
3. Had any loan to or from the enterprise or any officer, director, or principal stockholder thereof. This latter proscription does not apply to the following loans from a financial institution when made under normal lending procedures, terms, and requirements:
   (a) Loans obtained by a member or his firm which are not material in relation to the net worth of such borrower.
   (b) Home mortgages.

(c) Other secured loans, except loans guaranteed by a member's firm which are otherwise unsecured.

B. During the period covered by the financial statements, during the period of the professional engagement, or at the time of expressing an opinion, he or his firm

1. Was connected with the enterprise as a promoter, underwriter or voting trustee, a director or officer or in any capacity equivalent to that of a member of management or of an employee; or

2. Was a trustee for any pension or profit-sharing trust of the enterprise.

The above examples are not intended to be all-inclusive.

[As amended March 31, 1978.]

INTERPRETATIONS UNDER RULE 101—INDEPENDENCE

.02 101-1—Directorships. Members are often asked to lend the prestige of their name as a director of a charitable, religious, civic or other similar type of nonprofit organization whose board is large and representative of the community's leadership. An auditor who permits his name to be used in this manner would not be considered lacking in independence under Rule 101 so long as he does not perform or give advice on management functions, and the board itself is sufficiently large that a third party would conclude that his membership was honorary.

[Note: The following modification of Interpretation 101-1 is to become effective with respect to fiscal years beginning after February 29, 1980.]

101-1—Honorary directorships and trusteeships. Members are often asked to lend the prestige of their names to not-for-profit organizations that limit their activities to those of a charitable, religious, civic or similar nature by being named as a director or a trustee. A member who permits his name to be used in this manner and who is associated with the financial statements of the organization would not be considered lacking in independence under Rule 101 so long as (1) his position is purely honorary, (2) it is identified as honorary in all letterheads and externally circulated materials in which he is named as a director or trustee, (3) he restricts his participation to the use of his name, and (4) he does not vote or otherwise participate in management functions.

It is presumed that organizations to which members lend only the prestige of their names will have sufficiently large boards of directors or trustees to clearly permit the member to limit his participation consistent with the foregoing restriction.

.03 101-2—Retired partners and firm independence. A retired partner having a relationship of a type specified in Rule 101 with a client of his former firm would not be considered as impairing the firm's independence with respect to the client provided that he is no longer active in the firm, that the fees received from such client do not have a material effect on his retirement benefits and that he is not held out as being associated with his former partnership.

.04 101-3—Accounting services. Members in public practice are sometimes asked to provide manual or automated bookkeeping or data processing services to clients who are of insufficient size to employ an adequate internal accounting staff. Computer systems design and programming assistance are also rendered by members either in conjunction with data processing services or as a separate engagement. Members who perform such services and who are engaged in the practice of public accounting are subject to the bylaws and Rules of Conduct.

On occasion members also rent "block time" on their computers to their clients but are not involved in the processing of transactions or maintaining the client's accounting records. In such cases the sale of block time constitutes a business rather than a professional relationship and must be considered together with all other relationships between the member and his client to determine if their aggregate impact is such as to impair the member's independence.

When a member performs manual or automated bookkeeping services, concern may arise whether the performance of such services would impair his audit independence—that the performance of such basic accounting services would cause his audit to be lacking in a review of mechanical accuracy or that the accounting judgments made by him in recording transactions may somehow be less reliable than if made by him in connection with the subsequent audit.

Members are skilled in, and well accustomed to, applying techniques to control mechanical accuracy, and the performance of the record-keeping function should have no effect on application of such techniques. With regard to accounting judgments, if third parties have confidence in a member's judgment in performing an audit, it is difficult to contend that they would have less confidence where the same judgment is applied in the process of preparing the underlying accounting records.

Nevertheless, a member performing accounting services for an audit client must meet the following requirements to retain the appearance that he is not virtually an employee and therefore lacking in independence in the eyes of a reasonable observer.

1. The CPA must not have any relationship or combination of relationships with the client or any conflict of interest which would impair his integrity and objectivity.

2. The client must accept the responsibility for the financial statements as his own. A small client may not have anyone in his employ to maintain accounting records and may rely on the CPA for this purpose. Nevertheless, the client must be sufficiently knowledgeable of the enterprise's activities and financial condition and the applicable accounting principles so that he can reasonably accept such responsibility, including, specifically, fairness of valuation and presentation and adequacy of disclosure. When necessary, the CPA must discuss accounting matters with the client to be sure that the client has the required degree of understanding.

3. The CPA must not assume the role of employee or of management conducting the operations of an enterprise. For example, the CPA shall not consummate transactions, have custody of assets or exercise authority on behalf of the client. The client must prepare the source documents on all transactions in sufficient detail to identify clearly the nature and amount of such transactions and maintain an accounting control over data processed by the CPA such as control totals and document counts. The CPA should not make changes in such basic data without the concurrence of the client.

4. The CPA, in making an examination of financial statements prepared from books and records which he has maintained completely or in part, must conform to generally accepted auditing standards. The fact that he has processed or maintained certain records does not eliminate the need to make sufficient audit tests.

When a client's securities become subject to regulation by the Securities and Exchange Commission or other federal or state regulatory body, responsibility for maintenance of the accounting records, including accounting classification decisions, must be assumed by accounting personnel employed by the client. The assumption of this responsibility must commence with the first fiscal year after which the client's securities qualify for such regulation.

.05 101-4—Effect of family relationships on independence. Rule of Conduct 101 proscribes relationships which impair a member's independence through direct financial interests, material indirect financial interests, or other involvements. Relationships which arise through family bloodlines and marriage give rise to circumstances that may impair a member's independence.

1. *Financial and business relationships ascribed to the member.* It is well accepted that the independence of a member may be impaired by the financial interests and business relationships of the member's spouse, dependent children, or any relative living in a common household with or supported by the member. The financial interests or business relationships of such family, dependents or relatives in a member's client are ascribed to the member; in such circumstances the independence of the member or his firm would be impaired under Rule 101.

2. *Financial and business relationships that may be ascribed to the member.*

Close Kin

Family relationships may also involve other circumstances in which the appearance of independence is lacking. However, it is not reasonable to assume that all kinships, per se, will impair the appearance of independence since some kinships are too remote. The following guidelines to the effect of kinship on the appearance of independence have evolved over the years:

A presumption that the appearance of independence is impaired arises from a significant financial interest, investment, or business relationship by the following close kin in a member's client: non-dependent children, brothers and sisters, grandparents, parents, parent-in-law, and the respective spouses of any of the foregoing.

If the close kin's financial interest in a member's client is material in relationship to the kin's net worth, a third party could conclude that the member's objectivity is impaired with respect to the client since the kinship is so close. In addition, financial interests held by close kin may result in an indirect financial interest being ascribed to the member.

The presumption that the appearance of independence is impaired would also prevail where a close kin has an important role or responsible executive position (e.g., director, chief executive or financial officer) with a client.

Geographical separation from the close kin and infrequent contact may mitigate such impairment except with respect to:

a. a partner participating in the engagement or located in an office participating in a significant portion of the engagement,

b. a partner in the same office or one who maintained close personal relationships with partners participating in a significant portion of the engagement,

c. a partner who, as a result of his administrative or advisory positions, is involved in the engagement, or

d. a staff member participating in the engagement or located in an office participating in a significant portion of the engagement.

If a member does not or could not reasonably be expected to have knowledge of the financial interests, investments and business relationships of his close kin, such lack of knowledge would preclude an impairment of objectivity and appearance of independence.

3. *Financial and business relationships that are not normally ascribed to the member.*

Remote Kin

A presumption that the appearance of independence is impaired would not normally arise from the financial interests and business relationships of remote kin: uncles, aunts, cousins, nephews, nieces, other in-laws, and other kin who are not close.

The financial interests and business relationships of these remote kin are not considered either direct or indirect interests ascribed to the member. However, the presumption of no impairment with remote kin would be negated if other factors indicating a closeness exist, such as living in the same household with the member, having financial ties, or jointly participating in other business enterprises.

Summary

Members must be aware that it is impossible to enumerate all circumstances wherein the appearance of a member's independence might be questioned by third parties because of family relationships. In situations involving the assessment of relationships with both close and remote kin, members must consider whether geographical proximity, strength of personal and other business relationships and other factors—when viewed together with financial interests in question—would lead a reasonable observer to conclude that the specified relationships pose an unacceptable threat to the member's objectivity and appearance of independence.

.06 101-5—Meaning of the term "normal lending procedures, terms and requirements." Rule 101(A)(3) prohibits loans to a member from his client except for certain specified kinds of loans from a client financial institution when made under "normal lending procedures, terms and requirements." The member would meet the criteria prescribed by this rule if the procedures, terms and requirements relating to his loan are reasonably comparable to those relating to other loans of a similar character committed to other borrowers during the period in which the loan to the member is committed. Accordingly, in making such comparison and in evaluating whether his loan was made under "normal lending procedures, terms and requirements," the member should consider all the circumstances under which the loan was granted including

1. The amount of the loan in relation to the value of the collateral pledged as security and the credit standing of the member or his firm.
2. Repayment terms.
3. Interest rate, including "points."
4. Requirement to pay closing costs in accordance with the lender's usual practice.
5. General availability of such loans to the public.

Related prohibitions (which may be more restrictive) are prescribed by certain state and federal agencies having regulatory authority over such financial institutions.

.07 101-6—The effect of actual or threatened litigation on independence. Rule of Conduct 101 prohibits the expression of an opinion on financial statements of an enterprise unless a member and his firm are independent with respect to the enterprise. In some circumstances, independence may be considered to be impaired as a result of litigation or the expressed intention to commence litigation.

Litigation between client and auditor

In order for the auditor to fulfill his obligation to render an informed, objective opinion on the client company's financial statements, the relationship between the management of the client and the auditor must be characterized by complete candor and full disclosure regarding all aspects of the client's business operations. In addition, there must be an absence of bias on the part of the auditor so that he can exercise dispassionate professional judgment on the financial reporting decisions made by the management. When the present management of a client company commences, or expresses an intention to commence, legal action against the auditor, the auditor and the client management may be placed in adversary positions in which the management's willingness to make complete disclosures and the auditor's objectivity may be affected by self-interest.

For the reasons outlined above, independence may be impaired whenever the auditor and his client company or its management are in threatened or actual positions of material adverse interests by reason of actual or intended litigation. Because of the complexity and diversity of the situations of adverse interests which may arise, however, it is difficult to prescribe precise points at which independence may be impaired. The following criteria are offered as guidelines:

1. The commencement of litigation by the present management alleging deficiencies in audit work for the client would be considered to impair independence.

2. The commencement of litigation by the auditor against the present management alleging management fraud or deceit would be considered to impair independence.

3. An expressed intention by the present management to commence litigation against the auditor alleging deficiencies in audit work for the client is considered to impair independence if the auditor concludes that there is a strong possibility that such a claim will be filed.

4. Litigation not related to audit work for the client (whether threatened or actual) for an amount not material to the member's firm [2] or to the financial statements of the client company would not usually be considered to affect the relationship in such a way as to impair independence. Such claims may arise, for example, out of disputes as to billings for services, results of tax or management services advice or similar matters.

Litigation by security holders

The auditor may also become involved in litigation ("primary litigation") in which he and the client company or its management are defendants. Such litigation may arise, for example, when one or more stockholders bring a stockholders' derivative action or a so-called "class action" against the client company or its management, its officers, directors, underwriters and auditors under the securities laws. Such primary litigation in itself would not alter fundamental relationships between the client company or its management and auditor and therefore should not be deemed to have an adverse impact on the auditor's independence. These situations should be examined carefully, however, since the potential for adverse interests may exist if cross-claims are filed against the auditor alleging that he is responsible for any deficiencies or if the auditor alleges fraud or deceit by the present management as a defense. In assessing the extent to which his independence may be impaired under these conditions, the auditor should consider the following additional guidelines:

1. The existence of cross-claims filed by the client, its management, or any of its directors to protect a right to legal redress in the event of a future adverse decision in the primary litigation (or, in lieu of cross-claims, agreements to extend the statute of limitations) would not normally affect the relationship between client manageagement and auditor in such a way as to impair independence, unless there exists a significant risk that the cross-claim will result in a settlement or judgment in an amount material to the member's firm [3] or to the financial statements of the client.

2. The assertion of cross-claims against the auditor by underwriters would not usually impair independence if no such claims are asserted by the company or the present management.

3. If any of the persons who file cross-claims against the auditor are also officers or directors of other clients of the auditor, the auditor's

---

[2] Because of the complexities of litigation and the circumstances under which it may arise, it is not possible to prescribe meaningful criteria for measuring materiality; accordingly, the member should consider the nature of the controversy underlying the litigation and all other relevant factors in reaching a judgment.

[3] See footnote 2.

independence with respect to such other clients would not usually be impaired.

Other third-party litigation

Another type of third-party litigation against the auditor may be commenced by a lending institution, other creditor, security holder or insurance company who alleges reliance on financial statements of the client examined by the auditor as a basis for extending credit or insurance coverage to the client. In some instances, an insurance company may commence litigation (under subrogation rights) against the auditor in the name of the client to recover losses reimbursed to the client. These types of litigation would not normally affect the auditor's independence with respect to a client who is either not the plaintiff or is only the nominal plaintiff, since the relationship between the auditor and client management would not be affected. They should be examined carefully, however, since the potential for adverse interests may exist if the auditor alleges, in his defense, fraud or deceit by the present management.

If the real party in interest in the litigation (e.g., the insurance company) is also a client of the auditor ("the plaintiff client"), the auditor's independence with respect to the plaintiff client may be impaired if the litigation involves a significant risk of a settlement or judgment in an amount which would be material to the member's firm [4] or to the financial statements of the plaintiff client. If the auditor concludes that such litigation is not material to the plaintiff client or his firm and thus his independence is not impaired, he should nevertheless ensure that professional personnel assigned to the audit of either of the two clients have no involvement with the audit of the other.

Effects of impairment of independence

If the auditor believes that the circumstances would lead a reasonable person having knowledge of the facts to conclude that the actual or intended litigation poses an unacceptable threat to the auditor's independence he should either (a) disengage himself to avoid the appearance that his self-interest would affect his objectivity, or (b) disclaim an opinion because of lack of independence as prescribed by Section 517 of *Statement on Auditing Standards No. 1*.[5] Such disengagement may take the form of resignation or cessation of any audit work then in progress pending resolution of the issues between the parties.

[4] See footnote 2.

[5] A new Statement on Auditing Standards has been proposed which will supercede Section 517. See Auditing Standards Board, *Proposed Statement on Auditing Standards: Association With Financial Statements* (New York: American Institute of Certified Public Accountants, 1979), par. 7.

Termination of impairment

The conditions giving rise to a lack of independence are usually eliminated when a final resolution is reached and the matters at issue no longer affect the relationship between auditor and client. The auditor should carefully review the conditions of such resolution to determine that all impairments to his objectivity have been removed.

Actions permitted while independence is impaired

If the auditor was independent when his report was initially rendered, he may re-sign such report or consent to its use at a later date while his independence is impaired provided that no post-audit work is performed by such auditor during the period of impairment. The term "post-audit work," in this context, does not include inquiries of subsequent auditors, reading of subsequent financial statements, or such procedures as may be necessary to assess the effect of subsequently discovered facts on the financial statements covered by his previously issued report.

.08 **101-7—Application of Rule 101 to professional personnel.** The term "he and his firm" as used in the first sentence of Rule 101 means (1) all partners or shareholders in the firm and (2) all full and part-time professional employees participating in the engagement or located in an office participating in a significant portion of the engagement.

.09 **101-8—Effect on independence of financial interests in nonclients having investor or investee relationships with a member's client.**

Introduction

Rule 101, Independence, provides in part that "A member or a firm of which he is a partner or shareholder shall not express an opinion on financial statements of an enterprise unless he and his firm are independent with respect to such enterprise. Independence will be considered to be impaired if for example, (A) . . . during the period of his professional engagement, or at the time of expressing his opinion, he or his firm . . . had or was committed to acquire any direct or material indirect financial interest in the enterprise . . . (B) during the period covered by the financial statements, during the period of the professional engagement, or at the time of expressing an opinion, he or his firm . . . was connected with the enterprise . . . in any capacity equivalent to that of a member of management . . ."

This interpretation deals with the effect on the appearance of independence of financial interests in nonclients that are related in various ways to a client. Some of the relationships discussed herein result in a financial interest in the client, while others would place the member in a capacity equivalent to that of a member of management.

Situations in which the nonclient investor is a partnership are not covered in this interpretation because the interests of the partnership are ascribed directly to the partners. A member holding a direct financial interest in a partnership that invests in his client has, as a result, a direct financial interest in the client, which impairs his independence.

Terminology

The following specially identified terms are used in this Interpretation as indicated:

1. **Client.** The enterprise with whose financial statements the member is associated.
2. **Member.** In this Interpretation the term "member" means (a) a partner or shareholder in the firm or (b) a full or part–time professional employee participating in the engagement or located in an office participating in a significant portion of the engagement.
3. **Investor.** In this Interpretation the term "investor" means (a) a parent or (b) another investor (including a natural person but not a partnership) that holds an interest in another company ("investee"), but only if the interest gives such other investor the ability to exercise significant influence over operating and financial policies of the investee. The criteria established in paragraph 17 of Accounting Principles Board Opinion Number 18 shall apply in determining the ability of an investor to exercise such influence.
4. **Investee.** In this Interpretation, the term "investee" means (a) a subsidiary or (b) an entity that is subject to significant influence from an investor. A limited partnership in which a client-investor holds a limited partnership interest would not be considered an "investee" subject to this interpretation unless the limited partner were in a position to exercise significant influence over operating and financial policies of the limited partnership.
5. **Material Investee.** An investee is presumed to be material if:
   a. the investor's aggregate carrying amount of investment in and advances to the investee exceeds 5% of the investor's consolidated total assets, or
   b. the investor's equity in the investee's income from continuing operations before income taxes exceeds 5% of the investor's consolidated income from continuing operations before income taxes.

When the investor is a nonclient and its carrying amount of investments in and advances to the client investee is not readily available, the investor's proportionate share of the client investee's total assets may be used in the calculation described in (a) above.

If the income of an investor or investee from continuing operations before income taxes of the most recent year is clearly not indicative of the past or expected future amounts of such income, the reference point for materiality determinations should be the average of the incomes from continuing operations before income taxes of the preceding 3 years.

If a member has a financial interest in more than one nonclient investee of a client investor, the investments in and advances to such investees, and the equity in the income from continuing operations before income taxes of all such investees must be aggregated for purposes of determining whether such investees are material to the investor.

The 5% guidelines for identifying a material investee are to be applied to financial information available at the beginning of the engagement. A minor change in the percentage resulting from later financial information, which a member does not and could not be expected to anticipate at the beginning, may be ignored.

    6. Material financial interest. A financial interest is presumed to be material to a member if it exceeds 5% of the member's net worth. If the member has financial interests in more than one investee of one investor, such interests must be aggregated for purposes of determining whether the member has a material financial interest as described in the preceding sentence.

Interpretation

Where a nonclient investee is material to a client investor, any direct or material indirect financial interest of a member in the nonclient investee would be considered to impair the member's independence with respect to the client. Likewise, where a client investee is material to a non–client investor, any direct or material indirect financial interest of a member in the nonclient investor would be considered to impair the member's independence with respect to the client.

The remainder of this Interpretation discusses whether, in the other situations listed below, a member's financial interest in nonclient investor or nonclient investee of an audit client will impair the member's independence.

These situations are discussed in the following sections:

    1. Nonclient investee is not material to client investor.
    2. Client investee is not material to nonclient investor.

Other relationships, such as those involving brother-sister common control or client-nonclient joint ventures, may affect the appearance of independence. The member should make a reasonable inquiry to determine whether such relationships exist, and where they do, careful consideration should be given to whether the financial interests in question would lead a reasonable observer to conclude that the specified relationships pose an unacceptable threat to the member's independence.

In general, in brother-sister common control situations, an immaterial financial interest of a member in the nonclient investee would not impair the independence of a member with respect to the client investee provided the member could not significantly influence the nonclient investor. In like manner in a joint venture situation, an immaterial financial interest of a member in the nonclient investor would not impair the independence of the member with respect to the client investor provided that the member could not significantly influence the non-client investor.

If a member does not and could not reasonably be expected to have knowledge of the financial interests or relationships described in this interpretation, such lack of knowledge would preclude an impairment of independence.

1. Nonclient Investee is not Material to Client Investor

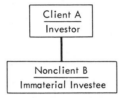

An immaterial financial interest of a member in Nonclient B (investee) would not be considered to impair the member's independence with respect to Client A (investor). A material financial interest of a member in Nonclient B would be considered to impair the member's independence with respect to Client A. The reason for this is that through its ability to influence Nonclient B, Client A could enhance or diminish the value of the member's financial interest in Nonclient B by an amount material to the member's net worth without a material effect on its own financial statements. As a result, the member would not appear to be independent when reporting on the financial statements of Client A.

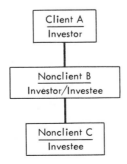

If Nonclient B (investee of Client A) had an investee, Nonclient C, the determination as to whether a financial interest in Nonclient C would be considered to impair the member's independence would be based on the same rules as above for Nonclient B, except that the materiality of Nonclient C is measured in relation to Client A, rather than to Nonclient B.

2. Client Investee is not Material to Nonclient Investor

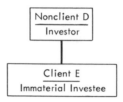

Except as indicated in the next paragraph, a financial interest of a member in Nonclient D (investor) would not be considered to impair the member's independence with respect to Client E (investee) even if the financial interest in Nonclient D were material to the member's net worth. The reason for this is that, since Client E is immaterial to Nonclient D, the member would not appear to be in a position to enhance his investment in Nonclient D.

If the member's financial interest in Nonclient D (investor) is sufficiently large to allow the member to significantly influence the actions of Nonclient D, the member's independence would be considered to be impaired. The reason for this is that a financial interest sufficient to allow the member to significantly influence the actions (operating and financial policies, intercompany transactions, etc.) of the investor could permit tbe member to exercise a degree of control over the client that would place the member in a capacity equivalent to that of a member of management. Such relationship would be considered to impair independence under Rule 101(b)(1).

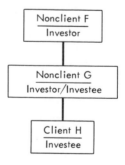

If Client H were an investee of nonclient G, who was an investee of another investor, Nonclient F, the determination as to whether a financial interest in Nonclient F would be considered to impair the member's independence would be based on the same rules as above for Nonclient G, except that the materiality of Client H is measured in relation to Nonclient F, rather than to Nonclient G.

Effective Date

To permit the orderly compliance with this Interpretation, the effective date is January 1, 1980 but earlier compliance is encouraged.

ET SECTION 102

Integrity and Objectivity

.01 Rule 102—Integrity and objectivity. A member shall not knowingly misrepresent facts, and when engaged in the practice of public accounting, including the rendering of tax and management advisory services, shall not subordinate his judgment to others. In tax practice, a member may resolve doubt in favor of his client as long as there is reasonable support for his position.

ET SECTION 201

General Standards

.01 Rule 201—General standards. A member shall comply with the following general standards as interpreted by bodies designated by Council, and must justify any departures therefrom.

- **A.** Professional competence. A member shall undertake only those engagements which he or his firm can reasonably expect to complete with professional competence.
- **B.** Due professional care. A member shall exercise due professional care in the performance of an engagement.
- **C.** Planning and supervision. A member shall adequately plan and supervise an engagement.
- **D.** Sufficient relevant data. A member shall obtain sufficient relevant data to afford a reasonable basis for conclusions or recommendations in relation to an engagement.
- **E.** Forecasts. A member shall not permit his name to be used in conjunction with any forecast of future transactions in a manner which

may lead to the belief that the member vouches for the achievability of the forecast.
[As amended March 31, 1978.]

INTERPRETATION UNDER RULE 201—
GENERAL STANDARDS

.02 201-1—Competence. A member who accepts a professional engagement implies that he has the necessary competence to complete the engagement according to professional standards, applying his knowledge and skill with reasonable care and diligence, but he does not assume a responsibility for infallibility of knowledge or judgment.

Competence in the practice of public accounting involves both the technical qualifications of the member and his staff and his ability to supervise and evaluate the quality of the work performed. Competence relates both to knowledge of the profession's standards, techniques and the technical subject matter involved, and to the capability to exercise sound judgment in applying such knowledge to each engagement.

The member may have the knowledge required to complete an engagement professionally before undertaking it. In many cases, however, additional research or consultation with others may be necessary during the course of the engagement. This does not ordinarily represent a lack of competence, but rather is a normal part of the professional conduct of an engagement.

However, if a CPA is unable to gain sufficient competence through these means, he should suggest, in fairness to his client and the public, the engagement of someone competent to perform the needed service, either independently or as an associate.

.03 201-2—Forecasts. Rule 201 does not prohibit a member from preparing, or assisting a client in the preparation of, forecasts of the results of future transactions. When a member's name is associated with such forecasts, there shall be the presumption that such data may be used by parties other than the client. Therefore, full disclosure must be made of the sources of the information used and the major assumptions made in the preparation of the statements and analyses, the character of the work performed by the member, and the degree of the responsibility he is taking.

ET SECTION 202

Auditing Standards

.01 Rule 202—Auditing standards. A member shall not permit his name to be associated with financial statements in such a manner as to

imply that he is acting as an independent public accountant unless he has complied with the applicable generally accepted auditing standards promulgated by the Institute. Statements on Auditing Standards issued by the Institute's Auditing Standards Board are, for purposes of this rule, considered to be interpretations of the generally accepted auditing standards, and departures from such statements must be justified by those who do not follow them.

INTERPRETATION UNDER RULE 202— AUDITING STANDARDS

.02 202-1—Unaudited financial statements. Rule 202 does not preclude a member from associating himself with the unaudited financial statements of his clients. The Rule states in part that "A member shall not permit his name to be associated with financial statements in such a manner as to imply that he is acting as an independent public accountant unless he has complied with the *applicable* [Italics provided] generally accepted auditing standards promulgated by the Institute."

In applying this provision to situations in which a member's name is associated with unaudited financial statements, it is necessary to recognize that the standards were specifically written to apply to audited financial statements. The fourth reporting standard, however, was made sufficiently broad to be applicable to unaudited financial statements as well.

The fourth reporting standard states in part:

". . . In *all* cases where an auditor's name is associated with financial statements, the report should contain a clear-cut indication of the character of the auditor's examination, *if any,* and the degree of responsibility he is taking." [Italics provided.]

Those sections of *Statements on Auditing Standards* and related guides which deal with unaudited financial statements provide guidance to members associated with such statements.

ET SECTION 203

Accounting Principles

.01 Rule 203—Accounting principles. A member shall not express an opinion that financial statements are presented in conformity with generally accepted accounting principles if such statements contain any departure from an accounting principle promulgated by the body designated by

Council to establish such principles which has a material effect on the statements taken as a whole, unless the member can demonstrate that due to unusual circumstances the financial statements would otherwise have been misleading. In such cases his report must describe the departure, the approximate effects thereof, if practicable, and the reasons why compliance with the principle would result in a misleading statement.

INTERPRETATIONS UNDER RULE 203—
ACCOUNTING PRINCIPLES

.02 203-1—Departures from established accounting principles. Rule 203 was adopted to require compliance with accounting principles promulgated by the body designated by Council to establish such principles. There is a strong presumption that adherence to officially established accounting principles would in nearly all instances result in financial statements that are not misleading.

However, in the establishment of accounting principles it is difficult to anticipate all of the circumstances to which such principles might be applied. This rule therefore recognizes that upon occasion there may be unusual circumstances where the literal application of pronouncements on accounting principles would have the effect of rendering financial statements misleading. In such cases, the proper accounting treatment is that which will render the financial statements not misleading.

The question of what constitutes unusual circumstances as referred to in Rule 203 is a matter of professional judgment involving the ability to support the position that adherence to a promulgated principle would be regarded generally by reasonable men as producing a misleading result.

Examples of events which may justify departures from a principle are new legislation or the evolution of a new form of business transaction. An unusual degree of materiality or the existence of conflicting industry practices are examples of circumstances which would not ordinarily be regarded as unusual in the context of Rule 203.

.03 203-2—Status of FASB interpretations. Council is authorized under Rule 203 to designate a body to establish accounting principles and has designated the Financial Accounting Standards Board as such body. Council also has resolved that FASB Statements of Financial Accounting Standards, together with those Accounting Research Bulletins and APB Opinions which are not superseded by action of the FASB, constitute accounting principles as contemplated in Rule 203.

In determining the existence of a departure from an accounting principle established by a Statement of Financial Accounting Standards, Ac-

counting Research Bulletin or APB Opinion encompassed by Rule 203, the division of professional ethics will construe such Statement, Bulletin or Opinion in the light of any interpretations thereof issued by the FASB.

ET SECTION 204

Other Technical Standards

.01 Rule 204—Other Technical Standards. A member shall comply with other technical standards promulgated by bodies designated by Council to establish such standards, and departures therefrom must be justified by those who do not follow them.
[As amended March 31, 1978.]

ET SECTION 301

Confidential Client Information

.01 Rule 301—Confidential client information. A member shall not disclose any confidential information obtained in the course of a professional engagement except with the consent of the client.

This rule shall not be construed (a) to relieve a member of his obligation under Rules 202 and 203, (b) to affect in any way his compliance with a validly issued subpoena or summons enforceable by order of a court, (c) to prohibit review of a member's professional practices as a part of voluntary quality review under Institute authorization or (d) to preclude a member from responding to any inquiry made by the ethics division or Trial Board of the Institute, by a duly constituted investigative or disciplinary body of a state CPA society, or under state statutes.

Members of the ethics division and Trial Board of the Institute and professional practice reviewers under Institute authorization shall not disclose any confidential client information which comes to their attention from members in disciplinary proceedings or otherwise in carrying out their official responsibilities. However, this prohibition shall not restrict the exchange of information with an aforementioned duly constituted investigative or disciplinary body.

INTERPRETATION UNDER RULE 301—
CONFIDENTIAL CLIENT INFORMATION

.02 301-1—Confidential information and technical standards. The prohibition against disclosure of confidential information obtained in the course of a professional engagement does not apply to disclosure of such information when required to properly discharge the member's responsibility according to the profession's standards. The prohibition would not apply, for example, to disclosure, as required by Section 561 of Statement on Auditing Standards No. 1 [AU section 561], of subsequent discovery of facts existing at the date of the auditor's report which would have affected the auditor's report had he been aware of such facts.

ET SECTION 302

Contingent Fees

.01 Rule 302—Contingent fees. Professional services shall not be offered or rendered under an arrangement whereby no fee will be charged unless a specified finding or result is attained, or where the fee is otherwise contingent upon the findings or results of such services. However, a member's fees may vary depending, for example, on the complexity of the service rendered.

Fees are not regarded as being contingent if fixed by courts or other public authorities or, in tax matters, if determined based on the results of judicial proceedings or the findings of governmental agencies.

ET SECTION 501

Acts Discreditable

.01 Rule 501—Acts discreditable. A member shall not commit an act discreditable to the profession.

INTERPRETATIONS UNDER RULE 501—
ACTS DISCREDITABLE

.02 501-1—Client's records and accountant's workpapers. Retention of client records after a demand is made for them is an act discreditable to the profession in violation of Rule 501. The fact that the statutes of the state in which a member practices may specifically grant him a lien on all client records in his possession does not change the ethical standard that it would be a violation of the Code to retain the records to enforce payment.

A member's working papers are his property and need not be surrendered to the client. However, in some instances a member's working papers will contain data which should properly be reflected in the client's books and records but which for convenience have not been duplicated therein, with the result that the client's records are incomplete. In such instances, the portion of the working papers containing such data constitutes part of the client's records, and copies should be made available to the client upon request.

If a member is engaged to perform certain work for a client and the engagement is terminated prior to the completion of such work, the member is required to return or furnish copies of only those records originally given to the member by the client.

Examples of working papers that are considered to be client's records would include:

a. Worksheets in lieu of books of original entry (e.g., listings and distributions of cash receipts or cash disbursements on columnar working paper).

b. Worksheets in lieu of general ledger or subsidiary ledgers, such as accounts receivable, job cost and equipment ledgers or similar depreciation records.

c. All adjusting and closing journal entries and supporting details. (If the supporting details are not fully set forth in the explanation of the journal entry, but are contained in analyses of accounts in the accountant's working papers, then copies of such analyses must be furnished to the client.)

d. Consolidating or combining journal entries and worksheets and supporting detail used in arriving at final figures incorporated in an end product such as financial statements or tax returns.

Any working papers developed by the member incident to the performance of his engagement which do not result in changes to the clients' records or are not in themselves part of the records ordinarily maintained by such clients, are considered to be solely "accountant's working papers" and are not the property of the client, e.g.:

The member may make extensive analyses of inventory or other accounts as part of his selective audit procedures. Even if such analyses have been prepared by client personnel at the request of the member, they nevertheless are considered to be part of the accountant's working papers.

Only to the extent such analyses result in changes to the client's records would the member be required to furnish the details from his working papers in support of the journal entries recording such changes unless the journal entries themselves contain all necessary details.

Once the member has returned the client's records to him or furnished him with copies of such records and/or necessary supporting data, he has discharged his obligation in this regard and need not comply with any subsequent requests to again furnish such records.

If the member has retained in his files copies of a client's records already in possession of the client, the member is not required to return such copies to the client.

.03 501-2—Discrimination in employment practices. Discrimination based on race, color, religion, sex, age or national origin in hiring, promotion or salary practices is presumed to constitute an act discreditable to the profession in violation of Rule 501.

ET SECTION 502

Advertising and Other Forms of Solicitation

.01 Rule 502—Advertising and Other Forms of Solicitation. A member shall not seek to obtain clients by advertising or other forms of solicitation in a manner that is false, misleading, or deceptive.

INTERPRETATIONS UNDER RULE 502— ADVERTISING AND OTHER FORMS OF SOLICITATION

.02 502-1—Informational Advertising. Advertising that is informative and objective is permitted. Such advertising should be in good taste and be professionally dignified. There are no other restrictions, such as on the type of advertising media, frequency of placement, size, artwork, or type style. Some examples of informative and objective content are—

1. Information about the member and the member's firm, such as—
   a. Names, addresses, telephone numbers, number of partners, shareholders or employees, office hours, foreign language competence, and date the firm was established.
   b. Services offered and fees for such services, including hourly rates and fixed fees.
   c. Educational and professional attainments, including date and place of certifications, schools attended, dates of graduation, degrees received, and memberships in professional associations.
2. Statements of policy or position made by a member or a member's firm related to the practice of public accounting or addressed to a subject of public interest.

.03 502-2—False, Misleading, or Deceptive Acts. Advertising or other forms of solicitation that are false, misleading, or deceptive are not in the public interest and are prohibited. Such activities include those that—

1. Create false or unjustified expectations of favorable results.
2. Imply the ability to influence any court, tribunal, regulatory agency, or similar body or official.
3. Consist of self-laudatory statements that are not based on verifiable facts.
4. Make comparisons with other CPAs.
5. Contains testimonials or endorsements.
6. Contain any other representations that would be likely to cause a reasonable person to misunderstand or be deceived.

.04 502-3 [Deleted]

.05 502-4—Self-Designation as Expert or Specialist. Claiming to be an expert or specialist is prohibited because an AICPA program with methods for recognizing competence in specialized fields has not been developed and self-designations would be likely to cause misunderstanding or deception.

.06 502-5—Engagements Obtained Through Efforts of Third Parties. Members are often asked to render professional services to clients or customers of third parties. Such third parties may have obtained such clients or customers as the result of their advertising and solicitation efforts.

Members are permitted to enter into such engagements. The member has the responsibility to ascertain that all promotional efforts are within the bounds of the Rules of Conduct. Such action is required because the members will receive the benefits of such efforts by third parties, and members must not do through others what they are prohibited from doing themselves by the Rules of Conduct.

ET SECTION 503

Commission

.01 Rule 503—Commission. A member shall not pay a commission to obtain a client, nor shall he accept a commission for a referral to a client of products or services of others. This rule shall not prohibit payments for the purchase of an accounting practice or retirement payments to individuals formerly engaged in the practice of public accounting or payments to their heirs or estates.

INTERPRETATION UNDER RULE 503—COMMISSIONS

.02 503-1—Fees in payment for services. Rule 503, which prohibits payment of a commission to obtain a client, was adopted to avoid a client's having to pay fees for which he did not receive commensurate services. However, payment of fees to a referring public accountant for professional services to the successor firm or to the client in connection with the engagement is not prohibited.

ET SECTION 504

Incompatible Occupations

.01 Rule 504—Incompatible occupations. A member who is engaged in the practice of public accounting shall not concurrently engage in any business or occupation which would create a conflict of interest in rendering professional services. [As amended March 31, 1978.]

ET SECTION 505

Form of Practice and Name

.01 Rule 505—Form of practice and name. A member may practice public accounting, whether as an owner or employee, only in the form of a proprietorship, a partnership or a professional corporation whose characteristics conform to resolutions of Council.

A member shall not practice under a firm name which includes any fictitious name, indicates specialization or is misleading as to the type of organization (proprietorship, partnership or corporation). However, names of one or more past partners or shareholders may be included in the firm name of a successor partnership or corporation. Also, a partner surviving the death or withdrawal of all other partners may continue to practice under the partnership name for up to two years after becoming a sole practitioner.

A firm may not designate itself as "Members of the American Institute of Certified Public Accountants" unless all of its partners or shareholders are members of the Institute.

INTERPRETATION UNDER RULE 505—
FORM OF PRACTICE AND NAME

.02 505-1—Investment in commercial accounting corporation. A member in the practice of public accounting may have a financial interest in a commercial corporation which performs for the public services of a type performed by public accountants and whose characteristics do not conform to resolutions of Council, provided such interest is not material to the corporation's net worth, and the member's interest in and relation to the corporation is solely that of an investor.

Management
Advisory Services
Practice Standards[1]

MS SECTION 101

Management Advisory Services Practice Standards

INTRODUCTION

.01   CPAs have historically been business consultants to their clients. The Council of the American Institute of Certified Public Accountants specifically encourages all CPAs to perform "the entire range of management services consistent with their professional competence, ethical standards and responsibility."

.02   The Institute recognizes a need for a separate set of standards specifically applicable to the practice of management advisory services. Management advisory services are described as follows:

The function of providing professional advisory (consulting) services, the primary purpose of which is to improve the client's use

[1] *AICPA Professional Standards,* vol. 1, MAS Sections 101, 110, 120, 130, 140, 150, 160, 170, and 180. Copyright © by the American Institute of Certified Public Accountants, Inc.

of its capabilities and resources to achieve the objectives of the organization. . . . In providing this advisory service, the independent accounting firm applies an analytical approach and process which typically involve—

- Ascertaining the pertinent facts and circumstances,
- Seeking and identifying objectives,
- Defining the problem or opportunity for improvement,
- Evaluating and determining possible solutions, and
- Presenting findings and recommendations,

and, following the client's decision to proceed . . .

- Planning and scheduling actions to achieve the desired results, and
- Advising and providing technical assistance in implementing . . . to produce solutions. . . .

.03 These Standards apply only to management advisory services engagements as described above. They are not intended to apply to "informal advice," which has been described as follows:

During the course of providing any type of service, independent accounting firms are called upon to give informal advice on many diverse questions. . . . This type of service differs from the structured approach to management advisory services . . . in that the nature of such services is informal and therefore no presumption should exist that an extensive study has been performed to identify and consider pertinent facts and alternatives. Further, no responsibility is assumed for seeking to achieve client action or for seeking to assure that any ensuing action will be effective. Here, the appropriate role is simply to respond as practicable at the moment and to express the basis for the response so that such informal advice is offered and accepted for what it is.

.04 The Code of Professional Ethics (Rule 101) [ET section 101.] precludes a member or his firm from expressing an opinion on the financial statements of an enterprise which he or his firm serves in any capacity equivalent to that of a member of management or of an employee. In rendering management advisory services to audit clients, members must take this into account.

.05 The definitions set forth in the March 1, 1973, Code of Professional Ethics are applicable throughout these standards. The term "practitioner" as used herein pertains to all those, whether CPAs or not, who perform management advisory services in CPA firms.

LIST OF MANAGEMENT ADVISORY SERVICES
PRACTICE STANDARDS

.06 **1.** *Personal Characteristics.* In performing management advisory services, a practitioner must act with integrity and objectivity and be independent in mental attitude.

2. *Competence.* Engagements are to be performed by practitioners having competence in the analytical approach and process, and in the technical subject matter under consideration.

3. *Due Care.* Due professional care is to be exercised in the performance of a management advisory services engagement.

4. *Client Benefit.* Before accepting an engagement, a practitioner is to notify the client of any reservations he has regarding anticipated benefits.

5. *Understanding with Client.* Before undertaking an engagement, a practitioner is to inform his client of all significant matters related to the engagement.

6. *Planning, Supervision, and Control.* Engagements are to be adequately planned, supervised, and controlled.

7. *Sufficient Relevant Data.* Sufficient relevant data is to be obtained, documented, and evaluated in developing conclusions and recommendations.

8. *Communication of Results.* All significant matters relating to the results of the engagement are to be communicated to the client.

MS SECTION 110

Personal Characteristics

Standard No. 1—In performing management advisory services, a practitioner must act with integrity and objectivity and be independent in mental attitude.

.01 The CPA, while performing management advisory services, practices in a unique professional environment, evolving from his traditional role in the attestation to the fairness of financial statements. His professional stature, and the reliance of his clients upon that stature, depend to a large extent upon his integrity and objectivity, and on his ability to be independent in mental attitude on all matters relating to client service.

.02 Integrity is a highly personal characteristic which ensures that the practitioner's statements of findings and recommendations are free of intentional distortions or misstatements. Objectivity is the ability to avoid bias and to maintain an impartial attitude on all matters under review.

.03 A practitioner may undertake only those engagements in which he can maintain an independent mental attitude. This requirement is based on the practitioner's obligation to the client and on the need to avoid impairment of public confidence in the profession.

.04 The role which a practitioner assumes in a management advisory services engagement is fundamental to his maintaining integrity, objectivity, and an independent mental attitude. In all aspects of the practitioner's performance of management advisory services, he must avoid assuming the role of management, limiting his services to those of an objective researcher, analyst, or advisor, rather than a decision maker.

.05 In developing recommendations for a client, the practitioner should study the problem involved, gather the information needed, consider alternative solutions to achieving the client's objective, and present his professional judgment. Any management decision made as a result of such activities must be made by the client.

MS SECTION 120

Competence

Standard No. 2—Engagements are to be performed by practitioners having competence in the analytical approach and process, and in the technical subject matter under consideration.

.01 In each technical area in which a practitioner performs management advisory services, the services performed are to be of a professional quality. Competence in professional work involves (a) the technical qualifications of the practitioners and (b) the ability to supervise the personnel assigned, to evaluate the quality of work performed, and to accept responsibility to the client for successful completion of the engagement.

.02 Competence in performing management advisory services is the ability to identify and define client needs, to utilize the analytical approach and process, to apply knowledge of the technical subject matter under consideration, to communicate recommendations effectively, and to assist in implementing the recommendations.

.03 The evaluation of competence in management advisory services is sometimes subjective. With respect to a specific engagement, this evaluation can require careful assessment of background and ability to determine whether a particular engagement should be undertaken.

.04 Competence is acquired and maintained through a combination of education and experience. Education, beyond that which is initially required for admission to the profession, includes formal and informal instruction and self-study. Experience relates to the knowledge and judgment acquired by personal participation in management advisory services engagements and other business affairs. Competence may be augmented by research and by consultation with others.

MS SECTION 130

Due Care

Standard No. 3—Due professional care is to be exercised in the performance of a management advisory services engagement.

.01 The concept of due care is concerned with what the practitioner does and how well he does it. It involves diligence and appropriate attention in carrying out the assignment. It does not imply infallibility. It does require systematic critical review by the practitioner, throughout the engagement, of work accomplished and judgments exercised.

.02 Due professional care requires that all work be done within the provisions of the Code of Professional Ethics and other professional standards of the AICPA.

MS SECTION 140

Client Benefit

Standard No. 4—Before accepting an engagement, a practitioner is to notify the client of any reservations he has regarding anticipated benefits.

.01 Problem definition, identification of objectives, and benefits to be derived should be considered in structuring the engagement. While in some cases the potential benefits are obvious both to the client and to the practitioner, an assessment of anticipated benefits often requires sufficient exploratory work to establish their reasonableness, and also requires the exercise of judgment. Some benefits can be quantified in financial or statistical terms, but many others are less tangible.

.02 The client's willingness to accept recommendations, and his ability to implement them, should be considered by the practitioner. Unwillingness to accept or inability to implement appropriate recommendations could impair realization of potential benefits.

.03 If during the course of the engagement the relationship between anticipated benefits and costs changes significantly, the client should be informed.

MS SECTION 150

Understanding with Client

Standard No. 5—Before undertaking an engagement, a practitioner is to inform his client of all significant matters related to the engagement.

.01 The significant matters related to an engagement generally include (a) the engagement's objectives, (b) its scope, (c) the approach, (d) the role of all personnel, (e) the manner in which results are to be communicated, (f) the timetable, and (g) the fee.

.02 A preliminary discussion or investigation is generally necessary to develop sufficient information for formulating engagement objectives and identifying scope. The engagement objectives reflect the results expected to be derived. There should be a clear expression by the practitioner as to both the engagement objectives and the extent and nature of the practitioner's involvement.

.03 Engagement scope should be broad enough to encompass matters likely to be significant in developing appropriate recommendations and producing desired results. Particular attention should be given to informing the client of possible consequences of significant constraints.

.04 The respective roles and responsibilities of the practitioner and the client should be defined. Where a third party is involved, it is especially important to establish which party—the practitioner or the client—assumes responsibility for third-party performance.

.05 Definition of major tasks to be performed, the methods to be used in reporting engagement status and achievements, and the timing of such reporting should be established. There should be a clear statement as to what will constitute completion of the engagement and as to the content of the end product.

.06 There should be an expression of when work will commence, the estimated completion date, and the fee and expense arrangements.

.07 These matters should be recorded in writing, particularly for engagements of significant duration or complexity. This can be done in a formal contract, in a letter of understanding, or in a file memorandum summarizing the terms of an oral agreement with the client. Should a significant aspect of the engagement change as work progresses, there should be a new arrangement with the client and a written record thereof.

MS SECTION 160

Planning, Supervision, and Control

Standard No. 6—Engagements are to be adequately planned, supervised, and controlled.

.01   Planning, supervision, and control are based directly on the practitioner's understanding with the client as to the engagement and as to the role of all personnel concerned.

Planning

.02   Planning is the translation of engagement objectives into a structured set of activities and events within a targeted time schedule. The resultant engagement plan is to be used in supervising and controlling the engagement.

.03   The practitioner is usually responsible for engagement planning. The greater the problem complexity and the larger the number of persons involved, the more formal and detailed the engagement plan should normally be. Both the practitioner and the client should recognize the provisional nature of any plan and the need for monitoring and possible revision throughout the engagement.

Supervision

.04   Engagements must be performed and supervised by competent personnel. The practitioner in charge must exercise judgment as to the appropriate amount of supervision, based on the experience of the persons involved and the complexity of the assignment.

Control

.05   Effective control requires measurement of progress in meeting the engagement plan and objectives. Adequate documentation should be maintained to permit measurement and assessment of progress at significant engagement points. Evaluation of progress should be made in terms of accomplishments, time schedule, and quality of work.

MS SECTION 170

Sufficient Relevant Data

Standard No. 7—Sufficient relevant data is to be obtained, documented, and evaluated in developing conclusions and recommendations.

.01 A practitioner must exercise his professional judgment in determining the type and amount of data required. Such determinations take into consideration the nature and scope of the engagement and related circumstances. The source and reliability of the data, and any limitations with respect thereto, must be considered in formulating conclusions.

.02 The amount and formality of documentation will vary according to the nature and scope of the engagement. The documentation should demonstrate that due care has been exercised. It should record, as appropriate, (a) the evidential matter obtained and its source, (b) the alternatives considered, and (c) the analytical process leading to specific recommendations.

MS SECTION 180

Communication of Results

Standard No. 8—All significant matters relating to the results of the engagement are to be communicated to the client.

.01 The principal findings, recommendations, and accomplishments, and the major assumptions relied upon, should be conveyed to the client, together with any limitations, reservations, or other qualifications.

.02 Reports to a client may be written or oral. When a practitioner does not issue a written report to the client, he should prepare a file memorandum documenting the significant recommendations and other pertinent information discussed with the client.

Interim Communications

.03 Interim communications are desirable. Interim communication encourages the involvement of management, helps preserve management's role as decision-maker, and keeps management informed of progress towards the final conclusions, recommendations, and accomplishments.

.04 Interim communications should normally summarize (a) findings to date, (b) work accomplished in relation to plan, and (c) when appropriate, tentative recommendations. They are also used to review problems encountered, to obtain management decisions, and to reassess priorities.

Final Report

.05 A final report should be made to the client upon completion of an engagement to ensure that results and recommendations are communicated. Reports should be responsive to the objectives and scope of the engagement. The nature of work performed and the extent of interim communications will influence the degree of detail of the final report.

.06   Reports should describe the significant alternatives considered by the practitioner and the rationale supporting any recommendations. Related significant facts and assumptions, and their source and bases, should be disclosed.

Appendix

3

Statements
on Responsibilities
in Tax Practice[1]

TX SECTION 101

Introduction

I. The Program

.01 The program contemplates publication of a numbered series of Statements on Responsibilities in Tax Practice by the Institute's Division of Federal Taxation.

II. The Significance of Statements

.02 The series of statements is intended to constitute a body of advisory opinion on what are good standards of tax practice, delineating the extent of a CPA's responsibility to his client, the public, the Government and his profession. Each statement will cover a particular aspect of tax practice. . . .

TX SECTION 111

Signature of Preparer

I. Introduction

.01 Is it proper for a certified public accountant to prepare a Federal tax return and deliver it to the taxpayer without having signed the preparer's declaration?

II. Statement

.02 A CPA should sign as preparer any Federal tax return which requires the signature of a preparer if he prepares it for and transmits it to the taxpayer or another, whether or not the return was prepared for compensation. . . .

TX SECTION 121

Signature of Reviewer: Assumption of Preparer's Responsibility

I. Introduction

.01 Frequently, a certified public accountant is engaged to review a Federal tax return by a taxpayer who seeks added assurance that it has been prepared properly. In many such instances, the taxpayer requests that the CPA sign or cosign the preparer's declaration on the return.

.02 This statement considers whether a CPA who is not the preparer of a return, and therefore is not required to sign the preparer's declaration, nevertheless in his discretion may sign and thus assume the preparer's responsibility.

.03 TX section 111 discusses the signature requirement for a CPA who is the preparer of a Federal tax return.

II. Statement

.04 If the CPA is not the preparer of a Federal tax return, he is not required to sign the preparer's declaration. However, in his discretion, the CPA may sign the declaration on a return prepared by the taxpayer or another if he reviews the return and, in the course of the review, acquires knowledge with respect to the return substantially equivalent to that which he would have acquired had he prepared the return. Unless such review is made, the CPA should not sign the preparer's declaration. . . .

TX SECTION 131

Answers to Questions on Returns

I. Introduction

.01 May a certified public accountant sign the preparer's declaration on a Federal tax return where one or more questions on the return have not been answered? The term "questions" is considered to include requests for information on the return which are not stated in the interrogatory form.

II. Statement

.02 A CPA should sign the preparer's declaration on a Federal tax return only if he is satisfied that reasonable effort has been made to provide appropriate answers to the questions on the return which are applicable to the taxpayer. Where such a question is left unanswered the reason for such omission should be stated. The possibility that an answer to a question might prove disadvantageous to the taxpayer does not justify omitting an answer or a statement of the reason for such omission. . . .

TX SECTION 141

Recognition of Administrative Proceeding of a Prior Year

I. Introduction

.01 This statement considers whether a certified public accountant may sign the preparer's declaration on a Federal tax return in which the treatment of an item differs from that consented to by the taxpayer for a similar item as a result of an administrative proceeding concerning a prior year's return. This statement refers to an administrative proceeding which was concluded by the execution of a waiver by the taxpayer.

.02 An "administrative proceeding" includes an examination by a revenue agent, a district conference or an appellate conference relating to a return or a claim for refund.

.03 The term "waiver" includes a waiver of restrictions on the assessment of a deficiency in tax, the acceptance of the Internal Revenue Service's findings by a partnership, fiduciary or Subchapter S corporation, and the acceptance of an overassessment.

.04 Any reference to "item" or "year" is intended to cover the plural of those terms.

II. Statement

.05 The selection of the treatment of an item in the course of the preparation of a tax return should be based upon the facts and the rules as they are evaluated at the time the return is prepared. Unless the taxpayer is bound as to treatment in the later year, such as by a closing agreement, the disposition of an item as a part of concluding an administrative proceeding by the execution of a waiver for a prior year does not govern the taxpayer in selecting the treatment of a similar item in a later year's return. Therefore, if justified by the facts and rules then applicable, a CPA may sign the preparer's declaration on a return containing a departure from the treatment of an item arrived at as a part of concluding an administrative proceeding regarding a prior year's return. Such departure need not be disclosed. . . .

TX SECTION 151

Use of Estimates

I. Introduction

.01 This Statement considers the responsibility of a certified public accountant in connection with the use of estimates in the preparation of a Federal tax return which he signs as preparer.

II. Statement

.02 A certified public accountant may prepare tax returns involving the use of estimates if such use is generally acceptable or, under the circumstances, it is impracticable to obtain exact data. When estimates are used, they should be presented in such a manner as to avoid the implication of greater accuracy than exists. The CPA should be satisfied that estimated amounts are not unreasonable under the circumstances. . . .

TX SECTION 161

Knowledge of Error: Return Preparation

I. Introduction

.01 This Statement considers the responsibility of a certified public accountant when he learns of an error in a client's previously filed Federal tax return, or of the failure of a client to file a required Federal tax return. As used herein, the term "error" includes an omission.

.02 For purposes of this Statement, the client will not be considered to have made an error in cases where there is reasonable support for the position taken by the client or there was reasonable support at the time the return was filed.

.03 This Statement applies whether or not the CPA prepared the return which contains the error.

II. Statement

.04 A. A CPA shall advise his client promptly upon learning of an error in a previously filed return, or upon learning of a client's failure to file a required return. His advice should include a recommendation of the measures to be taken. Such advice may be given orally. The CPA is neither obligated to inform the Internal Revenue Service nor may he do so without his client's permission.

B. If the CPA is requested to prepare the current year's return and the client has not taken appropriate action to rectify an error in a prior year's return that has resulted or may result in a material understatement of tax liability, the CPA should consider whether to proceed with the preparation of the current year's return. If he does prepare such return, the CPA should take reasonable steps to assure himself that the error is not repeated. Furthermore, inconsistent double deductions, carryovers and similar items associated with the uncorrected prior error should not be allowed to reduce the tax liability for the current year except as specifically permitted by the Internal Revenue Code, Regulations, Internal Revenue Service pronouncements and court decisions.

C. Paragraph B is concerned only with errors that have resulted or may result in a material understatement of the tax liability. Moreover, that paragraph does not apply where a method of accounting is continued under circumstances believed to require the permission of the Commissioner of Internal Revenue to effect a change in the manner of reporting the item involved. . . .

TX SECTION 171

Knowledge of Error: Administrative Proceedings

I. Introduction

.01 This Statement considers the responsibility of a certified public accountant in administrative proceedings when he learns of errors in returns which are the subject of the proceedings. As used herein, the term "error" includes an omission.

.02 This Statement is concerned only with errors that have resulted or may result in a material understatement of the tax liability. For purposes of this Statement, the client will not be considered to have made an error in cases where there is reasonable support for the position taken by the client or there was reasonable support at the time the return was filed. Moreover, it does not apply where a method of accounting is continued under circumstances believed to require the permission of the Commissioner of Internal Revenue to effect a change in the manner of reporting the item involved.

.03 This Statement applies whether or not the CPA prepared the return which contains the error.

II. Statement

.04 When the CPA is representing a client in an administrative proceeding in respect of a return in which there is an error known to the CPA that has resulted or may result in a material understatement of tax liability, he should request the client's agreement to disclose the error to the Internal Revenue Service. Lacking such agreement, the CPA may be under a duty to withdraw from the engagement. . . .

TX SECTION 181

Advice to Clients

I. Introduction

.01 This Statement discusses certain aspects of providing tax advice to clients and considers certain circumstances in which the certified public accountant has a responsibility to communicate with his client when subsequent developments affect advice previously provided.

II. Statement

.02 In providing tax advice to his client, the CPA must use judgment to assure that his advice reflects professional competence and appropriately serves the client's needs. No standard format or guidelines can be established to cover all situations and circumstances involving written or oral advice by the CPA.

.03 The CPA may communicate with his client when subsequent developments affect advice previously provided with respect to significant matters. However, he cannot be expected to have assumed responsibility for initiating such communication except while he is assisting a client in implementing procedures or plans associated with the advice provided. Of course, the CPA may undertake this obligation by specific agreement with his client. . . .

TX SECTION 191

Certain Procedural Aspects of Preparing Returns

I. Introduction

.01 This Statement considers the responsibility of the CPA in connection with the following procedural aspects of preparing Federal tax returns:

1. Examination of supporting data.
2. Use of prior years' returns.
3. Modification of the preparer's declaration.

II. Statement

  .02 In preparing a return, the CPA ordinarily may rely on information furnished by his client. He is not required to examine or review documents or other evidence supporting the client's information in order to sign the preparer's declaration. Although the examination of supporting data is not required, the CPA should encourage his client to provide him with supporting data where appropriate.

  .03 The CPA should make use of his client's returns for prior years whenever feasible.

  .04 The CPA cannot ignore the implications of information known by him and, accordingly, he is required to make reasonable inquiries where the information as presented appears to be incorrect or incomplete.

  .05 If a CPA prepares a Federal return, he should sign it without modifying the preparer's declaration. . . .

TX SECTION 201

Positions Contrary to Treasury Department or Internal Revenue Service Interpretations of the Code

Introduction

  .01 This Statement discusses whether a CPA should provide in tax returns information about positions taken therein that are contrary to the Internal Revenue Code or to interpretations of it by the Treasury Department or the Internal Revenue Service.

Statement

  .02 In preparing a tax return a CPA may take a position contrary to Treasury Department or Internal Revenue Service interpretations of the Code without disclosure, if there is reasonable support for the position.

  .03 In preparing a tax return a CPA may take a position contrary to a specific section of the Internal Revenue Code where there is reasonable support for the position. In such a rare situation, the CPA should disclose the treatment in the tax return.

  .04 In no event may a CPA take a position that lacks reasonable support, even when this position is disclosed in a return. . . .

Appendix

4

The Institute
of Internal Auditors
Code of Ethics[1]

INTRODUCTION:

Recognizing that ethics are an important consideration in the practice of internal auditing and that the moral principles followed by members of *The Institute of Internal Auditors, Inc.*, should be formalized, the Board of Directors at its regular meeting in New Orleans on December 13, 1968, received and adopted the following resolution:

WHEREAS the members of *The Institute of Internal Auditors, Inc.*, represent the profession of internal auditing; and

WHEREAS managements rely on the profession of internal auditing to assist in the fulfillment of their management stewardship; and

WHEREAS said members must maintain high standards of conduct, honor and character in order to carry on proper and meaningful internal auditing practice;

---

[1] Copyright © by the Institute of Internal Auditors, Inc., 249 Maitland Avenue, Altamonte Springs, Florida 32701 U.S.A. Reprinted with permission.

THEREFORE BE IT RESOLVED that a Code of Ethics be now set forth, outlining the standards of professional behavior for the guidance of each member of *The Institute of Internal Auditors, Inc.*

In accordance with this resolution, the Board of Directors further approved of the principles set forth.

INTERPRETATION OF PRINCIPLES:

The provisions of this Code of Ethics cover basic principles in the various disciplines of internal auditing practice. Members shall realize that individual judgment is required in the application of these principles. They have a responsibility to conduct themselves so that their good faith and integrity should not be open to question. While having due regard for the limit of their technical skills, they will promote the highest possible internal auditing standards to the end of advancing the interest of their company or organization.

ARTICLES:

I. Members shall have an obligation to exercise honesty, objectivity, and diligence in the performance of their duties and responsibilities.

II. Members, in holding the trust of their employers, shall exhibit loyalty in all matters pertaining to the affairs of the employer or to whomever they may be rendering a service. However, members shall not knowingly be a part to any illegal or improper activity.

III. Members shall refrain from entering into any activity which may be in conflict with the interest of their employers or which would prejudice their ability to carry out objectively their duties and responsibilities.

IV. Members shall not accept a fee or a gift from an employee, a client, a customer, or a business associate of their employer without the knowledge and consent of their senior management.

V. Members shall be prudent in the use of information acquired in the course of their duties. They shall not use confidential information for any personal gain nor in a manner which would be detrimental to the welfare of their employer.

VI. Members, in expressing an opinion, shall use all reasonable care to obtain sufficient factual evidence to warrant such expression. In their reporting, members shall reveal such material facts known to them, which, if not revealed, could either distort the report of the results of operations under review or conceal unlawful practice.

VII. Members shall continually strive for improvement in the proficiency and effectiveness of their service.

VIII. Members shall abide by the bylaws and uphold the objectives of *The Institute of Internal Auditors, Inc.* In the practice of their profession, they shall be ever mindful of their obligation to maintain the high standard of competence, morality, and dignity which *The Institute of Internal Auditors, Inc.,* and its members have established.

Appendix

5

Statement of Responsibilities of Internal Auditors[1]

NATURE

Internal auditing is an independent appraisal activity within an organization for the review of operations as a service to management. It is a managerial control which functions by measuring and evaluating the effectiveness of other controls.

OBJECTIVE AND SCOPE

The objective of internal auditing is to assist all members of management in the effective discharge of their responsibilities by furnishing them with analyses, appraisals, recommendations and pertinent comments concerning the activities reviewed. Internal auditors are concerned with any phase of business activity in which they may be of service to management. This involves going beyond the accounting and financial records to obtain a full understanding of the operations under review. The attainment of this overall objective involves such activities as:

---

[1] Copyright © by the Institute of Internal Auditors, Inc., 249 Maitland Avenue, Altamonte Springs, Florida 32701 U.S.A. Reprinted with permission.

- Reviewing and appraising the soundness, adequacy, and application of accounting, financial, and other operating controls, and promoting effective control at reasonable cost
- Ascertaining the extent of compliance with established policies, plans, and procedures
- Ascertaining the extent to which company assets are accounted for and safeguarded from losses of all kinds
- Ascertaining the reliability of management data developed within the organization
- Appraising the quality of performance in carrying out assigned responsibilities
- Recommending operating improvements

RESPONSIBILITY AND AUTHORITY

The responsibilities of internal auditing in the organization should be clearly established by management policy. The related authority should provide the internal auditor full access to all of the organization's records, properties, and personnel relevant to the subject under review. The internal auditor should be free to review and appraise policies, plans, procedures, and records.

The internal auditor's responsibilities should be:

- To inform and advise management, and to discharge this responsibility in a manner that is consistent with the Code of Ethics of The Institute of Internal Auditors
- To coordinate internal audit activities with others so as to best achieve the audit objectives and the objectives of the organization

In performing their functions, internal auditors have no direct responsibilities for nor authority over any of the activities reviewed. Therefore, the internal audit review and appraisal does not in any way relieve other persons in the organization of the responsibilities assigned to them.

INDEPENDENCE

Independence is essential to the effectiveness of internal auditing. This independence is obtained primarily through organizational status and objectivity:

- The organizational status of the internal auditing function and the support accorded to it by management are major determinants of its range and value. The head of the internal auditing function, therefore, should be responsible to an officer whose authority is sufficient to assure both a broad range of audit coverage and the adequate consideration of and effective action on the audit findings and recommendations.

■ Objectivity is essential to the audit function. Therefore, internal auditors should not develop and install procedures, prepare records, or engage in any other activity which they would normally review and appraise and which could reasonably be construed to compromise the independence of the internal auditor. The internal auditor's objectivity need not be adversely affected, however, by determining and recommending standards of control to be applied in the development of the systems and procedures being reviewed.

Appendix

6

Standards for
the Professional Practice
of Internal Auditing[1]

100 INDEPENDENCE—*INTERNAL AUDITORS SHOULD BE IN-DEPENDENT OF THE ACTIVITY THEY AUDIT.*

    110 Organizational Status—*The organizational status of the internal auditing department should be sufficient to permit the accomplishment of its audit responsibilities.*

    120 Objectivity—*Internal auditors should be objective in performing audits.*

200 PROFESSIONAL PROFICIENCY—*INTERNAL AUDITS SHOULD BE PERFORMED WITH PROFICIENCY AND DUE PROFESSIONAL CARE.*

    The Internal Auditing Department

    210 Staffing—*The internal auditing department should provide assurance that the technical proficiency and educational background of internal auditors are appropriate for the audits to be performed.*

[1] Copyright © by the Institute of Internal Auditors, Inc., 249 Maitland Avenue, Altamonte Springs, Florida 32701 U.S.A. Reprinted with permission.

220   **Knowledge, Skills, and Disciplines**—*The internal auditing department should possess or should obtain the knowledge, skills, and disciplines needed to carry out its audit responsibilities.*

230   **Supervision**—*The internal auditing department should provide assurance that internal audits are properly supervised.*

The Internal Auditor

240   **Compliance with Standards of Conduct**—*Internal auditors should comply with professional standards of conduct.*

250   **Knowledge, Skills, and Disciplines**—*Internal auditors should possess the knowledge, skills, and disciplines essential to the performance of internal audits.*

260   **Human Relations and Communications**—*Internal auditors should be skilled in dealing with people and in communicating effectively.*

270   **Continuing Education**—*Internal auditors should maintain their technical competence through continuing education.*

280   **Due Professional Care**—*Internal auditors should exercise due professional care in performing internal audits.*

300   **SCOPE OF WORK**—*THE SCOPE OF THE INTERNAL AUDIT SHOULD ENCOMPASS THE EXAMINATION AND EVALUATION OF THE ADEQUACY AND EFFECTIVENESS OF THE ORGANIZATION'S SYSTEM OF INTERNAL CONTROL AND THE QUALITY OF PERFORMANCE IN CARRYING OUT ASSIGNED RESPONSIBILITIES.*

310   **Reliability and Integrity of Information**—*Internal auditors should review the reliability and integrity of financial and operating information and the means used to identify, measure, classify, and report such information.*

320   **Compliance with Policies, Plans, Procedures, Laws, and Regulations**—*Internal auditors should review the systems established to ensure compliance with those policies, plans, procedures, laws, and regulations which could have a significant impact on operations and reports and should determine whether the organization is in compliance.*

330   **Safeguarding of Assets**—*Internal auditors should review the means of safeguarding assets and, as appropriate, verify the existence of such assets.*

340   **Economical and Efficient Use of Resources**—*Internal auditors should appraise the economy and efficiency with which resources are employed.*

350   **Accomplishment of Established Objectives and Goals for Operations or Programs**—*Internal auditors should review*

operations or programs to ascertain whether results are consistent with established objectives and goals and whether the operations or programs are being carried out as planned.

400 PERFORMANCE OF AUDIT WORK—*AUDIT WORK SHOULD INCLUDE PLANNING THE AUDIT, EXAMINING AND EVALUATING INFORMATION, COMMUNICATING RESULTS, AND FOLLOWING UP.*

 410 Planning the Audit—*Internal auditors should plan each audit.*

 420 Examining and Evaluating Information—*Internal auditors should collect, analyze, interpret, and document information to support audit results.*

 430 Communicating Results—*Internal auditors should report the results of their audit work.*

 440 Following Up—*Internal auditors should follow up to ascertain that appropriate action is taken on reported audit findings.*

500 MANAGEMENT OF THE INTERNAL AUDITING DEPARTMENT—*THE DIRECTOR OF INTERNAL AUDITING SHOULD PROPERLY MANAGE THE INTERNAL AUDITING DEPARTMENT.*

 510 Purpose, Authority, and Responsibility—*The director of internal auditing should have a statement of purpose, authority, and responsibility for the internal auditing department.*

 520 Planning—*The director of internal auditing should establish plans to carry out the responsibilities of the internal auditing department.*

 530 Policies and Procedures—*The director of internal auditing should provide written policies and procedures to guide the audit staff.*

 540 Personnel Management and Development—*The director of internal auditing should establish a program for selecting and developing the human resources of the internal auditing department.*

 550 External Auditors—*The director of internal auditing should coordinate internal and external audit efforts.*

 560 Quality Assurance—*The director of internal auditing should establish and maintain a quality assurance program to evaluate the operations of the internal auditing department.*

Appendix

7

Association of Government Accountants Code of Ethics[1]

---

a. *Introduction.* The Association of Government Accountants is a national professional organization most of whose members are primarily engaged in government accounting, auditing, budgeting, and related financial management activities.

The membership represents most government agencies as well as industrial, educational, and private personal service organizations having an interest in government programs.

The Association of Government Accountant's major program objectives are to:

> Unite professional financial managers in government service to perform more efficiently for their own development and thereby for the benefit of the government and society.

> Encourage and provide an effective means for interchange of work-related and professional ideas.

> Aid in improving general financial management and accounting and auditing techniques and concepts.

[1] National Bylaws, Article I, Section 3.

Improve financial management education in all levels of government and universities.

b. *Purpose of the Code.* In order to foster the highest professional standards and behavior, and exemplary service to the government, this Code of Ethics has been developed as guidance for the members of the Association of Government Accountants, and for the information of their employers.

c. *Definitions.* In instances where reference is made to a member, it is intended to include all classes of membership. Where reference is made to employer, it is intended to apply to a government agency as an entity, and to a non-government organization to the extent the principle is considered applicable.

d. *Explanations.* To better understand each ethical principle, a justification or explanation is provided to indicate where and how motivation or proscription of action is intended.

e. *Ethical Principles.*

Personal Behavior

1. A member shall not engage in acts or be associated with activities which are contrary to the public interest or discreditable to the Association of Government Accountants.

(This principle cautions members to avoid actions which adversely affect the public interest and the professional image of the Association.)

2. A member shall not engage in private employment or hold himself out as an independent practitioner for remuneration except with the consent of his employer, if required.

(This principle identifies a restriction against earnings which result from the use of a member's professional qualifications, without the express approval of his employer, if required.)

3. A member shall not purposefully transmit or use confidential information obtained in his professional work, for personal gain or other advantage.

(This principle prohibits the improper use of official position or office for strictly personal purposes, monetary, or otherwise.)

4. A member shall adhere to the Standards of Conduct promulgated by his employer.

(This principle, for example, endorses the commitment of Federal employees to recognize the Standards of Conduct prescribed by their government agencies pursuant to Executive Order 11222 of May 8, 1965, (30 F. R. 6469), and the Code of Ethics for government services adopted by the Congress on July 11, 1958.)

5. A member shall strive to perform the duties of his position and supervise the work of his subordinates, with the highest degree of professional care.

(This principle emphasizes the requirement for a member to give special attention to the professional aspects of his work, and not to condone substandard performance at any level within his responsibility.)

6. A member shall continually seek to increase his professional knowledge and skills, and thus to improve his service to employers, associates and fellow members.

(This principle stresses the importance of professional development and the use of professional skills in helping his colleagues and employers.)

7. A member shall render opinions, observations or conclusions for official purposes only after appropriate professional consideration of the pertinent facts.

(This principle stresses the importance of avoiding unsupported opinions involving professional judgments which could cause inappropriate official actions.)

8. A member shall exercise diligence, objectivity and honesty in his professional activities and be aware of his responsibility to disclose improprieties that come to his attention.

(This principle places the responsibility upon a member to exercise moral and independent judgment and to disclose to appropriate authorities illegal, improper or unethical practices noted in the course of his work.)

9. A member shall be aware of and strive to apply requirements and standards prescribed by authorized government agencies, which may be applicable to his work.

(This principle recognizes that special professional criteria are promulgated by authorized government agencies at the Federal, State and Local levels which require attention in certain assignments.)

Responsibility to Others

10. In the performances of any assignment, a member shall consider the public interest to be paramount.

(This principle stresses a member's foremost concern for the public interest in any specific work situation involving competing interests.)

11. A member shall not engage in any activity or relationship which creates or gives the appearance of a conflict with his responsibilities to his employer.

    (This principle cautions against becoming involved in situations where a member's official or personal activities are inconsistent with his responsibilities to his employer.)

12. In speaking engagements or writings for publication, a member shall identify personal opinions which may differ from official positions of his employer.

    (This principle stresses the need to avoid inappropriate interpretations by the public from speeches or articles by members which reflect personal rather than official viewpoints of their employers.)

Appendix

8

Standards for
Audit of Governmental Organizations,
Programs, Activities,
and Functions[1]

INTRODUCTION

PURPOSE

This statement contains a body of audit standards that are intended for
application to audits of all government organizations, programs, activities,
and functions—whether they are performed by auditors employed by Federal, State, or local governments; independent public accountants; or others
qualified to perform parts of the audit work contemplated under these
standards. These standards are also intended to apply to both internal
audits and audits of contractors, grantees, and other external organizations
performed by or for a governmental entity. These audit standards relate to
the scope and quality of audit effort and to the characteristics of a professional and meaningful audit report.

The American Institute of Certified Public Accountants (AICPA) has
adopted standards and procedures that are applicable to audits performed
to express opinions on the fairness with which financial statements present

---

[1] Comptroller General of the United States, *Standards For Audit of Governmental Organizations, Programs, Activities, and Functions* (United States General Accounting Office, 1972).

the financial position and results of operations.[2] These standards are generally accepted for such audits and have been incorporated into this statement. However, the interests of many users of reports on government audits are broader than those that can be satisfied by audits performed to establish the credibility of financial reports. To provide for audits that will fulfill these broader interests, the standards in this statement include the essence of those prescribed by the American Institute of Certified Public Accountants and additional standards for audits of a broader scope as will be explained subsequently.

SCOPE

A fundamental tenet of a democratic society holds that governments and agencies entrusted with public resources and the authority for applying them have a responsibility to render a full accounting of their activities. This accountability is inherent in the governmental process and is not always specifically identified by legislative provision. This governmental accountability should identify not only the objects for which the public resources have been devoted but also the manner and effect of their application.

This concept of accountability is woven into the basic premises supporting these standards. These standards provide for a scope of audit that includes not only financial and compliance auditing but also auditing for for economy, efficiency, and achievement of desired results. Provision for such a scope of audit is not intended to imply that all audits are presently being conducted this way or that such an extensive scope is always desirable. However, an audit that would include provision for the interests of all potential users of government audits would ordinarily include provision for auditing all the above elements of the accountability of the responsible officials.

Definitions of the three elements of such an audit follow.

1. *Financial and compliance*—determines (a) whether financial operations are properly conducted, (b) whether the financial reports of an audited entity are presented fairly, and (c) whether the entity has complied with applicable laws and regulations.
2. *Economy and efficiency*—determines whether the entity is managing or utilizing its resources (personnel, property, space, and so forth) in an economical and efficient manner and the causes of any inefficiencies or uneconomical practices, including inadequacies in

---

[2] The basic standards are included in "Statements on Auditing Standards," issued by the American Institute of Certified Public Accountants.

management information systems, administrative procedures, or organizational structure.

3. *Program results*—determines whether the desired results or benefits are being achieved, whether the objectives established by the legislature or other authorizing body are being met, and whether the agency has considered alternatives which might yield desired results at a lower cost.

The audit standards are intended to be more than the mere codification of current practices, tailored to existing audit capabilities. Purposely forward-looking, these standards include some concepts and areas of audit coverage which are still evolving in practice but which are vital to the accountability objectives sought in the audit of governments and of intergovernmental programs. Therefore the audit standards have been structured so that each of the three elements of audit can be performed separately if this is deemed desirable.

It should be recognized that a concurrent audit of all three parts would probably be the most economical manner of audit, but often this may not be practical. Furthermore, it may not be practical or necessary to perform all three elements of the audit in particular circumstances. For most government programs or activities, however, the interests of many potential government users will not be satisfied unless all three elements are performed.

In memorandums of engagements between governments and independent public accountants or other audit organizations, the arrangement should specifically identify whether all, or specifically which, of the three elements of the audit are to be conducted. Such agreements are needed to ensure that the scope of audit to be made is understood by all concerned.

BASIC PREMISES

The following certain basic premises underlie these standards and were considered in their development.

1. The term "audit" is used to describe not only work done by accountants in examining financial reports but also work done in reviewing (a) compliance with applicable laws and regulations, (b) efficiency and economy of operations, and (c) effectiveness in achieving program results.

2. Public office carries with it the responsibility to apply resources in an efficient, economical, and effective manner to achieve the purposes for which the resources were furnished. This responsibility applies to all resources, whether entrusted to the public officials by their own constituency or by other levels of government.

3. A public official is accountable to those who provide the resources he uses to carry out governmental programs. He is accountable both to other levels of government for the resources such levels have provided and to the electorate, the ultimate source of all governmental funds. Consequently he should be providing appropriate reports to those to whom he is accountable. Unless legal restrictions or other valid reasons prevent him from doing so, the auditor should make the results of audits available to other levels of government that have supplied resources and to the electorate.

4. Auditing is an important part of the accountability process since it provides independent judgments of the credibility of public officials' statements about the manner in which they have carried out their responsibilities. Auditing also can help decisionmakers improve the efficiency, economy, and effectiveness of governmental operations by identifying where improvements are needed.

5. The interests of individual governments in many financially assisted programs often cannot be isolated because the resources applied have been commingled. Different levels of government share common interests in many programs. Therefore an audit should be designed to satisfy both the common and discrete accountability interests of each contributing government.

6. Cooperation by Federal, State, and local governments in auditing programs of common interest with a minimum of duplication is of mutual benefit to all concerned and is a practical method of auditing intergovernmental operations.

7. Auditors may rely upon the work of auditors at other levels of government if they satisfy themselves as to the other auditors' capabilities by appropriate tests of their work or by other acceptable methods.

An inherent assumption that underlies all the standards is that governments will cooperate in making audits in which they have mutual interests. For many programs that are federally assisted, it would be neither practical nor economical to have every auditor at every level of government do his own background research on the laws, regulations, objectives, and goals of his segment of the program. Therefore, to provide the auditor with the necessary background information and to guide his judgment in the application of the accompanying standards, Federal or State agencies that request State, local, or other levels to make audits are expected to prepare broad, comprehensive audit instructions, tailored to particular programs or program areas.

The content of such audit guidance should include a digest of, or as a minimum, citations to applicable statutes, regulations, instructions, manuals, grant agreements, and other program documents; identification of specific audit objectives and reporting requirements in terms of matters of primary interest in such areas as program compliance, economy, and effectiveness; and other audit guidelines covering specific areas in which the auditor is expected to perform.

GENERAL STANDARDS

1. The full scope of an audit of a governmental program, function, activity, or organization should encompass:
   a. An examination of financial transactions, accounts, and reports, including an evaluation of compliance with applicable laws and regulations.
   b. A review of efficiency and economy in the use of resources.
   c. A review to determine whether desired results are effectively achieved.
   In determining the scope for a particular audit, responsible officials should give consideration to the needs of the potential users of the results of that audit.
2. The auditors assigned to perform the audit must collectively possess adequate professional proficiency for the tasks required.
3. In all matters relating to the audit work, the audit organization and the individual auditors shall maintain an independent attitude.
4. Due professional care is to be used in conducting the audit and in preparing related reports.

EXAMINATION AND EVALUATION STANDARDS

1. Work is to be adequately planned.
2. Assistants are to be properly supervised.
3. A review is to be made of compliance with legal and regulatory requirements.
4. An evaluation is to be made of the system of internal control to assess the extent it can be relied upon to ensure accurate information, to ensure compliance with laws and regulations, and to provide for efficient and effective operations.
5. Sufficient, competent, and relevant evidence is to be obtained to afford a reasonable basis for the auditor's opinions, judgments, conclusions, and recommendations.

REPORTING STANDARDS

1. Written audit reports are to be submitted to the appropriate officials of the organizations requiring or arranging for the audits. Copies of the reports should be sent to other officials who may be responsible for taking action on audit findings and recommendations and to others responsible or authorized to receive such reports. Unless restricted by law or regulation, copies should also be made available for public inspection.

2. Reports are to be issued on or before the dates specified by law, regulation, or other arrangement and, in any event, as promptly as possible so as to make the information available for timely use by management and by legislative officials.

3. Each report shall:

   a. Be as concise as possible but, at the same time, clear and complete enough to be understood by the users.

   b. Present factual matter accurately, completely, and fairly.

   c. Present findings and conclusions objectively and in language as clear and simple as the subject matter permits.

   d. Include only factual information, findings, and conclusions that are adequately supported by enough evidence in the auditor's working papers to demonstrate or prove, when called upon, the bases for the matters reported and their correctness and reasonableness. Detailed supporting information should be included in the report to the extent necessary to make a convincing presentation.

   e. Include, when possible, the auditor's recommendations for actions to effect improvements in problem areas noted in his audit and to otherwise make improvements in operations. Information on underlying causes of problems reported should be included to assist in implementing or devising corrective actions.

   f. Place primary emphasis on improvement rather than on criticism of the past; critical comments should be presented in balanced perspective, recognizing any unusual difficulties or circumstances faced by the operating officials concerned.

   g. Identify and explain issues and questions needing further study and consideration by the auditor or others.

   h. Include recognition of noteworthy accomplishments, particularly when management improvements in one program or activity may be applicable elsewhere.

   i. Include recognition of the views of responsible officials of the organization, program, function, or activity audited on the auditor's findings, conclusions, and recommendations. Except where the possibility of fraud or other compelling reason may require different treatment, the auditor's tentative findings and conclusions should be reviewed with such officials. When possible, without undue delay, their views should be obtained in writing and objectively considered and presented in preparing the final report.

j. Clearly explain the scope and objectives of the audit.

k. State whether any significant pertinent information has been omitted because it is deemed privileged or confidential. The nature of such information should be described, and the law or other basis under which it is withheld should be stated.

4. Each audit report containing financial reports shall:

a. Contain an expression of the auditor's opinion as to whether the information in the financial reports is presented fairly in accordance with generally accepted accounting principles (or with other specified accounting principles applicable to the organization, program, function, or activity audited), applied on a basis consistent with that of the preceding reporting period. If the auditor cannot express an opinion, the reasons therefor should be stated in the audit report.

b. Contain appropriate supplementary explanatory information about the contents of the financial reports as may be necessary for full and informative disclosure about the financial operations of the organization, program, function, or activity audited. Violations of legal or other regulatory requirements, including instances of noncompliance, and material changes in accounting policies and procedures, along with their effect on the financial reports, shall be explained in the audit report.

SUPPLEMENTAL STANDARDS

1. The auditor shall actively participate in reviewing the design and development of new data-processing systems or applications, and significant modification thereto, as a normal part of the audit function.

2. The auditor shall review general controls in data-processing systems to determine that (A) controls have been designed according to management direction and legal requirements, and (B) such controls are operating effectively to provide reliability of, and security over, the data being processed.

3. The auditor shall review application controls of installed data-processing applications to assess their reliability in processing data in a timely, accurate, and complete manner.

Appendix
9

Statements of Principles with Respect to the Practice of Law Formulated by Representatives of the American Bar Association and the AICPA

PREAMBLE

In our present complex society, the average citizen conducting a business is confronted with a myriad of governmental laws and regulations which cover every phase of human endeavor and raise intricate and perplexing problems. These are further complicated by the tax incidents attendant upon all business transactions. As a result, citizens in increasing numbers have sought the professional services of lawyers and certified public accountants. Each of these groups is well qualified to serve the public in its respective field. The primary function of the lawyer is to advise the public with respect to the legal implications involved in such problems, whereas the certified public accountant has to do with the accounting aspects thereof. Frequently the legal and accounting phases are so interrelated and interdependent and overlapping that they are difficult to distinguish. Particularly is this true in the field of income taxation where questions of law and accounting have sometimes been inextricably intermingled. As a result, there has been some doubt as to where the functions of one profession end and those of the other begin.

For the guidance of members of each profession the National Conference of Lawyers and Certified Public Accountants recommends the following statement of principles relating to practice in the field of federal income taxation:

1. Collaboration of Lawyers and Certified Public Accountants Desirable

It is in the best public interest that services and assistance in federal income tax matters be rendered by lawyers and certified public accountants who are trained in their fields by education and experience, and for whose admission to professional standing there are requirements as to education, citizenship and high moral character. They are required to pass written examinations and are subject to rules of professional ethics, such as those of the American Bar Association and American Institute of Certified Public Accountants, which set a high standard of professional practice and conduct, including prohibiting of advertising and solicitation. Many problems connected with business require the skills of both lawyers and certified public accountants and there is every reason for a close and friendly cooperation between the two professions. Lawyers should encourage their clients to seek the advice of certified public accountants whenever accounting problems arise and certified public accountants should encourage clients to seek the advice of lawyers whenever legal questions are present.

2. Preparation of Federal Income Tax Returns

It is a proper function of a lawyer or a certified public accountant to prepare Federal income tax returns.

When a lawyer prepares a return in which questions of accounting arise, he should advise the taxpayer to enlist the assistance of a certified public accountant.

When a certified public accountant prepares a return in which questions of law arise, he should advise the taxpayer to enlist the assistance of a lawyer.

3. Ascertainment of Probable Tax Effects of Transactions

In the course of the practice of law and in the course of the practice of accounting, lawyers and certified public accountants are often asked about the probable tax effects of transactions.

The ascertainment of probable tax effects of transactions frequently is within the function of either a certified public accountant or a lawyer. However, in many instances, problems arise which require the attention of a member of one or the other profession, or members of both. When such ascertainment raises uncertainties as to the interpretation of law (both tax law and general law), or uncertainties as to the application of law to the transaction involved, the certified public accountant should advise the taxpayer to enlist the services of a lawyer. When such ascertainment involves difficult questions of classifying and summarizing the transaction in a significant manner and in terms of money, or interpreting the financial results thereof, the lawyer should advise the taxpayer to enlist the services of a certified public accountant.

In many cases, therefore, the public will be best served by utilizing the joint skills of both professions.

4. Preparation of Legal and Accounting Documents

Only a lawyer may prepare legal documents such as agreements, conveyances, trust instruments, wills, or corporate minutes, or give advice as to the legal sufficiency or effect thereof, or take the necessary steps to create, amend or dissolve a partnership, corporation, trust, or other legal entity.

Only an accountant may properly advise as to the preparation of financial statements included in reports or submitted with tax returns, or as to accounting methods and procedures.

5. Prohibited Self-designations

An accountant should not describe himself as a "tax consultant" or "tax expert" or use any similar phrase. Lawyers, similarly, are prohibited by the canons of ethics of the American Bar Association and the opinions relating thereto, from advertising a special branch of law practice.

6. Representation of Taxpayers before Treasury Department

Under Treasury Department regulations, lawyers and certified public accountants are authorized, upon a showing of their professional status, and subject to certain limitations as defined in the Treasury rules, to represent taxpayers in proceedings before that Department. If, in the course of such proceedings, questions arise involving the application of legal principles, a lawyer should be retained, and if, in the course of such proceedings accounting questions arise, a certified public accountant should be retained.

7. Practice before the Tax Court of the United States

Under the Tax Court rules non-lawyers may be admitted to practice.

However, once upon issuance of a formal notice of deficiency by the Commissioner of Internal Revenue a choice of legal remedies is afforded the taxpayer under existing law either before the Tax Court of the United States, a United States District Court, or the Court of Claims. It is in the best interests of the taxpayer that the advice of a lawyer be sought if further proceedings are contemplated. It is not intended hereby to foreclose the right of non-lawyers to practice before the Tax Court of the United States pursuant to its rules.

Here also, as in proceedings before the Treasury Department the taxpayer, in many cases, is best served by the combined skills of both lawyers and certified public accountants, and the taxpayers, in such cases, should be advised accordingly.

8. Claims for Refund

Claims for refund may be prepared by lawyers or certified public accountants, provided, however, that where a controversial legal issue is involved or where the claim is to be made the basis of litigation, the services of a lawyer should be obtained.

9. Criminal Tax Investigations

When a certified public accountant learns that his client is being specially investigated for possible criminal violation of the Income Tax Law, he should advise his client to seek the advice of a lawyer as to his legal and constitutional rights.

CONCLUSION

This statement of principles should be regarded as tentative and subject to revision and amplification in the light of future experience. The principal purpose is to indicate the importance of voluntary cooperation between our professions, whose members should use their knowledge and skills to the best advantage of the public. It is recommended that joint committees representing the local societies of both professions be established. Such committees might well take permanent form as local conferences of lawyers and certified public accountants patterned after this conference, or could take the form of special committees to handle a specific situation.

Appendix

10

American Bar Association
Statement of Policy
Regarding Lawyers' Responses
to Auditors' Requests
for Information[1]

NOTE: This document, in the form herein set forth, was approved by the Board of Governors of the American Bar Association in December 1975, which official action permitted its release to lawyers and accountants as the standard recommended by the American Bar Association for the lawyer's response to letters of audit inquiry.

PREAMBLE

The public interest in protecting the confidentiality of lawyer-client communications is fundamental. The American legal, political and economic systems depend heavily upon voluntary compliance with the law and upon ready access to a respected body of professionals able to interpret and advise on the law. The expanding complexity of our laws and governmental regulations increases the need for prompt, specific and unhampered lawyer-client communication. The benefits of such communication and early consultation underlie the strict statutory and ethical obligations of the lawyer to preserve the confidences and secrets of the client, as well as the long-recognized testimonial privilege for lawyer-client communication.

Both the Code of Professional Responsibility and the cases applying the evidentiary privilege recognize that the privilege against disclosure can

[1] *The Business Lawyer*, vol. 31, No. 3, April 1976, pp. 1709–1715.

be knowingly and voluntarily waived by the client. It is equally clear that disclosure to a third party may result in loss of the "confidentiality" essential to maintain the privilege. Disclosure to a third party of the lawyer-client communication on a particular subject may also destroy the privilege as to other communications on that subject. Thus, the mere disclosure by the lawyer to the outside auditor, with due client consent, of the substance of communications between the lawyer and client may significantly impair the client's ability in other contexts to maintain the confidentiality of such communications.

Under the circumstances a policy of audit procedure which requires clients to give consent and authorize lawyers to respond to general inquiries and disclose information to auditors concerning matters which have been communicated in confidence is essentially destructive of free and open communication and early consultation between lawyer and client. The institution of such a policy would inevitably discourage management from discussing potential legal problems with counsel for fear that such discussion might become public and precipitate a loss to or possible liability of the business enterprise and its stockholders that might otherwise never materialize.

It is also recognized that our legal, political and economic systems depend to an important extent on public confidence in published financial statements. To meet this need the accounting profession must adopt and adhere to standards and procedures that will command confidence in the auditing process. It is not, however, believed necessary, or sound public policy, to intrude upon the confidentiality of the lawyer-client relationship in order to command such confidence. On the contrary, the objective of fair disclosure in financial statements is more likely to be better served by maintaining the integrity of the confidential relationship between lawyer and client, thereby strengthening corporate management's confidence in counsel and encouraging its readiness to seek advice of counsel and to act in accordance with counsel's advice.

Consistent with the foregoing public policy considerations, it is believed appropriate to distinguish between, on the one hand, litigation which is pending or which a third party has manifested to the client a present intention to commence and, on the other hand, other contingencies of a legal nature or having legal aspects. As regards the former category, unquestionably the lawyer representing the client in a litigation matter may be the best source for a description of the claim or claims asserted, the client's position (e.g., denial, contest, etc.), and the client's possible exposure in the litigation (to the extent the lawyer is in a position to do so). As to the latter category, it is submitted that, for the reasons set forth above, it is not in the public interest for the lawyer to be required to respond to general inquiries from auditors concerning possible claims.

It is recognized that the disclosure requirements for enterprises subject to the reporting requirements of the Federal securities laws are a major concern of managements and counsel, as well as auditors. It is submitted that compliance therewith is best assured when clients are afforded maximum encouragement, by protecting lawyer-client confidentiality, freely to consult counsel. Likewise, lawyers must be keenly conscious of the importance of their clients being competently advised in these matters.

STATEMENT OF POLICY

NOW, THEREFORE, BE IT RESOLVED that it is desirable and in the public interest that this Association adopt the following Statement of Policy regarding the appropriate scope of the lawyer's response to the auditor's request, made by the client at the request of the auditor, for information concerning matters referred to the lawyer during the course of his representation of the client:

(1) *Client Consent to Response.* The lawyer may properly respond to the auditor's requests for information concerning loss contingencies (the term and concept established by Statement of Financial Accounting Standards No. 5, promulgated by the Financial Accounting Standards Board in March 1975 and discussed in Paragraph 5.1 of the accompanying Commentary), to the extent hereinafter set forth, subject to the following:

(a) Assuming that the client's initial letter requesting the lawyer to provide information to the auditor is signed by an agent of the client having apparent authority to make such a request, the lawyer may provide to the auditor information requested, without further consent, unless such information discloses a confidence or a secret or requires an evaluation of a claim.

(b) In the normal case, the initial request letter does not provide the necessary consent to the disclosure of a confidence or secret or to the evaluation of a claim since that consent may only be given after full disclosure to the client of the legal consequences of such action.

(c) Lawyers should bear in mind, in evaluating claims, that an adverse party may assert that any evaluation of potential liability is an admission.

(d) In securing the client's consent to the disclosure of confidences or secrets, or the evaluation of claims, the lawyer may wish to have a draft of his letter reviewed and approved by the client before releasing it to the auditor; in such cases, additional explanation would in all probability be necessary so that the legal consequences of the consent are fully disclosed to the client.

(2) *Limitation on Scope of Response.* It is appropriate for the lawyer to set forth in his response, by way of limitation, the scope of his engage-

ment by the client. It is also appropriate for the lawyer to indicate the date as of which information is furnished and to disclaim any undertaking to advise the auditor of changes which may thereafter be brought to the lawyer's attention. *Unless the lawyer's response indicates otherwise, (a) it is properly limited to matters which have been given substantive attention by the lawyer in the form of legal consultation and, where appropriate, legal representation since the beginning of the period or periods being reported upon, and (b) if a law firm or a law department, the auditor may assume that the firm or department has endeavored, to the extent believed necessary by the firm or department, to determine from lawyers currently in the firm or department who have performed services for the client since the beginning of the fiscal period under audit whether such services involved substantive attention in the form of legal consultation concerning those loss contingencies referred to in Paragraph 5(a) below but, beyond that, no review has been made of any of the client's transactions or other matters for the purpose of identifying loss contingencies to be described in the response.**

(3) *Response May Be Limited to Material Items.* In response to an auditor's request for disclosure of loss contingencies of a client, it is appropriate for the lawyer's response to indicate that the response is limited to items which are considered individually or collectively material to the presentation of the client's financial statements.

(4) *Limited Responses.* Where the lawyer is limiting his response in accordance with this Statement of Policy, his response should so indicate (see Paragraph 8). If in any other respect the lawyer is not undertaking to respond to or comment on particular aspects of the inquiry when responding to the auditor, he should consider advising the auditor that his response is limited, in order to avoid any inference that the lawyer has responded to all aspects; otherwise, he may be assuming a responsibility which he does not intend.

(5) *Loss Contingencies.* When properly requested by the client, it is appropriate for the lawyer to furnish to the auditor information concerning the following matters if the lawyer has been engaged by the client to represent or advise the client professionally with respect thereto and he has devoted substantive attention to them in the form of legal representation or consultation:

(a) *overtly threatened or pending litigation,* whether or not specified by the client;

(b) a *contractually assumed obligation* which the client has specifically identified and upon which the client has specifically requested,

---

* As contemplated by Paragraph 8 of this Statement of Policy, this sentence is intended to be the subject of incorporation by reference as therein provided.

in the inquiry letter or a supplement thereto, comment to the auditor;
(c) *an unasserted possible claim or assessment* which the client
has specifically identified and upon which the client has specifically requested, in the inquiry letter or a supplement thereto, comment to the
auditor.

With respect to clause (a), overtly threatened litigation means that a potential claimant has manifested to the client an awareness of and present
intention to assert a possible claim or assessment unless the likelihood of
litigation (or of settlement when litigation would normally be avoided)
is considered remote. With respect to clause (c), where there has been
no manifestation by a potential claimant of an awareness of and present
intention to assert a possible claim or assessment, consistent with the
considerations and concerns outlined in the Preamble and Paragraph 1
hereof, the client should request the lawyer to furnish information to the
auditor only if the client has determined that it is probable that a possible
claim will be asserted, that there is a reasonable possibility that the outcome
(assuming such assertion) will be unfavorable, and that the resulting
liability would be material to the financial condition of the client. Examples
of such situations might (depending in each case upon the particular circumstances) include the following: (i) a catastrophe, accident or other
similar physical occurrence in which the client's involvement is open and
notorious, or (ii) an investigation by a government agency where enforcement proceedings have been instituted or where the likelihood that they
will not be instituted is remote, under circumstances where assertion of
one or more private claims for redress would normally be expected, or
(iii) a public disclosure by the client acknowledging (and thus focusing
attention upon) the existence of one or more probable claims arising out
of an event or circumstance. In assessing whether or not the assertion of
a possible claim is probable, it is expected that the client would normally
employ, by reason of the inherent uncertainties involved and insufficiency
of available data, concepts parallel to those used by the lawyer (discussed
below) in assessing whether or not an unfavorable outcome is probable;
thus, assertion of a possible claim would be considered probable only when
the prospects of its being asserted seem reasonably certain (i.e., supported
by extrinsic evidence strong enough to establish a presumption that it
will happen) and the prospects of non-assertion seem slight.

It would not be appropriate, however, for the lawyer to be requested
to furnish information in response to an inquiry letter or supplement
thereto if it appears that (a) the client has been required to specify unasserted possible claims without regard to the standard suggested in the
preceding paragraph, or (b) the client has been required to specify all or
substantially all unasserted possible claims as to which legal advice may
have been obtained, since, in either case, such a request would be in

substance a general inquiry and would be inconsistent with the intent of this Statement of Policy.

The information that lawyers may properly give to the auditor concerning the foregoing matters would include (to the extent appropriate) an identification of the proceedings or matter, the stage of proceedings, the claim(s) asserted, and the position taken by the client.

In view of the inherent uncertainties, the lawyer should normally refrain from expressing judgments as to outcome except in those relatively few clear cases where it appears to the lawyer that an unfavorable outcome is either "probable" or "remote"; for purposes of any such judgment it is appropriate to use the following meanings:

> (i) *probable*—an unfavorable outcome for the client is probable if the prospects of the claimant not succeeding are judged to be extremely doubtful and the prospects for success by the client in its defense are judged to be slight.

> (ii) *remote*—an unfavorable outcome is remote if the prospects for the client not succeeding in its defense are judged to be extremely doubtful and the prospects of success by the claimant are judged to be slight.

If, in the opinion of the lawyer, considerations within the province of his professional judgment bear on a particular loss contingency to the degree necessary to make an informed judgment, he may in appropriate circumstances communicate to the auditor his view that an unfavorable outcome is "probable" or "remote," applying the above meanings. No inference should be drawn, from the absence of such a judgment, that the client will not prevail.

The lawyer also may be asked to estimate, in dollar terms, the potential amount of loss or range of loss in the event that an unfavorable outcome is not viewed to be "remote." In such a case, the amount or range of potential loss will normally be as inherently impossible to ascertain, with any degree of certainty, as the outcome of the litigation. Therefore, it is appropriate for the lawyer to provide an estimate of the amount or range of potential loss (if the outcome should be unfavorable) only if he believes that the probability of inaccuracy of the estimate of the amount or range of potential loss is slight.

The considerations bearing upon the difficulty in estimating loss (or range of loss) where pending litigation is concerned are obviously even more compelling in the case of unasserted possible claims. In most cases, the lawyer will not be able to provide any such estimate to the auditor.

As indicated in Paragraph 4 hereof, the auditor may assume that all loss contingencies specified by the client in the manner specified in clauses (b) and (c) above have received comment in the response, unless otherwise therein indicated. The lawyer should not be asked, nor need the lawyer undertake, to furnish information to the auditor concerning loss contingencies except as contemplated by this Paragraph 5.

(6) *Lawyer's Professional Responsibility.* Independent of the scope of his response to the auditor's request for information, the lawyer, depending upon the nature of the matters as to which he is engaged, may have as part of his professional responsibility to his client an obligation to advise the client concerning the need for or advisability of public disclosure of a wide range of events and circumstances. The lawyer has an obligation not knowingly to participate in any violation by the client of the disclosure requirements of the securities laws. In appropriate circumstances, the lawyer also may be required under the Code of Professional Responsibility to resign his engagement if his advice concerning disclosures is disregarded by the client. The auditor may properly assume that whenever, in the course of performing legal services for the client with respect to a matter recognized to involve an unasserted possible claim or assessment which may call for financial statement disclosure, the lawyer has formed a professional conclusion that the client must disclose or consider disclosure concerning such possible claim or assessment, the lawyer, as a matter of professional responsibility to the client, will so advise the client and will consult with the client concerning the question of such disclosure and the applicable requirements* of FAS 5.

(7) Limitation on Use of Response. Unless otherwise stated in the lawyer's response, it shall be solely for the auditor's information in connection with his audit of the financial condition of the client and is not to be quoted in whole or in part or otherwise referred to in any financial statements of the client or related documents, nor is it to be filed with any governmental agency or other person, without the lawyer's prior written consent.† Notwithstanding such limitation, the response can properly be furnished to others in compliance with court process or when necessary in order to defend the auditor against a challenge of the audit by the client or a regulatory agency, provided that the lawyer is given written notice of the circumstances at least twenty days before the response is so to be furnished to others, or as long in advance as possible if the situation does not permit such period of notice.†

(8) *General.* This Statement of Policy, together with the accompany-

---

* Under FAS 5, when there has been no manifestation by a potential claimant of an awareness of a possible claim or assessment, disclosure of an unasserted possible claim is required only if the enterprise concludes that (i) it is probable that a claim will be asserted, (ii) there is a reasonable possibility, if the claim is in fact asserted, that the outcome will be unfavorable, and (iii) the liability resulting from such unfavorable outcome would be material to its financial condition.

† As contemplated by Paragraph 8 of this Statement of Policy, this sentence is intended to be the subject of incorporation by reference as therein provided.

ing Commentary (which is an integral part hereof), has been developed for the general guidance of the legal profession. In a particular case, the lawyer may elect to supplement or modify the approach hereby set forth. If desired, this Statement of Policy may be incorporated by reference in the lawyer's response by the following statement: "This response is limited by, and in accordance with, the ABA Statement of Policy Regarding Lawyers' Responses to Auditors' Requests for Information (December 1975); without limiting the generality of the foregoing, the limitations set forth in such Statement on the scope and use of this response (Paragraphs 2 and 7) are specifically incorporated herein by reference, and any description herein of any 'loss contingencies' is qualified in its entirety by Paragraph 5 of the Statement and the accompanying Commentary (which is an integral part of the Statement)."

NOTE: An extensive Commentary accompanies this Statement of Policy and is an integral part of it. Those interested in using this Appendix should consult it in conjunction with the Commentary.

Index

A

"Academic Preparation for Professional Accounting Careers," 18, 19
Accountability, 15–16, 52, 103, 148, 426, 428
Accountant-client privilege, 190, 312, 314, 315–33
Accounting control, 98–99, 110–22, 112 (*see also* Internal accounting control)
Accounting principles, 23, 24, 25, 57, 58, 59, 60, 69, 92–93, 181, 182–83, 387–88
Accounting Principles Board, 58, 182
Accounting profession:
education requirements, 17–21
structure of, 8–11, 22
Accounting programs, 9, 19–21, 22
Accounting Research Bulletins, 58, 182, 388
Accounting and Review Services Committee, 119
Accounting schools, 8, 9, 19
Accounting Series Releases, 13, 14, 24, 44

Accounting services, 373–75
Accounting standards, 15–16, 22, 23, 24, 25, 26, 27, 57, 61–63, 66–67, 84–89, 385–86 (*see also* Auditing standards; Technical standards)
Accreditation, 21, 139, 141
Actuarial services, 162, 163–64
Administrative control, 98, 99, 104, 110–11
Administrative proceedings, 407, 408, 409–10
Admonishment, 138, 370
Advancement, 150
Advertising, 16, 27, 143, 154, 155–56, 157–58, 175, 214, 392–93, 433
Advice, 397 (*see also* Legal advice; Management advisory services; Tax advice)
Aerospace Industries Association, 88
Agent, enrolled, 360
Agran v. *Shapiro*, 346–49
AICPA, 10, 12, 86, 88, 173, 174
accountant's responsibilities to colleagues, 126–28
Accounting Research Board, 10

445

AICPA (cont.):
Accounting and Review Services Committee, 119
accounting standards, 15–16, 22, 61–63, 66–67
and American Bar Association, cooperation between, 432–35
auditing standards, 11, 15, 26, 42–46, 58, 63–64, 425–26
auditor's independence, 42–46
Code of Professional Ethics, 6, 10, 11, 30, 32, 37, 39, 49, 62, 63, 65, 127, 131, 136, 137, 138, 153, 155, 158, 161, 162, 174, 179, 183, 184, 312, 321, 370, 397, 400, 433
Committee on Accounting Research, 10, 58
Committee on Education and Experience Requirements for CPAs, 17
discipline, 135–49
Division for CPA firms, 9, 10, 137, 144, 145, 148, 149, 151, 162
education requirements, 9, 17–19, 21
expert testimony, 226
expulsion from, 138, 370
internal control, 102
law, practice of, 432–35
membership termination, 135–36
Peer Review Committee, 151
Practice Review Committee, 131
Private Companies Practice Section, 137, 139, 141
Professional Ethics Division, 131, 136–37
Public Oversight Board, 138, 139, 162
Quality Control Standards Committee, 137, 149, 151
response to criticism, 25–26
responsibilities to clients, 92–93
Rules of Conduct, 32, 39–42, 60, 61, 65, 95, 120, 129, 130, 133, 154, 156, 158, 160, 161, 174, 179, 369–95
sanctions, 138, 139
SEC Practice Section, 137, 138, 146, 162
SEC Practice Section Organizational Document, 162
Statement on Auditing Procedures, 209
Statements on Auditing Standards (see Statements on Auditing Standards)
subpoena powers, 146
suspension from, 135–36, 138
Trial Board, 370, 389
violations, 136, 137
Voluntary Quality Control Review Program, 149, 151
"Aiding and abetting," 273–74, 275, 276

Affiliated Ute Citizens v. United States, 281
Alteration, of records and documents, 68
American Accounting Association, 10, 21, 29, 88
American Assembly of Collegiate Schools of Business, 21
American Bar Association, 175, 203, 362, 363, 432–35, 436–43
American Institute of Accountants, 176–77, 178, 363
American Institute of Certified Public Accountants (see AICPA)
Anticompetition, 25, 26, 213, 214
Antifraud (see Fraud)
Antitrust laws, 143, 214 (see also Sherman Act)
APB Opinion, 388
Appeals, 136
Apprenticeships, 218, 219
Armed Services Procurement Regulation, 85
Assessments, 80–83, 84
Assets, misappropriation of, 67, 68, 69
Assistance, 128, 132
Association of Government Accountants, 10, 421–24
Attorney-client privilege, 312, 313, 314–15, 323, 326–32
Audit:
cost of, 72
governmental, 171–72
limitations of, 72–73
quality of, 168–70
Audit failures, 172–73
Auditing standards, 11, 15, 22, 25, 26, 27, 42–46, 48, 49, 58–61, 63–64, 386–87, 412–14 (see also Technical standards)
accountability, 426, 428
computer-based accounting systems, 107–14
governmental, 425–31
letter from legal counsel, 79–84
reporting clients' illegal acts, 74–79
Auditing Standards Board, 58
Auditing Standards Executive Committee, 11, 386
Auditor:
advertising, 155–56
computer audit specialist, 109–110
data-processing specialist, 109, 110
general staff, 108–9, 110
image, 170
independence (see Independence, auditor's)
integrity, 32–33, 35, 37, 38, 39, 52

Auditor (cont.):
  internal (*see* Internal auditor)
  predecessor, 132–35
  responsibilities, 17, 25, 26, 93–94, 108–14, 128–29
  standards (*see* Auditing standards)
  successor, 132–35
  technical proficiency, 108–110

B

Bankruptcy, 147, 223, 316, 321, 323
Bar, 336, 354
Baylor v. Mading-Dugan Drug Company, 317–18
Bencivenga, J. V., 47
"Benefit of the bargain" theory, 237, 282
Bercu case, 347, 357, 358, 359, 360 (*see also In Re New York County Lawyers Assoc.*)
Bid-rigging, 210
Bill of Rights, 324–26
Board on Standards for Programs and Schools of Professional Accounting, 19
Boards of accountancy, 9, 144, 146, 173
Bonds, 247, 259 (*see also* Securities)
Bookkeeping, 43, 177, 219, 373
Breach of contract, 195, 196, 201, 204, 223–24, 241–42, 248, 253
Bribery, 75, 101, 148
Burden of proof, 224, 261, 267, 270, 283, 289
Burkett v. Adams, 197–99
Business failures, 23, 24, 147, 148

C

Canons of Professional Ethics, 339
Carmichael, D. R., 47
Caveat emptor, 234
Censure, 138, 144
Certificate of interest, 259
Certification, 9, 18, 66, 135–36, 141, 144, 145, 146, 199, 215–19
Certified management accountant, 7–11
Checklists, 70
CIA (*see* Internal auditor)
C.I.T. Financial Corporation v. Glover, 206–8
Civil liability, 139, 141, 143, 144, 272, 275, 287
Claims, 80–83, 84

Code of ethics, 10, 30–31, 32, 38, 63, 136, 139–40, 195, 342, 433
  AICPA (*see* AICPA, Code of Professional Ethics)
  government accountants, 421–24
  internal auditors, 412–14, 416
Code of Professional Responsibility, lawyer's, 83, 175, 203, 436
Cohen, Manuel F., 17, 25
Cohen commission, 25, 26, 103, 160, 165–66, 173
Colleagues, 128–31
Collusion, 68, 72
Commission on Auditor's Responsibilities, 17, 25, 103, 145, 160, 165–66
Commissions, 143, 155, 156, 393
"Common honesty," 235, 251
Communications:
  confidential (*see* Confidential communications)
  management advisory services, 403–4
  privileged (*see* Privileged communications)
Community activities, 173
Compensation, 63, 154, 155, 156–57, 192–96
Competence, 57, 58, 59, 60, 61, 64, 66, 70, 93, 132, 143, 154, 155, 166, 169, 170, 199, 219, 253, 385, 386, 399–400, 414
Competition, 21, 25, 26, 143, 166, 196–204, 209, 212, 214
Competitive Associates, Inc. v. Laventhol, Krekstein, Horwath & Horwath, 279–82
Complexity theory, 346–52
Computer audit software, 169
Computer audit specialist, 109–10, 169
Computer "block time," 373
Computer programming, 373
Computers, 107–14
Computer systems design, 373
Concentration, 21, 25
Confidential communications, 190, 311, 312, 313, 314, 315, 320, 321, 322, 323, 327, 328, 330, 332, 333, 436 (*see also* Privileged communications)
Confidential information, 93, 94, 96, 133, 143, 389, 413
Confidentiality (*see* Confidential communications)
Confirmations, 71
Conflict of interests, 143, 155, 160–61, 174, 195, 394, 413 (*see also* Incompatible occupations)
Conglomerates, 23

Congress, 14–17, 24, 25, 85–86, 145, 146,
    148, 259, 314, 315–16, 333, 360
Conscience, 4
Constitution, U.S., 5, 312, 315, 316, 324,
    326, 360
Consulting, 22, 149–50, 171, 386
Contempt of court, 337, 341
Continental Vending case, 142, 289
Contingent monetary effects, 77
Continuing education, 9, 64, 137, 138,
    150, 419
Contracts (*see* Employment contracts;
    Federal contracts; Law of con-
    tracts)
Controller, 131
Controlling person, 260
Controls, 62, 168–69
    accounting (*see* Accounting control)
    administrative (*see* Administrative con-
        trol)
    business, 69
    compensating, 112
    internal (*see* Internal control)
    management advisory services, 398,
        402
Corporations, 15–16, 52, 141, 158–59,
    316, 337, 361, 394, 395, 434
Cost accounting standards, 84–89
Cost Accounting Standards Board, 10, 58,
    84–88
Couch v. *United States,* 303, 324–26
Council of the American Institute of Ac-
    countants, The, 347
Court of Claims, 434
Courteen Seed Co. v. *Hong Kong &
    Shanghai Banking P. Corp.,* 246
Courtesy, professional, 4, 21, 127, 143
CPA Letter, The, 15
Credibility, 170
Crime, 135, 190, 287, 288
Criminal liability, 258, 260, 271
    criminal intent, 287–88, 300–302
    false statements, federal, 308
    mail fraud, 307–8
    Securities Act of 1933, 288–89
    Securities Exchange Act of 1934, 289–
        300
    tax return preparation, 303–7
Customer lists, 333

D

Damages, 139, 144, 146, 210, 222, 237–
    38, 253, 282–83

Data, 57, 61, 62, 67, 107, 108, 385, 398,
    402–3
Data processing, 43, 62, 373, 431 (*see
    also* Computers)
Data-processing specialist, 109, 110
Debentures, registration statement, 263–
    67
Deceit, 234, 235, 247, 378, 379
Deceptive practices, 143
Defalcation, 67, 68
Defamation, 313–14
Defense contractors, 10
Defense contracts, 58, 85–89
Defense Procurement Act, 85
DeMarco, Victor F., 51
Dignity, 64, 414
Directorships, honorary, 372
Disbarment, 14
Discipline:
    of firms, 137–39, 140, 141
    of individuals, 135–37, 140, 141, 142
    by institutions, 145–47
    misconduct, types of, 142–43
    peer review programs, 149–51
    of a profession, 139–49
    of public accounting profession, 140–41
    sanctions, 138, 139, 140, 141, 144
    by state societies, 136, 141
Disclaimers, 49–50, 73, 78, 117, 118, 119,
    204–9, 237, 379
Disclosure, 24, 25, 49, 59, 77, 81, 83, 84,
    86, 88, 93, 107, 118, 119, 162, 177,
    180, 207, 377, 389
    of accounting principles, 181, 182–83
    criminal liability, 289, 298, 299, 302
    of loss contingency, 79, 80, 439
    privileged communications, 312, 313,
        320, 321, 322, 327, 328, 330, 332,
        333, 436–37, 438
    statutory liability, 259, 274, 277, 281
    tort liability, 233, 235, 236
Discrepancies, 71
Discovery process, 331
Discrimination, 391
Discs, 114
Distortions, intentional, 67, 68
District court, 315, 316, 318
Diversity of citizenship, 315–16, 317,
    318–20
Division for CPA Firms, 9, 10, 137, 144,
    145, 146, 148, 149, 162
Due diligence, 167–68, 270, 271, 274,
    278–82, 283, 289, 400
Due process clause, 218
Due professional care, 57, 58, 59, 61, 62,
    64, 66, 67, 142, 143, 253, 385,
    398, 400, 418, 419, 429

Duggins v. *N.C. St. Bd. of C.P.A. Examiners,* 215–19
Duty to speak, 233, 234, 235, 236, 275 (*see also* Disclosure)
Dyer v. Young, 202

E

Eavesdropping, 313
Ebbeskotte v. *Tyler,* 203
Education, 8, 9, 17–21, 22, 27, 64, 137, 138, 399–400, 419
Edward I, 342
Embezzlement, 239, 311
Employment, right to seek, 197
Employment contracts, 191, 192, 196, 197, 198, 200–204, 205
Energy crisis, 24–25
Energy Policy and Conservation Act, 14
Equal protection clause, 218, 219
Equity Funding case, 300
Erie doctrine, 319
Ernst & Ernst v. *Hochfelder et al.,* 275–78
Errors, 61, 67, 68, 69–74, 96, 106, 108, 112, 142, 148, 194, 195, 197, 206, 253, 274, 300, 301, 408–10
Escott v. *Barchris Construction Corporation,* 261–70
Estates, 174, 361
Estoppel, 204
Ethics, 4, 28, 30–31, 33 (*see also* AICPA, Code of Professional Ethics; Code of ethics)
Evidence, 224–25, 226, 301, 312, 319, 320
Evidential matter, 113–14, 134, 159
Examinations, CPA, 9, 18, 19, 335
Experience, 215–19, 399, 400
Expulsion, 138, 370
External auditor, 131–32

F

Falsification of records or documents, 68, 72
Family relationships, 33–34, 374–76, 382–83
FASB (*see* Financial Accounting Standards Board)
Faw, Casson & Co. v. *Cranston,* 200–204
Federal contracts, 58, 85–89
Federal Corrupt Practices Act of 1977, 97, 100, 101

Federal courts, 315–18, 319
Federal False Statements Statute, 308
Federal Government Accountants Association, 88
Federally assisted programs, 428
Federal Mail Fraud Statute, 307
Federal Rules of Civil Procedure, 319
Federal Rules of Evidence, 318, 319
Federal Securities Acts, 12
Federal Trade Commission, 25
Federation of Schools of Accountancy, 8
Fees, 96, 138, 154, 155, 162, 171, 173, 192, 195, 196, 209–14, 283, 328, 336–37, 340, 362, 363, 390, 392, 393, 413
Felony, 135, 143, 209
Field staff, 217
Field work, 59, 98, 108, 110, 113
Fifth Amendment, 312, 323, 324, 325, 326
Financial Accounting Foundation, 10, 23
Financial Accounting Standards Board, 10, 12, 13, 14, 23, 24, 57, 58, 60, 86, 88, 388, 438
Financial executive, internal control and, 101–7
Financial Executives Institute, 10, 21, 88, 160
Financial statements:
association with, 117–18
compilation of, 119, 120, 121–22
content, responsibility for, 176–80, 181, 182–83, 184
disclosure of accounting policies, 182
of non-public entities, 119–22
procedures during year, 181
of public entities, 117–19
review of, 119–21
revision of predecessor auditor's, 135
Fines, 138, 144
Firms, operating characteristics, 22–23
Fischer v. *Kletz,* 233–36
Forecasts, 57, 58, 65, 120, 385, 388–89
Foreign Corrupt Practices Act of 1977, 101–2, 103
Forgery, 68, 72, 245, 288
Foster, Jesse R., 101
Fourteenth Amendment, 316, 324, 325
Fourth Amendment, 324, 325, 326
Fraud, 61, 66, 67–74, 103, 142, 143, 147, 180, 191, 227, 237–38, 303, 304, 306, 307–8, 322, 378, 379 (*see also* Securities, fraud)
Free choice, 4
Freedom of Information Act, 333
Friendships, 33, 173

G

Gardner v. *Conway*, 340–46, 347
General Accounting Office, 85, 171, 172
Gifts, 33, 413
Glanzer v. *Shepard*, 245, 246, 250
Goldberg, Arthur, 52
Goldfarb et Ux. v. *Virginia State Bar et al.*, 210–14
Good faith, 235, 251, 297, 413
Goodwill, 197, 198
Government accountants, 421–24
Governmental auditing, 171–72
Government contracts (*see* Federal contracts)
Grace v. *Allen*, 357–59
Graese, C. E., 170
Great Depression, 258
Guttry, Harvey V., Jr., 101

H

Hanson, Walter E., 53
Harno, Albert J., 3
Health, Education and Welfare, U.S. Department of, 212
Hickman v. *Taylor*, 331
Hiring, 150
Holmes, Oliver Wendell, 325
Horizons for a Profession, 8, 18
House Commerce Committee's Subcommittee on Oversight and Investigations, 145, 173
Howell, C., 85

I

Illegal acts, by clients, 74–79
Imprisonment, 144
"Improving the Accountability of Publicly Owned Corporations and their Auditors," 15
Income tax advice (*see* Tax advice)
Income Tax Law, 435
Income Tax Regulations, 63
Income tax returns, 62–63, 96, 135, 240, 300–307, 323, 326, 328, 331, 343, 344–45, 346, 347–48, 352, 353, 354, 355–56, 361, 362, 406–11, 432, 433–35
Incompatible occupations, 161, 174, 393–94 (*see also* Conflict of interests)

Independence, 30, 31–36, 37–39, 40, 41, 50, 96, 143, 149, 166, 371–84, 399
accountant's, 177, 179–80, 183
auditor's, 31–34, 35, 36, 37–39, 42–46, 47–51, 93, 101, 161–62, 165, 168, 172–74, 178–80, 184, 332
financial interests, effect on, 380–85
impairment of, 379–80
of internal auditor, 37–39, 51–54, 416–17, 418
lack of, 47–51
litigation, effect on, 377–80
of management advisory services, 138, 164–74
of management consultant, 34–36
of officer of company, 50–51
perceptions, 42–46
SEC on, 42–46
Information systems, 108, 168–69
Injunctions, 141, 144, 200, 201, 208
Injury, 237–38, 343
In Re New York County Lawyer's Assoc., 352–56, 358
Inspection, 150–51
Institute of Internal Auditors, Inc., 9, 10, 22, 63, 64, 412–14
Instructions, 70
Insurance companies, 163–64, 319–20, 379
Insurance policies, 163, 164
Integrity, 30, 32–33, 34, 35, 37, 38, 39, 40, 41, 42, 52, 70, 71–72, 93, 96, 98, 132, 134, 155, 166, 172, 173, 373, 385, 398–99, 413
Intention to mislead, 227–28, 253 (*see also* Scienter)
Interim financial information, 114–17
Internal accounting control, 69–72, 74, 76, 94, 97, 98–99, 102, 104, 131, 132 (*see also* Internal control)
Internal auditing department, 418–19, 420
Internal auditor, 7–8, 37–39, 51–54, 131–32, 412–17, 418–20
Internal control, 68, 69–72, 74, 76, 94, 97, 100–102, 103, 104–6, 107, 112–14, 169–70, 173
auditor's responsibilities, 98–101
auditor's technical proficiency, 108–110, 113
and computer, 107–14
and EDP environment, 110–12
and financial executive, 101–7
legislation, 101–3
management's responsibility, 104–105
Internal professional, 63–66, 97, 98, 122–23, 159–60

Internal Revenue Code, 303, 307, 323, 354, 409, 411
Internal Revenue Service, 332, 359, 360, 361, 362, 409, 410, 411
Internships, 18
Interstate commerce, 211, 212, 213, 273, 274, 288, 323
Inventories, 178, 181
Investments, 103, 258, 259, 260, 380–85, 395 (*see also* Securities)
Investment trusts, 258
Irregularities, 61, 67, 69–74, 195

J

Jaillet v. *Cashman*, 246
Jancura, Elise G., 107
Joint Trial Board Division, 136
Judgment, professional, 70, 142, 183, 373, 385, 386, 400, 413
Jury, trial by, 224, 225, 226, 232, 239, 283, 301, 315, 316
Justice Department, 25, 362
Justice of the peace courts, 337

K

Kentucky State Bar Association v. *Bailey*, 338–39
Kin, 375–76 (*see also* Family relationships)
Klion, Stanley R., 164

L

Lavin, David, 43, 46
Law:
dual practice with accounting, 174–75
patent, 360
practice of, 432–35
before the IRS, 360–61
before the Tax Court, 361–62, 434
defined, 336, 337–39, 346
federal licensing, 360–62, 363
legal advice, 330, 332, 336, 337–39, 346, 347, 353, 355
regulating, 336–37, 360–62
procedural, 316
substantive, 316–17, 319
tax (*see* Tax law)

Law (cont.):
unauthorized practice of, 190, 335–36, 337, 339, 362–63
complexity theory, 346–52
state statutes, 335–37, 360
theories in deciding cases, 340–59
Law of contracts, 191
agreements not to compete, 196–204
breach of contract, 195, 196, 201, 223–24, 241, 248, 253
contract and tort cases, difference between, 224
disclaimers, 204–9
employment, 191, 192, 196, 197, 198, 200–204, 205
exculpatory clauses, 204–9
licensing, professional, 215–19
price-fixing, 209–14
privity of contract, 249, 250, 254
qualification, 204, 208–9
right to compensation, 192–96
withdrawal, 195–96
Lawsuits, 23, 24, 27, 147, 225–26, 227, 283, 331, 378 (*see also* Law of contracts; Litigation; Tort liability)
Lawyer-client communications, 84, 436–38
Leases, 181, 197, 198
Legal advice, 330, 332, 336, 337–39, 346, 347, 353, 355, 361, 362, 363
Legislation, 101–3, 140, 145, 146
Letters:
audit inquiry, 81–83
engagement, 180–81, 184, 196
representation, 159–60, 175–84
Liability, 144, 145, 146, 147, 159, 178, 179, 190, 196, 208, 209
civil, 187, 258, 260–61, 271 (*see also* Statutory liability)
common law, 254
criminal (*see* Criminal liability)
securities, 160–63, 272–74, 283
Statutory (*see* Statutory liability)
third-party, 208, 209, 241–53, 254
tort (*see* Tort liability)
Liability insurance, 137, 159
Libel, 311, 313, 314
Licenses, 9, 31, 135–36, 139, 140, 144, 199, 215–19, 336, 339, 342, 360–62
Lilly, Fred L., 107
Litigation, 24, 79–83, 84, 146, 148, 180, 189–90, 311, 314, 324, 337, 339, 362, 377–80, 435, 437 (*see also* Criminal liability; Law of contracts; Tort liability)

Loans, 376–77
Lockheed Aircraft Corp., 15
Loss contingencies, 77, 79, 438, 439–41
Loss reserves, 163
Lukee Enterprises Inc. v. *New York Life Insurance Co.*, 319–20

M

MacNeill, James H., 8
Magnetic tapes, 114
Malpractice, 139, 140, 146, 147, 148,
    189, 190, 223–24, 249, 253
Management advisory services, 138, 161–
    62, 166–67, 370, 396–404
  audit independence, 172–74
  audits, quality of, 168–70
  client benefit, 170–72, 398, 400–401
  communication of results, 398, 403–
    4
  compatibility, 164–74
  competence, 398, 399–400
  control, 398, 402
  due professional care, 398, 400
  independence, 164–74
  personal characteristics, 398–99
  planning, 398, 402
  relationship to audit practice, 164–66,
    172
  role of practitioner, 167–68
  standards, list, 398
  sufficient relevant data, 398, 402–403
  supervision, 398, 402
  understanding with client, 398, 401
Management Advisory Services Practice
    Standards, 34, 138, 173, 396–98
Management consultant, 34–36, 61–62,
    94–96, 129–31, 157–58
Manipulation, 68, 122–23, 277–78
Manners, 4, 5
Master of Business Administration pro-
    grams, 19
Material fact (*see* Materiality)
Materiality, 77, 265–67, 271, 272–73,
    274–75, 277, 281, 288, 289, 306–7
Material weakness, 100, 103
Mautz, Robert, 86
McClenon, Paul, 87
Mergers, of accounting firms, 22, 23
Metcalf, Lee, 166
Metcalf Subcommittee on Reports, Ac-
    counting and Management, 15, 17,
    166, 173
Misconduct, 142–43

Misrepresentation, 66, 68, 71, 72, 143,
    232–36, 237, 249, 250, 251, 252,
    273, 274–75, 281, 290, 385
Mistakes (*see* Errors)
Mistatement (*see* Misrepresentation)
Monopoly, 213, 363
Moonlighting, 160
Morality, 4, 64, 414
Moss, John E., 24, 145
Moss subcommittee, 16, 17, 145, 173
Moss Subcommittee Report, 103
Moulton, Lord, 4
Murphy v. *Waterfront Commission of
    New York Harbor,* 325

N

Name, firm, 394–95
National Association of Accountants, 10,
    21, 88
National Association of Securities
    Dealers, 16
National Association of State Boards of
    Accountancy, 9
National Conference of Lawyers and
    Certified Public Accountants, 347,
    363, 432
National Organization of SEC Accoun-
    tancy, 16
National Review Board, 136, 137
Negligence, 194, 195, 196, 205, 206, 208,
    209, 223–24, 225, 228, 230, 236,
    237, 238–53, 270, 273, 275, 276,
    277, 278, 283, 300, 302, 322
Negligent nonfeasance, 276
Negligent words, 246
New York case, 356 (*see also In Re New
    York County Lawyer's Assoc.*)
New York Stock Exchange, 16
Nondisclosure (*see* Disclosure)
Nonprofit organizations, 372

O

Obedience, 4, 5
Objectivity, 30, 31, 34, 35, 37, 39, 40, 41,
    42, 93, 132, 155, 173, 174, 179,
    373, 375, 379, 380, 385, 398–99,
    413, 416, 417, 418
Occupational Safety and Health Act, 75
Oil well interests, 259
Olson, Wallace E., 21, 139

Omissions, 68–69, 239, 261, 263, 265, 274, 275, 281, 408, 409
1136 Tenants' Corp. v. *Max Rothenberg & Co.,* 240
Opinions, 195–96, 232, 245, 332, 377, 414
"Out of pocket," 237, 282

P

Parker v. *Brown,* 210, 211, 214
Parliament, 342
Partnerships, 141, 158, 196, 197, 259, 361, 371, 372–73, 380–81, 394, 434
Peer review, 137, 138, 141, 144, 149–51, 162
Peer Review Committee, 151
Penn Central Corp., 15, 23
Perjury, 307
Personality conflicts, 195–96
Personnel, 104, 149
Petroleum industry, 24–25
Planning, 57, 58, 59, 61, 62, 64, 67, 385, 398, 402
Planning Executives Institute, 10
Police power, 336
Political contributions, 75, 148
Pound, Roscoe, 198
Practice:
  form of, 394–95
  scope of, 161–64
Practice Review Committee, 131
Precedents, 349, 356
Price-fixing, 209–14
"Primary benefit," 251
Privacy, right of, 143, 313
Private Companies Practice Section, 10, 137, 139, 141
Privileged communications, 190, 323 (*see also* Confidential communications)
  accountant-client, 312, 314, 315–33
  attorney-client, 312, 313, 314–15, 323, 326–32, 436–37
  Bill of Rights, 324–26
  client, 320–21
  discovery process, 331
  diversity of citizenship, 315–16, 317, 318–20
  federal question cases, 316–18
  self-incrimination, 312, 313, 323, 324–27
  state statutes, 313, 315, 316, 318, 319, 320–23

Privileged communications (cont.):
  work-product, 331–32
Privity, of contract, 249, 251, 254, 261, 270, 274
Profession:
  defined, 198
  distinguished from other occupations, 213
Professional, CPA as, 7–11
Professional associations, 10, 127, 139, 154
Professional development, 150
Professional development courses, 136–37
Professional Ethics Division, 131, 136–37
Professionalism, evolution of, 21–28
Professional organizations, 144
Professional societies, 127, 128, 173
Profit-sharing, 259
Pro forma, 288
Proprietorships, 158, 394
Pro se, 337
Prosser, Dean, 234, 235
Proxmire Report, 103
Public inspection, of accounting firms, 138
Public officials, 427–28
Public Oversight Board, 138, 139, 146, 161, 162
Punishment, 139, 140 (*see also* Discipline)

Q

Qualification, 208–9, 240
Quality controls, 24, 27, 137, 144, 147, 149, 150, 151
Quality Control Standards Committee, 137, 149, 151
Quantum meruit, 192, 193, 196
"Quantum of proof," 225
Questionable payments, 101, 102
Questionnaires, 70

R

Racine v. *Bender,* 203
Real estate, 211, 212–13
Real estate broker, 343
Record-keeping, 373
Records, clients', 390–91
Recruiting, 162, 163, 170
Referrals, 128, 129–31, 156–57, 393

Regulation S-X, 13
Reliance, 236–37, 273, 274, 275, 277–82, 299
Reporting, standards of, 59, 122–25, 430–31
Reports, 97–98, 103, 104, 122–23, 139, 160, 403–4, 430–31
Representations, 178, 179, 180
Reprimands, 135, 137, 138
Rescision, mutual, 196
Research design, 43–44
Research and development, 60
Restatement of Torts, 248, 250, 251, 252, 254
Restraint of trade, 196, 198, 202, 203, 209, 212, 213
Rickover, Hyman, 85
Rotation, 33, 137
Roy, Robert H., 8
Rules of Conduct (*see* AICPA, Rules of Conduct)
Rutsch Factors, Inc. v. *Levin,* 249–50
Ryan v. *Kanne,* 193–95

S

Sale of a business, 196, 197, 198
Sale of a practice, 199
Sanctions, disciplinary, 138, 139, 140, 141, 144, 146
Schoenhaut, Arthur, 87
Scienter, 227–32, 238, 246, 271, 273, 275–78
Scope paragraph, 48
Scott v. *Gillis,* 203
SEC (*see* Securities and Exchange Commission)
SEC Practice Section, 10, 137, 138, 141, 146
SEC Practice Section Organizational Document, 162
Securities, 97, 138, 272
communications, 260, 261, 288
damages, 282–83
defined, 259
due diligence, 267–68, 270, 271, 274, 278–82, 283
fraud, 260, 270, 273, 274, 275, 276–77, 278, 279–80, 281, 282, 283, 288, 289, 290
liability, 260–63, 272–74, 283
manipulation, 277–78
materiality, 265–67, 271, 272–73, 274–75, 277, 281, 288, 289, 290

Security (cont.):
prospectus, 259, 260, 261, 263, 274, 283
proxy solicitation, 272
registering, 272
registration statement, 260, 261, 262, 263–65, 271, 283, 288
regulation of, 258, 259, 260–61 (*see also* Securities and Exchange Commission)
reliance, 273, 274, 275, 277–82, 298, S-1 review, 268–70
statute of limitations, 271
Securities Act of 1933, 15, 259–71, 288–89
Securities Act of 1938, 116
Securities Exchange Act of 1934, 15, 97, 272–83, 289–300
Securities and Exchange Commission, 8, 10, 24, 26, 35, 86, 88, 100–101, 103, 116, 144, 177–78, 205, 226, 316, 323, 374
auditor's independence, 42–46
authority of, 11–14, 15, 16, 24, 31, 258
disciplinary action, 141, 143, 144, 145, 146, 148
materiality, 265, 271
registration statements, 260, 261, 262, 263–65, 271, 283, 288
Self-incrimination, 312, 313, 323, 324–27
Self-regulation, of a profession, 140, 141, 145, 146, 148
Senate Committee on Governmental Affairs, 16
Separation of powers, 336
Services:
accounting, 373–75
advisory (*see* Management advisory services)
executive recruiting, 162, 163
insurance actuarial, 162, 163–64
price-fixing, 209–14
scope of, 161–64
Shareholders, 158, 196, 260, 322, 371, 378–79, 394
Shatterproof Glass Corporation v. *James,* 251
Sherman Act, 209, 210, 211, 213, 214
Signatures, 159–60, 406–7, 408, 411
Silence, 233, 234, 235, 274, 275
Sixth Amendment, 362
Slander, 311, 313, 314
Slush funds, 148
Small claim courts, 337
Solicitation, 21, 27, 143, 154, 157, 272, 392–93, 433

S-1 review, 268–70
Standards, 226
    accounting (*see* Accounting standards)
    auditing (*see* Auditing standards)
    education, 17–21, 22
    reporting, 47–51, 122–23
    technical (*see* Technical standards)
Standards for Accounting and Review
    Services, 119
Standards of Conduct, federal, 422
Standards for the Professional Practice
    of Internal Auditing, 37, 38
State courts, 315, 316, 318
Statement on Auditing Procedures, 209
Statement of Principles Relating to Prac-
    tice in the Field of Federal Income
    Taxation, The, 347
Statement of Responsibilities of Internal
    Auditors, 37, 38, 415–17
Statements on Auditing Standards, 11,
    58, 100, 102, 104, 106, 108, 110,
    111, 112, 113, 114, 117, 119, 120,
    133, 178–80, 183, 184, 386, 387,
    389
Statements of Financial Accounting Stan-
    dards, 81, 83, 388, 438
Statements on Management Advisory
    Services, 62, 94, 130, 162, 167
Statements on Responsibilities in Tax
    Practice, 62, 63, 96, 405–11
State Street Trust Co. v. *Ernst,* 227–32
Statistical sampling, 226
Statutes, state, 313, 315, 318, 319, 320–
    23, 335–37, 360
Statutory liability (*see also* Securities)
    Securities Act of 1933, 259–71
    Securities Exchange Act of 1934, 272–
        83
Stock exchanges, 258, 272
Stockholders (*see* Shareholders)
Study on Establishment of Accounting
    Principles, 23
Subcommittee on Interstate and Foreign
    Commerce, 16
Subcommittee on Reports, Accounting
    and Management, 15, 16
Subpoenas, 324, 389
Sufficient relevant data, 57, 61, 62, 67,
    385, 398, 402–3
Summonses, 324, 389
Supervision, 57, 58, 59, 61, 62, 64, 67,
    150, 385, 398, 402
Supremacy clause, 360
Supreme Court, 315, 331, 360, 362, 363
Suspension, 14, 135–36, 138, 139, 140,
    141, 143, 145, 146, 370

T

Tax accounting, 356
Tax advice, 240, 332, 352, 356, 370, 410
Tax consultant, 345, 355, 356, 434
Tax Court, 354, 360, 361, 362, 434–35
Tax credits, 181
Tax evasion, 307, 336
Tax expert, 345, 363, 434
Tax investigations, 435
Tax law, 343–44, 348, 352, 353, 354, 355,
    356, 358, 363, 435
Tax practitioner, 34–36, 61–62, 96, 129–
    31, 157–58, 332
Tax returns (*see* Income tax returns)
Technical skills, 169
Technical standards, 10, 57, 58, 59, 64,
    66, 67, 142, 143, 382–83, 389
Technology, 5
Teich v. *Arthur Andersen & Co.,* 237–38
Testimony, 223, 224, 225–26, 323
Testing, 72, 108
Tests, 70, 71, 76, 99–100, 111, 113, 132
Texas case, 360 (*see also Grace* v. *Allen*)
Theft, 114, 245
Third-party beneficiary, 206, 242, 248,
    254
Times Mirror, 105–6
Title examination, 212, 213
Title insurance, 247
Tolerance, 5
Tort liability, 204
    admissibility of evidence, 224–25
    burden of proof, 224–25
    damage, 223, 237–38
    defined, 22–23
    expert testimony, 225–26
    fraud, 227–38, 239, 241, 243, 244,
        246–47, 248, 249, 251, 253
    injury, 237–38
    justifiable reliance, 236–37
    malpractice theories, 223–24
    misrepresentations, 232–36, 237, 249,
        250, 251
    negligence, 238–53, 254
    scienter, 227–32, 238, 246, 253
    third-party liability, 241–53, 254
    Ultramares doctrine, 241–53, 254
Torts, 222–23, 227, 249
Trade secrets, 332, 333
Training programs, 24
Trans World Airlines, 52
Treasury Decision 5000, 85
Treasury Department, 332, 347, 348, 354,
    356, 359, 360, 361, 411, 434
Treasury Rules, 348, 434

Trial Boards, 136, 137, 370, 389
Trusteeships, honorary, 372
Trusts, 361, 434

U

Ultramares Corp. v. *Touche,* 242–48
Ultramares doctrine, 241–53, 254
Unemployment compensation boards, 337
Uniform Commercial Code, 191
United States Criminal Code, 303, 307
United States v. *Benjamin,* 302
United States v. *Brown,* 329–31
United States v. *Natelli,* 301
United States v. *Schmidt,* 326–29
United States v. *Simon,* 142, 290–300, 302
United States v. *Warden,* 303–307
Unrecorded transactions, 68, 72
Utility holding companies, 258

V

Values, 5
Veterans Administration, 212

Vinson-Trammel Act, 85
Voluntary Quality Control Review Program, 149, 151

W

Waiver, 204, 323, 332, 407, 408, 437
Wheat commission, 23
Whiskey receipts, 259
White-collar crimes, 190, 287
Withdrawal, 195–96
Worker's compensation boards, 337
Working papers, 134, 390–91
Work-product privilege, 331–32
Work sheets, 181, 391
Wright, Howard, 87

Z

Zelkin v. *Caruso Discount Corporation,* 349–52